to the spirit of
gregory bateson

Student   *I want to ask a question.*

G.B.   *Yes.*

Student   *It's — do you want us to*
learn what you are telling us?
Or is it all a sort of example,
an illustration of something else?

G.B.   *Yes, indeed.*

— Steps to an Ecology of Mind

Foreword

What is language? Or better, what is "language"? Whatever is asked here, it is language we need for an answer; and, of course, we need language to ask that question on language. Hence, if we did not know the answer, how could we have asked the question in the first place? And if indeed we did not know it, what will an answer be like that answers itself?

How would a dictionary handle this case that is so different from most others? At the instant it is to tell what is language, it must turn mute for reasons we know now well. I was particularly curious how my favorite dictionary, *The American Heritage Dictionary of the English Language*, would do it. After the entry "language" will it leave, say, two inches of blank space? Or will it have a small mirror pasted at this place so that I can see my own puzzled face? Or what?

Apparently the editors decided against employing such warnings. After an account of the noises (or scribbles) associated with language spoken (or written) they adopted the following definition:

> *The transmission of meaning, feeling, or intent by significance of act or manner.*

If one had no idea about "meaning," "feeling," and "intent," one could think of these nouns to stand for some kind of commodity that can be packaged and transmitted. (In fact this seems to become now a popular belief. Take for instance, "information processing," "information storage and retrieval," and other ailing metaphors.) Hence, I was going to check on "meaning." I got:

> mean•ing (mē'ning) n. 1. *That which is signified by something; what something represents; sense; import; semantic content: 'Pending a satisfactory explanation of the notion of meaning, linguists in the semantic field are in the situation of not knowing what they are talking about.'* (Willard V. Quine)

This precisely was (and approximately still is) the state of affairs when Gregory Bateson and a small group of people around him sensed that certain psychological disorders of an individual could be traced to linguistic pathologies of this individual's social environment, and that these disorders resisted all orthodox approaches because the attempted therapies themselves suffered from the same linguistic pathologies.

To me it seems that the crucial step toward the success of Bateson and his co-workers was that at the outset they rejected a terminology that would admit notions of "transport," "transfer," "transmission," "exchange," etc., in an epistemology of communication, and instead turned at once to communication's underlying process, namely, to interaction.

Shifting attention from a specific to a more general form of behavior, and, at the same time, brushing aside the semanticist's problem of "meaning" seeems, at first glance, to be trivial and naive.

Not so!

There is indeed a fundamental difference between the orthodox perspective and the interactional view, a difference Bateson must have seen very early, and which he put in various ways in his many writings. Let me demonstate this, and the power of this view, on one of Bateson's charming vignettes he called *Metalogues*, fictitious (or perhaps not so fictitious after all) conversations of a father (I hear Bateson talking) with his inquisitive daughter. Here is the one entitled

What is an Instinct?

D: *Daddy, what is an instinct?*

If I had to answer this question I may have been easily seduced — as perhaps many amongst us — to come up with sort of a lexical definition: "Instinct is the innate aspect of behavior that is not learned, is complex, etc. . . ." Bateson, however, ignores semantic links (they can be found easily somewhere else), and alerts us to the, shall I say, strategic, political, functional, "interactional" consequences when "instinct" is evoked in a conversation. Thus father replies:

F: *An instinct, my dear, is an explanatory principle.*

I like to refer to this contextual somersault as "The Batesonian Shift from Semantic to Functional Signifcance." Of course, it does not satisfy Daughter.

D: *But what does it explain?*

F: *Anything — almost anything at all. Anything you want it to explain.*

I wish to invite the reader to reflect for a moment what it means to have arrived at something that explains "almost everything." Does something that explains anything explain anything at all? Maybe such a thing explains in fact nothing at all. Perhaps there is nothing that explains anything? What has Daughter to say about that explanatory principle that explains almost anything?

D: *Don't be silly. It doesn't explain gravity.*

Excellent! How will father get out of this?

F: *No. But that is because nobody wants "instinct" to explain gravity. If they did, it would explain it. We could simply say that the moon has an instinct whose strength varies inversely as the square of the distance . . .*

D: *But that's nonsense, Daddy.*

F: *Yes, surely. But it was you who mentioned "instinct," not I.*

Okay. So Father got himself out all right. However, I would like to draw the reader's attention to two points: (i) in contrast to the great didactic dialogues of our literary heritage, for instance, the Socratic Dialogues, or Galilei's *Dialoghi (delle nueve scienze)*, etc., etc., in which the partners mutually support one another by assent, confirmation, complement, agreement, etc., (semantic continuity), this metalogue, by kicking the semantics around, thrives on personal involvement (functional continuity); (ii) explanations — should we like to have one — are in the descriptive domain: ". . . we could simply *say* that the moon . . ." More of this later. Right now, let's hear Daughter again:

D: *All right — but then what does explain gravity?*

F: *Nothing my dear, because gravity is an explanatory principle.*

D: *Oh.*

Who would not join in Daughter's exasperated "Oh!"? But she recovers quickly, and I shall not interrupt now the fast exchange that follows. I only ask the reader to contemplate the profound consequences of Bateson's insistence on seeing explanations, hypotheses, etc., purely in the descriptive domain. Watch his use of "say": "If you *say* there was a full moon. . ." and not: "If there was a full moon. . ." etc.

D: *Do you mean that you cannot use one explanatory principle to explain another?*

F: *Hmm . . . hardly ever. That is what Newton meant when he said, "hypotheses non fingo."*

D: *And what does that mean? Please.*

F: *Well, you know what "hypotheses" are. Any statement linking together two descriptive statements is an hypothesis. If you say that there was a full moon on February 1st and another on March 1st; and then you link these two observations together in any way, the statement which links them is an hypothesis.*

D: *Yes — and I know what* non *means. But what's* fingo?

F: *Well,* fingo *is a late Latin word for "make." It forms a verbal noun* fictio *from which we get the word "fiction."*

D: *Daddy, do you mean that Sir Issac Newton thought that all hypotheses were just* made up *like stories?*

F: *Yes — precisely that.*

D: *But didn't he discover gravity? With the apple?*

F: *No, dear. He invented it.*

D: *Oh. . .*

With this epistemological somersault the Laws of Nature become inventions, rigor is married to imagination, and Nature is fiction, made up by us acting together: Interacting. Ultimately this means

Seeing oneself
through the eyes of the other

Thanks to Gregory Bateson's perceptions, the seventeen pieces that follow facilitate this vision.

Heinz Von Foerster
Pescadero, California
March, 1981

Preface

From February 15th to 18th 1979, 100 scholars from 40 institutions in 25 states gathered at Asilomar Conference Grounds in Pacific Grove, California, for a conference in honor of Gregory Bateson. This book began at that meeting, and we hope it transcends the genre of conference proceedings, yet captures something of the context that was "Asilomar."

Asilomar, in 1979, was a meeting whose year had apparently come, bringing together for the first time many of the best of the current generation of human communication scholars with a collection of theoretical mentors, centrally Gregory Bateson and Kenneth Burke.

The conference was borne of failure. Paul Watzlawick was unable to accept an invitation to speak at the 1978 Speech Communication Association convention in Minneapolis, and Carol Wilder-Mott's subsequent proposal to organize a small invited conference on the West Coast to "bring the mountain to Mohammed," as Barnett Pearce put it, was endorsed by colleagues in the Interpersonal Communication division of the International Communication Association at that group's 1978 meeting in Chicago.

One thing led to another, and events seemed to take on a life of their own. Arthur Bochner, Herbert Simons, Robert Norton, and Wilder-Mott conferred by telephone and travels about the conceptual shape of the conference and the list of formal paper invitees from the ICA/SCA network. This list eventually included Dean Barnlund, San Francisco State University; Arthur Bochner, Temple University; Barnett Pearce and Vernon Cronen, University of Massachusetts; Donald Cushman, State University of New York at Albany; Donald Ellis, then of Purdue University; Leonard Hawes, University of Utah; C. David Mortensen, University of Wisconsin; Robert Norton, Purdue University; L. Edna Rogers, Cleveland State University; Herbert Simons, Temple University; John Wiemann and Clifford Kelly, University of California at Santa Barbara and University of the Pacific, respectively; and Frederick Williams, The Annenberg School of Communications — University of Southern California. Peter Andersen of West Virginia University, B. Aubrey Fisher of the University of Utah, Lynn Segal of the Mental Research Institute, and Carlos Sluzki of the University of California at San Francisco agreed to be respondents. Two paper slots were opened for competition among conference registrants, and papers by Linda Harris and by Kenneth N. Leone Cissna and Evelyn Sieburg were chosen by committee. The remaining space for participant observers filled before announcements in ICA and SCA newsletters went to press. The original limit of 60 was revised to 80, with a waiting list even longer.

By this time, late Summer of 1978, the International Communication Association, Speech Communication Association, and San Francisco State University had offered their names as conference co-sponsors and had provided seed funding. Rhetorical theorist Kenneth Burke, biophysicist/cybernetician Heinz Von Fœrster, communication theorist/therapist Paul Watzlawick, and clinical anthropologist John Weakland agreed to address the conference.

In the Spring of 1978 Gregory Bateson, in whose honor the conference was organized, was told that he had an advanced cancer and that "time might be short." Both public and private sources indicated that Bateson was turning away all requests to devote his final months, at Esalen Institute, to the completion of *Mind and Nature*. But in August 1978, his illness in remission, Bateson responded to the conference invitation writing: "Heck, I can't sit and sulk at Esalen while the boys talk nonsense at Asilomar. Send more information, please." Wilder-Mott spent three days with Bateson at Esalen discussing ideas related to the conference, and so it came to be that the guest of honor at Asilomar became, indeed, a guest. In the end, even California Governor Jerry Brown, a Bateson student, responded to a request for a message to be presented at the conference banquet by presenting it himself.

All of this made for a special atmosphere which little can survive the transforms through time, space, and medium to you, the reader of this book. But we hope that some of this spirit, as well as specifics, may come through in some of these essays. The lessons of Bateson's work and life are in the early stages of being taken seriously, when at all, by the academic community, and missteps are inevitable. We believe that this volume includes some rare and graceful insights which complement Bateson's thinking as well as its share of "talking nonsense": altogether a reflection of how far we may have come and how much farther we may go. We leave it for you to learn, as we have, by sifting the wheat from the chaff.

Most of the major Asilomar papers and presentations are included here. Several authors have chosen to publish elsewhere. We have allowed the original tone of the author to stand. In some cases, chapters are formal academic papers; in other cases revisions of oral presentations. Gregory Bateson's revision of "Paradigmatic Conservatism" was completed six months before his death on July 4th, 1980. Heinz Von Foerster's "Foreword" and Wilder-Mott's introductory essay were written after the conference especially for this volume. Stephen Toulmin's "The Charm of the Scout" was not related to Asilomar at all, but appeared first in the *New York Review of Books*. Arthur Bochner brought Toulmin's piece to our attention, and we were so taken by its own charm we decided that even if it .wasn't written for the book, it should have been. We are very pleased to have permission to include it.

We have organized *Rigor and Imagination* into four sections, and offer brief introductory remarks for each. *Context* sketches the historical, social, and conceptual domain of the book. Essays in the *Theory* section address a variety of current issues related to the interactional view in particular and human communication studies in general. The essays under the rubric of *Research* review several of the most widely studied aspects of the interactional model and suggest directions for future work. In the final section, each essay offers *Provocations* which challenge conventional ways.

Many contributed, directly or indirectly, to making this book possible. First, for the Asilomar conference itself, we would like to acknowledge the sponsorship of the International Communication Association (Board of Directors and Interpersonal Communication Division), the Speech Communication Association, and San Francisco State University (Department of Speech and Communication Studies, Forensics Union, School of Humanities, and Office of the President).

Personal thanks are due to Keiko Yamamoto, Randi Nydish, Mike Griffin, Rosie Kontur, Cynthia Hartley, Herb Ferrette, K. C. Schillhahn, Pete Seel, Garth O'Donnell, Ann Nova Young, Paul Romberg, Lawrence Ianni, Leo Young, Lawrence Medcalf, Griff Richards, Nancy McDermid, Bill Work, Anita Taylor, Cathy Waxman, Bob Cox, Hank McGuckin, Frank Moakley, Val Sakovich, Bob Norton, Don Ellis, Art Bochner, Herb Simons, Barnett Pearce, Lynn Segal, Carlos Sluzki, Claire Bloom, Dean Barnlund, John Herr, Ted Keller, Hugh Brady, Nancy Dawson, Richard Kuhn, Gillian Ellenby, and Mai Von Foerster. And to Timothy, on the second cybernetic frontier. And to Anna.

For support in the preparation of this book, we are indebted first to a San Francisco State University Affirmative Action Faculty Development Grant which provided Wilder-Mott with four units of released time during the Spring 1980 term. Edwin Scharf Priewert and Michael Lloyd-Davies provided informed editorial assistance at several stages. Sharon Lucas translated our scratchings into typescript with competence and good cheer. Finally, the Mental Research Institute gave us space, warmth, collegiality, and a Don D. Jackson Memorial Award for manuscript preparation.

This volume is written largely by and for scholars of human communication, but we hope it speaks also to colleagues in other disciplines. And especially to our students and children, who will make the next difference — if a difference is to be made — in our ways of thinking, forms of explanation, and ethics for action.

C. W.-M.
J. H. W.
Palo Alto, California
March 1981

Contents

THEORY

RESEARCH

PROVOCATIONS

AFTERWORD

APPENDICES

CONTEXT

Without context, words and actions have no meaning at all. This is true not only of human communication in words but also of all communication whatsoever, of all mental process, of all mind, including that which tells the sea anemone how to grow and the amoeba what he should do next.

　　　　　　　　　　　　　　　　　　　　— Gregory Bateson

"Without context," wrote Bateson, "there is no communication." As knotty as the notion of context becomes upon examination, the value of placing ideas within a framework is evident. Each essay in this section, in some sense, sketches the social and conceptual domain for the remainder of the book. In another sense, these three chapters — very different in tone and level — are unified by an implicit attempt to demonstate the value of direct consideration of the interactional context which informs scholarly activity. Each essay is both an explication and demonstration of patterns of contextualizing social and ideational phenomena.

In "Rigor and Imagination," Carol Wilder-Mott begins by sketching "The Context of Human Communication Studies" in order to provide an historical framework within which the interactional view of communication can be understood developmentally. A section entitled "Help Stamp Out Nouns" presents three of the premises which characterize the interactional model: a premise of systemic description, a premise of pragmatism, and a premise of verbal realism. In the concluding section of the chapter, "Lessons from Gregory Bateson," Wilder-Mott narrates an account of learning, and sometimes not learning, from Bateson's example.

John H. Weakland, Bateson's student, colleague, and friend over more than thirty years, presents his own account of how "One Thing Leads to Another." As a member of the ground-breaking 1952-1962 Bateson research team which, among other things, formulated the double bind theory, Weakland offers an insider's look at the research process of this creative and prolific group. Contrary to the persistent myth that major conceptual breakthroughs are the outcome of tidy, cumulative, linear thinking, Weakland proposes that the actual process may be very different.

In "*Forming Warm ideas,*" Arthur P. Bochner presents a series of provocative propositions aimed at explicating the nature of scientific activity implicit in Bateson's thought and method. Bochner argues that scientific activity is inherently codificational; that scientific progress requires ingenuity, passion, intuition, and courage; that science is an open system in continual change; and that scientific activity is recursive. Further, data cannot speak for themselves, and "ideas are as important as facts and nowhere is it evident that they are inducible from them." Finally, Bochner offers a summary of Bateson's perspective on social scientific work, leading to the conclusion that we should "aim for catalytic conceptualizations; warm ideas are contagious."

C.W. M.

Rigor and Imagination

Carol Wilder-Mott

Ideas have a lifetime. Like the people who mind them, ideas come to be and pass away, suffer the vicissitudes of fate and the determinations of will, and remain forever creatures of context.

This essay is just such a creature, and not a cover piece which is designed necessarily to introduce what follows. Rather, acting from my part as organizer of the 1979 Asilomar conference in honor of Gregory Bateson where this book began, the present chapter is my own account of the personal and professional contexts which have given meaning to that experience. As such, what I have to say should not be taken to represent a consensus of collaborating authors, who in some cases may take exception to my argument or tone or both. The essays in this book are woven together by a slender thread of varying degrees of affinity for the ideas of Bateson and the derivative "interactional view" of human communication. Each essay is, thus, a product of its author's context and will stand or fall on its own merits, present company included.

I begin here by characterizing the context of the evolution of ideas, as I have learned and lived them, in scholarship about human communication. This first section includes a cursory account of ancient and contemporary trends in rhetorical and communication theory and research, and may be of little interest to colleagues in related disciplines. Indeed, it may be of even less interest to the communication scholar whose framework is ahistorical. But I, for one, have found the larger view of value in placing my more immediate concerns into perspective.

One of these immediate tasks is to sketch the context and premises of the interactional view of communication and change which has evolved largely out of the work of Gregory Bateson. And, finally in this essay, to share some of the lessons in learning to learn that I have derived from the example of Bateson himself, which is the heart of the matter.

While it may be true that these three topics — the context of communication studies, the premises of the interactional view, and the epistemology of Gregory Bateson — are linked strongly only in my own scheme of things, I hope to suggest to the reader who persists that there may be more to it all than that.

I. THE CONTEXT
OF HUMAN COMMUNICATION STUDIES

Classical Communication Theory

For the better part of twenty-five centuries, theory and informed practice of human communication were dominated by the model articulated in the *Rhetoric* of Aristotle and embellished by the work of Cicero and Quintilian. While viewing Aristotle's treatise within his larger philosophy illuminates the relation of oratory to human affairs, this relationship was not the only concern of the ancients nor to most of their interpreters through the ages. As commonly (mis)construed out of philosophic context, Aristotle's *Rhetoric* is a handbook on public speaking designed to teach leaders in politics, law, and entertainment how to be persuasive orators. The emphasis is upon assisting speakers in "discovering the available means of persuasion" through analysis of the intended audience and the construction of effective logical, emotional, and speaker credibility-related appeals. In order to achieve success the speaker must discover and invent persuasive arguments, organize them sensibly, clothe them in appropriate language, and deliver the package in a befitting manner.

Following this classical communication paradigm, a *speaker* constructs a *speech* and delivers it to an *audience*, which in turn serves as judge of the presentation's effectiveness. Rhetorical theorists of different eras have emphasized varying dimensions of this procedure, often with telling results for the interpretation of their time and culture as a whole, but the main point has nearly always been the development of the orator, whether through clearer apprehension of the "good" and "true" or through finer construction of the enthymeme, or heightened aesthetics of the trope, or practiced movement of the brow. Even "whole" rhetorics in the Ciceronian tradition which attended equally to canons of invention, arrangement, style, memory, and delivery promoted (wittingly or not) an elemental, linear, speaker-centered view of communication process; protocol for what Quintilian termed the "good man speaking well."

This classical paradigm, in modern dress, is employed by Nancy Harper as the unifying framework for her synthesis of *Human Communication Theory: The History of a Paradigm*. In Harper's words:

> As a model of the communication act, the [classical] paradigm can be understood as follows: An individual, whether a sender or a receiver, (1) perceives data — phenomena — which he or she classifies and stores for future use [the classical canon *memory*], (2) assigns meaning to the data in light of some present concern [the classical canon *invention*], (3) represents the meaning in symbols [the classical canon *style*], (4) adapts the symbols to social contingencies [the classical canon *arrangement*], and (5) embodies the message in some physical form [the classical canon *delivery*] (1979:3).

Even given Harper's suggestion that this model must be understood "holistically," because of the "interactive and simultaneous relationship of the five parts," taken together the parts comprise a monadic conception of communication process which focuses upon the *individual* as speaker or listener rather than upon the interactional *relationship* between communicators. While the classical paradigm could be stretched to make this point, as has been done in some contemporary rhetorical theory, during the long history from 500 B.C. to 1900 which Harper surveys, such was rarely the case. In fact, classical *dialectical* theory is in many ways a more interactional model of communication than classical *rhetorical* theory. Rhetoric is, indeed, the counterpart of dialectic, as Aristotle (to little consequence) insisted.

The value of rhetorical theory as a humane tradition was never to be found in formulary practical advice to would-be orators. Rather, the role and esteem of rhetoric from age to epoch has always been a gauge more reliable than most of a culture's social, political, and spiritual climate. Thus, philosophically minded rhetorics flourished in times of enlightenment, stylistic rhetorics in times of decline and transition, and scholastic rhetorics in times of stability or stagnation. Analysis of the nature and function of human communication provides a window for the study of culture, and in every century until the twentieth this analytic window framed a view of communication from the *one* to the *many*. Rhetorical analysis in this tradition employed qualitative concepts and methods much like those of the literary or historical scholar, an approach codified in Thonssen and Baird's work on *Speech Criticism* (1948).

Contemporary Communication Theory

The development of science and technology during this century altered both the methods and substantive concerns of communication scholars. On one hand, the introduction of telephone, radio, television, and recently laser, satellite, and computer technologies, transformed the communication environment in ways unimagined a generation ago, spawning a large field of interest in "mass" communication. On the other hand, students of face-to-face communication turned toward the scientific study of interactional systems; couples, families, work groups, friendship networks, formal organizations, and the like. The student of public address, not long ago nearly alone in a preoccupation with human communication, was suddenly not so much alone as lonely, all but engulfed by communication scholars interested in either mass-mediated or interpersonal communication.

Attention to mass communication and interpersonal communication is quite recent in the stream of things, comprising but about 25 out of 2500 years of concern with human discourse. This note on the infancy of our concerns offers not an excuse for sloppy thinking, but rather an incitement to innovation in both the substance and methods of our work. For surely there is a long way to go despite the surface impression that much of the research territory is staked out and most of the issues uncovered.

Contemporary communication studies did not substantially emerge until after World War II when the brillance of Kenneth Burke's "neo-Aristotelianism" began to refresh rhetorical theory, Alfred Korzybski's "non-Aristotelian" general semantics turned attention toward matters of meaning, Norbert Weiner's cybernetics and Shannon and Weaver's information theory introduced models thought to be applicable both to human and technical systems, the work of Harry Stack Sullivan and George Herbert Mead turned psychology and sociology in a communicational direction, and, perhaps most influentially, social psychologists such as Carl Hovland launched an era of systematic studies of persuasion using the "new" scientific methods of experimental psychology.

Hovland's famous "Yale Studies" of persuasion (Hovland, Janis & Kelley, 1953) were important in several ways. World War II provided an impetus (not to mention funding) for American scholars to study the nature and effects of propaganda, thus Hovland's research concerns were with human influence through communication — *persuasion* — for centuries the exclusive province of rhetorical studies. This convergence of rhetoric and psychology was most apparent in Hovland's studies of "source credibility," and in his operational breakdown of the construct which coincided remarkably with Aristotle's ancient analysis of rhetorical *ethos*. But there is a more important point. For while Hovland was not the first in this century to "psychologize" persuasion, he was among the first to "scientize" communication research. This he accomplished by using the empirical and experimental *methods* of the psychology lab, ushering in an epistemological revolution which established the study of human communication as a legitimate area of study in behavioral science while concomitantly laying the foundation for a methodological stranglehold by the very tools which conferred legitimacy in the first place. And soon the masters of these methods became their slaves. The qualitative rhetorical approach which had long dominated communication studies began a fall into disfavor, rendered (at least temporarily) defenseless in the face of the rising cultural eminence of science.

Speech teachers and scholars have long found themselves on shaky ground within the academy — right from the days when Plato, in the *Gorgias*, attacked the Sophists for valuing *results* over the pursuit of *Truth* and the Roman satirist Lucian wrote "A Professor of Public Speaking," through the bifurcating influence of Peter Ramus in the sixteenth century and the delivery-obsessed Elocutionary Movement of the nineteenth century, to the Dale Carnegies and pseudo-psychologists of our own time. And what better way to firm at last the foundation than by becoming epistemologically reborn as communication *scientists?*

The trend toward a science of communication developed slowly during the 1950s as scholars outside of "speech" issued communication treatises. In addition to Hovland's contribution, influential scientifically-oriented works on communication included George Miller's *Language and Communication* (1951), Elihu Katz and Paul Lazarsfeld's *Personal Influence* (1955), Osgood, Suci and Tannenbaum's *Measurement of Meaning* (1957), Leon Festinger's *Theory of Cognitive Dissonance* (1957), and the most comprehensive work of the decade, Colin Cherry's *On Human Communication* (1957). It is ironic that Cherry, a British telecommunications engineering professor, published a work as definitive as any on the emerging American field of *human* communication studies. While it would be unfair to accuse Cherry, informed as he was of linguistic, semantic, and information theory, of urging the quantification of communication research, the book certainly "looked" scientific and leaned in a technical direction. *On Human Communication* included scant reference to any direct observation of naturally occurring *human* events, its title notwithstanding. Indeed, the book was even wryly dedicated to the author's dog.

Social psychology's orgy of experimental studies of attitude change during the 1950s (see McGuire, 1969) was probably most directly responsible for the quantification of communication studies and the decline of rhetorical approaches to persuasion. Newcomb (1963) provided conceptual leadership with "balance theory," Osgood and colleagues broke through with the semantic differential as an operational measure for "congruity theory," and especially, Festinger's ideas about "cognitive dissonance" led to a veritable binge of experimental and quasi-experimental studies. This was right up the alley of fallen-away rhetorical scholars — now rather than the *qualitative* study of persuasion, speech could be *quantified* and explored as *experimental* public address. We could remain true to the ancient concern with persuasive public speaking *and* earn a rightful place as behavioral scientists.

During this seduction of communication scholars by experimental social psychology, a whole intellectual movement such as general semantics could be virtually ignored, perhaps because Korzybski's radical constructivism was by definition resistant to operationalism, and hence to "scientific" treatment. It may be that Korzybski made a fundamental miscalculation not so much in the zealous excesses of his advocacy of "non-elementalistic, non-Aristotelian" science, but rather in his belief that "simple yet powerful structural factors of sanity can be found in science" at all (1948:lxix). Korzybski, it turned out, believed in a science which would reject his ideas as beyond the pale of feasible research in a era when the doctrine of operationalism was firmly entrenched. Of course, these same blinders also deprived most students of human communication of participation in the early years of cybernetics and information theory.

As Arthur Bochner has pointed out, during the 1950s and 60s communication research was an orderly enterprise, dominated by the building block view of science, the paradigm of experimental research, and a linear causality implied by the accepted antecedent-consequent relationship of independent-dependent variables. "It was assumed," writes Bochner, "that scientific knowledge could be accumulated progressively and that the steady, methodical accumulation of facts would withstand the test of time" (1977:325).

Rhetorical studies during this period were likewise more predictable than not. A typical rhetorical analysis of public communication would include consideration of speaker, speech, audience, and occasion with further attention to the development of one or more of the classical canons of invention, arrangement, style, and delivery. The contemporary-minded relied instead upon Kenneth Burke's dramatistic framework which directed attention to the communication act, scene, agent, agency, and purpose (Burke, 1969). But in either case the research mode was qualitative, critical/analytic, historical, sometimes literary in flavor.

Events of the 1960s, from the 1963 presidential assassination through the 1970 killings at Kent State, ended this steady state of scholarly detachment. From the beginning of Western thought, the focus of human communication studies has been a product of its time and social context. Of the classical period, Harper writes:

> As with most significant innovations in human history, the study of communication as a science came into existence as a practical response to social exigencies. Initially, the impetus was the legal entanglement resulting from the overthrow of the tyrants of Syracuse. The later proliferation of communication study throughout Greece was in response to the demands of the Greek social structure, which was oral, democratic, and communal (1979:17).

This context-bound nature of communication studies is no less true now than then. Three trends of the 1960s (in addition to the rise of "mass communication" and the "information explosion") altered the terrain of human communication studies: greatly increased methodological sophistication, a shift in both research and teaching from "persuasion" to "interpersonal communication," and a move toward expansion and social relevance for rhetorical theory and criticism.

Quantification of Communication Studies

Increasingly widespread availability of computer technology during the 1960s triggered a quantum leap in the complexity of statistical methods. In the 1950s, chi-square, simple analysis of variance and correlational statistics had to suffice for most quantitative research, with calculations often done by hand. By the 1960s more complicated techniques such as factor analysis became feasible with computer assistance. From then on, a Pandora's box of multivariate techniques, nearly impossible to perform without machine aid, were within reach of any researcher who had a number at the university computer center. Multivariate analysis of variance, multidimensional scaling, canonical correlation, path analysis, and the like entered the vocabulary of communication researchers. This has been a mixed blessing, leading in some quarters to a tyranny of method over meaning in research.

As Gerald Miller has cautioned, despite the many positive aspects of increased methodological rigor, "unquestioning acceptance of such methodologies impels the researcher to subscribe to the notion that, in principle, communication is a marvelously complex phenomenon, and the only way of advancing knowledge is to look for more and more complex methodologies to describe and analyze communication" (1977a:12). "What," Miller asks, "is the scientific utility of explaining 90 percent of the variance with 65 variables; what kind of elegance and parsimony does that give us? While it may be mathematically interesting and nice to plug into a computer, I don't know what we can do with that 65 or 70 variable empirical generalization once it is constructed" (1977a:17). Indeed, Miller reports that no less a statistician than John Tukey has indicated that human communication research is in "such a state conceptually and theoretically that most researchers would be better off running repeated analyses of variance to protect the Alpha level and looking for straightforward, simple relationships" (1977a:12).

Accompanying this trend toward methodological complexity was a sustained move to further scientize communication research and teaching. This is apparent in the recommendations of the 1968 New Orleans conference which addressed conceptual frontiers in speech communication research and instruction. The conference, sponsored by the U.S. Office of Education and organized by the Speech Communication Association, brought together the most prominent behaviorally-inclined people in the field. The first recommendation of the conference, adopted with mild dissent, stated that "within the scope of a central focus on spoken symbolic interaction, the conference participants recommend that the importance of scientific approaches in speech-communication research be stressed" (Kibler & Barker, 1969:20). Also, conferees encouraged "the use of scientific approaches to inquiry in many areas of speech-communication which have traditionally used different approaches — such as rhetorical criticism, oral interpretation and theatre" (p. 21). Addressing curriculum and instruction, New Orleans participants urged academic departments "to develop a scientifically based instructional program in speech-communication" (p. 27). Whatever else this document suggests about the thinking of leaders in the field of communication only a decade ago, an infatuation with the sound of "science" is evident. This was best stated by the unidentified conference participant who dissented on one recommendation, saying:

> I oppose the resolution not because I endorse any other method than the one which is scientific; it is just that we might as well say we endorse excellent research, because the word scientific has become nothing more than an honorific term which people who are insecure about their status try to appropriate in order to define themselves in the realm of acceptability (Kibler & Barker, 1969:21).

From Influence to Interaction

Another trend of the 1960s changed the conceptual emphasis in communication research and teaching from "persuasion/attitude change" to "interpersonal communication." This paradigmatic shift from public influence to interpersonal interaction owed something to interpersonal and group studies in social psychology and much to the "human potential movement" of the 1960s and 70s. This fire was further fanned by the radical romanticism of the hippie movement and the political intensity of women, blacks, and assorted "new left" groups. "Interpersonal communication" took hold both in the research arena and in the classroom, albeit in very different guises.

Serious research attention to interpersonal communication can probably be dated roughly from Dean Barnlund's classic synthesis *Interpersonal Communication: Survey and Studies* (1968). Whereas during the 1950s and 60s scientifically-oriented communication research almost always looked at persuasive communication, by the 1970s quantitative persuasion studies gave way almost entirely to studies of interpersonal interaction, which typically employed one or more multivariate statistical procedures. Research commonly followed, more or less, what Barnett Pearce has termed the "objective scientific" approach. Pearce suggests that:

> As implemented in the study of interpersonal communication, an objective scientific approach is characterized by a mechanistic model of man, a reductionalistic-atomistic selection of the appropriate units of observation, a deterministic concept of behavior, and an epistemology which stresses 'variable testing' research in highly contrived situations (1977:105).

This was the same epistemology which had guided most quantitative experimental work in attitude change, but with a shift of focus to dyadic and group communication.

Meanwhile, in the classroom appeared a different manifestation of interpersonal communication. When communication scholars had studied primarily persuasive public communication, the basic course in speech communication had likewise been "public speaking." During the late 1960s, courses in interpersonal and small group communication proliferated, challenging (if not eclipsing) curricular emphasis on public communication. Most of these interpersonal communication courses operated from a model antithetical to the objective scientific approach of interpersonal communication research. This orientation, dubbed by Pearce the "humanistic celebration approach" to interpersonal communication, has an affinity with "the essentially nonacademic aspects of small group participant training, such as Tavistock and NTL-style T-groups; clinical and 'humanistic' psychologies; various 'awareness' producing activities such as values-clarification, assertiveness training, consciousness raising, self-acceptance; and Eastern philosophies such as Taoism which endorse a nonintrusive *laissez faire* life style" (Pearce, 1977:106). This approach is heavily value-laden, politically utopian, and on the whole distinctly anti-intellectual. It is geared toward inculcating attitudes about what "humanistic psychologists" believe *should be* the case when persons communicate, rather than surveying with less fervor what typically *is* the case.

William Gorden identifies concepts such as feedback, self-disclosure, nonverbal communication, openness, trust, and self-actualization taught through methods of "experiential learning" as central to the humanistic celebration approach. Gorden attended and wrote about T-groups, Tavistock, and est training as representative influences upon the interpersonal communication curriculum. He concluded that, despite many worthwhile aspects of his experiences, "I am, nevertheless, convinced that educators in the classroom and trainers within industry and community organizations must guard against utilizing these potent techniques for the very reason they are appealing — that is, because they feed on human hurt and conflict." Furthermore, Gorden admonishes, "an additional serious charge against the advocates and practitioners of the human potential movement is that they promote a new hedonism" (1979:48). This is the sort of self-absorption Tom Wolfe found in the "Me Decade" and Christopher Lasch in the "Culture of Narcissism." All of which is not even to mention that very few communication instructors were trained as therapists to deal professionally with the consequences of dredging the depths of student psyches. While much interpersonal communication research from the "objective scientific" model may be at worst irrelevant, interpersonal communication pedagogy from the "humanistic celebration" orientation may be at best irresponsible. Further, the radically divergent paradigms (call it "methods vs. morals") which guide research and teaching under the same "interpersonal communication" rubric is one of the sorrier contemporary features of our field. Pearce calls for convergence toward a "humane scientific" approach for the classroom, but the gulf between research and teaching in interpersonal communication is wide and seldom forded and there remains an inverse relationship between professional prestige and visible attention to matters of communication pedagogy.

Toward a Contemporary Rhetoric

During the 1960s and early 70s, while communication researchers were responding to methodological development in the behavioral sciences and speech communication teachers found affinity with the human potential movement, rhetorical scholars (somewhat under siege within the discipline) reacted swiftly and dramatically to the social and political movements which abounded. Traditional rhetorical studies had typically employed historical methods to assess the logic and persuasive effects of "great" single orators from the past (Edmund Burke, Jonathan Edwards, Daniel O'Connell, FDR). Rhetorical studies during the 60s turned toward the analysis of collective behavior (especially social movements and political campaigns), often from a participant observer or participant point of view, and toward study of the rhetoric of "non-oratorical" forms such as small group interaction, song, film, and literature (Tompkins, 1969; Simons, 1970; Bowers & Ochs, 1970; Campbell, 1972; Chesebro, 1973; Chesebro & Hamsher, 1975).

In 1970, rhetoricians and philosophers held their counterpart of the "New Orleans" conference, sponsored by the Speech Communication Association and funded by the National Endowment for the Humanities. The central question of these two "Wingspread Conferences" was "What is the essential outline of a conception of rhetoric useful in the second half of the twentieth century?" (Bitzer & Black, 1971:v). Conference participants were all distinguished rhetorical theorists or philosopher-rhetoricians, only three or four of whom had been involved in any way with the more "scientifically" oriented New Orleans meeting two years earlier. (The lines between "rhetoric" and "communication" were, by this time, clearly drawn.)

Wingspread participants reached consensus on four major statements regarding the shape of a contemporary theory of rhetoric: (1) It is imperative that rhetorical studies be broadened to explore communicative procedures and practices not traditionally covered (e.g., the non-discursive as well as the discursive, the nonverbal as well as the verbal, the event or transaction which is unintentionally as well as intentionally suasive); (2) Our recognition of the scope of rhetorical theory and practice should be greatly widened (i.e., rhetorical analyses should be applied even to things — the products of science and technology); (3) A clarified and expanded concept of reason and rational decision-making must be worked out [affirming faith in reasoned discourse as opposed to "clamorous protest"]; and (4) Rhetorical invention should be restored to a position of centrality in theory and practice, having been "largely neglected since the eighteenth century when theorists influenced by revolutions in science and philosophy dismissed *inventio* as trivial on the assumption that a single methodology—namely the new science—should be used by sensible people in all kinds of investigations and deliberations" (Bitzer & Black, 1971:238-239).

These statements reveal a sensitivity both to the social context of 1970 and to the threat which scientific studies of communication were posing to the very existence of rhetorical studies within departments where "rhetoric" and "communication" frequently had to compete for resources. It is doubtful that the New Orleans recommendation that "scientific approaches" be applied to rhetorical criticism would have been well received at Wingspread, where conferees concluded to the contrary that "it seems clear to us that methods of discovery and proof far wider than empirical methods need to be elaborated, taught, and widely used. Only a small fraction of problems . . . admit of scientific analysis and resolution" (Bitzer & Black, 1971:239).

Marie Hochmuch Nichols once wrote that "the humanities without science are blind, but science without the humanities may be vicious"(1963). It is regrettable that humanistic rhetoricians and communication scientists came to see their interests as almost mutually exclusive; communication scientists, especially, seemed more than willing to throw out the baby of rhetoric along with the bathwater of its excesses and defects. But wait. As Bateson has written:

> The would-be behavioral scientist who knows nothing of the basic structure of science and nothing of 3,000 years of careful philosophic and humanistic thought about men — who cannot define either entropy or a sacrament — had better hold his peace rather than add to the existing jungle of half-baked hypotheses (1972:xxi).

And it was precisely the *rhetorical* tradition which long served (albeit indirectly) to educate communication scholars in the history of Western philosophic and humanistic discourse.

Then a funny thing happened in the field of "Speech," or "Speech Communication," or "Human Communication," as it had become known by the mid-70s. While "rhetoric" and "communication" squabbled and mass communication split off into its own booming business, through the back door appeared all manner of curious theoretical animals which had not been tamed and taxonomized by the field: semiotic, structuralism, critical theory, hermeneutic, phenomenology, interpretative social science, systems theory, cybernetics, symbolic interactionism, ethnomethodology, discourse analysis, constructivism, rules theory, dialectical theory, natural language philosophy, and other creatures great and small. Most of these ideas had been around for some time, but they were not learned in the field because, simply, they were not taught. So suddenly the question was no longer "Is this or that *Science?*" but "What *is* 'science' anyway, especially as regards human behavior?"

Thus ensued in the mid-70s the era of the great "metatheoretical debate" ("What theoretical posture is most appropriate to the objects/relationships of our study?") and the less great "metametatheoretical debate" ("What is all this metatheoretical debate about, anyway? Let's get on with the research.") In 1977, even Gerald Miller, probably the most respected "empirical" researcher the field has produced, succumbed by writing both a metatheoretical paper on the relative value of laws, rules, situational and developmental approaches to communication research (1977a), *and* a metametatheoretical paper offering "a note of skepticism" about the " 'pervasiveness' and 'marvelous complexity' of human communication" (1977b). In the latter essay, Miller decries the "present spate of metatheoretical essays and the current paucity of research" expressing concern with the self-important tone of most metatheoretical statements (e.g., "To accept the view presented here portends a crisis comparable to the one that has occurred in modern physics") and, especially, assailing many of the essays for "the illiterate, second-rate philosophy of science posture adopted, particularly when attacking the arch-ogres, logical positivism and behaviorism" (1977b:9-10). Miller makes a strong point, but then many of the metatheoreticians who are holding forth with ill-informed philosophy of science were trained in the very departments which banished rhetorical theorists and other "humanists" to corner offices in the basement of the Phys Ed building, there to be alone with Plato and Aristotle, Toulmin and Burke.

One of the current ironies is that many of the "new" approaches to communication coming to the fore through efforts of, in some cases, disenchanted conventional communication scientists, bear a striking resemblance in tone to the humanistic bent of classical rhetorical theory. Semiotics, for instance, is qualitative, speculative, critical/analytic in method.

We have entered a promising era in the study of human communication where the tendency toward theoretical and methodological dogmatism appears to be giving way to respect for a pluralism which may allow multiple perspectives to flourish (e.g., Fisher, 1978). This is a healthy sign, especially if we now take care to keep our research feet on the ground while our metatheoretical heads are in the clouds.

II. "HELP STAMP OUT NOUNS"

One of the theoretical and ideological perspectives which has come to the attention of communication scholars in recent years has no name, at least not in the sure-sounding sense of "ethnomethodology" or "hermeneutics." Some of the names attempted for this collection of ideas have been the "New Communication" (Weakland, 1967), the "Pragmatic Perspective" (Fisher, 1978), "Batesonian Interactionism" (Simons, in this volume), and "Palo Alto Group Communication Theory." The misrepresentation suggested by several of these terms could fill its own book, and perhaps will some day when the history of this intellectual movement is written.

But namelessness is not necessarily a sorry state of affairs. "Words are dangerous things," warned Bateson, for to name a new idea is inevitably to tempt reification and misplaced concreteness. When faced with a vague notion unready to be brought into "strict expression," Bateson used a certain trick of thought and speech whereby he coined some brief colloquial term — the "stuff" or "bits" or "feel" of culture — as a reminder that "the concepts behind them are vague and await analysis" (1972:84). This approach, he suggested, can be used to train scientists to "tie knots in their handkerchiefs whenever they leave some matter un-formulated — to be willing to leave the matter so for years, but still leave a warning sign in the very terminology they use, such that these terms will forever stand not as fences hiding the unknown from future in-vestigators, but rather as signposts which read: 'UNEXPLORED BEYOND THIS POINT' " (1972:87).

John Weakland tied an appropriately loose knot by coining the term "Interactional View" to title a collection of papers from the Mental Research Institute (MRI), which he edited with Paul Watzlawick, in 1977. Significant here is the choice of "view" over "theory" to characterize the perspective being developed at MRI and elsewhere. To profess the presentation of a "theory" within the current research milieu is to connote that a set of ideas and their relationships are rather thoroughly worked out; to profess a "view" stakes a more modest claim which says "here are some of the ideas we've come up with which seem to fall into a pattern of sorts, but the territory is 'unexplored beyond this point'." The choice of "view" was also intended to signify that what was offered was a way of viewing or viewpoint, one of but many possible perspectives for observation and analysis.

This is not to say that the interactional view does not embrace a strongly held set of premises; as we shall see, it does. Rather, that these premises are as much *ideological* as *theoretical* in nature. Scholars outside of the U. S. often do not distinguish theory from ideology. Such a posture is less accepted in the objective scientific mode of U. S. research which largely resists, if not rejects, the ideological character and implications of scientific theorizing about human behavior. In any event, "ideology," according to Webster, is in the first case "visionary theorizing," a characterization that most people related to the interactional view would find congenial.

Before explicating some basic premises of the interactional view, an historical note is in order. As Jay Haley has pointed out repeatedly (1976a:92; 1976b:ix; and in Lipset, 1980:227) there never was, strictly speaking, a "Palo Alto Group." Rather, there were from 1952-1962 the Bateson projects in Menlo Park and Palo Alto (which included Gregory Bateson, John Weakland, Jay Haley, and William Fry with Don D. Jackson as first a consultant and later a member) and, separately, from 1959 on, the Mental Research Institute in Palo Alto, founded by Jackson, which in the early years included Jules Riskin, Virginia Satir, and Paul Watzlawick. While there was considerable informal interplay between these groups, and they even shared quarters for a brief time, Bateson preferred to maintain his autonomy, and emphatically declined to have his project subsumed by the MRI. As Haley reports, "He didn't want to have his consultant [Jackson] over him as director" (Lipset, 1980:227). When the Bateson project ended in 1962, both Haley and Weakland went to MRI (Haley left for Philadelphia in 1967). But by this time Bateson was preparing to work with dolphins and octopuses at John Lilly's Communication Research Institute in the Virgin Islands, and had largely disowned the psychiatric community. Thus, not only were there some strong differences *within* the Bateson group during his Palo Alto years and some stronger differences *between* Bateson and the MRI group, but Bateson soon altogether abandoned direct involvement with psychiatry.

These personal and professional differences may seem trivial from a distance, but the closer one gets to following the conceptual development of Bateson and others through the literature, the more salient such differences seem as it becomes apparent that many different voices are speaking in only approximately the same vocabulary, and not always on the same subjects. All that can probably safely be said of everyone involved with the Bateson and MRI groups in the early years is that they shared an interest in studying human communication and behavior with the aid of ideas from systems theory and cybernetics, along with a preference for naturalistic research methods rather than laboratory experimentation. Certainly, most of them maintained a focus on human problems in relation to psychotherapy, but this was notably not the case with Bateson, for whom psychiatry was but one context of many in which he pursued his epistemological studies.

During the 1960s, the Bateson project disbanded, Haley and Weakland turned specifically to the process of therapeutic change, applying and extending the ideas of their mentors — Bateson, Jackson, and the great hypnotherapist Milton Erickson. Haley's *Strategies of Psychotherapy* (1963) and Watzlawick, Beavin and Jackson's *Pragmatics of Human Communication* (1967) introduced the ideas developed during the 50s to a wide community of therapists and scholars at a time when Bateson's writings were still widely scattered and largely unknown, except for those who had stumbled upon *Communication: The Social Matrix of Psychiatry* (Ruesch & Bateson, 1951). Bateson, of course, was well away from the scene by the 60s, but his influence was still deeply felt. Don Jackson's untimely death in 1968 ended another era in the development of the interactional view, and since then Watzlawick, Haley, and Weakland have been the most visible continuing spokesmen from the earlier years, although their paths have also been independent.

All of this is by way of demonstrating that any summary account of the interactional view (see, e.g., Greenberg, 1977; Wilder, 1979; Bodin, 1980), including this one, must be taken as a series of open conclusions regarding our dim understanding of human communication, behavior, and change, rather than as the codification of any final "word."

In a special 1967 edition of *American Behavioral Scientist* on "Communication in Behavior and Behavioral Science," issue editor John Weakland made the following points to characterize what has become the general orientation for the interactional view, suggesting that communicational thinking about behavioral research carries the following implications:

(1) Focusing behavioral research on directly observable communication — with a realization that important and observable messages may be very subtle and hard to see. (2) Deliberate concern with the influential aspects of communication, of which 'information' is only one. (3) Keeping in mind that even the hardest 'facts' and the clearest messages are subject to differing interpretations. (4) Attention to the complexities, including contradiction, in communication situations — even if these can at first be characterized only roughly — rather than inappropriate atomization and oversimplification to fit observational or statistical tools already available. (5) Especially, attention to the whole system involved in any communicative interaction, even when this means that the experimenter or observer must take account of himself equally with his subject (Weakland, 1967:2).

If we recall the characterization of predominant trends in 1960s communication research drawn earlier in this chapter, Weakland stands in contradistinction on every point. Against the prevailing trend toward contrived experimentation, he advocates research on natural communication events; against the shift from "persuasion" to "interpersonal communication," he professes concern with communicational influence; against the trend toward precise operationalism, he takes a constructivist position on message interpretation; against the tendency toward reductionism and methodological determinism (the "iron law of the hammer"), he directs attention to phenomenological complexity; against the prevailing linear independent-dependent variable model of causality from an objective scientific stance, he points to a recursive systemic model of communication which must consider the influence of the observer. It can even be said that in drawing attention to communication subtlety and contradiction he stands in contrast to the humanistic celebration of openness, honesty, and "direct" communication.

These are not minor quibbles; taken as a whole Weakland's view suggests a significant paradigmatic shift for both the territory which communication research might include and the perspective from which inquiry is conducted. The positivist mood turns tentative, research becomes exploration, innovation, and adventure, not from lack of confidence but instead from the boldness to walk the alley that may be blind, to put aside the crutches of convention and be willing to fall occasionally between the steps of progress. From this view the ".05" unachieved or the "variance unaccounted for" or the "noise" in a system are not demons to clarity and understanding, but harbingers of creative thinking which remind us that the matter is "unexplored beyond this point."

During the 1970s, the interactional view was refined in theory and extended in practice, primarily in psychotherapeutic practice. The founding of MRI's Brief Therapy Center in 1967 by Richard Fisch, John Weakland, Paul Watzlawick, and Arthur Bodin, signalled an era when the theoretical notions earlier developed in the service of communicational *analysis* of behavior were applied in the service of behavioral *change*. This has been the main line of development of the interactional view during the past decade at MRI and, separately but similarly, by Jay Haley and his associates on the East Coast (see especially Watzlawick, Weakland & Fisch, 1974; Weakland, Fisch, Watzlawick & Bodin, 1974; and Haley, 1976b). Again, the interactional approach includes almost as much divergence as convergence, but at the risk of oversimplification I would argue that in addition to Weakland's 1967 characterization three major premises or orientations guide the current enactment of the interactional view: (1) a premise of systemic description; (2) a premise of pragmatism; and (3) a premise of verbal realism.

Premise of Systemic Description.

Any model of the world provides a frame of reference, a perspective, a lens through which to view events. Applied to the "same" set of observations, differing models predispose one toward differing conclusions and consequences. Marxism, Feminism, Christianity, "Science," Zen Buddhism; each provides such a model. In psychotherapy, for instance, the monadic intrapsychic Freudian model long dominated: problems had their origin in an individual's past and unconscious, and change was predicted to occur when the individual became aware of these hidden forces through the help of the therapist. Conversely, a systemic model of behavior and change focuses upon what is currently happening within the interactional system of one's interpersonal network with little regard for forces "inside" the individual or for uncovering deep past traumas. Increasing the *number* of individuals considered does not compel a systemic view: for instance, Freudian-psychoanalytic assessment can be done with all family members rather than one. As Jackson pointed out, "it is only when we attend to *transactions between* individuals as primary data that a qualitative shift [from an individual to an interactional] conceptual framework can be achieved" (1965:5).

Systemic description and explanation is based in part upon the principles of nonsummativity (the whole is more than the sum of parts; complexity increases exponentially rather than additively) and nonisolability (variables — or individuals — cannot be understood out of context). Systemic description directs attention toward the discovery of interactional forms, patterns, rules, themes; such patterns are identified through the observation of redundancy in behavioral sequences. Systemic description is rooted in the metaphor of "information" rather than the metaphor of "energy."

Watzlawick writes along these lines:

> Since approximately the end of World War II, a very different epistemology has gained increasing acceptance. Rather than basing itself on the concept of energy and its undirectional causality, it is founded on the concept of *information*, that is, of order, pattern, negentropy, and in this sense the second law of thermodynamics. Its principles are cybernetic, its causality is of a circular, feedback nature, and with information being its core element, it is concerned with the process of communication within systems in the widest sense — and therefore also with human systems, e.g., families, large organizations, and even international relations (Watzlawick & Weakland, 1977:xii).

From a systemic cybernetic perspective, forms of feedback, recursion, and self-reflexiveness take on special interest. One must communicate to communicate about communication. Syntactic, semantic, or pragmatic recursion can produce paradox. I am a part of the context I am trying to embrace and apprehend as an observer. As Heinz Von Foerster puts it, "I am the observed relation between myself and observing myself...'I' am the infinite recursive operator" (1972:19). Stated by R. D. Laing, "The truth I am trying to grasp is the grasp that is trying to grasp it" (1967:190).

The subject — predicate — object structure of Indo-European language itself presents a serious obstacle to systemic description because of the way it predisposes expressions of *acting upon* rather than *interacting with*. This is the problem mathematician Anatol Holt was pointing to when he proclaimed "HELP STAMP OUT NOUNS!" (M. C. Bateson, 1972), those little linguistic devils which ground an epistemology of substance vs form, quantity vs pattern. Don Jackson recognized a similar problem when he wrote in 1967 that the entire psychiatric nosology is descriptive of the *individual* rather than the *interaction*. Jackson argued for a shift in terminology "from description of the 'nature of' someone to descriptions of the 'relationships between' someone and someone else." Dean Barnlund touches upon the same issue when he writes in this volume that "conjunctivitis, in the grammatical rather than the optical sense, is as important to cultivate in our research as in our lives."

More practically speaking, systemic description suggests that relational problems and promise are most usefully explained within an interactional context. Human problems are thus seen to be engendered, maintained, and changed through systemic processes. Not only does cybernetic explanation help to account theoretically for the complexities of play, humor, religion, art, and madness, but the model also carries direct implications for practical matters of human development and change.

Premise of Pragmatism.

Bateson, in later years, moved away from the anthropological orientation which had long kept his thinking linked closely to direct observation of data, toward a form of highly speculative philosophical idealism wherein concrete exemplifications were invoked primarily in the service of demonstrating a larger epistemological theme. Conversely, in recent years, the interactional view, especially as developed at MRI, has been refined to address practical human problems, with theory invoked in the service of guiding specific actions. Brief therapy was developed in response to the practical exigencies confronting psychotherapists as designated change agents. While Bateson's question became something like "What is the largest possible framework I can sketch to encompass my thinking about thinking?," the interactional therapy question became something more like "What is the smallest possible intervention that can be designed to alter this interactional system?"

Brief therapists are interested primarily in *doing* the process of change, and but secondarily with *explaining* the doing, and even then with the caveat that descriptive metaphors, analogies, and the like are at best approximate mappings. Pragmatism is rooted in *praxis*, action, doing, and the thought that we *do* more than we *know*. We can speak a proper sentence without being able to parse it; tie a knot with no knowledge of the neurophysiology involved; bake a cake understanding neither chemistry nor thermodynamics. And even knowing these things does not fully account for the poetry of the sentence, the strength of the knot, or the taste of the cake. Likewise, we have but the slightest understanding of how human behavior, communication, and change work. But work they do, for better or worse. Thus any theoretical account is a partial account, any explanatory metaphor sheds light from only certain angles.

Whatever theoretical parsimony, coherence, or elegance has evolved during the development of the interactional view has always been the consequence of a secondary objective. Similarly, the theoretical *incon-sistencies* of the interactional view are in some measure the result of a maverick disregard for conventional canons of theory construction, due partly to the fact that therapists deal directly with spontaneous communication in all its muddled glory rather than with the sterilized abstractions and reductions of talk which provide the basis for much communication research. "Virtual communication" (e.g., self-reports of attitudes) is much more amenable to formal modeling than "actual communication." To accommodate studies of actual communication, John Weakland has suggested that rather than considering the constructs of the interactional view as building blocks for some monistic theory, they might be more appropriately construed as a series of "self-reflexive interventions" which reframe our own implicit and largely uncriticized rules for understanding communication "as we hitch ourselves up one notch at a time out of the mud" (Wilder, 1979:184). This sort of sea-level thinking, characteristic of Weakland's approach, is a long way from Bateson's lofty "ecology of mind," but it brings into focus an important difference between Bateson the idealist and the path of his proteges.

What was important to Bateson was sketching the outlines of "the pattern which connects" all living things; most important to Weakland and his colleagues is the development of practical strategies for the clarification and resolution of human problems. Both of these orientations employ the language of systemic description, but within different domains and with objectives of different scope.

Corollary to the pragmatic perspective is what may be termed a *premise of possibility*. This is articulated in Watzlawick's exposition of the "utopia syndrome" as a problem-engendering pattern resulting when the *ideal* is mistaken for the *possible* (Watzlawick, Weakland &

Fisch, 1974:47-61). This position is based upon the belief that life, at best, is fraught with difficulties and challenges. Even the most joyous events — marriage, childbirth, milestones of professional achievement — carry with them stressful changes. In courting accomplishment of any sort, one is often inclined to overlook the heightened pressure, expectations, and complexity that accompany successful attainment. The darker side of "self-actualization" has been little explored. The myths of Horatio Alger, Hollywood, and the human potential movement still prevail in middle-class American culture, promoting the belief that anything less than a life which moves from peak experience to peak experience is somehow lacking. While it might be unreasonable to suggest working for less than the best life, more brutal to the human spirit is the relentless pursuit of chimerical bliss. In situations where change in the realities of circumstance is all but impossible, Watzlawick writes, "it is the premise that things *should be* a certain way which is the problem and which requires change, not the way things *are*. Without the utopian premise, the actuality of the situation might be quite bearable" (Watzlawick, Weakland & Fisch, 1974:61).

It is likely that Watzlawick and his colleagues in affluent Palo Alto see more than their share of utopian clients in therapy, but whatever the case the premise of possibility guides their problem-oriented, behaviorally-focused, goal-directed approach to interactional therapy. In contrast to many contemporary humanistic therapies which lead one to believe that by focusing upon life's miracles its problems will vanish (when in fact it is often the miracles which vanish under scrutiny), the message here is more like "attend sensibly to life's difficulties, and the miracles will take care of themselves."

The premise of possibility does not compel one to abandon hopes, dreams, ideals, or visions of the best human condition; rather it directs one simply to consider the difference between what is possible to achieve within a given set of constraints and what is not, and to act accordingly.

The pragmatic orientation also carries implications for communication research. The typical first steps in any research enterprise include stating the question to be explored and defining the scope of the problem to be addressed. All research does this, either directly or by implication, but the problem is with the nature of the "problems" themselves. It is difficult to maintain that the outcome of most interpersonal communication research should be knowledge for the sake of knowledge, but this is the impression generated by the empty elegance of many well-executed projects which take us through what Janet Beavin Bavelas calls "beautiful routes to nowhere in particular" (1980). In reviewing such studies, the pragmatist might ask "But what's the *problem?*" Research from the pragmatic perspective is grounded in the quest to explicate the processes of creation and resolution of felt human problems, remaining as close to observable behavior as possible. *Always*, the problem takes precedence over methodological aesthetics.

Premise of Verbal Realism.

As a third-grader, I became engaged in an argument with my teacher over when it was safe to cross at a signalled intersection. She taught that we should cross when the light was green; I insistently countered that it was safe to cross when the light was red. Apparently, this was her last straw with me, as mother was called to school and the three of us marched to the nearest intersection presumably to show, once and for all, who was "right." As it turned out, of course, we had been looking at different lights; she at the one in the direction of the cross, myself at the signal controlling the traffic perpendicular to one's direction. I lost the argument on the basis of sheer power, a valuable lesson in its own right, while privately maintaining my belief in the superior safety of "crossing on red." (After all, it's the perpendicular traffic that runs over you, regardless of the stop or go of parallel cars.) But the more important lesson learned was that "rightness" and "reality" depend largely upon one's point of view in a situation. That might makes right so frequently may obscure this, but not diminish its pervasive truth.

It is not *power* that corrupts, Bateson cautioned, but the *idea* of power. Likewise, it is not "reality" that enlivens and endangers our daily social world so much as our symbolic reifications. Speaking along these lines, Kenneth Burke tells of when his young son asked "Is the Easter Bunny *real?*" "Think about it and come up with your own answer," the father suggested. Some time later the son returned: "I've got it. There *is* an Easter Bunny but it isn't *real.*".

The premise of verbal realism suggests that social reality is, in large measure, constructed through communication. Even first-order "physical" realities are not apart from this construction. While few would doubt the "reality" of words on paper in my typewriter were they with me as I write this, a schizophrenic or clever colleague could walk in and ask what the alphabet soup I'm cooking here will taste like, and one or both or neither may laugh if I respond that I'm prepared to eat my words. Watzlawick submits:

> ... Our everyday, traditional ideas of reality are delusions
> which we spend substantial parts of our daily lives shoring
> up, even at the considerable risk of trying to force facts to fit
> our definition of reality instead of vice versa. And the most
> dangerous delusion of all is that there is only one reality.
> What there are, in fact, are many different versions of reality,
> some of which are contradictory, but all of which are the
> results of communication and not reflections of eternal objec-
> tive truths (1976:xi).

While communication as we understand it could not proceed at all
without some stability in our consensus about reality, it is easy to forget
that we are the architects of this construction. "Facts do speak," writes
Weakland, "but not for themselves" (1967:2).

The idea of the social construction of reality has received much lip-
service in social science, especially since the argument was cogently advanced by Berger and Luckman (1966), but has yet to be taken seriously
within the research domain, so enormous seem the problems of
characterizing (as Laing has several times attempted) multi-
perspectivity. Be that as it may, within the more open clinical domain,
the premise of verbal realism has become a cornerstone belief in exploring strategies of psychotherapeutic change from the interactional view.
If one accepts that social reality can be defined quite variously in dialectical interplay with circumstantial constraints, then a rose by any other
name becomes something else again. Is a certain behavioral pattern
nagging or reminding? Oppression or loving protection? Helping or
domineering? Failure or learning experience? Is the glass half-empty or
half-full? It all depends, of course, upon one's point of view. Taking this
position to heart has resulted in the development of a variety of very potent strategies for change which offer the beginnings of a novel theory of
persuasion that makes a sort of "uncommon sense."

The premise of verbal realism has led, for instance, to the development of a range of "reframing" techniques which alter not the "facts" of
a situation, but rather the *meaning attributed to* the facts. To reframe
"means to change the conceptual and/or emotional setting or viewpoint
in relation to which a situation is experienced and to place it in another
frame which fits the 'facts' of the same concrete situation equally well or
even better, and thereby changes its entire meaning" (Watzlawick,
Weakland & Fisch, 1974:95). Social context is thus redefined in a more

life-promoting way. To persuade a person to accept the reframing, one learns to "speak the patient's language" — to frame the new frame — by presenting advice and opinions using appropriate communication channels, and reasoning in terms of the person's own logic and belief systems (Watzlawick, Weakland & Fisch, 1974:104; Bandler & Grinder, 1975). To use *resistance* to change to *promote* change, the therapist may use Selvini's technique of "positive connotation," which frames all behaviors within an interactional system as functional (Selvini, *et al.*, 1978:55-56). Or one can reframe through the "Confusion Technique" of Milton Erickson (Erickson, 1964) which uses inappropriate responses to create vulnerability during distraction. This is not the place to discuss the implications of these and similar change strategies, but only to point out that such approaches are all based on a belief in the premise of verbal realism.

Now, is the premise of verbal realism itself "real?" From the pragmatic perspective, this is the wrong question, an inevitable artifact of linguistic recursion. To state that "there is no single reality" includes this statement itself within its own scope. However, if paradox is understood as central to systemic description, such a loop contains a truth in its own right and need not be untied so as to lie in a straight line. Given the constraints of prose and even poetry, it is difficult if not impossible to characterize an anti-reification perspective in a non-reifying fashion. But given the choice of retreating to either an ashram or to academic analysis, most of us are still inclined (however marginally) toward the latter.

The interactional view is a collection of ideas developed by a network of people working together and apart over the past thirty years along the lines of exploring in a very wide sense human communication, behavior, and change. Taken roughly as an aggregate, this perspective is distinct both from other approaches to human communication and from the later path of its theoretical mentor, Gregory Bateson. The interactional view has set out a few context markers on territory that is "unexplored beyond this point." Further conceptual innovation, research, experience and argument are needed to continue the search to discover "how much all of us have to learn about what each of us already knows" (Bochner & Krueger, 1979:208).

III. LESSONS FROM GREGORY BATESON

In 1973 I was teaching at Oberlin College in Ohio and completing a Ph.D. thesis which argued a Marxian-dialectical framework for the analysis of social conflict and change, a position which had evolved naturally in graduate studies at Kent State University during the extraordinary years there from 1969 to 1972. An Oberlin colleague, Christian Koch, offered to take a look at the thesis and give his opinion. I knew little about Chris except that he taught courses on such esoteric topics as "Semiotic and Structuralism" and "Ecology and Ideology," which attracted a small but fervent band of loyalists who, as far as I could tell, by half-way through any one of Koch's seminars, spoke in strange tongues and only to each other.

Koch's feedback was immediate and direct: "You've got it all wrong. What we need is a morphogenetic event. Here, read this," he said, handing me the just-published *Steps to an Ecology of Mind.* I knew vaguely of Gregory Bateson, had read some of *Communication: The Social Matrix of Psychiatry* years earlier, so I bought a copy of *Steps,* browsed it, read a few pages here and there, and put it down for three years. This man, too, was speaking in tongues, and I was having enough difficulty mastering the language of dialectical materialism (already chosen at some peril over the language of statistics) to switch epistemologies midthesis, as it were.

In 1976, having moved to Palo Alto, California, a series of synchronicitous events led me to dig out *Steps* and, this time, read it cover to cover. And I haven't put it down for long since (something of a mistake, as I shall point out), so tantalizing is the way of thinking it demonstrates. I now know what Stewart Brand meant when he wrote "a good many people I know consider Bateson maddeningly obscure. Some of those later found him maddeningly clear and they started paying attention. I don't know anyone who stopped paying attention once they started" (1978:5).

In these five years of reading and writing and teaching "about" Bateson, I have learned a great deal about learning from Bateson, mostly from having gotten so many things wrong. A large part of this difficulty in learning from Bateson comes, I believe, from the fact that in nearly every phase of my formal education I was taught to learn in the wrong way and about the wrong things (indeed, about "things" at all) to prepare me to approach an epistemology of pattern. I have known at least since the third-grade incident at the stop light that something was amiss with an education which bore such a low correlation with life as I understood it from my own experience. Along these lines, Heinz Von Foerster tells of a conversation he had as a young boy in Vienna with his uncle, Ludwig Wittgenstein. Wittgenstein asked the boy what he wanted to be when he grew up. "I want to be a *Naturforscher*," said Heinz. The uncle replied, "You will have to learn many, many things to be a *Naturforscher*." "But I know them already," insisted the boy. "Ah," said the uncle, "but you will have to learn very much to know that you know."

Reaction to Bateson's work typically takes one of three forms, which I present here as a way of teaching about (my) learning from Bateson, possibly making the path easier for others: *disregard*, *consecration*, and — to tie a loose knot — *"doing"* Bateson. Sometimes these forms appear as developmental stages — as they did for me and probably do for most academics — but in the case of people with less to unlearn, understanding of Bateson comes more rapidly. (My students apprehend Bateson much more easily than did I, or do my colleagues.) While Bateson insisted that all taxonomies are misleading, in the words from *Rebel Without a Cause*, "You've gotta do *something*." Bateson himself remarked, when asked what he got out of his work, that "90 percent is in the process; the rest isn't worth much." And learning from Bateson is indeed a process, often so subtle that you don't know when you do know, and just when you think you understand you learn that you didn't.

Disregarding Bateson

"All change," Joseph Heller advises in *Good as Gold*, "is for the worse." This Heller half-truth reminds us that even learning, progress, and enlightenment, carry with them the seeds of destruction of the secure known, untenable as that known may be. One of the best documented occurrences in psychotherapy is resistance to the very change professed to be most desired; the painful pathology of the known often holds powerful check over chancing the unpredictable consequences of improvement (e.g., Jackson, 1957). Similarly, intellectual curiosity and exploration carry greater risk of failure and rejection than does faithful servitude to the current epistemological party line. For instance, the social conformity required to attain advanced degrees, and later professional tenure, often ensures that once such freedom of academic expression is secured, one has nothing imaginative or challenging left to express. Perhaps it is more than coincidence that neither Bateson nor Kenneth Burke ever earned a Ph.D. or held a tenured university position.

Stephen Toulmin notes in this volume that because of the peculiarities of Bateson's expression, those scholars who might most benefit from his thinking are, alas, those most likely to ignore or dismiss it. To approach Bateson's work seriously takes an open mind borne of a certain malaise with more conventionally codified ways of thinking about communication, behavior, and change. And even then, Bateson isn't of much immediate help, speaking as he did in a patois informed of biology, anthropology, cybernetics, aethetics, and mysticism, with never an apology and seldom a revision or explanation. Even his vocabulary is vexing. The language of digital and analogic modes of communication, deutero- and proto-learning, symmetrical and complementary interaction, report and command levels of communication, entropy, difference, dormitive hypothesis, double bind, stochastic process, and double description is a strange tongue indeed. These are complex ideas taken even singly, and more baffling yet when taken as a whole.

"Bateson knows something which he does not tell you," or "There's something behind what Bateson says, but he never says what it is," his students would complain (Bateson, 1972:xvii). He told me he was always asked, "Bateson can't you say it more clearly, or in an easier way?" "But I don't know how to say it in any other way," was his response. Bateson believed that part of the problem with understanding his work was that people did not believe he really meant what he said. But as Bochner rejoins, to say " 'I mean what I say' does not say what is meant." And thus to the end of his life Bateson felt deeply misunderstood, as perhaps he was and is. "The seeds I have sown have grown as dragon's teeth," he said. "Where have I gone wrong?"

John Weakland suggests that Bateson was hard to follow for at least two reasons. First, since he was always breaking new ground, his words and ideas appeared strange almost by definition, as he struggled against the boundaries of language. Secondly, Bateson seemed to have some ambivalence about being understood. As Jay Haley commented, "Bateson sometimes seemed to give the impression that if you understood him, he wasn't being profound enough." But Weakland adds, "nevertheless he *did* communicate, or others would not have taken up and developed his ideas" (Weakland, 1980). And it is important to point out that while Bateson was the prime mover, he was by no means the *only* mover among his colleagues. Ironically, without the success of the very revisionists he ridiculed, the magnitude of his own public recognition and esteem would have been greatly restricted.

The reach of Bateson's thought seemed often to exceed the grasp of his expression, a condition not helped by his intellectual isolationism. During all of his peripatetic professional life — in Britain, Bali, New Guinea, New York, Boston, Hawaii, the Virgin Islands and California — he never looked back to engage either his critics or followers. Jack of many disciplines, he was master of none in a traditional sense. He wrote and published fitfully on a wide range of topics in a curious and astonishing array of journals—including *Junior College Journal, Journal of American Folklore, Impulse — Annual of Contemporary Dance, American Journal of Occupational Therapy*, and *Art Bulletin*, as well as journals in the fields of biology, genetics, anthropology, sociology, political science, psychiatry, psychology, science, philosophy of science, semantics, communication, and evolution.

According to Haley (1976a), Bateson knew just about everyone who was anyone in most disciplines. But when he worked in collaboration it was usually with students rather than with peers, a tendency which increased markedly through the years. As Toulmin notes, Bateson seemed to be addressing the audience of his "great precursors down the ages" rather than the audience of his contemporaries. There is more than a hint here of British hubris; a spirit of intellectual imperialism common to the context of Bateson's birthright into a family, a social class, a culture, and an era where the sun never set on the empire and self-assurance knew no opposite.

And there were blind spots. It took Bateson nearly thirty years, from the early 1950s to the very end of *Mind and Nature*, to recognize the limitations, well known to others during that time, of one of his key metaphors, Bertrand Russell's "theory of types," as well as to recognize one pervasive form of his own thought as "dialectical." The original double bind paper (Bateson, Jackson, Haley, and Weakland, 1956) was read (if not intended) as a lineal formulation of binder to victim and allowed a tendency toward reification that even later restatements of the idea (Bateson, Jackson, Haley & Weakland, 1963; Weakland, 1974) have failed to chase away. Also, some of Bateson's early allies in anthropological relativism remain perplexed by his final turn toward the search for "eternal verities of life." Finally, it was not until 1970, at the age of 66, that Bateson realized "the abiding intellectual project of his life — to pioneer a science of mind" (Lipset, 1980:272), a "moment of lucidity" achieved during preparation of that year's Alfred Korzybski memorial lecture, published as "Form, Substance, and Difference" (1972:448-465). And from then this very grandness of purpose suggested standards for the measurement of his own accomplishment which are truly attained by few.

Bateson's categorical repudiation of inductive empirical science, his avoidance of scholarly debate, the singular path of his personal and professional life, along with the eccentricities of his manner and often place of expression, make his contribution easy to disregard. Disregard is no doubt the prudent course for many, but "for those of us who respect his approach to natural philosophy, and who find many of his ideas congenial and appealing," writes Toulmin, "that is a matter for particular regret."

"Batesonian Consecration"

In February 1980, I traveled to Esalen Institute in Big Sur, California, to attend what was to be one of Bateson's last weekend "Ecology of Mind" seminars. Esalen had taken in the Bateson family after his cancer was diagnosed in 1978. It was at Esalen that he completed *Mind and Nature* with the assistance of his daughter Cathy, living in a round house — built for Fritz Perls — on a Pacific cliff, revered as resident sage. Bateson, the towering intellectual, was a curious figure at Esalen, once epicenter of the human potential movement. The weekend of the seminar we shared the premises with a "basic encounter group" and a "couples encounter group," strange bedfellows indeed alongside the rarefied cerebral aura surrounding Bateson. While Esalen may be derided as a psychological theme park ("Disneyland of Northern California"), it is hard to deny that there is something magical about the place, set as it is on the country's most magnificent coastline, and that the Esalen environment may have lengthened Bateson's life.

A friend of mine who had not met Bateson once asked another who had: "How tall is he?" "Six-foot-five by the tape," was the reply, "and about ten feet tall in person." Such truly appeared to be the case during his last years in a cultural context which included Esalen, the University of California Board of Regents, the San Francisco Zen Center, and Governor Jerry Brown's circle of confidants introduced to Bateson through new age impresario Stewart Brand.

Bateson always attracted an interesting collection of people, and the "Ecology of Mind" seminar participants were no exception: a feminist, a film-maker, a solar energy entrepreneur, mind-explorer John Lilly and his wife Toni, university students, the usual smattering of mental health professionals, several visitors from other countries, and a few surprised people who enrolled in the Bateson seminar because the encounter groups were full.

We had all been waiting for some time when Bateson shambled into Esalen's Huxley Room to convene on Friday evening. I squirmed through the awed silence which greeted him, but such was often the response his demeanor evoked, and even more so at that moment when it was plain to those who had known him that his strength was rapidly waning. Bateson began by reading, unannounced, a passage from T. S. Eliot's *Four Quartets*, long among his favorite poems. I was put privately at ease because I recognized the selection, as I was to recognize most all of his references during the weekend as the conversation ranged through symmetry in nature, end-linkage between U.S. and British childrearing practices, Mary Poppins and the double bind, intercultural communication problems with the Mideast, form and pattern in Japanese tradition, "eternal verities of life," multiple levels of river otter communication, and trance induction in Bali. I had studied my Bateson so dutifully and well it was not until the end of the second seminar day that I realized I had absolutely nothing to contribute aside from page references, painfully trivial knowledge in this context. Far richer were those who had glimpsed Bateson's work in their peripheral vision and focused then not between the lines, but rather beyond them, bringing back to bear on the matters at hand a wide range of anecdotes and experience through which to advance the circles of dialogue. Once again, my approach to learning had failed me. Having finally mastered the role of good student, able to recite chapter and verse, it was stunning to realize that to understand this man I must learn to learn in a new way. Bateson suffered fools more gladly than he suffered revisionists. It was time to put away the books for a while.

"Batesonian Consecration" (and he predictably abhorred the adjective "Batesonian") typically takes one of two forms: *reification* or *deification*.Reification is most readily seen in the twenty-five year history of double bind research, where the spirit of the double bind as a crude epistemological matrix suggestive of the shape of systemic description of interactional phenomena has been almost entirely overlooked in favor of attempts to operationalize the construct in order to "count" double binds. Gina Abeles, in a review of double-bind studies, correctly suggests that the greater contribution of the double bind lies in its heuristic value, while adding that "meanwhile it presents itself as a theory with derivable hypotheses, and as such continues to invite empirical validation" (1976:137). Contrary to Clifford Geertz's claim (1973:5), the doctrine of operationalism is far from dead in behavioral research.

Reification of Bateson's thinking is also manifest in seminars, books, and review articles which attempt to tidy the muddle by taxonomizing or otherwise reducing his ideas, rather than expanding them laterally to other contexts. Bateson despised textbooks for the false sense of completion they offer (Lipset, 1980), and his critique of an otherwise well-received "Palo Alto Group" review essay of my own (Wilder, 1979) was characteristic. "While," he wrote, "you should not feel yourself to be worse than the average when you find yourself somewhat stuck in the swamps of confusion," the essay was nonetheless, "yet another attempt to clean the Augean stable where, you will remember, the horses made the task difficult even for Hercules by continued shitting" (Bateson, 1978). It was not until later I learned that I was in excellent company being admonished in this fashion, and not until the Esalen "Ecology of Mind" seminar, my fourth visit, I knew fully that understanding Bateson was not to be had by reading between the lines, but rather by venturing beyond them.

The second mode of "Batesonian Consecration," deification, is a phenomenon probably particular to contemporary culture in Northern California, where in his last years Bateson came to be adulated especially within the Esalen and Zen communities by followers who were untouched by his scholarship but utterly captured by his charisma. Bateson reacted paradoxically by passively playing the part while actively scorning the role. He was at once a benevolent teacher and merciless critic, unable to quite grasp his own contribution to the twin fates of deification and reification. But, after all, how is one to take a scientific mystic? A poetic scientist?

Odious as both deification and reification were to Bateson, each has a place in the evolution of ideas. Deification, surely a form of love, stirs the energy and even passion required to sustain interest in a vulnerable emergent way of thinking. Reification provides a measure of contemporary scientific epistemology against which new ideas can be assessed as to whether they can be accommodated by existing paradigms or will be found to account for anomalies of such significance that paradigmatic change is demanded. Geertz writes, along related lines, that after a powerful new idea (the second law of thermodynamics, the principle of natural selection, the notion of unconscious motivation, the organization of the means of production — and perhaps the double bind or the "pattern which connects"?) has "burst upon the intellectual landscape with tremendous force" to hold for a time the status of "the conceptual center-point around which a comprehensive system of analysis can be built," and is subsequently tamed through application and extension, we finally recognize that the idea "does not explain everything, not even everything human; and our attention shifts to isolating just what that something is, to disentangling ourselves from a lot of pseudoscience to which, in the first flush of its celebrity, it has also given rise" (1973:3-4).

"Doing" Bateson

More than thirty years ago, Bateson was John Weakland's first teacher of anthropology at the New School in New York. Weakland tells that it took him a long time to appreciate how different Bateson's teaching was from that which usually occurs. What usually happens is that students are inundated with one or both of two things: either "grand theories of the ancient masters of the art which tell you where it's all at so you can follow it and not question it," or "an enormous mass of data about this and that and the other thing from all over the world that there is no way one can make any real sense out of ." In contrast:

> What Gregory did was to assign to each of us, fledgling and new to anthropology as almost all of us were, a concrete project that we could do within the confines of a semester that involved going out and looking at some actual data with the aim of making some beginning sense of it and carrying that beginning sense as far as we could go within the confines of the situation, plus he offered some general guidelines as to how we might begin (Weakland, 1979).

Bateson attempted to teach *how* to think, not *what* to think. The maxim of this, if there is one, might be "Do as I do, not as I say." To "do as I say" leads straight into the traps of conventional revisionism, reductionism, and reification; dead-end thinking which proscribes discovery rather than promoting it.

But what does it mean, in Bateson's case, to "do as I do"? None of us *is* Bateson, after all, and few of us could mimic his visual, analogic, aesthetic, recursive style of expresson if even such imitation was to be desired. Bateson challenges us with what Umberto Eco terms an "open" rather than a "closed" text, which demands much of the reader in that its story line does not predictably satisfy our "hunger for redundancy" (1979:121).

Several things may be said with some confidence about Bateson's way of doing science. Bochner, in this volume, mentions some of the lessons to be learned from Bateson's approach: study life in its natural setting, think aesthetically, live with your data, resist dogmatic formalisms, be precise but remain open, and "aim for catalytic conceptualizations; warm ideas are contagious." The sum of this approach made Bateson's thinking at once intellectually rigorous, aesthetically pleasing, and practically applicable, a collection of attributes as powerful as it is rare.

More abstractly, following Bateson's lead, not only do we move from thinking about objects and elemental kinds of "things" to form and process, but we move to a realm where the distinctions often drawn between object and subject, form and process, make no difference except in the "difference" that they make. He taught not about "things" as "objects" of "thought," and not even really about first-order patterns, but rather about second-order patterns and beyond — about ways of thinking about ideas. And about ways of thinking about thinking about ideas. As Bateson has said, there are five kinds of creatures in the world. First, those that just are. Second, those that are and live. Third, those that are and live and move. Fourth, those that are and live and move and think. And finally, the creatures of interest to him and us: those that are and live and move and think and *think about thinking*.

In his pursuit of this epistemology for "thinking about thinking," Bateson's own patterns of mind finally emerged rather clearly. This is complex territory which I can do no more than point to in the present context, resisting the temptation to draw a diagram which, even given the virtues of formalism and visualization, would make the configuration of Bateson's mentality appear tidier and more static than it was.

Perhaps most evident among Bateson's forms of thought was a preference for hierarchies of description and explanation. (What one might term an "Epistemology of British Social Classism.") This is where Russell's "theory of types" came in handy to characterize logical levels of learning and communicaton, as set forth succinctly in "The Logical Categories of Learning and Communication" (Bateson, 1972:279-398). We think in patterns of contexts of differences. We learn and we learn to learn. We communicate and we communicate about communication. (After the third-order transform — e.g., communicating about communicating about communicating — the pattern is of little practical value, although Bateson asserted cryptically to me that "learning three and four tell you that learning one and two are all screwed up.") The hierarchical metaphor is where Bateson's "metas" come from, and he uses more than a dozen of them — metacommunication, metacontext, metapattern, metarandom, metaslash, and so on. "A man's reach should exceed his grasp, or what's a meta for?" he punned (Brockman, 1977:246). While Bateson recognized by the early 1960s that the logical types model was not a simple unbranching ladder in that it must include "propositions about the relations *between* classes of different logical types" (1972:307), it was not until *Mind and Nature* he fully saw that "instead of a hierarchy of classes, we face a hierarchy of *orders of recursiveness*" (1979:209). The ladder is looped, not lineal. Paradox is embraced rather than exorcised. And the theory of types is no longer an adequate metaphor.

Also, in both action and argument, Bateson strongly preferred deduction over induction, and often a form of lateral thinking — abduction — over both. In teaching, he discovered that "a difference between my habits of thought and those of my students sprang from the fact that they were trained to think and argue *inductively* from data and hypotheses, but never to test hypotheses against knowledge derived by *deduction* from the fundamentals of science or philosophy" (1972:xviii). And he believed "that it is simply not true that the fundamentals of science begin in induction from experience" (1972:xxii).

But Bateson's natural form of argument most frequently took the shape of what C.S. Peirce termed "abduction" — the "lateral extension of abstract components of description" — whereby it is possible to describe some thing or event "and then look around the world for other cases to fit the same rule that we devised for our description" (1979:142). Bateson's training in natural science deserves credit for this inclination toward abduction which served a "very important motif" in his thinking — "a habit of constructing abstractions which refer to terms of comparison between entities" (1972:79). Bateson borrowed homology, homonomy, and analogy from zoology to use as terms of description for a wide range of phenomena (1972:80; 1979:166-172). The product of this abductive way of thinking was often an array of cases from different contexts presented in order to examine patterns of relationship.

Abduction leads directly to a more complicated form of Bateson's thought which he made much of in later years — a dialectical process of "double description." Bateson first identified his "double habit of mind" in a 1940 paper "Experiments in Thinking about Observed Ethnological Material," a lucid personal account of how he at that time thought that he thought about anthropological data. This is where he sketches the dialectic of "loose and strict thinking" that occurred when the double habit of mind "led me into wild 'hunches' and, at the same time, compelled more formal thinking about these hunches" (1972:75). He also demonstrated this pattern in discussing the relationship between "data" and "fundamentals" (1972:xvii-xxvi). And by 1979 this dialectical mode had led him to the central questions: "In what way can two or more items of information or command work together or in opposition?" (1979:64) and "What bonus or increment of knowing follows from *combining* information from two or more sources?" (1979:67). By 1979 he could declare "the manner of the search [of my fifty years of science] is plain to me and might be called the *method of double or multiple comparison*" (1979:87). Much of *Mind and Nature* proceeds in this manner, for beyond the major argument to establish six criteria of mind, the remainder of the book "is about different sorts of what I called *double description* and ranging from binocular vision to the combined effect of the 'great' stochastic processes and the combined effect of 'calibration' and 'feedback.' Or call it 'rigor and imagination' or 'thought and action' " (1979:212).

Hierarchies of orders of recursiveness and a dialectic of double description — what we have here is a reflexively shaped dynamic epistemology wherein discovery moves simultaneously in many directions. Bateson's own work is, or course, the most definitive demonstration we have of these forms of thought as enacted by a scientist. What's unusual is not that he uses these methods — somewhat standard procedures for poets and mystics — but that he uses them *as a scientist*. Be he prophet or fool or both may not be known for some time, but in any case the legacy of Gregory Bateson is one of vision, integrity, and courage. As Stewart Brand wrote, "If I could count on Gregory's company in heaven, and I could get to heaven by being good, I'd be good" (1980:1).

Whatever paths we choose as scholars and people in the natural world, we may at least agree to hope, with Bateson, that as each year passes "we shall know a little more by dint of rigor and imagination, the two great contraries of mental process, either of which by itself is lethal. Rigor alone is paralytic death, but imagination alone is insanity" (1979:219).

To Bateson, the scientist, "ultimate unity is aesthetic," compelling a quest in one's fashion:

> Trying to use new words, and every attempt
> Is a wholly new start, and a different kind of failure
> Because one has only learnt to get the better of words
> For the thing one no longer has to say, or the way in which
> One is no longer disposed to say it. And so each venture
> Is a new beginning, a raid on the inarticulate
> With shabby equipment always deteriorating
> In the general mess of imprecision of feeling,
> Undisciplined squads of emotion. And what there is to
>   conquer
> By strength and submission, has already been discovered
> Once or twice, or several times, by men whom one cannot
>   hope
> To emulate — but there is no competition —
> There is only the fight to recover what has been lost
> And found and lost again and again; and now, under
>   conditions
> That seem unpropitious. But perhaps neither gain nor loss.
> For us, there is only the trying. The rest is not our business.
>
> T.S. Eliot
> *East Coker*

One Thing Leads to Another

John H. Weakland

Since I'm just a West Virginia country boy, when I was asked to speak at the beginning of the Asilomar conference, naturally I sought guidance. So I asked Carol Wilder-Mott what she wanted, and she said, "Well, you know, just sort of a talk about how all this thing developed." And I said, "Yes, but what in detail?" "Well, you know, anything." So I said, "How long?" And she said, "Well, whatever you want." Having received that guidance, I thought it over some, and here we are.

What I would like to offer is a personal account of the series of research projects on the nature and significance of communication that Gregory Bateson directed from 1952 to about 1961, what has developed from them, and then touch on where I think we might go from here. My account will focus not only on the content or subject matter of those projects, but also — perhaps more — on some of the features most responsible for their remarkable productivity and fertility. That brings up one sense in which this account will be personal. It is my individual view, one among many.

I don't claim that I am necessarily precise in what I'm going to present here. The best I can say is that regardless of where I arrived, I gave it considerable serious thought — more thought in general than in specific detail. In talking primarily about the ideas and examinations of data about communication that made up the Bateson projects, it is rather appropriate to lay the main stress on what is *general* rather than on what is more *specific*. Because if there was anything that was characteristic about that project, anything significant, it was that we were trying to get a handle on some broad ideas and broad points of view, rather than "Let's make sure we get the details straight first, and then hope it will lead to something larger eventually." Thus this account will focus on things in terms of what I think was of general significance and general importance, over the course of my nearly ten years involvement in that project. Then we will lead into a few things about what I see as having developed from it. There are certainly other views.

There are some relevant things by Bateson here and there on the project, a good bit of it in *Steps to an Ecology of Mind* (1972), but nothing very specific or extensive. I have written several things that touch on it, but these again are not comparable in scope to Jay Haley's view published in Carlos Sluzki's and Don Ransom's book on the double bind (1976). I might mention the piece I wrote on "The Double Bind Theory by Self-Reflexive Hindsight" (1974), which indicates what I thought of these things in most general terms, after I'd had time to think about it and see what other people thought about it. There is a little bit in the piece I wrote and published in Phil Guerin's volume on family therapy, entitled *Communication Theory and Clinical Change* (1976). Don Jackson himself wrote very little on the project. Bill Fry wrote very little on it. So it turns out that there are several views. There's one large view, some partial views, and some people who have not been heard from explicitly.

While giving you my personal view of the project, I plan to cover three topics. After a little bit on where we started from, I will offer my view of how our project developed. I will say a bit about where developments might go from their current state and then discuss the factors that, in my opinion, made the project as productive, as pathbreaking as I estimate it to have been. And in the middle, I will give you a surprise.

"Where Do We Start?"

Where do we start? That's an important question for several reasons. It is certainly my strong impression that in the two fields that we were concerned with and that our work overlapped — the fields of communication and of psychopathology and therapy — things were very different twenty-five years ago than they are now. In those days it was very clear — by which I mean it was the received wisdom — that problems of psychopathology were specific to individual patients, and were internally located. That much was agreed on, even though there were two very different camps; a mentalistic camp and a physiological camp. But the one thing they could get together on was that the problem was *in* the patient. And behavior was just some sort of surface manifestation of what was deep within — sort of an epiphenomenon.

It's not that those views don't exist strongly now. The difference is that in those days there wasn't anything else, essentially. So that when people began to think about interaction and talk to families, they were considered crazy by orthodox psychiatry and psychology. Family therapy is something that began as an underground movement. And for some years it was only mentioned if you went to a national meeting and you met an old friend you hadn't seen for some time because he worked in a different part of the country. After a long day of meetings, you got together and had three or four drinks. Then, loosened up, one confided, "You know, I saw some family members of one of my patients." And the other would say, "You know, I did that too!" That's the way it was.

There are some other things I can say about the way it was. In those days, the things that became of particular interest to us, and remain so, basically were ruled out from the realm of study. That is, crazy behavior, by being labeled "crazy" was essentially labeled "nonbehavior." It was not to be considered behavior in the sense that any other behavior should be considered. It was put beyond the pale. And the same thing with schizophrenic speech: Once you say it's "word salad," that makes it plain that whatever it is, it's not communication. The whole area of "psychopathology" — a vast area — was just put out of the usual picture of human behavior. As far as therapy goes, the only thing that was clear was that things are very complex. What was thought to be needed was lengthy study to clarify this complexity so that it could be conveyed, insight would result, and insight would somehow produce change. It's a very different picture now.

As far as communication studies go, I knew a bit more then about what was done with mass communication — which was a large part of communication studies — than I did anything else, because I was doing content analysis of a sort with cultural documents, mainly films. What I was interested in related to what I did later, but it was very different from what other people were doing. Others were breaking things down into smallest units, or if not to smallest units then *next*-to-smallest units — and then adding up how many of each of them there were. What I was trying to do was to see the themes and patterns that repeat in films, and how they relate to each other. I had a little to do with linguistics, being originally an anthopologist. But something always puzzled me: linguistics seemed to have nothing to do with the users of language! It was just language floating up there by itself. But I knew that I was always looking at things strangely. One other thing was then common to studies of language and communication: there was an enormous focus on the *ideal*, on how things *should* be, even though this focus was often implicit, and covered up with terms like "normality." Normality wasn't what people really do. Normality was an implicit ideal in the minds of psychiatrists and psychologists. Nobody paid enough attention to what people actually *do* to have much of a concept of what might be normal in the sense of everyday behavior. Normality was an ideal of rational speech. If you tape anybody's speech, it doesn't come out anything like that ideal of normal rationality, even if they've never been in a hospital or fallen into the clutches of a therapist. It's just not that way in ordinary usage.

One reason that where we started from is important is because it was so different. Another thing that I think is important is that I do not see what we have done — what we did in this project and what we've done since — as really all that much a matter of discovering new truths. As I attempted to write in the paper "Pursuing the Evident into Schizophrenia — and Beyond," (Weakland, 1978) — which I delivered in 1977 at the "Beyond the Double Bind" meeting in New York (to little attention) — what I now see is that our work, more than anything else, was a process of digging ourselves out of the holes constituted by a bunch of preconceptions which prevented people from getting anywhere, holes that were dug by the received wisdom. So that more and more I've come to subscribe, rather devotedly, to the point of view that was once presented by one of our greatest psychologists, Mark Twain. He said, "It is not so much what people *don't* know that makes trouble, as what people know that ain't so." And twenty-five years ago we knew a hell of a lot that wasn't so.

"Gregory, What Is This Project All About?"

How did the whole thing get started? You always have to take an arbitrary starting point. Bateson had been interested in behavior, then communication, ever since he got into anthropology. He was my first teacher of anthropology. Like various other things, this proceeded from a misconception. I had been an engineer, and I started looking for a change. I was interested in social sciences and I'd read something of his. I got very daring one day in 1947 and phoned him in New York. I began very tentatively, "I'm just an engineer, but I've been reading some of your stuff and I had a thought about calling you." And he interrupted me and said, "Come right down." I was flabbergasted. The reason he asked me to come right down was at that time he was involved in the Macy Foundation Cybernetics Conferences. He had the unfounded idea that as an engineer, I could straighten out all the mathematics of cybernetics that was proving rather troublesome to him. I'm not sure that I helped him much with the mathematics of cybernetics. But it began things. So I was his student, and became his friend.

He sought out and received a grant from the Rockefeller Foundation in 1952. This happened through rather fortuitous circumstances, as I think is probably often the case for things that are not along the conventional tracks of thinking, research, and practice. At that time, the head of the Rockefeller Foundation was Chester Barnard, who had just finished a long term as head of New Jersey Bell Telephone. Barnard wasn't your everyday executive. He was a bright man and a thinker who wrote a very interesting book called *The Functions of the Executive* (1938). Somewhere along the line he had come across a book that very few other people had noticed entitled *Naven*, by Gregory Bateson (1937). He had found it rather interesting, so he had gotten in touch with Bateson. Then later, when Bateson was looking for financing for a project on communication, he submitted his grant proposal to Barnard. My understanding has always been, essentially, that Barnard personally put the thing through Rockefeller, and that it probably would not have gotten through any other way. I knew that this was going on. When it looked imminent Gregory came to New York to see about the wrap-up, and stayed in our apartment.

One day he came home and said, "It's set; I've got a project. How about going out to dinner?" My wife and I said fine, so we went around the corner in the Village. And after dinner Gregory said, "Would you like to come to California and work on my project?" Since I was interested in his project, and since I was having great difficulty trying to cook up a dissertation that would unite the departments of sociology and anthropology at Columbia, which I later realized didn't want to be united, and since I was getting mighty tired, I said "Sure." So we moved to California and began work in early 1953 — Gregory, myself, Jay Haley, who came into things from having contacted Gregory as a student working toward an M.A. in the communication department at Stanford (with his thesis around analysis of a fictional film) and Bill Fry, who was a young psychiatrist just completing his residency.

The title of the project was "The Significance of the Paradoxes of Abstraction in Communication." Gregory was already interested in the idea of levels of abstraction, which later were related to ideas about levels of classification, and to levels of communication in a more pragmatic, functional context. It took off from the more abstract view of levels of "Logical Types" in Whitehead and Russell, gradually attaching to that the idea of levels of classification and levels of abstraction in actual communication. There was something about the project that was both an advantage and a disadvantage. This was perhaps best indicated by the fact that for several months in a row, at least once a week, when we had our morning discussions over coffee, the question would arise from Jay or myself or both, or Bill Fry, "Gregory, what is this project all about?" Now, that kind of uncertainty indicates certain difficulties which are obvious. We were trying to get a fix on "What are we supposed to be doing? Where are we supposed to be headed?" But I wouldn't underestimate the advantages of that uncertainty either. We had a lot of elbow room, a lot of territory to work in, and we had some general guidance: it had something to do with communication, and it had something to do with the fact that communication is not simple — there are complexities in it, and one of the complexities is that there are different levels of some sort.

Perhaps that doesn't sound like much to go on, but there are a lot of people who had a lot more to go on and haven't come out with as much.

So, while we were trying to get an answer to that question of what we were supposed to be doing, we had to do something with the parts of the day when we were not discussing the question. One of the things we did was to look at data and look for descriptive and analytic terms. We developed various sorts of terms throughout the history of the project. In some ways we came up with more sets of almost synonymous, but not quite synonymous, terms for various things we were looking at than anybody else has yet done. For example, in the primary area we would sometimes talk about "Logical Types," sometimes we would talk about "levels of abstraction," sometimes we would talk about "levels of communication," sometimes we would talk about "messages and meta-messages," and sometimes we would talk about "meta-communicative levels." It was never quite clear what the differences and distinctions were, but in a way I think this was reasonable. We were groping for handles on things that were of significance but were hard to pin down. And maybe it's just as well we didn't pin them down too hard and fast too soon.

I keep getting reminded, when I think about this whole project, about a paper that Bateson wrote which is included in *Steps to an Ecology of Mind*. I had a hard time finding it there because its title in my mind was not the title that's on the paper in the book. The title actually on the paper in the book is "Experiments in Thinking about Observed Ethnological Material." In this paper Gregory gives a description as best he can of how he works back and forth between data and ideas. The title I had in my mind is taken from a phrase later on in the paper in which he talks about "strict and loose thinking." He also talks about strict and loose terminology, and basically points out that there is a place for each — that if you can tie something down precisely, it's a mistake to refer to it loosely. But it's an equal mistake to tie something down tightly when you really can't. And you'd better use a loose term to remind yourself that you're somewhere in the area but you don't quite know where. That's one of the reasons why it seems to me relevant that we were using a variable set of terms. We continued to do so over six or eight years, for one thing or another. We were always looking for a way to get a handle on something that was new to us, and it seemed to me that what probably looked particularly from the outside like terminological confusion, was appropriate to the enterprise.

"One Thing Leads to Another"

We were also getting involved with data of all sorts. We were going to the zoo in San Francisco to watch otters playing and monkeys on the monkey island, and Gregory was filming them. Gregory went up to San Rafael to watch them train guide dogs for the blind. He became interested in how the trainers would deliberately give two different and contradictory messages at the same time. Dr. Fry was working on an analysis of humor from the standpoint of levels. We somehow located a doctor in San Francisco (a proctologist — I don't know if that has any relevance) whose hobby was ventriloquism; so we went up and studied him while he communicated and interacted with his puppet. Well, one thing leads to another. Gradually, we were led into studying some curious communication that was going on all around us. The project, although it was funded through Stanford, was housed in the Veterans Administration Hospital in Menlo Park. A large portion of the patients there were labeled schizophrenic. There was a lot of strange talk and behavior going on. If you were curious about communication and were not confined to ordinary sorts of data, there was a lot of data at hand there.

Before long, we had become interested in schizophrenia. We were probably pushed somewhat by Jay Haley, who always wanted to try something a step further. In getting into this, somehow or other, we were looking at all of these things from a natural history, ecological approach. We used this viewpoint partly because both Bateson and I came out of anthropology, and partly because somehow we'd gotten into reading Lorenz and Tinbergen on animal ethology.

We were looking at all these things, and published a couple of papers about two years after we got started. We were already talking about paradoxes, and play, and fantasy, and therapy — how they all went together. Again, one thing led to another. We got the idea that in relation to levels of communication, messages modify each other. First we had the idea that there were messages and meta-messages. And the meta-message tells you how to interpret the message. It sort of frames the message.

For awhile we were toying with thoughts about, "Well, let's look at the Gestaltists; they've talked about figure and ground, but they haven't gone far enough." Figure and ground obviously refer — at least by analogy — to pictures. But there's something else about a picture. What about the *frame?* So we had some fun with that for awhile. I still think that it was pursued usefully. If you don't talk about the frame you're losing something important. But mainly, it led us to thinking further about how messages qualify each other. You can't understand the message unless you know what's around it. Are there any related messages? One thing leads to another: as soon as you see that, you're on the road to seeing, "Yeah, but there might be another message." And you are moving toward realizing that you can't ever understand a message in itself. The only way you can ever begin to understand a message is by considering its *context.* Then you begin to think, "Okay, what is its context?" Its context may be another message, but it may be not only another *verbal* message — it can be a tone of voice which qualifies the message. It can be physical behavior of the speaker. Or it can be something about the broader context, the social setting.

So without intending to, we slid into more and more interest in the context of messages. This is a very important step. It's completely opposed to the idea that: "We must cut out something as *the* pure message and understand it in itself." This is so much in line with the general thrust of what is considered "real" science in the world. The way we were going, that didn't make any sense. We didn't really know how to study contexts. But we chose to proceed with something that seemed relevant. And we did it as best we could rather than do something that didn't look to us to make any sense — even if a more conventional approach might be used to fund the next renewal of the project.

"And On We Went"

And it *would* have been used because our Rockefeller grant ran out at the end of the second year. Indeed, we couldn't get any more money out of Rockefeller. Barnard had resigned. Our angel was gone, and we were up the creek. But by this time we had begun to get into schizophrenia. So we wrote another grant proposal which focused on schizophrenia: language in schizophrenia, levels of meaning, paradoxes, and so forth. Gregory had a couple of other friends. This time we got some money from the Josiah Macy Foundation in New York. We could breathe and eat for another couple of years. And on we went.

I can't tell you much of the details, or even all of the general lines of how we went on in this limited space, but I will summarize some of it — at least by exemplification of the sort of things we did, and the sort of ideas we had.

In the early days we talked about communication — at least deliberate communication — as something that had evolved gradually out of the automatic sorts of things that the animal ethologists were talking about. Things that could be labeled as mood signs or simply a visible part of behavior — and to which response was automatic. We discussed how things could move more and more over time in the direction of these behaviors being taken as signals: being more separable from other behavior; being subject to control; therefore, being subject to interpretation. We talked about classification of messages by other messages. Then we began to talk about schizophrenia in terms of its "as if" nature: this behavior, or this talk, looks *as if* it could be understood as such-and-such.

From there we moved on to talking about schizophrenic speech. Schizophrenic speech makes a lot better sense if you don't try to put it in the literal framework implied by ideals of rational speech: if you instead look at it in terms of "Could this be metaphorical speech?" But metaphorical speech that is difficult to recognize, because you don't have the usual signs indicating that it is metaphorical. It's not common metaphor. If someone says, "I have butterflies in my stomach," you don't have a problem. If someone says, "I have cement in my stomach," you think, "What's the matter? He's crazy." Yet in terms of language, one is a commonly used and understood figure of speech, and the other isn't. But they are structurally parallel.

The metaphors of the schizophrenic are not labeled. They don't say, "It's like." They don't make it a simile. In fact, you might say that the "as if" is probably concealed a large portion of the time. But if one deliberately attempts to think of them in metaphorical terms, they begin to make sense. Jay Haley heard his patient come in and say "my stomach is full of cement." Instead of arguing with him, which was the usual response of the psychiatrist or psychologist, Jay reacted differently. Psychiatry labels such argument "clarification" or "indicating reality." It's argument, no matter how you label it. In essence you are saying, "No, your stomach is not really full of cement. Don't you understand that?" Jay realized that the interview was at 1:00 p.m. and that the patient had probably just come from lunch. We all know what institutional food is like. So Jay said, "The food is probably pretty bad around here." This way you don't put the patient on the defensive by insisting that he speak in a literal fashion. To some degree or other, the patient begins to get with you because you are reading him. What Jay said was important not only in terms of reality or logic but also in terms of pragmatic results.

This brings out another basic theme underlying much of our work, which probably received less explicit emphasis than other matters: communication is not just a process of conveying information, but also of influencing others' behavior. This basic idea is foreshadowed in Bateson's earlier statement that "...every message is both a report and a command... " (Ruesch & Bateson, 1951).

"Somewhere Along This Line the Double Bind Came In"

From there we went on to other thoughts about schizophrenia.

Somewhere along this line the double bind came in: I don't quite know how. I know how it got published, but I don't recall how it arose. It got published because when we began to move from levels of communication and communication in general to more of a focus on schizophrenia, we thought that this meant talking to patients. One thing we did was deal with data at first hand and repetitively. We went out and observed or talked to subjects; we made films and tapes, and we went over them. Okay, we thought, now we've got to talk with some schizophrenics if we're going to study them. We can't just sit way off somewhere and look at them through a telescope. Or maybe use one of those big parabolic dishes that the CIA uses to pick up what somebody is saying way over there. We didn't know much about dealing with them, so we brought in Don Jackson, who had had a great deal of experience in trying to treat schizophrenics. He also had a good deal of experience — being somebody who worked in a town the modest size of Palo Alto — working with their relatives. As we later learned, he had even begun to meet with patients and members of their families.

It was Don, seconded by Jay, who suggested that we publish our ideas. Don was quite a practical and promotional sort of guy. I don't know how long it would have taken us to publish "Toward a Theory of Schizophrenia" (Bateson, *et. al.*, 1956) if it hadn't been for Jackson. Even then, it took a good deal of fitting together of four or five somewhat different viewpoints among the members of the project to get it off the ground. That had its usefulness too, and I'll refer to it later.

The idea of the double bind came out of a very mixed background. We mixed in a little bit of direct contact with patients, a good deal of thinking about communication and its complexities and its different levels, Russell's Theory of Logical Types, and how things fitted together and what might lead to what. Lord knows it was a strange combination of observation and speculation, but I still think that it was useful. It got a lot of things further off the ground. After we had this idea about communication and schizophrenics, as described in terms of the double bind, we wondered about its sources. Because of our largely anthropological background, we naturally thought of things — in this case a style of communication — not in terms of what is *innate* in human nature, but in terms of how people *learn to behave* in the way they do. Once you begin to think in that direction, you consider the social context in which they've learned things, even schizophrenic speech.

Again, one thing led to another. If you think about the social context, you think about the family. If you think about the family, you consider "Well, maybe we'd better check up on this. How about if we get some of these people in to talk with members of their family? We can't go back to the earliest years because those are over. But at least we can try to bring in the family members and see how they talk to each other. We don't know what's going to happen, but at least we can try to make some sense out of it and ask if it fits with the ideas we've had. So we did.

Lo and behold, it looked to us as if we didn't *have* to go back to the time when the patients were little kids. It seemed that in a number of respects, we could discern and describe how the crazy ways the patients are talking *now* hang together with — in a way make sense or fit with — the way the other family members are talking *right now*. So it did seem to be systematic. It seemed to fit together.

One thing led to another again. Having got these people in, we got into attempts at treatment. This is where the family therapy thing began at least in our part of the world. When we got the family in, we were somewhat humanitarian so we wanted to help where we could. Also, we wanted to offer them something as a reward for coming in. Finally, when you deal with families of schizophrenics you are — or at least, I was — motivated to try to get them to behave in a more sane way before they drive *you* crazy. All of these things led to family therapy. Once you'd worked with families of schizophrenics you felt, what the hell, any other family couldn't be more difficult. You might as well try it. And so family therapy spread, and other things spread also. The other things that spread were (1) a clearer idea that we were talking about a new epistemology based on interaction — a circular, cybernetic rather than a linear model of causality; and (2) beginnings of refinement of study of the family to focus more and more on what is crucial, rather than just "the problem has something to do with the family as a whole."

Now let me give you the surprise I promised, then say a few words about why I think this project was productive. The surprise is this: I mentioned that we had a lot of data, some general ideas, and some varied people. I may have mentioned also that we discussed things a lot among ourselves. We brought our different experiences and viewpoints to bear on whatever seemed of particular interest at the time. This covered a rather wide range during the course of our studies. I would say that these intensive and extensive discussions were one of the three main factors accounting for the productivity of our work. The other two were the close and repeated study of raw, concrete behavioral data, guided but not confined by some very broad ideas about the nature and importance of communication.

I haven't mentioned much about the sources of information and ideas that we had, or that we had become interested in hypnosis early on in the project, particularly Jay Haley and myself. I had latched onto the observation that if you read any of the classic texts like Bleuler, or even earlier, you get lists of basic symptoms of schizophrenia. These, naturally, are supposed to be far-out since they're signs of a very dread disease. But reading any of the classic texts of the hypnotists on the sort of phenomena that they produce in trance, they are almost directly parallel to the list of symptoms of schizophrenia; positive and negative hallucinations, anaesthesias, parasthesias — the whole bloody list. You can go right down it, item by item.

One begins to wonder about this. In one case it's supposed to be terribly pathological, and only produced by the most extreme, long continued sort of traumatic circumstances. On the other hand it's supposed to be something that's rather an accomplishment. It can be done in anywhere from five minutes to an hour with a hypnotist and a subject. That aroused our interest. Also, Jay Haley was interested in Milton Erickson, both as a hypnotist and as one of the very few people who was willing to work at the time in psychotherapy with schizophrenics. John Rosen (1953) was about the only other one who was at all prominent, and we had something to do with him as well. So we proposed to Gregory, "We'd like to go to Phoenix and talk with Milton Erickson about these topics." Gregory was always rather agreeable; and though he didn't want to have much to do with hypnosis himself, he said okay. So we began to visit Erickson.

My surprise is a transcription of a project group discussion which took place after one return from Phoenix. Don't ask me how this piece of tape was preserved when Lord knows how many hours of tape have disappeared, but this happened to be in my office closet for some reason. This particular day in about 1954 that I have on tape, Gregory and Don Jackson and Jay and I were discussing some things about hypnosis, schizophrenia, manipulation, and other topics.

Let me first summarize a few segments of this particular staff discussion. First, there is reported how a confusion technique was applied by Erickson's three-year-old daughter. Another daughter a year or two older wants the girl to do something. But the little girl instead keeps looking around and saying, "Where's the comb? Where's the comb?" Finally, the elder child says, "What comb?" The younger daughter says, "*That* comb." But the elder daughter loses track of the whole thing and forgets about the task. Jackson contrasts this confusion business with an opposite — a very sharp, direct, forceful sort of clarity that he cites from an episode involving Harry Stack Sullivan. Jackson was a little leery of the manipulative side of Erickson's confusion techniques, although Jackson was pretty good at it himself. Then there is some discussion relating to a story that Erickson told about deliberately producing an amnesia, a communication story.

Erickson was in a seminar with a group of young residents. He was leading the seminar, but they were all taking part. Sitting on his left was one resident whom Erickson knew to be a very heavy smoker — practically a chain smoker. Erickson had colluded in advance with the resident sitting to his right. When Erickson started, he got out his pack of cigarettes and offered a cigarette to the heavy smoker on his left. At which point the resident said something to him and Erickson turned to answer, taking away the cigarettes as he turned his body. This was repeated in one form or another fifteen or twenty times. Then Erickson turned to the heavy smoker and said, "Would you like a cigarette?" And the smoker said, "No." And Erickson said, "Why not?" "Well, I don't really know, but I haven't been thinking about cigarettes lately and I just don't want one," he said. Further questioning indicated that the repeated procedure had blotted the whole thing out of the patient's mind.

After this there is further discussion of trance and manipulation, of how and why people go into trance, and, particularly, examples of inductions in which trance is set up as a sort of escape hatch to avoid some threatened ordeal. Even this brief segment illustrates some features that were typical of our project discussions. It is plain that, while there were a few general themes of shared common interest, the range of specific materials brought in for illustration or analysis was very wide. And considerable difference of opinion was made manifest.

Weakland   [The "schizophrenogenic mother"] covers up the truth and
              then, correspondingly gives you a help in interpreting it
              this particular way, which binds you tighter and tighter.

Haley: Most of the devices of hypnosis — distraction and such —
              could be used to just play hell with the kid finding out
              [what's what].

Weakland: ... the confusion technique, and some ... even some of
              Mrs. S's stuff, which ... How do you get at the subject,
              the different subjects — she isn't there anymore, or she's

over here. Or if she's over here, she's over there.

Haley: Well, Erickson's older daughter said to the little four-year-old, "Pick up your toys all over the floor." The little three-year-old started to play with the four-year-old, starting to putter around a little bit, and said, "Where's the comb? Where's the comb? Where's the comb?" . . . And the older daughter finally said, "Did you find the comb?" And the little girl said, "What comb?" And the older daughter said, "The comb you were talking about." And the little girl said, "Oh, *that* comb." And the whole business of picking up the toys was totally forgotten. [General laughter.] If you can imagine a mother talking in that style . . .

Bateson: And Milton is very proud of this:

Weakland: . . . And the older girl was confused even later when she was telling about it. She still didn't know what the hell had happened to her. [More laughter.]

Jackson: Sullivan gives an example in his book on the interview — I think it's in that book — of something that I've used a fair amount, and that is that he's in a . . . This is just a little incident where he was in a busy drug store that he frequently went into, and there was this particular soda fountain jerk that likes to ignore people, and get their orders mixed up and so on . . . So Sullivan is in a hurry for lunch or something, and he orders a Coca-Cola and a tuna sandwich or something. And a little while later he sees the guy and he says, "Where's my order?" And the guy says, "Oh, What did you order?" And Sullivan says very sharply and loudly to him, "You know exactly what I asked for," whereupon the guy promptly produced a tuna sandwich and a coke. That is, by creating a . . . I'm getting it confused with Zen Buddhism — I can see the stick over here. Suppose that with the . . . In the cigarette experiment, when the guy says, "What cigarette?" he then made it another painful penalty on top of that if he doesn't remember. Would he then remember the cigarette? is what I'm saying. Such as by fear coming into it — an intimidating tone of voice and so on . . . What I'm trying to say is that there's an opposite way to react from manipulation. To me, Erickson is a manipulator. The mother of the schizophrenic is a manipulator. And this leads to a double bind situation: The non-manipulator that says, "You *know* what I mean." You know, there's no fooling around. He gets a different kind of a response, a non — the opposite of trance, if there is a non-trance . . .

Weakland: Well, in a way, didn't Freud play that both ways in the early days, in which he put people in a trance when he was still using hypnosis? And he would get certain things under hypnosis, and then he would bring them out, and *insist they could remember,* until they finally remembered.

Jackson: What's the opposite of a trance? Isn't the opposite of a trance to experience the same situation but with painful affect and reality?

Bateson: In trance we have the affect all right.

Jackson: But it isn't . . .

Haley: It's what Rosen does somehow. Except the difficulty is that Erickson read Rosen's "Arthur" interview, and said "This guy works very much like I do." Rosen's done a hell of a lot of manipulating.

Jackson: Oh yeah.

Haley: But he's shocking guys awake in a sense, out of the trance.

Jackson: He's playing both ends.

Weakland: Well, that's also true. I mean, this isn't the whole story on what Erickson's doing, by any means.

Jackson: Well now look . . .

Haley: Erickson works with the trance to get them out of trance . . .

Jackson: No, I'm using it loosely, and I still think that we've got two things here: You are dealing with another person.

Something unpleasant comes up, which you notice. All right, you ignore it. We could make up all kinds of reasons why you might. What is the result of ignoring it? Either it is some kind of phenomenon that could be compared to a trance, I mean, such as you might get sleepy, you might get bored, you might find yourself suddenly fatigued ... I mean, something could happen as a result — or would happen as a result of this suppression. What is the opposite of that? To be aware of what the other person did, to respond to it emotionally, and painfully. You see ... if say the other person was someone you needed.

Weakland: To be consciously aware of what the reality is ...

Jackson: Yeah, but you'd have reality. You'd have the pain, but you'd also have reality. Now is the trance and the double bind the avoidance of this kind of anxiety?

Haley: Yeah, I think it is.

Weakland: Yeah.

Jackson: I mean, if we could do something with this kind of thing, I think ...

Haley: The trance is when you're faced with something that you don't want, or it's impossible, and you avoid it by going into a trance. Like seeing it differently, which is sense.

Bateson: This is the anaesthetic aspects of trance; it's what LeCron uses it for in dentistry — without anaesthesia.

Haley: It can be that, yes.

Weakland: Well, you can have anaesthesia of various kinds by — simply not noticing, by seeing it all a different way ...

Bateson: Yes, but anaesthesia after all is only negative hallucination — and I presume dis-anaesthesia is ...

Haley: Well, it is a negative hallucination produced by positive hallucination. You see yourself outside the door looking in at yourself in the dentist's chair, or something like that is often what occurs. Erickson ... We have on tape a subject he put in trance in which he describes how she did this by standing outside the window looking through the pane at herself in the dentist chair.

Jackson: Well, and why do you get hypnotized in that situation? So that you can avoid the pain ... In the event you certainly choose to join with the devil.

Weakland: Well, even in my story — there's a bind in that —

Jackson: Which story?

Haley: John obviously wanted to go into a trance. He asked Erickson, and then he asked him again, and then he moved over in the chair where Erickson usually hypnotizes people ... And Erickson was reluctant to do it with us, he said, because he said we'd get an unconscious awareness of what was involved and what we were after was a conscious awareness. So he'd rather bring in the subject and have us observe. But John was so obviously ready to go into a trance. And so Erickson sat up straight in the chair and then started to go like this. [Rocks back and forth.] And John started to go back and forth like this with him, and Erickson started to say, "You're on a ship, and the ship is rolling, and the sea's getting pretty rough, and you're beginning to feel a little bit sick." And then he said, "There's seagulls up in the air, and you can see land. Green land on the blue water." And John's eyes closed, and he told him his eyes would get heavier and close, and they did. And then Erickson ...

Weakland: This was against the background of I'd already said something about ... that we had done some work but that a real visualization was difficult for me.

Haley: And then Erickson brought him out of it, and John said, "Oh, I was hoping you'd bring me out of it before I got much sicker." And then we talked about how John had difficulty with visualization, and Erickson said, "Well, I think you would have much rather been a seagull in the sky than sitting there sick." And he was posing those alternatives; John really had to really clearly see that land, or he could be a seagull looking down at the land, or he was going to be sick.

Jackson: I think that's the dentist with the pain . . .

Bateson: Yeah. Now, on the other hand, presumably in trance, you would also hallucinate pain.

Weakland: Yeah.

Bateson: Which when hallucinated has all the reality of any other hallucination.

Jackson: Yeah. But that's no problem; Faust didn't solve his dilemma either, you know. I like the analogy, somehow.

Haley: Whenever Erickson wants a really quick induction, apparently he uses tricks like that, so you escape from worse things by going into a trance.

Jackson: The very escape makes you vulnerable to the things that you were trying to escape from.

Bateson: Yeah.

Jackson: Gambling in order to give up trying to give up gambling.

Haley: Vulnerable to something else, maybe. And that's the thing that's underscored.

Jackson: Oh no. I disagree.

Haley: The students in the seminar wanted a quick induction, regression, and anaesthesia. He took a subject and gave him the old knuckle squeeze, which is very painful.

Jackson: Gave him a what?

Haley: He squeezed his knuckles, which is very painful. And
            before he did it, he said "The easiest thing for you to do
            . . . And if you sit in this chair, it's going to be very painful
            as I squeeze your knuckles. And the easiest thing for you
            to do is to not be in the chair. And over there in the cor-
            ner," and he talked about not being in the chair. He gets
            out of the chair — and over there in the corner. "And over
            there in the corner is a dolly. And I wonder if you'd pick
            up that dolly and play with it," and he squeezed. And that
            guy felt, apparently, no pain at all. And was over there in
            the damn corner as a child playing with the dolly.

Jackson: But the kid plays it his way, didn't take his hand away.
            This is why it's a perfect double bind situation.

Weakland: Yeah . . . Just as in my case, I happened to be asking for it.

Jackson: Yeah, the same thing that wouldn't let him simply use that
            solution, is the same thing that makes him vulnerable.

Haley: He wanted to not feel the pain. It isn't that . . .

Jackson: I think we really have a beautiful analogy here . . .

Weakland: It's much closer than we thought when we left there.

Haley: And hour after hour on that tape there's stuff that's really
            close to all the stuff we're working with. I don't know
            anywhere we could've gone for data that would be more
            relevant, I think.

Jackson: No, if we'd gone to mother, she couldn't tell you what she
            was doing. [General laughter]
            But the next time you make the trip, why, I still won't go.

Haley: What, to see Erickson?

Jackson: Yeah.

Haley: He's a very benevolent guy — and really . . .

Jackson: Yes, I know — and that's the — he talks people into double
             binds . . .

"This Project Was All Over the Place"

Let me now say a few words about what I think the project was in
terms of how it proceeded. Then I will skip the matter about where
things will go from here, for while I think there's much left to be done,
that's more up to you all than it is to me.

The project did a lot of things, and while it can't be explained
altogether, some things can be pointed to. It's useful to point to them
because there's a lot of mythology about science and research, and that
mythology is not very helpful. Some mythologies may be useful, but I
don't think the mythology of very orderly progress in science is among
them.

This project was certainly not a matter of clear hypotheses formed in
advance and then tested step by step, confirmed or disconfirmed, and
then carefully rethought for the next step. *This project was all over the
place.* And the things that are going on as a result of it are still all over
the place. It certainly wasn't a matter of a focused, unified team of people, all with one common view and one common goal. There were differences among us, but there were also some commonalities. We had a
general field that we were concerned with and really interested in. We
had time to spend looking at things related to this field and talking
about them. When I think about the time we had to spend then, I
wonder why I'm running so hard now and probably doing less. We had
a lot of interplay of data and ideas — a wide range of data, a wide range
of ideas, and a lot of going back and forth between them without drawing our conclusions too fast.

We did a lot of checking back and forth between the different points
of view of the different members and we had something else that was
very useful — ignorance. We were all rather new to the fields we were
working in. Dr. Jackson was not new to psychiatry and schizophrenia,
but he was rather new to the communication business. The rest of us
were somewhat new to both, and it helped because we didn't know all
the answers before we began. There were many people who did know
"the answers," and they are still with those answers. I don't think that
those ideas are much good now, just as they weren't much good then.
So we had to ask questions about nearly everything we saw instead of
knowing where it was all at.

As I mentioned before, we used a variety of terms and concepts while we tried to deal with what we saw and thought about. I think that was useful. It was like trying things on for size. Along with our ignorance went a sort of natural history viewing: Let's look at what is directly observable, try to write down a description that is adequate to it, and try to see what hangs together. Let's build more general views out of those simple elements, rather than starting with a frame and putting these things into that frame, even if we've got to force them. So we started small and slow. Somehow or another, we were not terribly concerned with the idea that you have to do things the way the physical sciences claimed to proceed even if you are in the infancy of your work. We were concerned with making sense out of things rather than ruling them out as beyond the pale.

If somebody behaves in a way that is called crazy, well, let's at least try to see if we can't make sense out of the craziness instead of getting rid of it. Or pinning that label on it. In that sense we were helped by being, some of us, anthropologists rather than psychologists or psychiatrists. Making sense out of the crazy is the everyday work of the anthropologist because all the people he goes out to see look crazy to start with, and it's his job to understand why. We had freedom to explore what we wanted to, but always with the idea that somehow we would come back and relate it to what we were doing. Those are some of the ways in which I think that a group of somewhat unusual people — you can take that in either a positive or negative sense — came together and got off the ground a number of studies and ideas about problems and therapies specifically, but even more importantly, communication and behavior in general.

Forming Warm Ideas

Arthur P. Bochner

I

Like man himself, science, a creation of man, is unfinished, inconstant, and mutable. The public audience of science commonly assumes that the business of science is to "discover" laws by strictly applying a formal set of rules called the scientific method to observable phenomena called facts. Thus, in ordinary usage, the term scientific is equivalent to factual; the scientific method stands for the objective procedures by which truth is established; and scientific evidence is thought to be infinitely authoritative.

Of course, many people know better. They recognize that the public image of science is a fiction. After all, scientists are human beings. The phenomena which scientists seek to describe are not completely separable from themselves. The boundary separating internal from external, or subject from object is drawn arbitrarily. Scientific observations cannot result in "objective" descriptions because the phenomena observed must be *subjected* to the process of observation in order to be seen and described. Einstein convinced many of his contemporaries that a physicist's frame of reference conditioned observation, making it a relatively, rather than absolutely, objective process. Heisenberg further established the idea that scientific activity is recursive by noting that what has been seen also changes the one who is seeing. To these points can be added the vexing question of how observed and observer are transformed as time passes between observation of phenomena (so-called externals), recording of observations as "raw data," descriptions of these data as "findings" in formal scientific documents, and disseminations of the documents throughout a scientific community. How do these processes — observing, recording, reporting, disseminating — alter the original conception of the "findings?" The end products apparently can never be anything more or less than maps of maps of maps, to borrow Bateson's expression. No pure or simple facts, only apprehended appearances.

Over the course of the past two decades, historians have examined other fundamental premises about scientific activity and found them refutable. While some of their conclusions have been hotly contested, these historians have cast a shadow of suspicion over some firmly entrenched beliefs about the proper conduct of science and the nature of scientific progress. In science, progress is supposed to be cumulative. Step-by-methodical-step, the scientist trudges along, mounting new facts upon the shoulders of older established ones, building up a strong foundation of empirical observations that gradually leads to a theory befitting them. Although this metaphoric expression of how science progresses helps to create the impression that scientific inquiry is sturdy and its facts enduring, Kuhn showed rather convincingly "that is not the way a science develops" (1970:40). According to Kuhn, the building-block theory is not historically sound. Progress is not peaceful and serene, but conflictful and combative. The social climate among scientists must be ripe for revolution because prevailing beliefs must be undermined and converted. Scientific change requires skillful argument; innocent fact-finding, plodding along at research, will not suffice.

Phenomena cannot speak for themselves. They must be spoken for persuasively if science is to advance. Nowhere is this evidenced more clearly than in Feyerabend's controversial description of the Copernican revolution in physics. Galileo establishes that the earth moves, an outlandish assertion at the time it was first introduced. He accomplishes this feat, not by producing unequivocal facts, but by using ingenious argumentative ploys, trickery, and even propaganda. So preposterous and counterintuitive was his thesis that no amount of rational deliberation or "hard" facts would have captured for him the eyes and ears of his contemporaries. Even if they were available, and they were not, facts would have had no compelling force, since the epistemology of the day would have prevented observers from seeing them. Galileo had to change the way reality was construed. Orthodoxy would not turn the tide. So, he *ad hoced* his way through the case, defusing the cosmology of the day and subverting historically-derived cognitions by conducting a propaganda campaign, magically maneuvering the facts, and shielding an interesting hypothesis by taking liberty with the rules of scientific method. He was sloppy, devious, and superficial, and his muddleheadedness turned out to be bliss (Feyerabend, 1975). What would have happened if he had proceeded according to the rules, if he had let the facts speak for themselves? Feyerabend answers:

> Galileo succeeds because he did not follow these rules; his contemporaries with very few exceptions overlooked fundamental difficulties that existed at the time; and modern science developed quickly, and in the 'right direction' . . . because of this negligence. *Ignorance was bliss.* Conversely, a more determined application of the canons of scientific method, a more determined search for relevant facts, a more critical attitude, far from accelerating this attitude development, would have brought it to a standstill (1975:112).

Indeed, at nearly every bend in the road of scientific progress, there is evidence of departure from convention. No less an authority than the late Imre Lakatos remarked shortly before his death that:

> If we look at the history of science, if we try to see how some of the most celebrated falsifications happened, we have to come to the conclusion that either some of them are plainly irrational, or that they rest on rationality principles different from those we have just discussed (i.e., critical rationalism) (1970:114).

II

I am attempting to establish these three ideas:

(1) *Scientific activity — observation, analysis, reporting, etc. — is inherently codificational, symbolic, communicational.* All phenomena, no matter what we call them, are literally appearances. As Bateson implies (1972), we never see the territory because we cannot step onto the terrain without transforming it into a map. Science, then, is inescapably representational.

(2) *Scientific progress, especially theoretical advancement, requires ingenuity, passion, intuition, and/or courage.* It is doubtful whether these fall under the category of skills to be honed. Certainly, strict insistence on rules will not encourage imagination. Theorizing must be deformalized. The only common denominator among imaginative theorists seems to be artful dodging.

(3) *Science is an open system.* Like other developing systems, it continually changes. At each juncture in its evolution, a particular science will be confronted by the anguish of conflict accompanying its changing context. If strict rules are set and followed unyieldingly, adaptability will be threatened, creativity impaired, and progress halted. Direct clashes of ideas will not be easy to tolerate, but without them a science dies, its story ends.

In the remainder of this essay, I plan to examine the implications of these premises for the practice of theorizing and researching communicative processes, my special field of interest. These premises are starting points — steps, mental determinants, contexts — for extrapolating a larger story about scientific work on communication. They shall be used loosely to elaborate and distinguish what may constitute data, evidence, theory, and explanation in the study of communication. As I proceed, I will repeatedly make reference to some words or deeds of Gregory Bateson since my own thinking about communication has been profoundly influenced by his. There is no small risk in doing this, since I may ultimately find myself classified among the legion of interpeters accused of misunderstanding what Bateson means. To begin, it is appropriate to synthesize some Batesonian ideas.

III

It is not uncommon for reviewers of Bateson's work to say in one breath that his intellect and intuition are "imaginative," "novel," "penetrating," "expansive," and in the very next breath call his writing "unclear," "imprecise," "mysterious," "hard to understand." "The richness of Bateson's thought," wrote one perplexed admirer, "is equaled only by its elusiveness" (Elster, 1978:76). Bateson dismisses these reactions to his work as a failure to believe he means what he says. Yet surely, as the man most responsible for calling our attention to the multiple and potentially contradictory levels of meaning in discourse, he must recognize that meanings are not necessarily self-evident to readers. His readers' confusions cannot be so easily extricated. "I mean what I say" does not say what is meant.

The difficulty is not one of believability but of form. The form of Bateson's writing metacommunicates his meanings. This is problematic because occidental thinking is not generally conformable to that style. As his epistemology is monistic, so then is his expression of that epistemology. He does not fabricate dualisms, nor feign completeness. One can see in the thoughts he expresses a reaching outward, a stepping toward, a leaping after. The point is that even to approach an understanding of Bateson's epistemology, one must not only think it rationally but also experience its aesthetic qualities for he, like his father before him, is a scientist engaged in "a continuous struggle to satisfy his aesthetic tastes" (Lipset, 1977:38).

In "The Pattern Which Connects" Bateson revealed some clues for demystifying his epistemology:

> . . . there have been — and still are — in the world many dif-
> ferent and even contrasting epistemologies which have been
> alike in stressing an ultimate unity and, though this is less
> sure, have also stressed the notion that ultimate unity is
> *aesthetic*. From the diversity of these views, we may hope that
> perhaps the great authority of quantitative science may be in-
> sufficient to deny an ultimate unifying beauty (1978:14).

For Bateson, a science of living beings must be like a composition: aesthetically reasonable, rhythmical, qualitative. Throughout his scientific career, he consistently implored social scientists to search for form, look for relation, examine shapes. Connections, patterns, relations; or more metaphorically, steps, bridges, pathways — these are the differences that make a difference to interacting human organisms. He shows us that wherever there is learning, knowing, seeing, or sensing, there is classifying. Levels and hierarchies must be understood: patterns of patterns of patterns; maps of maps of maps. To think about phenomena incisively, one must be able to combine imaginative and rigorous thinking; heart and head must go hand in hand. Bateson's aesthetic sensibility being what it was, little wonder his scientific attention was drawn to the study of symbolic forms such as play, humor, religion, mythology, painting, and psychiatry. And how aptly Blake's words — "A tear is an intellectual thing" — often quoted by Bateson, summarize his holistic vision of social science.

Bateson showed an unusual affinity to attack problems with both sides of his brain, merging primary and secondary process into conceptual synthesis. Whether he was trying to make sense out of the exotic ceremonial customs of the Iatmul — *naven* — , interpreting how otters signal "play," analyzing disturbances in communicative functioning among the members of a family in which a child has been diagnosed as schizophrenic, explaining the logic of alcohol addiction and its treatment, or examining environmental crises, Bateson began by intuiting, sensing, imagining and/or visualizing the meta-patterns and configurations that contextualize the observed phenomena in question. Then, and only then, did he try to discuss his ideas more formally and precisely, but without closing off the possibility of wider application, further extrapolation, protracted meanings.

For Bateson a theory, even a whole field of science, ought to be judged by its catalytic effect. In a little known letter to the editor of *Science* (Bateson, 1959), he defined a *nontrivial* science thusly:

> It seems to me that a science has dignity and value insofar as it contributes to the next more abstract corpus of insights which lie behind it. [It ought to] enable any neighboring specialist to ask more searching questions in his special field (p. 294).

Here we have a context for understanding much of Bateson's activity as a scientist. The concepts he invented — double-binds, frames, schismogenic patterns of relationship — are visual analogies. Like an unkindled fire, they are dormant but combustible, capable of throwing great light and heat but only if energized by sources outside themselves.

Starting with "hunches," "mystical feelings," or "wild analogies," Bateson's pattern was to go only so far, until he had drawn a conceptual blueprint from which others could build, or give birth to an idea that others could nurture, or paved a road which others could traverse.

This is not to say that Bateson had no use for data or that he lacked methodological rigor, as some of his critics imply. He merely possessed a vastly different conception of theory and research — of what data are for and how methodologies ought to be used — different, that is, than most American educated social scientists. It is my impression that Bateson treated data inventively; not in order to *verify* preconceptions but to create postconceptions. In the original epilogue to *Naven*, Bateson reported that he had no special interest in studying the Iatmul, no reason for looking at some aspects of this culture rather than others, no clear sense, initially, of what questions were the right ones to ask. In fact, the written document itself is described as "an experiment in . . . methods of thinking about anthropological material." The material presented in the book, call it data if you wish, is aimed at developing a mental picture — a *mind* — capable of making sense of the culture, of achieving a gestalt that explained it. A similar strategy is reflected in the communication research project that constituted a major chapter in the saga of the double-bind concept. John Weakland, one of the original members of that research team, recounts his memories of how data were used by Bateson's group:

> Certainly it (the research project) involved a lot of thinking, and its essential accompaniment, discussion. But it should not be forgotten that this thinking occurred in conjunction with a great deal of examination of data, of many kinds. The fact that these were seldom statistical data is to me relevant in a positive sense. Certainly it is not easier work, for example, to listen closely and repeatedly to a tape of a therapy session than to hear a summary of what occurred in that session, based on his memory and conceptual scheme, or to make tabulations based on a number of such summaries. . . . When the aim is to get a fresh and fundamental view of any object of study, the natural history method of looking directly at raw observational data is often the most appropriate (1976:107).

Here, as elsewhere in reports by Bateson and his students, one is given the impression that a research team operates like a detective agency;

looking for configurations of clues, piecing together the parts of a puzzle, framing data. Data have no meaning without or until being placed into some context. Always there are data and meta-data; phenomena under consideration and the consideration of them. Data aren't analyzed in the statistical or actuarial sense in which most social scientists use that term. Rather, they are mulled, pondered, mused, ruminated. Reflecting on the way Bateson "distilled ideas," Margaret Mead remembered: "He has always emphasized that thinking grows from thinking, and that 'some data going through the system' is necessary but nevertheless it is not the nature of the data itself, but the process of mulling it over, sometimes very loosely, sometimes with extraordinary detail and precision, that provides the next step" (1977:171).

What, then, is theory and what is methodology? Which *things* are data and which are concepts? Not only does it appear impossible to tell for certain (or at best arbitrary), it seems wrong to ask — irrelevant, falsely dualistic, a confusion of substance and process, a substitution of things for activities, misplaced particularism. The modern word *method* derives from the original Latin *method-us* meaning "pursuit of knowledge" (*Oxford English Dictionary*), while the root of *theory* is a Greek word,[*theoria*], meaning a looking at, a viewing, a contemplation. The distinction between pursuing and contemplating in the context of research doesn't constitute a difference that makes a difference, especially if one's epistemology is holistic. Batesonian science is true to these meanings. Commenting on what he learned from Bateson, Birdwhistell (1977) reported that the most important lesson his mentor taught him was to think of theory *as* methodology and methodology *as* theory. Methodology and theory are carriers for moving from a specific research question to which they are categorically relevant to larger issues, newer questions, hidden insights, for which they may be modified, refined, and/or corrected.

Having considered Bateson's habitual application of visual analogies and his unorthodox resistance to particularizing theory and methodology, his perspective on explanation remains to be examined. To try to extract a precise statement of what Bateson means by explanation from what he has written is an exhausting experience in thinking. In the introduction to *Steps To An Ecology of Mind*, he defined "Explanation" as the mapping of data onto fundamentals. This looks like an uncharacteristically straight-forward conception; but it is not.

According to this prescription, to explain one must begin with *both* data and fundamentals, a fundamental being an empirical generalization or a tautological proposition. Immediately, Bateson clouded the issue by boldly asserting that "in the behavioral sciences ... scarcely a single principle worthy of a place on the list of fundamentals" (1972:xix) has been produced. Now this would not be so serious, were we to accept inductive reasoning as the basis for establishing fundamentals. The solution would then lie in getting more data. But Bateson flatly rejected the idea that fundamentals can be induced from experience. The matter is much more complicated. Empiricism, he argued, is an insufficient logic for arriving at fundamentals; and, as a demonstration, he developed an explanatory parable that contrasts how the origin of the universe is understood in two different cultures, one exotic and one familiar. Clearly, observation alone could not have produced the universal distinction between substance and form found in both cultures myths about creation, not unless one allows for illogical leaps of imagination. Accordingly, there must be two beginnings to explanation, observations *and* fundamentals. The two are nonsubstitutable; each is authoritative in its own right.

Here, then, is the dilemma. Explanation occurs by mapping data onto fundamentals. In the social sciences, however, the list of fundamentals is vacant. Without some fundamentals we can't explain. Further, it is a mistake to think that fundamentals are inducible from data, as the history of behavioral sciences sorrily reveals. Getting more data will not resolve the dilemma. Erroneously, social scientists have learned to confuse so-called heuristic constructs — anxiety, ethos, ego, competence, motivation — with fundamentals. These constructs may be parts or substances of the interacting system we are observing, but they are not equivalent to fundamentals. What we unknowingly end up with by proceeding in this fashion is, not two, but one starting point: data. Thus, explanation amounts to an exercise in mapping data onto data. What is needed, according to Bateson, are not empirically induced truths but *necessary* ones and the most necessary one he can imagine is the distinction between "pleroma" and "creatura" — the non-living and the living, substance and form, non-recursive and recursive systems.

Once it is understood that recursiveness is fundamental to the development of a science of "creatura," that is, human interacting systems, the character of explanation is somewhat simplified. Bateson states that matter directly:

> If our explanations or our understanding of the Universe is in some sense to match that universe, or model it, and if the universe is recursive, then our explanations and our logics must also be fundamentally recursive (1977:242).

Again, we have here a deceptively simple proposition. The hub of the matter is that explanation must conform to experience. Since human experience is necessarily recursive, explanations true to experience must be recursive. The necessity of recursion is dictated by the acceptance of a cybernetic description of how humans "know," what Von Foerster (1972) calls "an epistemology of living things." The process of human knowing, the way we objectify the world, is ruled by the operations performed by our sensory system. In a marvelously parsimonious expression of this process, Von Foerster notes: "Objects and events are not primitive experiences. Objects and events are representations of relations ... the postulate of an 'external (objective) reality' disappears to give way to a reality that is determined by modes of internal computations" (1972:6). Recursiveness enters when we recognize, as Bateson reminded us, that "we perceive only the products of our perceptions" (1977:7).

Once recursiveness is assumed, the focus of explanation shifts necessarily from the world of matter to the world of form. In recursive systems it is trans*forms* — distinctions, differences, representations — that are essential to explanation. A human response is a creation resulting from an internal representation that the person himself participates in. Events or objects cannot be said to cause human responses because events or objects are themselves representations, at least so far as we "know" them. The messages contained in events and objects (stimuli) are not transferred to us but rather are transformed by us. Thus, explanations must center not on the events and objects themselves but on the relations between them; that is, on *how* distinction and difference is carried. Information is not a material thing. Von Foerster (1972:6) bluntly asserts that "the environment contains no information; the environment is as it is." Information, then, is relative to how I apprehend, that is, how I operate on what is out there.

If it is the distinctions we ourselves make that are "causes," then it is how the outside gets to the inside, how the subjective gets objectified, how the territory gets mapped, that explains. The explanation — distinction, difference, views — becomes that which has to be explained. Hence, explanation becomes "fundamentally recursive." We must attend, then, to the processes of linking, relating, bridging and connecting, which appears to be precisely why *Mind* became "a necessary explanatory principle" for Bateson: "The world is joined together in mental aspects" (1978:15). Mind is not a material substance (no-thing). It is recursive, embodied in its own output; that is, the various representations it produces: ideas. Mind is the pattern which connects.

Bateson was also saying that explanation must be conformable to the way we operate on the world, make sense of it, know it. And the way we operate is as naming, classifying, distinguishing, languaging, symbolic animals. *In order to classify, it is necessary to contextualize, which is why Bateson implored us to look for explanations in the ever larger units rather than in the sorts of microscopic reductions that constitute explanations in the non-classifying, non-distinguishing world of physical things.* Whatever has meaning for us, has meaning for us by virtue of being placed into a larger context. On this score, he is clear:

> ...without context there is no communication (1972:482).
> Wisdom I take to be the knowledge of the larger interactive
> system (1972:133).

To summarize: In this section I have attempted to extract some of the main fibers of thought woven into the text of Gregory Bateson's essays and scientific papers. I have especially emphasized his views on the nature and goals of scientific activity in the behavioral sciences. Any attempt to synthesize, condense or simplify Bateson's thought is enormously difficult for two reasons. Firstly, because his work spans more than five decades, a period of time in which there have been many important shifts in the intellectual and socio-cultural forces influencing scientific scholarship. Consequently, one finds Bateson continually reinterpreting his previous work in terms of a new language — first cybernetics, then the theory of logical types, more recently the principle of mind. In each period of his work, there is a slight shift in the importance he assigns to a fundamental principle onto which he maps his data. He keeps saying to us, "I was doing this all the time but I didn't know I was doing it until I encountered Weiner, or read Russell and Whitehead, or heard Spencer Brown." Maybe. Surely, however, his later attempts to formulate a single, coherent epistemological statement give the impression of more continuity and deduction to his thinking than there probably was, and much more than one experiences while reading all of it.

Second, Bateson confined his writing largely to the form of articles and essays addressed to vastly different audiences. Tying many knots in many different handkerchiefs, he moved swiftly and confidently through the subject matter of anthropology, biology, information theory, cybernetics, learning theory, epistemology, psychiatry, environmental science, etc. As he tackled some new puzzle that engaged him, he authoritatively constructed explanatory parables that usually are both unfamiliar and convincing. He has an uncanny ability to penetrate to the core of his subject without much specialized or technical expertise in that subject matter. Trying to keep pace with him, however, leaves even the very broadly educated wheezing on the sidelines. When the reader begins to sense the manner in which Bateson's work weds occidental and oriental modes of reasoning, as I am convinced it does, the tendency either is to fall uncritically at his feet and beg for guidance or quit trying to understand him.

With these disclaimers in mind, I offer the following capsule summary of Bateson's perspective on social scientific inquiry — call them

BATESON'S RULES OF THUMB:

(1) Study life in its natural setting being careful not to destroy the historical and interactional integrity of the whole setting.

(2) Think aesthetically. Visualize, analogize, compare. Look for patterns, configurations, figures in the rug.

(3) Live with your data. Be a detective. Mull, contemplate, inspect. Think about, through, and beyond.

(4) Don't be controlled by dogmatic formalisms about how to theorize and research. Avoid the dualisms announced and pronounced as maximums by particularizing methodologists and theorists. (They'll fire their shots at you one way or the other anyhow.)

(5) Be as precise as possible but don't close off possibilities. Look to the ever larger systems and configurations for your explanations. Keep your explanations as close to your data and experience as possible.

(6) Aim for catalytic conceptualizations; warm ideas are contagious.

IV

These six points establish a set of nonformalistic rules of thumb for imaginative and catalytic thinking about the scientific study of social phenomena. They also say, metacommunicatively: If warm ideas are what you seek, you'd better sharpen your *critical* faculties. By warm ideas I mean ideas that compel us to move closer to our subject matter; ideas from which we can cast new rays of insight, open up new lines of thought, extend our territory into new avenues of inquiry, and amplify our understanding beyond what we knew before.

No matter how hard to understand or oblique one may consider Bateson's writing, no one can properly deny the longevity or impact of his ideas. In the twentieth year after the first paper on the double-bind, two conferences were held and three new books on the subject were published. The idea of framing generated a book-length monograph by a distinguished dramaturgical sociologist (Goffman, 1974) and an intriguing manual about change by some important psychotherapists (Watzlawick, Weakland & Fisch, 1974). The significance of hierarchy and classification in learning and in communication theory is now axiomatic. And the concepts of end-linkages and symmetrical and complementary patterns of interaction continue to be applied to problems of concern to many different disciplines.

Notwithstanding these achievements, Bateson's way of developing ideas and theorizing about communicating and knowing have had very little impact on the education and indoctrination of American social scientists. Assuming that my representation of his guiding principles — rules of thumb — is fair and accurate, I think it can be shown that not only do most scientists in my field practice research differently than Bateson, but also that if they were to begin to think and theorize in a Batesonian fashion, they would either suffer a psychotic break, be denied tenure, or end up radicalizing scientific work on communication.

My argument is that scientists studying speech and human communication rather than accepting the doctrine of science as representational, as nonformalistic and as an open system, act instead as if science were nonsymbolic, necessarily formalistic, and a closed system. To demonstrate, I shall examine briefly some representative work on speech and communication and evaluate it in light of the Batesonian Rules of Thumb. Before undertaking this task, however, let me clarify my presuppositions.

Without repeating the same arguments voiced by many critics of social science over the past few years, e.g., Gergen, Harre and Secord, Toulmin, Winch, Charles Taylor, etc., let me simply say that it does not take much insight to see that the inductive mode of theorizing reigns supreme in the social sciences, that the verificational model of theory-testing dominates the practice of empirical research, and that the adequacy and efficacy of concepts are judged by social scientists mainly according to psychometric and sociometric standards of adequacy, i.e., measurement models. As a result, the main controversies in the field consist either of methodological quibbling in which the arguing is over how best to measure a concept rather than whether it is worth measuring at all; or abstract, metatheoretical quarrelling over what formal rules should dictate the activity of theorizing, or what form and logic theories should follow, without much theorizing being accomplished.

The dissonances between what has proven imaginative and progressive in social science and the practices encouraged by prevailing norms are especially evident when considered in the context of my earlier arguments. Recall that:

(1) *Scientific activity is recursive.* To see phenomena a scientist must transform them; having transformed them, he or she is transformed by them.

(2) *Data cannot tell us what to ask of them, nor what they mean.* This suggests that the meaning of data is never beyond challenge, never closed to other meanings, never capable of absolutely falsifying or verifying. What we do to and/or with data is an intellectual activity.

(3) *Ideas are as important as facts and nowhere is it evident that they are inducible from them* (facts). We need imagination not rules; intuition not technique; warm ideas not cold facts. Particularly in the social sciences where the entire question of measureability of phenomena and lawfulness of behavior is so troublesome, what we need is inventive people not conformists, fertile thinking not rigid rules to follow.

These points suggest, first of all, that there will always be methodological disputes because no methodological tool can apprehend phenomena without representing them. We are arguing over maps, not over territory. The sense that something is really out there which once served as our source of orientation has been debunked and replaced by what Bateson urged us to think of as a creative subjectivity: "Somewhere between the two (objectivity and subjectivity) is a region where you are partly blown by the winds of reality and partly an artist creating a composite out of the inner and outer events" (1977:245).

Secondly, no data and no arguments are capable of *proving* that any given formalism (some of my colleagues favorites are rules, covering laws, and systems theories) will necessarily lead to productive theorizing or generative conceptualizations. Arguing these points from the perspective of the history of science, Feyerabend concluded:

No idea is ever examined in all its ramifications and no view is ever given all the chances it deserves. Theories are abandoned and superceded by more fashionable accounts long before they have had an opportunity to show their virtues ... knowledge is obtained from a proliferation of views rather than from a determined application of a preferred ideology ... Pluralism of theories and metaphysical views is not only important for methodology, it is also an essential part of a humanitarian outlook (1975:50-52).

A brief and selective examination of developments in the scientific study of human communication is now in order, the objective being to hint at the cleavage between a Batesonian practice of social science capable of generating warm ideas and a formalistic science of communication vacant of catalytic thinking.

Two patterns of scholarly activity in speech communication trouble me. The first is the tendency to generate explanations which move us away from the phenomena we are interested in explaining. The second centers on the habit of letting our statistical techniques and methodologies do our thinking for us, thus dulling our critical and imaginative faculties.

In the study of communication, our modes of explanation too often end up pulling us away from our phenomena rather than push us closer to them. Consider, for example, the question of how interpersonal relationships evolve over time. It is the assumption of almost every theorist and investigator of this subject that communication is the lifeblood of relationships; that what people say and do to one another is the sternest stuff of interpersonal life. I doubt that any writers on this subject would disagree with the premise that utterances and actions are what help make relationships work. Yet when I (Bochner,1982) closely examined the theories of relational development appearing in the literature of social psychology, sociology of the family, and speech communication, I found that explanations of the relational development process were, with one exception, cast into the framework and language of forces and substances so familiar to behavioral and physical science. Instead of saying that marriages became what they became largely as a result of their own activity — communication — theorists are prone to *reduce* explanation to reward/cost principles. Many even go so far as to argue that the outcome of a marriage or intimate relationship is predetermined by what each person brings to the relationship; their needs, motives, and values. I found many problems with this form of explanation, not the least of which was the erroneous assumption that the part can control the whole. Not only does this sort of explanation substitute one explanatory principle (rewards and costs) for another (that stern stuff called communication), but it also has the damaging effect of focusing our attention on commodities (things) rather than process (forms).

The compulsion for quantification also tends to rule out or restrict catalytic thinking, though this is more an emergent custom than an inherent quality of the quantifying activities of social scientists. Take, for example, the important question of judging the value of a concept. The prevailing practice is to determine a concept's efficacy almost entirely in terms of its measurement. Concepts are introduced into the field by establishing that they can be reliably measured, usually via some type of questionnaire. Claims of significance are demonstrated by mounting statistical evidence indicating that the concept "accounts for substantial amounts of variance in subjects' behaviors." Notice how this practice can dull critical thinking. Instead of thinking through the possible meanings of "per cent of variance accounted for" we take it as axiomatic that a factor analysis table *informs* us about how pure and important our concepts are. Why should we accept the notion that a concept which accounts for sizeable proportions of variance is "significant" without asking how much variance (relative to this domain of human behavior) there was to explain in the first place; or whether it is the absence of variance rather than its presence that is most interesting and most in need of explanation; or whether it is that proportion of the variance that is neither explained nor unique which is the important part, the essence of the phenomenon in question?

Why must we insist that empirical concepts be assessed and interpreted in terms of quantities? There is nothing inherent in the doctrine of operationalism (if it exists we can see it), so far as I know, that requires us to count, number and quantify. Seeing something does not mandate that we count it. Bateson argued that "quantities are precisely *not* the stuff of complex communication systems," yet we continue to judge concepts mainly according to the criterion of quantifiability.

Although I do not have sufficient space in this paper to do so, I think I could show that an enormous amount of the total research activity in the field of communication revolves not around theories or explanations but around measurement; we are more focused on data than on fundamentals. Our journals are filled with measures of new and old concepts. As soon as a new measure makes its way into print, efforts are engendered to correlate it with anything remotely connected with it, as long as that "thing" is measurable. By the time existing measures with which it can be correlated have been exhausted, some measure of a new pop variable has arrived on the scene and the hard-working empiricist can begin the same cycle of activity. Thus, research activity is stimulated not so much by ideas as by measures, and researchers are looking not so much for answers to theoretical dilemmas or troublesome puzzles as they are in locating neglected variables or explaining more variance (whatever that may mean). Check the literature of the last decade and you will find unexplainable (no anomalies) and sudden shifts in the topics (variables) being researched: first a wave of interest on opinion change and evidence; then a spurt of activity on credibility; then, trust and disclosure; next, communication apprehension and communicator style; now constructs are the thing.

Why do the subjects of our research shift so suddenly and continuously? No one can say for sure, but I sense that credibility research, to take one example, lost its appeal when agreement was reached about its basic dimensionality. Once you've found a substance what do you do with it? Even the constructivists, whose heads and hearts seem to be in the right place — whose basic assumptions about communicative phenomena seem conformable to the notions of difference and distinction emphasized by Bateson — tend in their research to represent *qualities* (hierarchies of constructs) with quantities and to treat research as a hypothesis-testing activity. I personally regard the nearly self-evident assumption that how people construe other people and events influences how they interact not as a hypothesis to be tested but as an idea to be extended.

The question is how to warm to the task of thinking catalytically. At the present time quantification rules. In my opinion, when quantitative methods control thinking (though they never have to do so), a social field of inquiry runs the risk of being not a marketplace for exhibiting, exchanging and evolving ideas, but a depository for dumping instruments, tools, and techniques.

THEORY

theory. 1. A sight, a spectacle. 2. Mental view, contemplation. 3. A conception or mental scheme of something to be done, or of the method of doing it. 4. A scheme or system of ideas or statements held as an explanation or account of a group of facts or phenomena. 5. Systematic conception or statement of the principles of something; often used as implying more or less unsupported hypotheses: distinguished from or opposed to practice.

6. A hypothesis proposed as an explanation: hence, a mere hypothesis, speculation, conjecture; an idea or set of ideas about something; an individual view or notion.

— *Oxford English Dictionary*

Each of the four essays in this section proposes a system of general principles which may serve to guide an understanding of human communication. The claims made vary both in scope and certitude, demonstrating a wide range of attitudes which can be brought to bear upon social scientific theorizing.

In "Toward an Ecology of Communication," Dean C. Barnlund posits "a way of looking at the phenomena called communication." He argues that the demonstrated limits of the classical communication model have left us reaching "across a paradigmatic divide" in search of a cosmology adequate to our consciousness. Barnlund sketches, in broad strokes, the outlines of the shape which a contemporary ecology of human communication might assume. It is a contextualist model: systemic, transactional, multidimensional, reflexive. To explicate this view, Barnlund explores "an ecology of contexts from the primary relations of the human being and the physical world to the more elaborate relations maintained with the world of other people," concluding with a consideration of some functional features of the relations between interacting systems. The assumptions examined in this essay are "far from trivial, for they define our field of inquiry, influence the investigative modes we favor and findings we respect, and are reflected in our personal manner of relating to others." "And," Barnlund suggests, "carry social and political implications as well."

"Who for, what for, metaphor?" asks Herbert W. Simons in "The Management of Metaphor." Metaphor, in its various guises, has long been problematic within the context of conventional science. Simons claims

that"*scientific theories are rhetorical constructions and their key terms are ineliminably metaphorical.*" Hence, scholars cannot escape from the ambiguities of metaphor: at best, metaphors can be managed. Simons proposes a dialectical model for the management of social scientific metaphors, involving metacommunication, rhetorical criticism, and modes of evaluation. Ignoring the ubiquity of metaphor in scientific discourse does not strengthen science, but rather may compromise its credibility. "*Metaphor presents itself as a Janus-faced object,*" Simons writes, "*a quintessential case of the dialectical tension between rigor and imagination in science generally.*"

"Communication Theory in a New Key" presents a theory of human communication developed in recent years by W. Barnett Pearce, Linda M. Harris, and Vernon E. Cronen. In this essay the authors first explore similarities between the "coordinated management of meaning" and the interactional view as perspectives on human communication. Both models, they suggest, are committed to a general systems framework, to hierarchically and temporally extended analysis of messages, to the concept of rule-governed action, and to the notion of the social construction of second-order reality. However, Pearce, Harris and Cronen claim that the coordinated management of meaning departs from the interactional view by identifying additional levels of context, by assuming greater flexibility in the organization of meaning, by analyzing relationship development in terms of changes in position among hierarchically structured elements, and by virtue of its distinctive treatment of paradox. The authors further explicate the coordinated management of meaning model, summarize relevant research, and present an extended case study undertaken from their theoretical stance. In sum, they argue that the coordinated management of meaning maintains some of the "virtues of science" — such as descriptive and explanatory power, some predictability, intersubjectivity and a rigorous verification procedure — without compromising Bateson's conception of communication.

B. Aubrey Fisher's position in "Implications of the Interactional View for Communication Theory" developed from his remarks as respondent to a set of theory-related papers presented at the Asilomar conference. Fisher offers some guiding assumptions for assessing the interactional view within the context of communication theory more generally. He points out that the interactional view is far from the mainstream of either communication theory or psychotherapy, and not a "theory" at all in conventional terms, but perhaps more aptly a "state of mind." By accepting this caveat, Fisher argues, one can better see the aspects of the interactional model which may, in fact, offer important implications for communication theory. These include the external (versus intrapsychic) locus of the interactional perspective, the notion of *hierarchies of contextualized meaning, recognition of the multidimensionality of human communication, increased attention to the significance of time in interaction, emphasis upon pattern identification, and consideration of issues of reflexivity in communication. The interactional view "treats the problematic as interesting," and thus not only do "the questions asked become more significant than the answers," but also "the asking of the questions is more interesting than the answers obtained."*

C.W.-M.

Toward an Ecology of Communication

Dean C. Barnlund

Each moment...
Is but a process in a process
Within a field that never closes;
As proper people find it strange
That we are changed by what we change
That no event can happen twice
And that no two existences
Can be alike...

Auden

Someone has suggested that the image of the behavioral sciences should be a snake biting its own tail. It is an image that is as provocative as it is amusing; an image that applies not to a single profession, but to every profession and to every human being. All of us are the authors and victims of the cosmologies we construct, suffering the pleasures and pains they make possible. We are all architects, fashioning from the materials of our lives and the grammars of our cultures, a framework that makes experience intelligible. It is only when the foundations of this assumptive world prove inadequate or the borders too confining that we are forced to evaluate its adequacy, install new footings, or enlarge its perimeter.

An architectural figure of speech aptly fits the comments to follow for we could not do better, in my view, than to seek a more enduring and liberating scaffold for the study of communication within the very process we seek to understand. Solutions tend to be implicit in problems. If architects begin by considering the character of the topography, activities to be housed, and the nature of available materials, should we not begin similarly by examining the assumptions that currently shape our view of communication? These assumptions are far from trivial for they define our field of inquiry, influence the investigative modes we favor and findings we respect, and are reflected in our personal manner of relating to others. And, I would suggest, carry social and political implications as well.

There can be no inquiry in the absence of a conceptual framework. Here we seek to describe the process of human communication: What needs does it serve? What resources does it employ? What patterns does it assume? What conditions facilitate or frustrate its aims? The object is neither to present a body of data nor a set of hypotheses, but to posit a way of looking at the phenomena called communication. Clearly communication deals not with objects, but with relations, with the way in which changes in organisms are related to changes in environments. To explicate this process we shall explore an ecology of contexts from the primary relations of the human being and the physical world to the more elaborate relations maintained with the world of other people. Finally, by examining some features of the relations between interacting systems we may be able to identify the conditions that promote optimal or pathological functioning.

ACROSS A PARADIGMATIC DIVIDE

The classical paradigm of communication was, and to most people still is, self-evident. The analytic framework emphasized the bounded, elementalistic, linear, additive, verbal and instrumental aspects of human interaction. Communication was a distinctive form of behavior, as much so as typing, shopping, swimming or knitting. One chose to communicate or not; talk signalled the start of this activity and silence its termination; one could communicate more or less, could succeed or fail to communicate. Three obvious elements were involved: a source, a message, and a receiver. They were linked in a linear pattern: sources articulated messages which influenced receivers. Meanings were transferred from source to receiver through the agency of symbols, and reflected the skill of the source. Messages were predominantly, if not exclusively, verbal. Sources were typically active, receivers passive.

Every cosmology creates its own events, placing some features in focus while placing others out. It is not surprising, then, that this paradigm triggered interest in public forms of discourse, for this type of communication involves structured settings, identifiable speakers, extended verbal messages, passive receivers and predominantly unilateral influence. Out of this analytic framework has come an appreciation of political advocacy and penetrating analyses of the structure of formal messages.

The incompleteness of this view of communication gradually became evident over time, very slowly and over a long time. If its usefulness in the study of public discourse was limited, its relevance in probing the less formal occasions that comprise most of life was even more striking. Roger Barker in *One Boy's Day* chronicled the events of a single day in the life of a young boy: Not a single experience involved a formal rhetorical setting. In some there was no speaker, in some no listener, in some no motive, in some it was absence or silence that occasioned the most significant meanings (1951).

The classical paradigm helped little in explicating the teasing of youngsters, the negotiating of contracts, or the unfolding of a love affair. It failed to explain communicative crises that appear in interpersonal, group and organizational contexts, even excluded such events as "not communication." And it is of little value in exploring communication in cultures that attach little importance to public deliberation, to rational analysis, or to words themselves. The specific and immediate effects of public advocacy alone fit its parameters and constitute its central domain.

The epistemological assumptions of any period or culture, of course, are rarely confined to a single discipline or sphere of activity; they tend to permeate every corner of life. Thus our inherited model of communication reflected the central premises of the classical world, and simply transformed these into a theoretical model of communication. Even today few recognize the extent to which this paradigm parallels the dominant models throughout the social sciences: the stimulus-response model, the object-perceiver model, and source-receiver models reflect such conceptual kinship as clearly to have sprung from the same epistemological ancestry. They are alike in their basic elements, alike in their postulated relations, alike in their social implications. All employ a cosmology that emphasizes structure over function, object over relation, element over variable, linearity over circularity, additivity over non-additivity; all reify object, stimulus or message, and all presume behavior to be externally determined. This reactive cosmology in which people are cast inevitably as victims or victimizers is, in my view, one of the vastly underestimated sources of twentieth century malaise.

A history of the intellectual revolution of the last hundred years is yet to be undertaken that will expose its complex tapestry of ideas. But it is not premature to characterize it as a period of unparalleled conceptual ferment, of transition to a new cosmology capable of transforming not only the physical and behavioral sciences, but of changing our image of what it is to be human. Clearly this is not traceable to a singular insight, but the result of simultaneous and parallel evolution across many fields of inquiry. Such a history, however, might expose its major themes and reveal the converging harmony one suspects is there.

The participants in this century-long dialogue represent every academic field, and the contributions often reflect the distinctive imprint of these fields. Now and then a voice rises that reaches beyond its own territorial boundaries — an Einstein, Freud, Marx, Picasso — but the record is far less an orderly series of solo speeches than a noisy, disorderly, confusing argument. In nearly every discipline — physics, anthropology, biology, philosophy, mathematics, linguistics — can be found traces of this ferment and the search for a new orientation. In the physical sciences there is the crossing of a paradigmatic divide from certainty to probability, from permanence to flux, from part to whole, from object to process, from objectivity to relativity. But the revolution in the arts has been no less radical: the impressionists turned hard edges into vibrations, the surrealists subordinated the objective to the subjective, the cubists insisted on a multifaceted and simultaneous experiencing of objects, and the kineticists replaced the objects with dynamic relationships. To accommodate such discoveries a host of hyphenated disciplines were born and new fields, like cybernetics and systems theory, arose to consolidate and extend them.

To exaggerate the revolutionary impact of these new assumptions is probably impossible. "When paradigms change," as Kuhn noted, "the mind itself changes with them" (1962:196). And the creation of a new mind is the creation of a new world. Here it is the articulation of these new premises and their application to human interaction that concerns us. The aim is to set forth the central postulates of this new cosmology with reference to the nature of human communication. It is important that such a cosmology remain as open and as tentative as possible for it will undoubtedly incorporate a myopia of person, place, time and particularly culture.

COMMUNICATION: PERSON-ENVIRONMENT

Communication as Intentional

Activity, or restlesssness, is an inherent feature of all forms of life. It is impossible to exist without acting; impossible to act without interpreting. Although born into a world without meaning, we invest it with significance through the discriminatory decisions we must make. In the *Myth of Sisyphus*, Camus notes that meanings are born out of "the confrontation between a human need and the unreasonable silence of the world" (1955:21). The word "communication" refers to this emergence of meaning as organisms attribute significance to external and internal conditions. If life becomes an endless "effort after meanings," it is because they are essential to actions, to growth and even to survival. Every discriminatory decision, of course, implies a direction. As May has written, "Each act of consciousness tends toward something, is a turning toward something, and has within it, no matter how latent, some push toward a direction for action" (1969:232). To define a situation and one's place in it is to give rise to purpose and to promote its achievement.

The work in cybernetics has been of immense heuristic value in demonstrating that static, determined, powered, self-initiating, programmed, homeostatic and ultrastatic systems each possess unique adaptive potentialities. With every level of organizational complexity there is an increase in the degrees of freedom. Human beings, the most complex of all systems, are capable of the greatest diversity of intentions and widest means of realizing them. Communication is a necessity in complex systems, and its function is the utilization of information for the maintenance and operation of such systems. The study of human communication concerns the process by which meanings are formed within and among people and of the conditions that determine their character and consequences.

Communication as Transaction

The world is possibility, no more, no less. We are born into an environment so varied, so complex, so devoid of inherent meaning as to overwhelm the senses. Yet no matter how chaotic it seems, we make it intelligible. As Morse Peckham argues: "Indeed there is no set of perceptual data so disparate that human perception cannot create order and unity out of it" (1973:30). Any object is capable of diverse interpretation, and diverse objects capable of generating similar interpretations. The fifteen stones of Ryoanji Temple appear absurd to one visitor, and awe-inspiring to the next. As Norbert Wiener once remarked, the world holds an infinity of "To Whom It May Concern" messages.

Clearly the locus of meaning is not in the objects or events that comprise the universe. Though born into a world devoid of meaning — neutral in very sense of the word — we invest it with whatever significance it acquires. Discriminatory decisions give structure to the flow of sensations, place perceptual boundaries around events, differentiate between noise (uninterpreted data) and information (interpreted data). Figure and ground are differentiated; some events are placed within operative categories and others excluded from them. It is, as Bateson so aptly put it, the creation of a difference that makes a difference (1972). The locus of such distinctions cannot be situated in the objects themselves, or in the space between them, for they are constructs invented to serve the interpreter. The painter, Georges Braque, put it this way: "I do not believe in any one thing. I do not believe in this or this . . . . I do not believe in things: I believe only in their relationship, in their circumstances" (1960:140). Or, as the architect Lyndon Herbert remarked, "What is important about the statement 'one' and 'one' makes 'two' is the 'and', not descriptions of 'one' and 'one' " (1972:75).

Two caveats are in order: One is that figure and ground are essential to each other: without figure there is no ground; without ground, no figure is discernible. The tenuous figures of Giacometti owe as much of their impact to the space that overpowers them as to their own insubstantiality. In that marvelous conversation, "Why Do Frenchmen?", Bateson and his daughter wisely conclude that when Frenchmen wave their arms in talking their gestures gain significance from their absence at other times, and their absence acquires significance from their expected presence (1972:9). Silence is as necessary in giving import to speech as speech is in endowing silence with meaning. The second caveat is that features of the real world never get into the nervous systems of interpreters nor, in fact, do the discriminations. Nothing at all gets *into* the interpreter: what occurs within the system — certain electrical-chemical changes - has been described as a "transform," "image," "abstraction," or "construct." All imply that we do not deal with the "real" world, but only with our constructions of it.

This process of organizing sensations is an active and creative one. For years it has been mistakenly described as "responding," "receiving," or "reacting" to the world.[1] That such a view pervades the behavioral sciences was documented in Allport's analysis of the vocabulary in texts on human behavior. Words like "reaction," "response," and "reception" far outnumbered proactive terms (1960). Chien has found the current scene largely unchanged, with the prevailing image of man that of a helpless, powerless reactor (1972).

One does not react to the world, for meanings do not reside in it. Nor is it accurate to say one interacts with the world, for there is no reciprocal interpretation by the environment. The process of communication is best described as a transaction in which people create meanings to fulfill emerging needs. Interpreters bring to each occasion a repertoire of experience and expectation and this, along with the resources of the setting, provides the materials of meaning. Physical and social environments can be regarded only as placing some constraints upon the scope and diversity of meanings.[2] It is out of this integration of inner and outer possibilities that any moment gains its unique significance. As Whitehead sensitively noted:

> Thus nature gets credit which should in truth be reserved for ourselves: the rose for its scent, the nightingale for its song, and the sun for its radiance... Nature is a dull affair, soundless, scentless, colorless, merely the hurrying of material, endlessly, meaninglessly (1953:70).

If the environment is without intrinsic meaning, human beings cannot be at the mercy of an external determinism; if their acts are not dictated by instincts, neither are they at the mercy of an inner determinism. Human behavior reflects an active and creative transformation of sensory material into meaningful events.

Communication as Intrapersonal

Although we do not occupy the center of the physical world, we clearly stand at the center of our experiential world. All meanings originate within us; they constitute an imaginative integration of past and present, a realization of potentials in the organism and environment. To say that communication is intrapersonal is to say it occurs in the presence or absence of other persons. While encounters between people may interest us most, it is critical to remember that meanings arise only in meaners.

The operations implicated in the attribution of meanings — sensing, organizing, recalling, evaluating — go on within the borders of the body. Yet the delineation of such functions is subject to certain qualifications: The listing of such functions must not imply a simple sequence of discrete operations for they are clearly overlapping and interdependent. Recent work suggests that an inductive, piece-by-piece construction of reality is almost the opposite of what happens. Bever concludes that "we organize our conscious perceptions of the world in terms of the highest available level of organization" (1974:169). Similarly, Shands notes that "relations precede objects" and concludes that "an object is a retrospective rationalization of an experienced relation" (1968:127).

An alternative to an identification of specific communicative functions is to substitute broader categories such as encoding and decoding. They are popular terms and seem to describe critical aspects of communication. The first refers to sensory discriminations that transform the organism in some way; the second refers to the expression of such internal states so they are accessible to others. We interpret the perceptual fields the environment provides; we create the perceptual fields others interpret. Even here, however, such a strict separation of functions while simplifying some problems complicates others for there is always a risk in dividing a process that operates as a whole and is without discernible internal boundaries.

The second caution concerns relations between communicative systems. The self-evident quality of the boundary that divides organism and environment becomes less and less obvious the closer we approach it. Bateson, in his classic example of the man-axe-tree circuit, suggests that only the total system of tree-eyes-brain-muscles-axe-stroke-tree has the quality of immanent mind. What occurs in this system is a series of transforms and what happens in the environment is as essential to the circuit as the sensory-muscular processes in the human participant. There is danger in separating meaning and context, or participant and setting, of falling into the trap of viewing one as independent variable and the other as dependent variable.

My own view agrees with his emphasis upon the idea that communication systems, particularly human ones, never exist out of context, that any analysis of behavior that disregards the matrix in which it occurs distorts its character in some respects. As he stresses, "in no system which shows mental characteristics can any part have unilateral control over the whole. In other words. the mental characteristics of the system are immanent, not in some part, but in the system as a whole" (1972:316). The issue here is whether to base the study of communication on the assumption of a hierarchy of systems in which each serves as context of the others, each having some unique features and some autonomy, or that the only communicative system is the universe as a whole and analytic units become "arcs of larger circuits." Whether this difference in conception makes a difference to scientific inquiry is not clear. However it is resolved, and my own preference is for regarding the universe as a hierarchy of communicative systems, both views emphasize the ecological nature of communication.

To see communication as an intrapersonal process carries practical and empirical consequences. It suggests that all meanings, since they are the creation of unique persons in unique settings, are distinctive. Further, that since our knowledge of the world is inescapably subjective, human interaction is about a transformed and imaged world. It is not the "real" world, but these private transforms that we fight about, laugh about, cry about. Our meanings are fictions, valued and useful fictions, but fictions nonetheless. Finally our identity is itself a construct, a highly valued and well protected one, but one that confirms Nietzsche's remark that "in the end we experience only ourselves."

Communication as Continuous

The process of communication is without clear lines of demarcation. It is not a thing, not an event, but a process that ebbs and flows with changes in the environment and in ourselves. The "stream of consciousness" is less a poetic metaphor than a literal description.

This process begins at birth or before, carries us forward from moment to moment, and terminates in death. It is a condition that inheres in all living forms. The "restless universe" of the physicist finds its counterpart in the "restless organism" of the physiologist and the "restless mind" of the communicologist. There is no way of starting or stopping this continuous traffic between organism and environment or between organism and organism.

Time is not a feature of nature, but an artifact of culture and conception. In nature there are no discernible, clearly bounded, events. Just as figure and ground await an organization of the field in space, so do events await an organization of the field in time. Subdividing human experience into occasions, events, episodes, and further distinguishing among working, playing or conversing, enables us to note them, preserve them, probe them, compare them, but it is vital in doing so to remember that we are working with maps not territories, that there is danger of obscuring the transient and continuous nature of human transactions with the world.

The study of behavior often fails to recognize that every act is both prologue and epilogue; a consequence of all preceding events and antecedent to all subsequent ones. The same is true of every moment within such events; every "message" reflects all prior ones and forms the context of all following ones. The principle is valid at even the most elementary level, each firing of a neuron is a report or comment, and equally a prediction or command. In a world of process there are, in effect, no products. Processes do not end in products; they end, as well as begin, in other processes. The continuous flow of human acts is something we seem more sensitive to as people than as scientists.

Communication as Evolutionary

Defining communication as a continual process of creating meaning leaves the communicologist in search of an adequate paradigm for studying it. Three conceptual models — linear, circular, and evolutionary — have dominated investigative efforts. The first focuses on three variables: source, message, and receiver. These fall into an obvious order suggesting that sources through messages transmit meanings to receivers. It is a mechanical model, isolating the parts that comprise the system, assuming an external control of meanings, and embodying a limited view of the nature of messages. Success or failure to inform or persuade is limited by the credentials and appeals of the source or by the ignorance and perversity of the receiver. That this model of communication has survived so long, still provokes inquiry, and elucidates many features of public discourse keeps it alive today. Its relevance for us lies in its directionality, and its emphasis on communication as a means of change.

The technological revolution of the last hundred years, and particularly work in cybernetics, forced an elaboration of this circuit, but one with immense heuristic consequences. The line was closed; linearity became circularity. Speakers not only articulated ideas, but monitored their performance in the interest of greater effectiveness. Messages could flow in both directions, sequentially or simultaneously; sources could become receivers and receivers sources; messages were no longer exclusively verbal. Positive feedback reinforced ongoing acts; negative feedback stabilized the system by counteracting error. The concept of homeostasis, deriving from the work of Claude Bernard and Walter Canon, was seen to be applicable to families, groups, organizations and cultures.

Many features of this model were liberating: structure gave way to function; linearity was replaced with circularity; simple causality became multiple causality; all forms of interaction became legitimate settings for communication research. Yet new difficulties appeared: the maintenance of homeostasis became a preoccupation; the shift from external to internal determinism merged with dynamic psychology to make defenses and pathologies the focus of students of communications; a completely circular system implied a defensively oriented one incapable of transcending its homeostatic script.

Something was still missing. Organisms seemed neither at the mercy of outer or inner compulsions. People were not simply adaptive, bent only on preserving their tenuous balance in a contingent universe. The model provided no explanation of the spontaneous and unpredictable acts of people. It failed to account for the accomplishments of "invulnerables," people who by genetic inheritance and social circumstances should be incompetent or criminal, but were not. It supplies little guidance in understanding the origin of languages, the formation of cultures, the creation of anything at all. People did not merely weather crises, but often transcended them in unforeseen ways. Worst of all, people manifested almost as much anxiety and illness when fully stabilized as when most challenged.

There are many ways of labeling the current paradigm: it has been referred to as an "ultrastatic" system, an "open" system, an "amplifying" system, an "homeorhetic" system, a "transactional" system. What is common to these labels is a commitment to viewing organisms as systems. These systems are complex, possessing both linear and circular properties. Human beings are seen as active, initiating organisms, seeking to realize their aims and in doing so giving birth to new aims; the meanings required to act intelligently are neither under the control of external events nor dictated by inner compulsions; people are linked to the universe both in a linear and a purposive way, but are sensitive also to constraints that keep the organism from exceeding its own limits; all meanings reverberate throughout a system, reinforcing or undermining existing behavior. Central in these models is the assumption that communication is an evolutionary process, that the system is in a continual state of semantic metamorphosis: there is both adaptation and elaboration. As Whyte notes, "the processes of living systems always display two aspects: a periodic or cyclic aspect which restores the normal state and leaves no net change, and a progressive or one-way aspect which results in the cumulative extension or multiplication of the organic patterns" (1946:114). There is, in short, evidence of both the maintenance of physical and semantic stability, and the potential for alteration and improvement.

Communication as Unrepeatable

That communication is unrepeatable derives from the nature of the environment and the nature of our relations with it. The world we inhabit is a world of particulars; no two objects or occasions are ever the same; all is unique and all is in flux. Every moment is a unique configuration of matter, space and time. It presents us, as Heraclitus noted, with fresh occasions for meaning.

If uniqueness and change characterize the world, interpreters of it are no less unique or changeable. The unrepeatability of communication derives, also, from the difference between systems that are deterministic or mechanical and those that are discretionary or spontaneous. In the former, the output of the system can be reliably predicted from knowledge of the input. The system obeys a rigid logic that is wired into it and cannot be revised through experience. In a closed system, the "same message" does produce the "same effect" for the system operates with minimal degrees of freedom. In spontaneous or open systems, the system is regulated by internal principles which are modifiable through experience. Identical inputs, if they could be arranged, may provoke variations in output for each experience changes the organism is some way and thereby alters the context of all subsequent experience. One cannot expect the "same message" to generate the "same meaning" for it is a different person who now interprets it. For humans, no novel, film, play, or remark can be experienced twice for the first time. The "same message" when repeated may bore or antagonize, but it is unlikely to prompt an identical meaning. As the artist Vincenzo Agnelli once remarked, "A word repeated becomes another word" (1972).

Carried to an extreme, unrepeatability would lead to totally random behavior and no science of communication would be possible. People do display consistencies in their relations with the environment and others; the extent of such consistency reflecting the similarity perceived in situations and the rigidity of these perceptual discriminations. But behavior rarely repeats itself exactly and this poses a challenge not only to scientists but to all who engage in social interaction.

Communication as Irreversible

In *The Human Condition*, Hannah Arendt speaks of the "predicament of irreversibility," of being unable to undo the consequences of acts whose outcomes were not, and could not, be known (1959:212). This predicament, a thoroughly human one, exposes another feature of communication. There are many systems — mechanical, physical, chemical, biological — that change from one state to another, but whose operations may be reversed so they can return to their original state. This is not true of the creation of meanings in human beings. As Wilder Penfield has noted, this process goes inexorably forward: "Time's strip of film runs forward, never backward, even when resurrected from the past" (1954:68). Although amnesia may mar the record or aphasia reduce the functioning of the mind, there is no going back. One can reflect on the past or anticipate the future, but both are in the service of the present.

This feature of communication carries serious implications for relations not only with the environment, but for relations with other people. One cannot insult or accuse or even praise someone without precipitating meanings that are irreversible. Meanings, once created, cannot be taken back. They may prompt still further meanings, but there is no way to restore an earlier innocence. It is the unpredictability and irreversibility of meanings that make interaction one of the more hazardous human enterprises, and they may have led Arendt to place the faculty of forgiving high among our most human attributes.

COMMUNICATION: PERSON-TO-PERSON

Communication acquires added dimensions when the attribution of meanings occurs in the presence of others, especially when it involves efforts to align such meanings through an interdependent and orchestrated series of complementary actions.

Communication as Coded

Although transactions with the world give rise to unique personal perceptions, to interact with others requires that such private meanings be convertible into public meanings. "There may be truths beyond speech," writes Arendt, "but men insofar as they live and move and act in the world can experience meaningfulness only because they can talk and make sense to each other" (1959:4).

To overcome the inherently subjective character of human experience it must be made accessible to others, and that requires that certain signals be endowed with sufficient commonality of reference to link the inner states of their users. Although the number of such signals is limited, because our capacity to master and to recall such signals is limited, the rules governing these codes greatly enrich their transformational possibilities.

The symbols that comprise such codes are obviously arbitrary, having no intrinsic connection with their referents.[3] Through constant repetition, norms evolve that constrain people to employ them with some consistency. Thus what the members of any linguistic community share is not the world so much as it is a similar way of construing the world; to the extent that persons inhabit a common universe of discourse they are capable of sharing a common universe of meaning (Barnlund, 1975).

The meanings associated with words and gestures are nothing but shared dispositions to act in similar ways in the presence of similar cues. If it can be said that it is impossible to transfer meanings from one person to another, it is equally impossible to transfer messages.[4] In contributing to a conversation one does not transfer anything at all, but transforms the context so as to encourage more or less equivalent attributions to their words or acts.

Such codes provide some means of transcending singular and subjective meanings: they help us to discover errors in our perceptions; they are a way of counteracting biases inherent in our interpretations of events; they permit empathic linkages among persons with diverse meanings; they make possible creative syntheses of partial views of reality; they expand enormously the scope of our experience, enabling us to plug into the knowledge of our contemporaries and of previous generations.

Yet as we use language, symbols tend to lose their status as tools for reporting experience and become the shapers of experience.[5] Events become so infused with symbolic significance that the name of something becomes more important that what it represents. Words acquire such authority that they not only define the world, but define the person who employs them, for one cannot define a relation *in* the world without simultaneously defining a relation *to* that relation. Once the master of our symbols, it is difficult to resist becoming their slaves.

If it can be said there are no ships nor sealing wax, no cabbages or kings in the mind, it can be said as well that there are no nouns, adjectives, verbs or conjunctions there either. Nor, we should add, any fists, winks, or frowns. Our repetoire of transforms includes not merely sensory discriminations of material things, but transforms of signs and symbols as well. When Bateson suggests we cannot be "frightened by a lion because a lion is not an idea," we must add that neither can we be frightened by the word "lion," or even an enactment of its roar, because these also are not ideas (1972:271).

Communication as Reflexive

The phonetic and acoustic properties of language usually give little trouble; it is the semantic properties — the transformation of meaning into signal and signal into meaning within separate assumptive worlds — that cause difficulty. To begin with, no symbol system has a structure that is isomorphic with the world; the map is not the territory, the pleroma is not the creatura. For this reason every statement is, in part, a lie. Every statement imposes a structure on events that derives from the grammar of the language, not necessarily from the grammar of events.

Another limitation arises from the small number of words — a few thousand at most — for naming and describing events. Each experience prompts unique meanings in each person, but this distinctiveness must be sacrificed to the requirements of coding. And each new human being multiples further the diversity of meanings to be accommodated by the same words. Language acquisition in children shows that while infants quickly acquire a vocabulary and soon master grammar, it takes many years to gain sufficient flexibility of reference to carry out cooperative tasks successfully (Glucksberg & Krauss, 1966).

To compress an infinity of meanings into a finite vocabulary requires that every word be capable of multiple meanings, often hundreds of meanings. The inherent ambiguity of symbols, then, makes every message a mystery, a pursuit of commonality using the vaguest of clues. "We want words to do much more than they can," Samuel Butler wrote, "we expect them to help us to grasp and dissect that which is as ungrippable as shadow" (1917:94). Communicants must learn to tolerate this ambiguity while narrowing referential gaps, or it becomes a source of confusion, deception or hostility.

Since there is no intrinsic link between symbols and the world, no binding relation between any word and its referent, language makes possible a hierarchy of meanings at various levels of abstraction. This feature has been noted in Russell's Theory of Logical Types, Korzybski's Reflexive Abstraction, Whorf's Theory of Linguistic Relativity, and in Bateson's concept of Framing. In all there is a recognition that symbols operate at various levels of abstraction; these authors differ only in their attention to the personal, interpersonal or cultural consequences of this feature.

In short, language permits observers to construct alternative interpretations of events, and also to frame these messages at different levels of generality. The meaning of a specific message is determined not solely by its content, but by how it may be framed at higher levels of abstraction. It is the proscenium that informs us the play is not life, the molding that distinguishes the painting from the wall. Peckham argues, for example, that it is impossible to define art by seeking it in some object or event; it is the framing of anything so that observers assume an aesthetic attitude toward it that defines the art experience (1973). The tradition in Japan of tying a rope or paper around a rock or tree of provocative form so that it will evoke appreciation illustrates this well. Such classifying behaviors in interpersonal encounters may have as their aim the framing of events, of relations, of motives, of contexts. It has taken over half a century of reiteration to recognize the importance of this attribute of symbolization.

The framings that interest us most are those employed in human interaction to create a specific stance in participants toward the acts they are perceiving, have perceived, or are about to perceive. Such framings may classify messages (metalinguistic), intentions (metacommunicative), interpersonal roles (metapersonal), or occasions (metafunction). They may be supplied explicitly or implicitly; they may be articulated by the actor or projected by the interpreter. Framing difficulties cannot be located within a particular message because, like all meanings, they are transactional phenomena that require some collaboration between the creator of the message and the creator of the meaning.

So much attention has focused on the negative consequences of reflexivity that its salutary functions are often ignored. It permits adoption of what Goldstein calls the "abstract attitude," one that allows people to change their point of view and thereby alter their conceptualizing of events (1963). It promotes what Flavell calls "decentering," the capacity to see oneself from the perspective of another (1963). Such reflexive role-taking seems indispensable in symbolic interaction: to encode requires not merely giving *some* form to inner sensations but, through predictive projection, giving it the particular form required by this setting, this moment, with this person; decoding requires an imaginative reconstruction of the relation between the source and the event symbolized (Mead, 1935). Finally, it is the reflexiveness of language that generates the confusions and contradictions which trigger new meanings and new relations between people and the world.

Among the difficulties that complicate human interaction are several that arise from the framing of discourse. And awkward as they are to describe, the effort is worth making. One is mystification. While lack of clarity is always confusing, failure to frame a message appropriately is more so. One may know what was said or done, but not know what sort of message it is, how it is to be taken, or what responses are expected. In disqualification, messages are so framed that interactants are not sure of who they are, what their relationship is to be, or how to reciprocate. The meta-message implies they are not to take themselves, nor will others take them, seriously. Finally there are paradoxical injunctions in which messages are framed in contradictory ways. This may be compounded when perceived to carry a superordinate framing that blocks any effort to clarify, revise, or integrate such contradictory frames (Watzlawick, 1967). In the latter case, the case of the double bind, one may gradually lose confidence in who one is, what one sees, what it means. In such circumstances people may become convinced of the absurdity of all interaction, thus moving toward a mechanical or autistic relation with the world.

Communication as Multichanneled

To say that interaction is coded, rather than simplifying matters, provokes new questions about the multiplicity of such codes, their interrelations, and their possible integration. We are, in effect, defining interaction as a linguistic or symbolic occasion, and at least three attitudes exist toward the study of such occasions.

One group, those who wish to preserve a narrow concept of language, we might call the "linguistic snobs." To them language consists of words and the structural rules governing their use in speech and writing. (It is this group which until recently opposed recognizing the signing of the deaf as a language.) For this group there is a primary code, the verbal, and all others are subordinate or supplementary to it.

A second attitude, belonging to what we are now forced to identify as "linguistic slobs," comprises two factions. Both recognize the multiplicity of codes employed in human interaction, and both accept that any cues that affect meanings should be incorporated in linguistic analysis. The first holds there are multiple codes operating in distinct channels — verbal, gestural, facial — and that each qualifies as a code in its own right. Although they play upon each other, each has distinctive properties and deserves separate study. The second holds that human acts are indivisible, that all the codes employed in manifesting or attributing meaning form a seamless whole. People do not employ a separate language of the face, the voice, the body, but speak a single language incorporating multiple cues in multiple channels. When a person uses a word, says Kelly, "he is expressing his own construction of events" (1958:42). To which one must add, so also is he in shrugging his shoulders, lowering his voice, or playing with a paperclip. Giving form to meaning and meaning to form, is an indivisible act. Interpretations of behavior are based not on a singular cue, not on a singular channel, not even on the interplay of channels, but on an integrated perception of the whole.

The idea of communication as a multichanneled process is another of those simple notions that fails to suggest its interactional ramifications. There is no simple, singular, identifiable message in human dialogue; any such notion disappears in a babel of inflections, pauses, gestures and raised eyebrows. "We comment on every utterance we make," writes Henry, "to make people understand that we 'mean' what we say or that we do not; that we feel it deeply or we do not; that we are honest about it or not" (1973:172). Clearly a number of channels play a part in human interaction. There is conscious control of some of these codes, such as words or gestures, less control of skin color and pupil size; at the interpretive end there is some control over whom we choose to meet or avoid as partners, but less control of our capacity to ignore highly contrasting sounds or sights.

The most serious interactional consequences arise from the relations among these channels. Three possibilities may complicate our interpretations of behavior. The first is where there is an interplay of cues in different channels but all are seen as operating at the same referential level: They may be redundant, carrying similar information; They may be consistent, reinforcing each other; They may be incompatible, with cues in one channel contradicting those in another. In the last instance, such contradiction may be provocative in a negative or positive sense.

The second relational possibility exists when signals in different channels function at different referential levels. It is not clear, then, which signal frames the other, which is message and which is metamessage. The interpreter and source may punctuate them differently, causing considerable confusion: "I heard what you said, but I don't know whether to take it as a joke (which your facial expression suggests) or to treat it as an order (which your voice suggests)." When this occurs repeatedly it is probably experienced as a lack of interpersonal compatibility.

The third, and to my knowledge unexplored relational feature, has to do with the timing of channel cues. Vocal, postural, facial cues may lead or lag each other, and for this reason be seen as framing or being framed by each other. A colleague in Japan, fluent in Japanese, found his remarks dismissed as English unless he first gave the slightest hint of a bow; this subtle postural shift announced that what would follow would be in Japanese. Finally, it may be that the cues in some channels consistently lead or lag others in a person, a family, or a culture, and thus frequently perform framing functions. Again, this could contribute to possible inconsistency of meanings.

Face-to-face conversation provokes such a variety of cues in such a variety of channels with such rich relational possibilities that they afford incredible means of manifesting and attributing meanings. Microscopic studies, particularly the work of Pittenger and Labov, give some intimation of the promise of analyses that relate verbal, physical, and vocal signals (1960,1977). While channels may be studied in isolation, and this may be a necessary investigative tactic at times, they rarely operate that way in life. It is almost impossible to express anger facially but not vocally, to make a threatening fist using only one's fist. Complicated as it makes the scientific enterprise, people orchestrate their meanings, and it is not the separate instruments employed, but their subtle integration that constitutes those meanings. Or, to put it another way, people perform their meanings, and are part of each other's performances. Nowhere is the inadequacy of a linear view of communication more apparent than in coping with the multiplicity of cues in a multiplicity of channels with all the potential combinations they make possible.

Communication as Multidimensional

The presumption of a singular message is compounded often by the presumption of a singular meaning. People speak not in a single tongue, but in a multitude of tongues, each clue to some nuance of meaning. Since every person — source, interpreter, observer — must view events from a unique perspective, using their own experience as a base, there will be as many interpretations as there are interpreters.

In life, sources usually claim final authority over the meanings of their own messages. This is understandable, but one can question if we are the only or the best judge of our intentions. Any meanings that are to be expressed arise from sensory-neural changes that are so subtle, occur so fleetingly, and are processed so unconsciously that one is scarcely aware of them. It is only in the process of articulating such inner states that people are able to recognize if they are giving authentic form to these states. And often not even then. A second reason is that we are in a poor position to monitor our own performance; it is difficult or impossible to observe one's own visual behavior, vocal inflections, or facial expressions, yet these are critical features of the messages over which we claim authority. Research has often indicated that we are far less able to recognize our own voices, postures, and manner of walking than are our associates and friends (Wolff, 1943). A third reason is the sheer number and instability of all meanings. Not every internal change can be outwardly displayed; only the peaks and valleys of experience may be encoded, or in some cases, never the peaks and valleys but only what lies between. Whatever a person expresses constitutes an edited version of their experience, one that is fit to the perceived requirements of this occasion, this partner, this moment. Finally, interpretations of all messages derive from the assumptive world of the interpreter. For this reason, evaluations of our own messages tend to have a self-justifying and self-fulfilling quality about them.

The effort to fix the meaning of any act, therefore, poses problems for participant and investigator as well. Messages not only lack objective meaning, but in their complexity and transience challenge the interpretive powers of all who scrutinize them. Everyone, inside and outside a conversation, attends to different cues, places them in different configurations, at different levels of abstraction, in different situational and motivational frames.

Multidimensionality is revealed in many ways: One can assume, for example, that every remark has both an external and internal locus of meaning. To regard communication as transactional is to see messages as reports of a relation between perceiver and perceived, and one cannot comment on either end of this relation without commenting on the other. Hence, messages inform us concerning both the inner and outer worlds of their authors. Also, since neither random acts nor totally controlled ones are possible, messages may be examined from what is consciously or unconsciously expressed. While the grosser aspects of behavior, such as clothing and vocabulary are capable of conscious manipulation, others, such as eye movements or autistic gestures, are less manipulatable. Acts thus contain not only edited, but unedited, clues to the past and present state of the organism. In most social encounters there is both a conscious and unconscious level of interaction.

In addition, the latent as well as manifest content of any act may be examined. There are several ways of doing this: one is to compare messages across settings so that larger consistencies and inconsistencies may be noted (life scripts, dominant metaphors). Another way is to vary the time frame employed in analysis: Microscopic study, employing a slower than normal time frame, and macroscopic study, where a faster than normal time frame is used, are two such approaches (Pittenger,

1960; Labov, 1977). In both, messages are examined to identify the deeper significance of preferred topics, choice of words, interpersonal tactics, and so on. Clearly no one has the final say over the meaning of any message, for what each interpreter creates is a secondary transform of a primary transform; every such interpretation reminds us of the depth and richness of human meanings.

Communication as Context-Bound

To say that communication is context-bound is to suggest that no human act carries semantic or pragmatic significance in isolation, but only from a construed relation to surrounding features. As the contemporary artist Gene Davis put it, "context is content" (1971:39). The significance of the vowel arises from surrounding vowels, a word from its ties to other words, a sentence from its position in an argument. Human acts are imbedded in a hierarchy of contexts such that each frames and thereby influences the meanings that arise within it.

The identification of any social occasion as, say, a "funeral" or "picnic," as "tragic" or "comic," does not derive from the event, but is a fiction of the participants and derives its force from the consistency of such attributions. Contextual definitions, like all definitions, tend to be self-fulfilling: Every naming of an event creates certain behavioral options and, at the same time, closes off others. To witness how easily a solemn occasion can become hilariously funny is to appreciate how fragile, and how dependent on social consensus, the social order is. If, as we now suspect, higher levels of meaning contextualize lower levels, the grammar of social occasions may be more critical in shaping human interaction than the grammar of codes employed in discourse itself.

Where the contexts of interaction can be assumed to be similar, differences in behavior can be attributed to differences in people; where the contexts of interaction are dissimilar, behavioral variance may be more attributable to environments than to people. Our ignorance, and our assumption, of contextual irrelevance in the study of human behavior may have exaggerated the differences in human beings. One should not assume that persons classified as normal, neurotic or psychotic differ, notes Haley, unless one can assume their social situations have been and are the same: "All attempts to classify individuals into types have assumed they face essentially the same situations and that therefore differences must be within them" (1977:41).

A number of taxonomies of contexts have been constructed: Some focus on settings — hospital, factory, church — and a defensible case for them can be made since architecture encourages or discourages certain activities and meanings; another is to order settings on the basis of the number of people involved — interpersonal, group, organizational — and, again, this has validity for the number of persons influences the pattern of their relationships and the forms of messages employed; efforts have been made also to define contexts on the basis of the dominant activity involved — problem-solving, game-playing, decision-making — or on the basis of the personal relationships they promote — co-presence, competition, collaboration — and these also seem critical in influencing both messages and meanings. Three different levels of contextual analysis will be noted here.

Perhaps the broadest contextual boundary used (aside from those of some ethnographers) is the "behavior setting." It consists of a "naturally defined" context using the same criteria people ordinarily use in recounting their daily activities. Such settings comprise a bounded juncture of place, time, activity, objects and persons, and the analytic approach is situation-centered rather than person-centered. The ecology of cultures, of communities, and of high schools has been studied using this approach. From an analysis of schools, for example, Barker found "we could predict some aspects of children's behavior more adequately from knowledge of the behavior characteristics of drugstores, arithmetic classes, and basketball games they inhabited than from knowledge of the behavior tendencies of particular children" (1968:4). Other studies have shown the influence of urban organization, neighborhood layout, domestic architecture and interior design on the regulation of interaction. Settings seem to have both a physical and semantic impact through the boundaries they impose and the meanings attributed to architectural features.

Another level of contextual analysis appears in studies of distinctive interactional occasions. Spatial and temporal variables are disregarded or held constant, and norms regulating the flow of messages in particular activities are examined. To define an occasion as a "party," "strike," or "trial" is to invoke expectations about how to act and how to interpret acts within that frame. As McHugh found, to define an activity as "therapy" prompted people to interpret even random replies of "Yes" or "No" as having therapeutic value (1968). Other studies probe a variety of tasks (problem-solving, factory production, decision-making) or those that elicit unique types of messages (self-disclosure, argument, therapy). Within such contexts grosser features of interactional structure are explored: Who interacts with whom? About what? In what way? For how long? With what effect? As Robert Bales, one of its exemplars, has noted, "a surprising amount of information is carried by the form of the interaction itself" (1974:235).

A third level of contextual analysis, and one with promise of exposing more of the emergent quality of meanings, focuses on the "episode" or interactional "segment." It examines a bounded series of exchanges with a common thematic focus. It is the structure of discourse itself — the way messages relate or fail to relate to each other and the interpretive consequences — that is the aim of investigation. From a distance, and often from inside them, conversations appear chaotic, disjointed, elliptical, but segmental and sequential analyses suggest there is more order to them than appears. Studies of this type may focus on greetings, apologies, turn-taking, criticism or compliments.

The context-bound nature of meanings, thus, may be explored at the level of kines and phonemes, or at the level of neighborhoods and cultures. All suggest a complex hierarchy of contexts that frame human interaction: meanings must be cast into codes; codes must be constituted into messages; messages must be positioned in sequences; sequences must be articulated into episodes; episodes must be linked to appropriate occasions; and these, in turn, must be fit to their settings. Each context while generating some options forecloses others, thereby playing a vital role in the enactment and interpretation of meanings.

Communication as Coordinated

It is not in transactions with the physical world that the greatest relational challenge arises, but in social encounters with people who are active creators of meanings themselves. To conduct a conversation involves a complex and coordinated exchange in which each participant must keep track of a mulitplicity of cues in a number of channels, must know and observe the norms that regulate participation, and must be able to act so as to sustain the overall direction of the conversation. But it requires, also, the capacity to project imaginatively the meanings that lie behind the messages of others and the capacity to anticipate the probable interpretations of ensuing acts of one's own. "Communication proceeds in the face of a number of uncertainties," writes Cherry, "and may be described as consisting of numerous inductive inferences being carried out concurrently" (1971:277). These inferences must take into account the actions of other participants to some extent and in some way: to what extent, and in what way, each act shapes the evolving relationship and all subsequent acts. This requires no postulation of some sort of social or group mind, but only a recognition that social acts differ from solitary ones; that private impulse and projected interpretations both enter into whatever behavior is exhibited.

Another feature of interaction is the emergent quality of meanings: nowhere is this more apparent than in the unfolding of a conversation. Each act and its context is replaced an instant later by a new act and new context. This transient quality makes it one of the most elusive phenomena to study. None of its features, aside from the words spoken, have conspicuous boundaries — where does a gesture begin or a smile end — and make the material of research as amorphous as a shadow. And these transient signals reflect an endless parade of inner doubts, images and impulses, only a few of which are singled out, given form and displayed to others. These become, for only an instant, the data on which other interactants may base the framing and manifesting of their own meanings.

The coordinating of human interaction is its most fascinating feature. To sustain any joint activity requires some shared rules, imposed or acquired, that will synchronize individual contributions. Interactants need to know when to speak, what to say, how to respond, when to be silent. Interactional rules arise to govern the form and sequencing of messages in human encounters. This grammar of discourse, like the grammar of language, is assimilated early and is so unconsciously employed that we are rarely aware of its existence. And just as the grammars of various languages display a certain relativity, so do the codes that regulate conversation vary from occasion to occasion and from culture to culture.

Some clues to appropriate regulative codes may be obtained from familiarity with the positions people occupy and the roles they perform in the social system. There is sufficient consistency in the behavior of mothers, teachers and store clerks to give some idea of how interaction with them will proceed. (It is also why the exchange of demographic and biographic details make up so much of the early stages of interaction.) In his "Postulate of Relational Continuity" Schutz suggests that in growing up people acquire a repertoire of role relationships (1960). What is critical in this is that they master a *relationship*, not simply one side of the relationship, but must assimilate both to interact successfully. This reinforces what was said earlier about the necessity of predictive projections to be understanding and understood. If we assimilate relationships, learning both roles simultaneously, then we become capable of displaying either *and* of comprehending either. We would assume that, in a similar way, one learns such interactional strategies as playing, arguing, teasing, apologizing, fighting, that are not situated in a particular role relation but that transcend specific settings. The continuity feature of this postulate suggests also that people prefer to employ strategies previously found to be rewarding and resist engaging in those that are unfamiliar or painful. Thus, any encounter is approached not merely with a set of predictive images of the other, but with a bias toward certain ways of defining a relationship and our place in it.

In his recent theory of the Coordinated Management of Meaning, Pearce has articulated an alternative to a role-based view of human interaction (1976). He argues: (1) There exist shared conventions (rules) that govern the sequence of messages, and the interpretive frames applied to them; (2) These are neither right or wrong, but limit the range of appropriate messages and make conversations intelligible; some are more and others are less resistant to change; (3) The existence of such rules make possible coordinated behaviors and the emergence of common meanings.

Just how commonality of meaning emerges from the observance of such rules is not entirely clear. One view is that it promotes the diffusion of information, comparison of perspectives, and convergence of interpretation. Watzlawick, for example, writes that "in a communicational sequence, every exchange of messages narrows down the number of possible next moves" (1967:131). This would seem to need some qualification for it suggests a semantic reductionism that would lead every conversation into a *cul de sac*. And, while meanings do undergo progressive change, there is no reason to presume that interaction might not broaden as well as narrow them.

A consistent, but somewhat different, explanation lies in the idea of sequential dependencies: "Given message *a*, its content delimits the probabilistic repertory of types of succeeding messages: For instance, if *a* is a question, it is more probable that the next message will be an answer than another question, and much more than an unrelated statement" (Sluzki & Ransom, 1976:223). Despite its common sense appeal, our exploratory efforts suggest there is only a modest probability that questions will always be followed by answers. And there is some danger here of returning to a linear and determinist view of human behavior. Still, the impossibility of conducting any social activity without conventions for coordinating individual acts, makes the assumption of a rule-based approach almost unavoidable.

But it is not necessary, and probably undesirable, to assume rules promote only a convergence of meanings. Social interaction serves a spectrum of needs in a variety of contexts: there are occasions when conversation is a satisfying end in itself; occasions when a consistent interpretation of events is critical; still others when the amplification of meanings is a measure of success.

An intriguing, discrepant, view posits that much conversation is an end in itself. We talk to go on talking. "Speakers are somehow able to proceed in an orderly fashion without paying a great deal of attention to the possible sense, meaning or intention of the actions of others," writes Jacobs, "they are continually proceeding in orderly ways in situations where none of the participants share anything like common understanding of what is going on" (1977:5). There is satisfaction simply in participating in a highly orchestrated series of symbolic acts. Ambiguity is not a problem, but an opportunity for alternative elaborations and inventions by others. It is, in my view, a refreshing perspective, but one that invites a qualification and a comment. The qualification is that meaning applies in two senses here, one referring to content, the other to process; while ambiguity in the former may not derail a conversation, ambiguity in the latter would make an interaction frustrating or impossible. The comment is that in such consummatory interaction, mutual misunderstanding is as rewarding as mutual understanding; indeed, as always, they are indistinguishable (except in their consequences outside the conversation).

However, the specific principles that fuse an assortment of acts into an orderly progression of messages remains puzzling. We know little about the interactional aspects of interaction. The most promising speculations appear in the work of Bateson (1972). Three can be cited here: The first, a concept of interactional relativity, extends the idea of framing to the interaction of sequenced acts. Every participant in a conversation punctuates any series of remarks in unique ways, each placing their own acts in the context of others and thereby giving them different interpretations. The passivity of one person is seen as requiring assertiveness of the other; the assertiveness of the other is seen as requiring passivity of the former. A further interpersonal consequence is that such sliding interpretive frames enable people to claim credit for their successes by attributing them to motives in themselves while disowning responsibility for their failures by casting themselves as the victims of the motives of others. Hence the powerful tendency toward a conspiratorial and manipulative view of human relationships.

The second, a principle of emergent reciprocity, suggests that interaction tends to encourage a symmetrical or complementary coupling of messages, in the former case a sequence of similar acts, in the latter a sequence of compensatory ones. The first tends to promote competitive relationships, the latter dependent ones. The distribution of such couplings in any encounter, their rewarding or punishing potentials, and their cultural implications, deserves much more study.

The third, the concept of reflexive contradiction, suggests that out of the sequencing of messages may arise a series of paradoxical injunctions that compound each other, placing their perceiver in an interpretive bind. Signals in various channels, or at various levels of abstraction, are seen to frame the interaction in self-contradicting ways. The resolution of such interpretive crises may be benign, giving rise to new ideas and artifacts, or pathological, undermining the capacity to relate to other people and, through interaction, to make life intelligible.

All of these formulations emphasize the need to look not at individuals, not at messages, not even at contexts, but at the integration of all variables that participate in the emergence of meanings.

SYSTEMIC CHANGE

Finally, something more may be learned of human potentials, and of the creative and crippling possibilities of human interaction, from exploring the nature of systems and particularly of their interrelations.

Communication as Contingent

Harold Laski, the British political economist, once observed that we lead "hyphenated lives." We never exist in isolation, but always in relation to a surrounding milieu of objects and people. That environment, at every moment, frees and constrains us, and by acting in it we are, in turn, bound by the consequences of our acts. In the vernacular, "we have met the problem and it is us."

One way of viewing this relation is to see the universe as a singular system, the only one with "immanent mind," one in which all other systems constitute the arcs and loops by which it maintains itself. Another is to view the universe as a series of systems within systems, processes within processes, a hierarchy of circles with overlapping perimeters in which each forms the context of the others. These two epistemologies are similar in most respects; they differ only in the assumed permeability of the boundaries and in the estimates of the degree of independence each system possesses.

Both emphasize that whatever sense of autonomy is perceived within any system — person, family, group, culture — is an artifact of framing. From one vantage point each system appears to act as an integrated whole and be capable of independent acts; from another it appears dependently trapped in a matrix of surrounding systems that control its behavior. "Looking down a system towards the subordinate level it seems a self-contained whole; but looking up toward the apex then a dependent part" (Herbert, 1972:115).

It is out of the nature of such systems, and particularly of their border relations, that contingency arises and gives to life its paradoxical quality. This is evident, first, in the ambiguity of the world, what Camus called its "silence." To live is to act and to act is to interpret, to confront this ambiguity in a particular way. As Pascal wrote, "to be born is for the individual the prime contingency, since it means to be born of this time, in this place, of these parents and this country — all of these brutally given facts on which his life has to seek to found itself" (1962:117). To be born is to be forced to choose, to think. And as Dewey recognized "Every thinker puts some portion of the stable world in danger as soon as he begins to think" (1962:19). The meanings we create tend to be self-serving, liable to error, and fated to be incomplete; our senses have a limited and fallible grasp, our inner circuitry formed to favor particular interpretations of events.

Even under the best of conditions we confront not merely an ambiguous world, but a restless, mutable one which, while it is being perceived, changes before our eyes. And the interpreter, like the interpreted, subject to that same mutability. The volatile nature of the physical and social world, its endless capacity for surprise, forces interpreters constantly to revise and reconstrue their views of it.

It is at the boundaries of systems that contingencies are most apparent for every boundary is a point of exchange with surrounding systems. A meaning that arises at any level is destined to reverberate throughout neighboring systems, lower order changes diffusing upward, and higher order changes diffusing downward. "Individual acts are framed within a cultural imperative, but cultures derive their imperatives from the acts of individuals" (Barnlund, 1975:vii).

The potential for crises is further intensified by the fact that never are two systems — cells, persons, groups, societies — alike in information or organization, nor are they changing at the same rate or in the same direction. And such changes, within or between systems, are complicative rather than additive; each change requiring compensatory changes elsewhere. The birth of a child or the hiring of a new employee disturbs existing roles and rules. To preserve a viable relation requires responsivity at either end; changes on one end must be reflected at the other or it ceases to be a relation. "A human being, in relating to another," writes Bateson, "has a very limited control over what happens in the relationship. He is part of a two-person unit and the control which any part can exert over the whole is strictly limited" (Bateson, 1972:267). The margin for unilateral action is small for the output of every system is the input of another. We are all creators and created, determining and determined.

Contingencies arise, then, not only from confrontation with an ambiguous world that offers no meanings yet insists upon them, but through our dialogical relations with other persons. The multiplicity of these couplings and the relativity of truth expands alternatives while underscoring the necessity of choice. If the world is a question, human acts are an answer, but an answer that takes the form of new questions giving rise to fresh possibilities. We exist in what Michael Hyde has called a "context of paradoxes" (1976). Each is forced to form a private vision, a singular meaning. Yet the necessity of being with others — to transcend the fallibility and incompleteness of our own vision, and to act with and through others — binds us to contradiction. To assume full dialogical responsibility is to accept the neutrality of the world, the relativity of meanings, and the interdependence of acts. It is to optimize the potentialities of all systems in a milieu where the acts of each are the context of all, and the acts of all are the context of each. Wisdom, and perhaps morality, lies in the effort to contextualize one's acts at the widest possible arc of these contingencies.

Communication as Stabilizing

Roger Shattuck, describing the revolutionary artists of the twentieth century, observed that they discovered what has never been sufficiently recognized, "that man is forever vacillating between passive inactivity (and the extinction of consciousness in habit) and insatiable restlessness (dissatisfaction with all his accomplishments)" (1968:344). Thrust into a world of endless sensation we are forced to make it intelligible, to make the amorphous recognizable, the uncertain predictable, the mysterious fathomable. This imperative prompts continual transformation of sensations into useable information.

This rage for order, for the comprehensibility of phenomena, is often dismissed as an unfortunate limitation. It is, instead, prerequisite for any action, routine or revolutionary. Cultural values, situational roles, interactional rules and language itself exist to promote the discernment of order. To deal with a random world is impossible. Placing boundaries over sensations, no matter how wide or narrow, how flexible or rigid, makes them transformable into decisions and actions. And there is not only necessity but delight in the discernment of order. Recognition of the familiar recalls earlier pleasures; a child's insistence upon word for word repetition of a familiar story manifests our pleasure in evoking past associations. Recognition that predictions have come true confirms our capacity to estimate the future. Yet there is always the risk of painful associations and the risk of disconfirmation. While predictive failure may always be somewhat painful, continuous disillusionment is probably intolerable.

If there is a rage for order, there is an equal countervailing rage for disorder. If total randomness is unbearable, so also is total redundancy. Orderliness so permeates human life that it is something we strive to overcome. The function of nearly every field of inquiry and learning — but particularly of the arts — as Peckham so incisively notes is "to offer the experience of disorientation" (1973:79). The craving of novelty operates even at the level of the mundane: no one, no matter how orderly it might make their lives, consumes the same food, reads the same book, repeats the same remark over and over if they can avoid it. The appeal of human conversation probably lies in its mixture of the obvious and ambiguous; meanings always seem to fall just short of, just beside, or just beyond the ones intended. Our games celebrate the pleasures of uncertainty: "A game is a way of making something hard for the fun of it," writes Ciardi, "no difficulty, no fun" (1964:18). The greater the challenge, the higher the stakes, the greater the effort demanded, the smaller the margin of success, the sharper the sense of aliveness they afford. The absence of problems, or solutions to all of them, characterize a system that is closed down. A world without challenge, surprise or mystery would be as painful to endure as one with no predictability at all.

It is the proportion of the familiar and unfamiliar that triggers psychological crises. People differ in their capacity to process information: their sensory acuity varies; they occupy environments of differing densities of information; they function in settings that offer varying proportions of negative and positive rewards. Over time each person becomes accustomed to a normal range of stimulation, a typical rate of input, a unique rhythm of activation. If these tolerances for handling new information are set too broadly, the organism underdiscriminates, if too narrowly, it overdiscriminates; if these tolerances are set too finely, the organism reacts prematurely, if too coarsely, it fails to respond soon enough.

Assuming adequate parameters, and adequate flexibility in control of them, the "normal" system can cope with a wide range of contingency. When confronted with information overload, with overwhelming challenges to existing meanings, it can "bank" the system to reduce input through exercising control over the environments, occasions, partners or topics it encounters. But given narrow tolerances or little elasticity in them, the person may manifest a pathology of overstimulation. Goldstein's patient who could not go even for a stroll because of the risk of unforeseen stimulation, and people whose lives consist of endless, mechanically performed routines, illustrate systems pushed to the limits of their semantic tolerances (1963:100).

At the other extreme, one of information underload, the "normal" person with broad tolerances and adequate control, can compensate by increasing input, again through their selection of settings, partners or activities. Saul Steinberg, that master of reflexive drawing, once said, "The life of the creative man is led, directed and controlled by boredom" (1978:92). Not only creative people, but even rats and chimpanzees, have been found to avoid monotonous environments and to seek some challenge to routine meanings. Heron, describing the work on sensory deprivation, notes that in the absence of sufficient information input there is a gradual decline from reflection to reminiscing to hallucinating and, finally, to loss of the capacity to perceive even size, shape and time (1957).

Humans appear to be at constant risk, poised between the threat posed by too much order and by too little order, between a pathology born of boredom and one born of excessive stimulation. If insufficient novelty contributes to deterioration and loss of systemic viability, an excess of novelty in the form of unassimilatable cues may contribute equally to paralysis. To be without adequate semantic challenge, or to be overwhelmed by it, may drive the system beyond its information handling capacity and threaten its survival.

Communication as Metastable

Systems vary in complexity and versatility, but one can broadly characterize them as closed or open. The former function within a limited range of input, have minimal capacity to adapt to environmental changes, and fail if their tolerances are exceeded. Their parameters, internal relations, and output characteristics are determined prior to their operation. Closed systems do not learn from experience, they perform the same actions in the presence of the same conditions. Their behavior is predictable from knowledge of their internal structure and external circumstances. Open systems generally have broader input range, acquire the principles that govern their operations through experience in varying contexts, and can modify these in light of their predicted consequences. Open systems, thus, are capable of learning. Their behavior, though consistent, is not completely predictable for the system is constantly undergoing change. Humans, with their capacity for symbolic transformation, interpreting and reinterpreting events, clearly possess the potential of open systems.

It is the quality of these transactions between persons and environments — and particularly their facilitative or destructive consequences — that interest the communicologist. Each person is born into a milieu saturated with cultural values, interactional roles, and symbolic codes. Each, however, acquires a distinctive history of transactions with their environment and, hence, a unique way of approaching events. Experience must yield patterns that are sufficiently stable to give the system some anchorage, enough flexibility to deal with contingencies, and latitude enough to transcend occasional failure. In some the course of such transactions leads to widening sensitivity and expanded flexibility of response; in others to a narrowing of discriminatory capacity and a rigidity of behavioral response.

The extent to which one capitalizes upon the potentials of an open system, thus, appears to turn on the quality of these transactions in infancy, childhood and throughout life. Every person learns to make certain discriminations, construe them in particular ways, select a course of action, and evaluate the consequences. This systemic learning appears to occur at three different reflexive levels and with different social consequences.[6] At the lowest level one learns to notice objects, words, people and, through trial and error, to link such perceptions to specific behaviors. This has been termed proto-learning (first-order learning), referential learning (extensionally-based discriminations) and pattern formation (giving form to sensation). It is localized and concrete, the categorizing of any event linked directly to a pattern of behavior. The number of such simple linkages may be great, limited only by our capacity for storing them. Since endless trial and error requires so much effort, and so many events manifest negligible differences, such learned actions are often turned over to unconscious regulation (habit). Although such routinizing of transactions with the environment conserves energy for other sorts of learning, it contributes to behavioral rigidity.

At a higher level, humans are capable of learning about learning; they can acquire insight into principles that govern whole areas of lower level discriminations. Learning of this type is called deutero-learning (second-order learning), reflexive learning (relations of relations) or pattern transformation (alternative interpretive constructs). People generalize concrete experiences at a more abstract level, acquiring insight into the dynamics of events in a variety of settings. Learning how to form a friendship, how to solve legal problems, or how to buy and sell apply across an immense variety of related situations. What prompts second-order learning is not clear; it may evolve out of the necessity of resolving ambiguities or contradictions at lower levels, because of the greater behavioral flexibility it provides, or it may simply be a latent potential of all symbolizing organisms. But it seems to differentiate closed and open systems. Where the former are at the mercy of surrounding conditions and their own determinism, the latter are capable of internal modification. Humans, thus, can create their own developmental options and choose among them. However, since every system tends to stabilize, open systems may become habituated to their second-order learnings as well. This may result from consistent reinforcement, or because the more abstract nature of such second-order rules makes them less vulnerable to critical evaluation. To the extent that such epistemological premises remain unconscious, open systems become less capable of changing their parameters and retaining their flexibility.

Learning at the third level occurs in those rare instances when experience is of such devastating impact that it provokes a paradigmatic shift, a radical change in underlying assumptions and values, a significant perceptual reorientation of the person. The ontological frames we acquire early in life and that shape the communicative style of each person are formed less consciously than all other meanings, and are the most profound in their consequences for they contextualize all experiences of the organism. They are deeply buried, resistant to change, and form the basis of our perceiving the world, making sense of it, and acting in it. Radical systemic upheavals may be induced by abrupt alterations in one's normal relations with the world, or from repeated and unrelievable failure in coping with events under existing assumptions. Interaction across such paradigmatic borders, as between mystic and empiricist, normal and abnormal, or between members of alien cultures is obviously complicated and precarious.

There are some provocative parallels between the pathologies of learning that occur in animals and humans. My first exposure to this occurred at about eight years of age. Having exhausted the more exciting attractions of the local fair, I visited the agricultural exhibits. Facing a marvelous caged rooster, I began to move my finger up and down the front of his cage. Soon the rooster was clucking its way up and down. Pausing, I started across from left to right, and soon the rooster learned to follow my gestures again. Then without thinking, I traced a circle on the front of the cage. The reaction was so sudden, noisy and violent that I ran from the barn to avoid being noticed. As Shands has also observed, to make an animal neurotic, we only need to isolate it, teach it some rules, place it in a situation where these rules conflict, and prevent its escape. "The animal," he writes, "has to be trained to be confused; he has to be put in a situation requiring action while clearly unable to plan action" (1968:130).

The situation for humans is not as simple, but there are striking parallels. Here, too, isolation from others or confinement with people who continually provoke contradictory meanings is a factor. Symbols, of course, enormously expand the diversity of meanings available to people but multiply the occasion for confusion and failure as well as for insight and success. No animal ever talks itself into trouble (even the rooster requires an intervening human), but humans do so regularly. Symbols may become so valued that they are prized over the territories they represent. Indeed, argued Shands, if people are to remain sane they must "lose the war with words, the sooner and more comprehensively the better" (1968:130). While providing for managing inconsistent meanings, language multiplies the number of occasions when people confront contradictions and threats to intelligibility.

The reflexivity of symbols makes possible hierarchial organization and assimilation of meanings. Disturbing meanings may be assimilated at lower, more concrete levels, or may gravitate to higher levels in search of integration. Semantic disturbances, what McReynolds calls "unassimilated percepts," tend to provoke ontological crises whose severity depends on the depth, duration and intensity of threat they pose to existing meanings. Such disturbances may stimulate new and creative syntheses or, if unassimilatable, radical changes in personality. These changes may be seen as constructive when they expand the potentials of the organism — via a new form of art, science, religion, invention, or behavior — but as destructive if they decrease its potential —

contributing to neurosis, phobia, illness, psychosis or suicide.[7]

In the former the organism, though stable, adapts itself to semantic disturbance by revising its operating rules. Symbols themselves offer a more flexible way of ordering events, and alternative ways of labeling such events may generate new options. Interaction, by requiring people to examine their own experience from the perspective of others encourages a reflexive attitude. The major means of any system gaining insight into its own premises is by getting outside itself, hence the desirability of interacting with other people, groups, and cultures to foster such insight.

In the latter case, where the system deteriorates or disintegrates, it appears to result either from the blocking of new information or through blindness to its own internal processes. Sluzki and Ransom, for example, speak of families whose balance is so precarious that any divergence of experience or meanings threatens their survival (1976). The introduction of new information into a system with inadequate ways of assimilating it is likely to intensify rather than ameliorate such crises. These two conditions — the resistance to new information and the lack of metarules by which the system might change itself — appear critical and are cited by Watzlawick as primary sources of systemic failure (1976:176).

Some of the conditions that provoke breakdowns in animals, then, have their parallel in human beings. Symbols may expand human potentials greatly and lead to the capacity to comprehend and empathize with the experience of others, to innovation in art and science, but they may contribute also to diminished capacity to realize that potential in transactions with the world and other people. Isolate persons, induce confusion and contradiction, block the flow of information, deprive them of the power to revise their premises, and they will suffer for it. Mystification, deception, disqualification and binding appear to be both the consequence and cause of failure. Prolonged involvement in a social context in which these interpersonal strategies prevail may promote mistrust of all messages (paranoia), concern only for literal meanings (hebephrenia) or retreat from interaction (catatonia). In extreme cases, the individual withdraws into an autistic world complete with a private set of symbols that cannot or will not be exposed to the exploitation of others. These sorts of human dysfunction, commonly identified as "mental" or "emotional" might more accurately be identified as "interactional failures" since they arise from and incapacitate one to participate in social occasions.

There must be ways of redirecting a process that produces endless pain and social inadequacy. Yet isolation of the conditions for constructive parametric and paradigmatic change has been less promising than hoped (Barnlund, 1968). Though far from definitive, the following would appear to contribute to the recovery of systemic viability: (1) Occasions in which new meanings are provoked so that integrative necessity arises; (2) Creation of supportive relationships more broadly confirming and less painful than existing relationships; (3) Sufficient semantic compatibility to favor decentering, and thus a more relativistic attitude that can reduce symbolic rigidity and reification. The maintenance of a flexible stability in a contingent universe, where ambiguity and contradiction are inescapable, seems to require the capacity to create and integrate meanings, to articulate and interpret them flexibly, and to assume responsibility for the process that promotes them.

CONCLUSION

It has become chic these days to deride the research of the past and to scoff at structural approaches, quantitative measures, and contrived experiments. True, we may have made too much of studies involving singular encounters, of short duration, between total strangers, carrying out arbitrary tasks, in sterile settings. But I am reluctant to join faddish movements, including this one. In reviewing thousands of studies over the past fifty years one cannot fail to be impressed with the growth of knowledge about human communication (Barnlund, 1968).

Yet an inspection of the architecture of our assumptions about communication does reveal some lack of empathy for the nature of our material. Rarely has the transactional, continuous, subjective and cumulative nature of meanings been the focus of our research. The interactional process has received slightly greater, though still spotty, attention. Language has been studied in great depth, though rarely as employed in actual conversation or in relation to surrounding codes and contexts. Interest is now developing in the structure of conversation and the rules that regulate interaction. And there is greater appreciation of the nature of human pathologies, their locus in the interactional matrix, and the nature of therapeutic interventions.

The prospect that holds the greatest excitement for me can be loosely defined as contextual analysis. The ethnocentric nature of nearly all our theories of human behavior becomes more glaring with each attempt to apply them to communication in other cultures (Barnlund, 1975). No level of research seems more provocative of fresh insights into human interaction than cross-cultural comparisons. A second neglected contextual variable is that of time: there is so much to be learned not only about the long-term evolution of human relationships, but about how meanings situated outside an encounter become accommodated inside it. In addition, the environmental dimension deserves far greater attention than it receives. Not only does the character of space and of buildings influence human alienation and attachment, but architecture plays a critical role in defining social occasions and in regulating behavior within such occasions.

Yet the contextualist approach, as Jenkins so incisively describes it, rejects the presumption of, and the search for, any singular, all-encompassing explanation of human behavior: "For the contextualist, no analysis is 'the complete analysis'. *All* analyses eventually 'sheer away' from the event into more extensive contexts. This argues that there is no one analysis, no final set of units, no one set of relations, no claim to reducibility, in short, no single and unified account of anything" (1974:787). What is critical, in science or life, is that any act be situated in a frame large enough to accommodate its relevant variables, those that shape its emergence and those that absorb its effects. Conjunctivitis, in the grammatical rather than the optical sense, is as important to cultivate in our research as in our lives: "We are all centers of each other's periphery" (Richards, 1964:110).

This search for an ecology of communication began with the lines of a notable Western poet; let me close with those of a notable Eastern poet. They bear a remarkable affinity for each other, yet the lines below hint of an even broader contextualization:

> To learn Buddhism is to know yourself
> To know yourself is to forget yourself
> To forget yourself is to identify yourself
> With the law of the universe — one with the universe
> To be one with the universe is to "drop" the notion
> That you are one with the universe
> Along with the body and mind of yourself and others.

> Dogen

NOTES

1. Terms like "sender," "receiver" and "response" will be avoided wherever possible. Their static and elementalistic implications are misleading and tend to confuse hopelessly the analysis of human interaction. The point of view developed here is, at best, awkward to articulate using the traditional terminology of the field.

2. As economic and social determinists have stressed, overstressed in my view, meanings arise out of the environment of inherited institutions, normative values, and expressive forms. Though true, this is an influence that is rarely unilateral: individual and society are locked in an endless dialogue, forming and being formed by each other. If there is little prospect of an entirely original act or idea, there may be equal improbability of an entirely unoriginal one. A twentieth-century musical genius, transplanted into the cultural milieu of two thousand years ago could never have composed a musical symphony, for society had not yet evolved this form of expression; neither could society have created such a form were it not for the unique contributions of individuals to its evolution. Private meanings are undoubtedly influenced by public meanings, but they also embody an inescapable uniqueness born of a particular person, particular event, and particular motive. No person ever inhabits the same world as another, nor even the same world they once did or will in the future. Occasions for meaning merely provide the opportunity for personal interpretation.

3. In talking of signs and symbols one has to guard constantly against their reification. There are, in effect, no such things. Anything may represent anything, but its capacity to do so lies not in it but in a commitment by its interpreters to act toward it in a particular way. It would be better if we spoke less of signs and symbols and more of signal and symbolic *behaviors*.

4. For stylistic reasons most writers on communication employ the term "message," and few have grappled with the confusion that lurks there. If there are no signs or symbols, but only dispositions to treat cues signally or symbolically, then "messages" composed of such cues have no objective existence either. No messages exist apart from the decision of some interpreter to so identify a set of phenomena in which case, of course, there are different messages for every interpreter — "sender," "bystander," "receiver," or "behavioral scientist." Rarely do people agree entirely on which verbal and nonverbal cues constitute the "message." Boundary disputes of this sort plague many if not all human dialogues to some extent.

5. The linguistic relativity hypothesis argues that every coding system incorporates epistemological assumptions in its structure, and all who use them are bound more or less to respect these assumptions. Major families of languages are thought to differ sufficiently in their assumptions that they create for their users somewhat distinctive perceptual orientations. During the decades of dispute over this theory critics seem always to remain trapped into comparisons of verbal systems alone while the hypothesis would seem to encompass all coding systems and would argue for the relativity of all codes. If so, linguistic relativity should be as detectable within cultures as between them. And no one has ever seriously proposed that equations could be translated into paintings, plays into

sculpture, or poetry into music. If this could be done there would have been no need to create such codes to accommodate the variety of ways humans have experienced the world. All modes of articulating meaning would seem to demonstrate the influence of every medium upon the user of that medium.

6.   Since programs of action are only potentialities of open systems, the success of the organism depends on the character of its learning. Two sorts of behavioral changes seem to occur: In the first, learning is incremental or cumulative; there is gradual improvement or gradual decline in performance. In the second there is a sudden, non-cumulative and novel integration of acts that were heretofore isolated or inefficiently combined. One "gets it" or "does not." Ashby refers to such radical and abrupt changes in the learning gradient as "step" functions while Rabkin has substituted the term "saltus" (1956, 1976). Cumulative learning tends to be associated with lower level learning, non-cumulative with higher levels of learning.

7.   That ontological crises can prompt creativity as well as pathology is nicely illustrated in Bateson's description of the trained porpoise. Failing to obtain further rewards from habituated behavior, the porpoise converts this crisis into an occasion for the invention of a sequence of novel and unprecedented performances (1972:277).

The Management of Metaphor

Herbert W. Simons

A line of demarcation should be drawn between "to use" and "to be used," lest we fall victim to metaphor, mistaking the mask for the face. In brief we must "expose" metaphor, "unmask" it. This proximity between use and abuse leads to a correction of the metaphors about metaphor. We have spoken of transference or transporting. That is true: facts are reallocated by metaphor; but such reallocation is also a misallocation. Metaphor has been compared to a filter, a screen, and a lens, in order to say that it places things under a perspective and instructs us to 'see as ....' Yet it is also a mask that disguises. It was said that metaphor integrates diversity; but it also leads to categorical confusion. It was said that it 'stands for ...'; it must be said as well that it is 'taken for.'

Paul Ricouer, *The Rule of Metaphor*

Who for, what for, metaphor? At a conference on metaphor that I attended recently, I chanced, during a break in the action, to meet the organizer of a conference on natural food labeling which was being held in an adjoining room. When I told him what we were about he suggested half-jokingly that our two conferences be merged. "No one seems to know anymore what a natural food really is," he said. "All we're doing is talking in metaphors."

Like my food labeling acquaintance I suspect that those of us who theorize about communication are a bit less sanguine these days about the "reality-content" of our own labels and a mite more willing than in times past to label at least some of our labels as metaphors. Yet I am not at all sure how far we would be willing to go in acknowledging our dependence on metaphor. Would we declare ourselves incapable of theorizing except in terms of metaphor? Would we go further and assert that, once having framed a theoretical perspective in metaphorical terms, we are inevitably imprisoned by it; that metaphor-laden theoretical propositions cannot be translated into theory-neutral, testable propositions? In the spirit of Watzlawick's (1976) *How Real Is Real?*, would we acknowledge that such concepts as "substance," "essence," "the real" are themselves metaphorical; that "All we're doing is talking in metaphors"? If so, what should we make of these acknowledgments? Is truth replaced by trope, given these conceptions, or are there "metaphorical truths" (Ricouer, 1977)? If we cannot "prove" metaphorical claims, can we at least offer "good reasons" in their support?

Both the term "metaphor" (i.e., the concept) and the "thing" metaphor (i.e., that which we agree is a metaphor) are problematic in scientific contexts. The term "metaphor" is problematic, in part, because it stands as genre to a wide variety of species (Booth, 1978). Witness the array of metaphors which metaphor theorists commonly use in defining metaphor: a "lens," a "filter," a "screen"; a form of "linguistic play," a "semantic fiction," a "false identity"; a term "foreign" to its context, a "displacement," a contextual "shift," a "carrying over" of meaning from one context to another. Witness, too, the array of functions embraced by the term: from simple comparison to figurative analogy, from perspective-defining as in the notion of a "lens" to emotional expression and ornamentation.

Some of the ambiguity in the term "metaphor" can be reduced by distinguishing between *structural* or *analogic* metaphors and *textual* metaphors (Fernandez, 1974). Predication is made in the former on the basis of isomorphic patterns of relationship (e.g., man as a servomechanism); in the latter on the basis of similarities in feeling-tone (e.g., hate as a smoldering fire). In speaking of metaphor in this chapter I shall primarily have reference to the structural or analogic metaphors which populate scientific discourse. Fernandez reminds us, however, that considerations of feeling-tone may underlie the choice of a structural metaphor. "For example, the Durkheimian mechanical and organic metaphors seem to have different emotional weights — the former an objectivity, an exteriority, a detachment; the latter a subjectivity, an interiority, an attachment" (122-123).

The foregoing distinction enables us to narrow our concern, but there remains the problem of borderline cases. Although all of us would agree that some theoretical constructs should be labeled as metaphors (e.g., the brain as a computer or telephone switchboard, the mind as a black box, groups as organs or organisms, behavior as driven, stimulus fields, double-binding messages, feedback loops), confusion persists as to the range of cases comprehended by the term. Particularly troublesome is the distinction between the metaphorical and the literal. On the one hand, virtually all metaphor theorists (e.g., Beardsley, 1962; Richards, 1965; Ricouer, 1977; Turbayne, 1962) speak of the two as qualitatively different forms of expression.[1] Literal terms are said to be "right" or "proper" in their contexts; they can be taken at "face value." Metaphorical terms are said to be "foreign" to their contexts; they produce the shock of absurdity or contradiction when taken at face value, thus leading the reader to search for hidden or implied meanings, suggested by the foreign term. Paradoxically, however, these same theorists claim that metaphors undergo a gradual process of literalization — a position which is at variance with the conception of the metaphorical and the literal as qualitatively different modes of expression. According to the gradualist view, "live" metaphors become "dead" metaphors over time, i.e., they become part of what we take to be literal usage. The movement toward literalization is said to involve both sense and reference: terms once considered foreign to a context are invested with a sense of propriety or ordinariness (e.g., *leg* of a table); and terms which once were conceived to be heuristic fictions are invested with "substance" (e.g., *mental* illness). Unfortunately, metaphor theorists do not tell us *how* "foreign" a term must be to qualify as a metaphor,[2] or at what point in its evolution toward literal status the term is invested with propriety or substance.[3] We shall see that the absence of clear markers for distinguishing the literal from the metaphorical can be a major source of confusion for readers of scientific discourse and that it offers an invitation to abuse by theorists.

Let us postpone further discussion of borderline cases and turn now to a set of problems associated with the *"thing"* metaphor; i.e., with terms such as those identified in the preceding paragraph, which all would agree are metaphors. These *"as-if"* constructs perform important heuristic and organizing functions in theory construction; indeed, it seems unreasonable to suppose that one could avoid metaphors entirely and still construct theories. Nevertheless, metaphors pose a number of problems, particularly at the point which theories are subjected to testing and comparison. Metaphors serve to organize scientific fact but they may easily be reified or in other ways confused with scientific fact. Metaphors serve to reflect and sharpen realities, but they simultaneously deflect attention from other realities. Metaphors serve to clarify the complex, but in doing so they also introduce complexity by evoking multiple interpretations, some of them unintended. In additon to the problem of unwanted or "surplus" meanings, there is the problem of incompleteness. Metaphors permit us to glimpse connections between things by telling us of the "thisness of that" and the "thatness of this" (Burke, 1969); but metaphors do not tell us in what respects the "this" is not a "that" and "that" is not a "this." Literally speaking, what we are left with upon hearing a metaphorical expression is a "false identity," one which is often most effective heuristically "when most wrong" (Geertz, 1973), and which we may judge to imply an apt analogy or an overextended one, but only on the basis of an aesthetic or rhetorical judgment. As Bruyn (1966) reminds us, there are no scientific tests for aptness.

The foregoing problems have been a major source of concern for philosophers of science. Not without cause, the British empiricists (Hobbes, Bentham, Locke) denounced metaphor as an instrument of deceit, a "perfect cheat," a device for obscuring the differences between "real" entities and "fictitious" entities. Although a few philosophers of science continue to speak of metaphor in such scathing terms, the fact of metaphoric ambiguity persists.[4] Indeed, the problem has become more manifest as faith in verificationist and strict falsificationist philosophies of science has waned.

Those among the scientifically orthodox who do not simply dismiss metaphor as a device of the poets and theologians attempted to harness the power of metaphor at the theory-building ("context of discovery") stage of science while translating or paraphrasing metaphorical expressions into theory-neutral, testable propositions at the theory-testing ("context of justification") stage (e.g., Scheffler, 1967). By most accounts, however, these efforts have failed. Indeed, the very assumptions of a rule-bound, deductive process leading to theory-neutral scientific tests (i.e., verifications or falsifications) has been called into question. Kuhn's (1970) well known history of scientific revolutions repeatedly evidenced the resistance to translation and comparison of rival metaphors and the consequent inability of adherents to "incommensurable" paradigms to resolve their differences on the basis of a fully rule-bound logic of justification. He concluded that while there may be "good reasons for being persuaded" to adopt a new paradigm (p. 199), "there is no neutral algorithm for theory-choice, no systematic decision-procedure which, properly applied, must lead each individual in the group to the same decision" (p. 200).

Much the same arguments have been presented by other scholars. Even so staunch a defender of Popperian falsification as Imre Lakatos (1970) has acknowledged that the elasticity of key theoretical metaphors enables scientists to defend their theories in the face of purported counter-evidence. Were this not the case, said Lakatos, our very best theories could not survive. Similarly, Macormac (1976) has argued that scientific theories are no less resistant to full formalization than the metaphor-laden claims put forth by theologians. Koch (1964) put the matter most strongly when he argued that "The scientific process is in principle, and at all stages, underdetermined by rule" (p. 22). Said Koch:

> If one wishes to fall back on the distinction between 'context of discovery' and 'context of justification,' one falls back on a distinction that any empirically apt account of inquiry shows to be unsupportable and that, indeed, no longer receives support in many expert quarters. Any detailed analysis of the 'justificatory' activities of scientists, for instance, will show justification at many points to depend as much on extra-rule determined processes as does discovery. Among the re-analyses of inquiry that are now shaping up there is no point-for-point consensus, but most agree in stressing the absurdity in principle of any notion of full formalization, in underlining the gap between any linguistic 'system' of assertions and the unverbalized processes upon which its interpretation and application are contingent (pp. 21-22).

What emerges, then, from these re-analyses of inquiry is a picture of the scientific process quite different from the model presented by verificationists and strict falsificationists. Scientific theories are rhetorical constructions and their key terms are ineliminably metaphorical. Far from being able to translate metaphorical claims into theory-neutral propositions, scientists appear to be *stuck* with metaphor, for good *and* for ill, throughout the scientific process.

On the basis of the foregoing arguments I have been led to the entrepreneurial metaphor in the title of this chapter. To speak of metaphor management is to recognize that metaphor is both ubiquitous in science and problematic; that scientific metaphors can at best be argued for or defended against through a process of persuasion and counterpersuasion in which, as Kuhn (1970:152) puts it, "there can be no proof." And it is to acknowledge that scientific propositions are valid only within the framework of a given paradigm; that some propositions which appear literally true today are certain to seem quaintly metaphorical again as scientific communities shift to new paradigms.[5] Metaphor presents itself as a Janus-faced object, a quintessential case of the dialectical tension between rigor and imagination in science generally.

In the remainder of this chapter I want first to argue that even our ostensibly most literal social-scientific terms and expressions exhibit some degree of metaphoricity. In making this argument I shall be commenting further on the ambiguities of metaphor, and on the additional ambiguities and paradoxes which result from the absence of clear markers for distinguishing the literal from the metaphorical. From a perspective on scientific discourse as rhetorical, I shall then offer suggestions as to how we might best manage social-scientific metaphors — this through a dialectical process involving metacommunications about metaphor, institutionalized criticism of metaphor, and ongoing evaluation in terms of a tradeoff among several evaluational criteria.

In particular, I shall be focusing upon the theorizing of the Batesonian Interactionists,[6] both as a subject worthy of analysis in its own right, and as an illustrative object. The Batesonians communicate metaphorically, they comment often about their use of metaphor, and they have done a good amount of theorizing about metaphor. Moreover, by their use of metaphor, the Batesonians are fairly representative of the newer, more interpretive breed of social-scientific epistemologies, perspectives such as the "rules" approach, dramatism, hermeneutics, ethnomethodology, French structuralism and semiotic, which reflect growing disenchantment among social scientists with verificationist and strict falsificationist philosophies of science. Proponents of these perspectives tend to use metaphor freely, both in their theorizing, and in the highly colorful examples from diverse contexts which they offer as illustrative support for their theories. Though we often find their metaphors attractive and their anecdotes seductive, it is reasonable to ask whether these perspectives are as corrigible to evidence and comparison as the more "simpleminded" variable-effects paradigm which dominated the social sciences for lo these many years. Thus the question of metaphor management looms as an especially important one for proponents of these perspectives.

RECOGNIZING METAPHOR: AMBIGUITIES AND PARADOXES OF CLASSIFICATION

In this section I want to defend a broad view of metaphor, consistent with my claim that metaphor is unavoidable in social-scientific theorizing. In particular I shall focus upon the issue of "dead" metaphors so as to exhibit some of the problems in interpretation which result when, in the absence of clear markers, we assume that there are qualitative differences between the literal and the metaphorical.

To begin with we can say that all social-scientific theories are reflective of one or another *root* metaphor. This is Pepper's (1942) way of saying that theories are but perspectives, each offering a "false identity" (e.g., the world is mechanical). Whenever we theorize, said Pepper, we reflect one of four rival root metaphors: formism, mechanism, organicism or contextualism. Others have added to Pepper's list. We might, for example, think of information as a root metaphor (e.g., Watzlawick, Beavin, & Jackson, 1967). To say that man is *driven* to behave is to reflect a mechanistic root metaphor. To say that behavior is genetically *coded* is to reflect an informational root metaphor.

At a lower level of abstraction are key theoretical constructs, examples of which were provided earlier in this chapter. Other examples include economic terms used to describe social exchanges, military terms used to describe battles between id and superego, and such mechanistic metaphors as the eye of the camera, the memory as a storage bin, and intrapsychic life as a hydraulic system. Black (1962) uses the constructs of Lewinian field theory as his examples: field, vector, phase-space, tension, force, boundary, fluidity, etc. In all of these instances we understand immediately that the terms are not to be taken at face value; that the theorist has been engaged in a kind of linguistic play; that there has been a deliberate carrying over from one context of usage to another.

Yet there are a great many other constructs in the social-scientific lexicon in which the shift in contextual usage is so subtle or so gradual that it goes virtually unnoticed. Included among them are terms such as *role* or *persona* as applied to interactions outside the theater, which some metaphor theorists might well label as "dead" metaphors. Although I do not detect a clear qualitative difference between the literal and the metaphorical in these examples, I believe it important that we recognize them as true metaphors; to do otherwise is to blind ourselves to the disanalogies between staged dramas and life's dramas.

In general I would argue that our so-called "dead" metaphors are often most in need of critical attention. Metaphor theorists are correct in asserting that language develops by metaphorical extension, our conception of the literal deriving from a kind of mass forgetfulness of metaphorical origins. Moreover, the examples they most frequently point to (e.g., "leg of a table") are generally unproblematic; we may safely treat them as purely literal expressions. Yet they mistakenly assume that we can become fully liberated from past usage; that what the structuralists (e.g., Hawkes, 1977) refer to as the *diachronic* or *vertical* meanings of terms have no influence on our collective psyches. With Burke (1969), De Man (1978), Harries (1978) and others, I would maintain that at least some "dead" metaphors continue to haunt us. If they are indeed "dead," they warrant resurrection, this so that we may examine their influence upon us.

The term "mental illness" provides a familiar example of a "dead" metaphor that refuses to lie quietly. As Szasz (1969) has argued, this seemingly technical term conceals a whole set of centuries-old understandings: that there is a direct parallelism between mind and body; that deviations are not freely chosen; that they are not "sins"; and so on. We understand how loaded this term is only by rediscovering its metaphorical origins.

Still another example of a "dead" metaphor which we too often take for granted is the term "public opinion." Edelman (1971) reminds us that the "voice" of public opinion is not one voice but many; that the idea of a univocal public evokes the fallacy of the "group mind"; that the metaphor fosters the image of decisiveness in the face of evidence that most people on most political issues are ambivalent or apathetic; and that, along with such other tropes as the "body politic," the "arm of the law," the "head of state," the term "public opinion" serves to personalize an essentially impersonal political system.

The term "self" provides yet another example, this one made popular by Skinner (e.g., 1957). Until I read Skinner I was convinced that I had a self and that the self had wishes, expectations, delusions, etc. Skinner argued that "self" necessarily *implied* the metaphorical notion of an homunculous, a little person residing within us that required another little person to explain it. My little person and his parts, said Skinner, are not very different from the souls and spirits that populate theological discourse. "Self," then, was an *implicit* metaphor, a conventionalized "substance" grounded on a metaphorical fiction.

After reading Szasz and Edelman and Skinner one is tempted to banish terms such as "mental illness," "public opinion" and "self" in favor of terms designating so-called "real" entities. This was the British empiricists' noble effort, and one finds traces of their metaphysical materialism in the work of the behaviorists such as Skinner. Yet, as Chomsky (1959) has so convincingly argued, Skinner cannot avoid metaphor in applying such terms as stimulus, response and reinforcement in nonlaboratory descriptions of verbal behavior. The basic metaphor here is implicit in Skinner's claim that all communication is behavior, a carrying over from the realm of meaning to the realm of motion (Burke, 1969). As Burke argues, metaphor is inescapable whenever one attempts to develop or extend a perspective.

Burke (1969) goes to the heart of the matter in his essay on "substance." He observes that, etymologically, there is a pun lurking behind the Latin roots. The word is often used to designate what some thing or agent intrinsically is — its essence or main elements or essential import. Yet, literally, "sub-stance" is something "that stands beneath or supports the person or thing." It refers not to the thing itself, but to some attribute of its context, to what it is not. Says Burke:

> Here obviously is a strategic moment, an alchemic moment, wherein momentous miracles of transformation can take place. For here the intrinsic and the extrinsic can change places .... We here take the pun seriously because we believe it to reveal an inevitable paradox of definition, an antimony that must endow the concept of substance with unresolvable ambiguity, and that will be discovered lurking beneath any vocabulary designed to treat of motivation by the deliberate outlawing of the word for substance (p. 24).

Burke states further that we may banish terms for substance or ignore their metaphorical origins, but we can only succeed in "*concealing* their functions." Hence, he admonishes us to dwell upon words such as "substance," considering "its embarrassments and its potentialities for transformation, so that we may detect its covert inflence even when it is overtly absent."

Burke's insights on "substance" enable us better to understand why metaphor has been an embarrassment to science. Those scientists who have attempted, as it were, to objectify "the real" have found that they have been unable to capture the intrinsic without reference to the extrinsic; unable, in other words, to tell us what something is except in terms of some metaphor-bound perspective on what it is not. And each such metaphor has revealed the paradox of substance in that, as Burke (1969:32) points out, the subject of the metaphor "both is and is not the same as the character with which and by which it is identified."

To be sure, there are scientists who have eschewed all terms for intrinsic substance, preferring instead to speak in comparative terms of system parameters or process variables and of relationships among systems or processes (e.g., Bateson, 1941; Bateson, 1970). In doing so, however, they neither escape the mediation of metaphor nor the paradox of substance. As De Man (1978) observes, the major tropological etymons in Indo-European languages tend to be closely inter-linked, and they tend to fall back upon conceptions of substance. Burke (1969) notes that the term "system" derives from the same Indo-Germanic roots as "substance." As for "process," my American Heritage dictionary defines it as a progression in time analogous to a movement from one place to another. De Man (1978) notes that "motion is a passage and passage is a translation; translation, once again, means motion, piles motion upon motion. It is no mere play of words that translate is translated in German as 'ubersetzen' which itself translates the Greek 'meta phorein' or metaphor" (p. 17).

We may note, finally, that the very term "substance" is an implicit metaphor as applied to nonmaterial entities (e.g., as in Descartes' famous depiction of himself as "thinking substance") in that it carries with it our visual conceptions of place or location in space. Not by accident "sub-stance" and "under-stand" derive from the same root, and "seeing" and "understanding" may, in some contexts, be used interchangeably. No wonder that orthodox empiricists typically demand visual evidence of a phenomenon before they grant that it has substance.

On the basis of this brief etymological excursion we may better understand the difficulties which the Batesonians and other communication theorists have had in distinguishing the form and content of even the simplest of messages. The content of a message — its "substance" — is assumed to be contrastable with the form of the message, as figure is to ground. But we inevitably find that we cannot describe message content except in terms of its form; hence content becomes form. By an inverse logic, we may also find ourselves asserting that form is content. Thus, for example, the Batesonians (e.g., Watzlawick *et. al.*, 1967) declare metaphorically that forms, and even contexts, "communicate" (or "metacommunicate"). And since contexts are always parts of larger contexts, it becomes fair to say, by a kind of metaphorical regress, that all that we do not communicate is presented in the texts of what we do communicate. This, as I gather it, is the semiologists' very serious dictum: All the world's a text, and every message ultimately requires a reading of the "all" for us to interpret it (e.g., Hawkes, 1977).

To their credit, the Batesonians are self-acknowledged metaphorists; indeed, Haley (1976) has argued that metaphor is essential in any account of person-person, as opposed to person-object or object-object, relations.[7] Just as Skinner proceeds metaphorically in converting meaning to motion, so the Batesonians proceed metaphorically when they assert that all behavior is communication (e.g., Watzlawick *et al.*, 1967:49-50); the shift in contexts of usage is simply in the reverse direction. Many of their expressions are clearly metaphorical; the phrase "ecology of mind" provides an example. But, like the rest of us, the Batesonians also use a great many metaphors of the implicit, ostensibly "dead" variety, commonplace terms such as "level" and "steps" which require a *mind's eye* conception of a physical relationship (i.e., as in levels and steps of a building) for us to understand their applications to incorporeal relationships. After warning of the dangers of hypostatizing reality, Watzlawick, Beavin, and Jackson (1967:260) hypostatize in turn when they allege as "fact" that a "hierarchy of levels seems to pervade the world we live in and our experiences of selves and others . . . ." The authors index nine different ways in which they employ this architectural metaphor in linguistic and communicational contexts.[8]

The Batesonians have also evidenced some awareness of the problems which arise when commonplace terms with long histories of usage are employed metaphorically in scientific accounts. In an essay highly revealing of his methods, Bateson (1941) described his initial flirtation with the term *"ethos"* and his subsequent decision to replace it with technical, comparative terms from biology such as "homology" and "homonomy." Like the many other old-but-not-quite-dead metaphors which I have been commenting upon in this chapter, *ethos* proved "dangerous" as applied in social-scientific texts. The danger with this Greek substantive was that it invited reification; led even Bateson to the error of investing the *ethos* of a culture with causal powers. Whereas "homology" and "homonomy" preserved the notion of analogy and captured well the structural relations Bateson sought to convey, *ethos* proved ambiguous, neither clearly metaphorical nor appropriately literal. Better, said Bateson, to speak "loosely" and clearly metaphorically of the "feel" of a culture than to speak semi-technically of its *ethos*.[9]

Bateson's essay illustrates well, not just the ambiguities of metaphor but also the paradoxes of its use by scientists. It is not simply that metaphorical expressions mean something other than what they literally assert — the universal paradox of substance — but that, in using metaphor, scientists metacommunicate simultaneously that they are engaging in a kind of verbal play and that, as scientists, they wish to be taken seriously. As if this oxymoron of *serious play* were not troublesome enough, they also use substantives like "levels" and "ethos" which, in some contexts, are not clearly metaphorical or clearly literal, and they frequently compound the problem by acting as though (and often believing) these terms refer literally to fixed entities or substances. In these latter cases, the reader is placed in a position much like that of the schizophrenics described by Bateson *et al.*, (1956), unable to distinguish the literal and the metaphorical. Like the dogs in the Pavlovian experiment described by Watzlawick, Beavin, and Jackson (1967:216-217), our ellipses become circles and our circles ellipses.

THE DIALECTICS OF METAPHOR: EXPLICATION, CRITICISM, AND EVALUATION

Beyond simply recognizing them, what shall we do to manage the metaphors that our social-scientific theories are riddled with? By way of a general answer, our metaphors must be subjected to argument and counterargument. Here the explication of key metaphors looms as highly important, as does rhetorical criticism of the metaphors put forth by others. Scientists are obligated to metacommunicate about metaphors: to classify them as metaphors, to interpret for us whether they are intended playfully or seriously (or both), and to indicate both the similarities and the dissimilarities in the similes and analogies which their metaphors imply.

But because metaphors are inherently ambiguous, and because scientists play games with metaphors, and because their metacommunications about metaphor are often more ambiguous than the terms and expressions they comment upon, there is need for critical analysis of their explicative rhetoric. Scientists, like other rhetors, are not above leaving readers hanging as to whether their constructs are to be understood literally or metaphorically, leaving indeterminate the rhetorical purpose of a metaphor, failing to explicate the comparisons implied by their metaphors, defending the introduction of vaguely defined terms on grounds that they are "only" being used metaphorically, reifying metaphors or inviting others to do so, and insisting that rival schools of thought adhere to standards of evaluation more rigorous than those they employ in defending the utility of their own metaphors.

The analysis of metaphorical usage should be part of a larger project in rhetorical criticism in which assessments are made, on an ongoing basis, of the force of extra-factual, extra-logical factors in scientific articles and books. In his illustrative analysis, Joseph Gusfield (1976) includes such factors as the mood and tone of the article, its entitlement terms, its modes of expressing identifications and divisions, and its overall arrangement. Says Gusfield:

> To be relevant or significant, data must not only be selected, they have to be typified and interpreted. In doing this, language and thought are themselves the vehicles through which such relevance is cast. In Burke's terms they are 'modes of action.' They lead us to conclusions and thus to new perspectives. It is not that Science is 'reduced' to Rhetoric, and thus rendered corrupt and useless. It is rather that the rhetorical component *seems* to be unavoidable if the work is to have a theoretical or policy relevance. Thus an analysis of scientific work *should* also include its rhetorical as well as its empirical component. Science is thus a form of action with meanings derived from its Art as well as its Science (p. 31).

The task of critically assessing metaphors need not be construed narrowly. As Wayne Booth has argued,

> A very large part of what we value as our cultural monuments can be thought of as metaphorical criticism of metaphor and the characters who make them. In this view, even the great would-be literalists like Hobbes and Locke are finally metaphorists — simply committed to another kind of metaphor, one that to them seems literal. Without grossly

overestimating we could say that the whole work of each philosopher amounts to an elaborate critique of the inadequacy of all other philosophers' metaphors. What is more, the very existence of a tradition of a small group of philosophies is a sign that hundreds of lesser metaphors for the life of mankind have been tested in the great philosophical — that is, critical — wars and found wanting (1978:66).

One important task of the rhetorical critic operating in scientific contexts is to resurrect so-called "dead" metaphors. The analyses of "mental illness" by Szasz (1969) of "public opinion" by Edelman (1971), and of "self" by Skinner (e.g., 1957) provide examples of what I mean.

A second function of rhetorical criticism in scientific contexts involves the counterposing of one metaphor with another. In place of mechanical metaphors to describe social systems, the critic may propose that social systems are better likened to homeostatic organisms or to channeled streams of energy. Capitalizing on the possibilities for metonymic extension and synecdochic development in these substitute metaphors, a second critic might insist that the social system as organism is not passive or dependent but self-generating and independent. Similarly, the turgid stream might be replaced by one that is turbulent, crooked, unmanageable, and that courses mysteriously below the surface of our awareness. These shifts within the framework of a given metaphor are of no small consequence. Indeed, Watzlawick, Beavin, and Jackson (1967) have maintained that the great leaps which have occurred in physics, molecular biology, chemistry and telecommunications took place when the metaphorical stream was reconceived as carrying a flow of information rather than energy.

A third function of rhetorical criticism involves detailed analysis of how metaphors operate within a given body of scientific discourse. In his analysis of "drunk-driver" studies, for example, Gusfield (1976) observed that their authors tended to affect a dry, non-metaphorical style ("a style of non-style") in the body of their reports and then burst forth with a profusion of metaphors in the concluding sections of these reports — thus creating the impression of technical neutrality while being forcefully persuasive in the same articles.

The foregoing functions of metaphor, of metacommunications about metaphor, and of rhetorical criticism of metaphor may be illustrated with respect to the Batesonian Interactionists.[10] The Batesonians typically provide numerous examples from varied contexts to convince us of the utility of a comparative term, and then, by metaphorical extension, and with additional examples and analogies, apply the term to previously uncharted relationships. Not uncommonly, they offer several metaphors and analogies as a way of providing a "fix" on a concept or phenomenon. In an essay contrasting Balinese and Iatmul value systems, for example, Bateson (1949) invoked cybernetic theory, Richardson equations, the orgasm metaphor, and Von Neumannian game theory — being careful all the while to indicate in what respects his analogies were also disanalogies.

The Batesonians are not always careful with their metaphors and analogies; like the rest of us, they need the correctives provided by rhetorical criticism. In a seminar paper (Simons, 1977) I gently chided the authors of *Change* (Watzlawick, Weakland & Fisch, 1974) for applying the mathematical distinction between first- and second-order change too literally to social relationships. In moving so facilely "from math to morals," I argued, Watzlawick *et al.*, had failed to heed a lesson which the Interactionists had helped teach us: that system characteristics are in the eyes of the beholder. Not only, for example, did they purport to identify a single "rule of the relationship" in highly complex, communist Russia, they also presumed to know which psychological problems are "real" and which are only "difficulties," which patterns of thinking are "errors" and which are "correct," which solutions are "utopian" (a "devil" term for them) and which are "realistic."[11]

No doubt Watzlawick and colleagues will want to counter with their own criticisms. "Suppose," they might ask, "that we had shouted on every page: 'These applications of Russell and Galois are purely metaphorical'. Besides taking us to task for writing unaesthetically, might not you, Simons, criticize us this time for speaking paradoxically, the 'metaphor' label functioning as a way of denying our own serious intent"? A fair question, I believe, one which illustrates that rhetorical critics are as vulnerable to criticism as the persons they are criticizing.

We come now to the very difficult task of comparing and evaluating rival metaphors. Although there are no neutral algorithms by which to determine the aptness of a given metaphor, there are some rhetorical yardsticks which we can apply in its evaluation. We can ask, for example, whether it is profound or trivial, relatively clear or hopelessly confusing, poetic or provocative or unaesthetic and uninteresting. A given metaphor may be justified on grounds that it has worked well in an allied discipline. Or that it enables us to glimpse the ineffable within our own discipline. Or that it expresses economically a complex set of relations. Or that it fits well with other terms in one's theory. More realistically, the proponent of a given metaphor may be obliged to argue that it offers an optimal *tradeoff* among these desiderata. All of us would grant, for example, that the double-bind metaphor is highly provocative and even poetic in its evocation of the image of someone literally bound in multiple knots. Yet, repeated efforts at disambiguation spanning two decades should convince us that the term is by no means clear.

Where possible, proponents and critics will want to bring evidence to bear on their evaluations of a theory's key organizing metaphors. The route from organizing metaphor to evidential support is not a fully deductive one; there are gaps in the road which must be bridged rhetorically. Still, at least some of the problems of incorrigibility, discussed earlier, can be ameliorated through research. It was counter-evidence, for example, which contributed to Robert White's (1959) abandonment of the "drive" metaphor as applied to exploration, mastery and activity. Linked from its inception in general psychology to the root of metaphor of organism-as-machine, the drive metaphor had, by common agreement, three ineliminable characteristics. The psychological drive had to function like a coiled spring which, when activated, provides directive force or energy to the organism. The release of that energy had to be followed by a period of satiation (i.e., equilibrium). And there had to be some mechanism by which the energy-producing potential of the psychological spring could be activated.

White's reading of the available evidence suggested that exploration, mastery and activity did not conform to these ineliminable drive characteristics. For example, it appeared that exploratory behavior was drive-increasing rather than drive-reducing. Moreover, the activity drive, when self-stimulated cortically, was found to be insatiable — leading the animal, literally, to kill itself through overactivity. After tinkering with possible modifications of drive theory, White elected a different metaphorical tack. The phrasing of his conclusion is instructive:

> Perhaps this is no more than a question of words, but I should prefer at this point to call it a problem in conceptual strategy. I shall propose that these three "drives" have much in common and that it is useful to bring them under the single heading of competence. Even with the loosening of the concept of drive, they are still in important respects different from hunger, thirst, and sex. It is in order to emphasize their

intrinsic peculiarities, to get them considered in their own right without a cloud a surplus meanings, that I prefer in this essay to speak of the urge that makes for competence simply as motivation rather than as drive (p. 305).

Note that White cannot compel the reader's assent and does not even try. Instead, he pleads the utility of what he refers to as a "conceptual strategy." White attempts persuasion rather than proof, but his argument for a limited rejection of the drive metaphor is nevertheless based on good reasons.[12]

Not all social-scientific metaphors can be evaluated in a manner comparable to the drive metaphor. Nor should they be. Elsewhere (Simons, 1978) I have sung praises to "muddleheaded anecdotalism," an umbrella term for all manner of social-scientific perspectives — Batesonian Interactionism among them — which make conspicuous and self-conscious use of metaphors, and which "evidence" their metaphors more by anecdote than by experimental test. Watzlawick gives point to my argument when he maintains that:

> There are two methods of scientific explanation. One is to expound a theory and then show how observable facts bear it out. The other is to present facts from many different contexts to make obvious, in a very practical way, the structure that they have in common and the conclusions that follow from them. In the first approach, the examples are used as proof. In the second, their function is metaphorical and illustrative — they are meant to demonstrate something, to translate it into a more familiar language, but not necessarily to prove anything (1976:xii).

The first method is, of course, the method of traditional social scientists — the method of those, like the drive theorists, who have operated within a verificationist mold. The second method is the method of the newer, more interpretive social-scientific perspectives which I referred to earlier in this chapter. Although the latter may not "prove anything" in the verificationist sense, they may, if their metaphors are well chosen and well illustrated, render the mysteries of social interaction more fathomable to us.

What, in the way of evidence, can we expect of the muddleheaded anecdotalists? I think we can ask that their key metaphors be "tested" across a wide range of contexts in terms of their capacity to evoke a sense of isomorphism among phenomena that might previously have seemed unrelated. This, as I see it, is a principal virtue of many of the Batesonian metaphors. When terms such as "feedback loop" are convincingly argued to have a goodness of fit in servomechanical, biological, cultural and even intrapersonal contexts, we begin to suspect that they are more than heuristic devices.[13]

The utility of an anecdotalist metaphor is also evidenced when it is used in what Geertz (1973:3-30) has referred to as "thick descriptions" of a particular phenonmenon; here the anecdotalist's interest is in richness of application rather than range of application. In Geetz's (1973) richly detailed depiction of Balinese cockfights as mixed-motive games, one gets a sense both of the power of the metaphor and of its appropriate limitations. Not by accident, Bateson (1949) drew upon this same metaphor in contrasting Iatmul and Balinese cultures.

Where, finally, a metaphorical term is used in a causal generalization, the gap between muddleheaded anecdotalism and simpleminded digitalism must be bridged. The creature produced by this coupling of epistemologies will not be a pretty one — a methaphorical figure disfigured by operational definitions, counting procedures, and the like — but it is nevertheless necessary. I would urge, for example, that the authors of *Change* (Watzlawick *et al.*, 1974) provide much more statistical data than they offered in their book about the rate and degree of success in therapy that they have achieved with various "reframing" devices. Having entered the digitalists' game by speaking of percentages of "cure," they must live by the digitalists' rules.

For the most part, however, the power of the anecdotalists' metaphors will not be evidenced in their statistical tables but in their capacity to enliven our imaginations. Like the poet, the anecdotalist must reach to the limits of language, thereby providing a glimpse of the differences between nature and what we say about it. This the Batesonians have done quite well.

What, now, of the many other social-scientific perspectives that contend for our adherence? Rather than choosing between the digitalists and the anecdotalists, or between the Batesonians and, say, the ethnomethodologists, I find myself committed to "perspectivalism," a kind of meta-perspective. There is irony in the perspectival position since, as Burke (1969:513) notes, it "requires that all of the sub-certainties be considered as neither true nor false, but *contributory*." So as to guard against the dangers of relativism inherent in the position, Burke urges us to take care that "the dialectic is properly formed" (p. 512).

My own dialectical contribution has been to the resolution of the tension between rigor and imagination in the use of metaphor. It has consisted in the following suggestions for metaphor management:

First, that we recognize the ubiquity of metaphor in social-scientific discourse. Try as we might to banish metaphors by speaking only of intrinsic substances, or to efface from our memories the metaphorical roots of ostensibly literal expressions, or to paraphrase metaphors into theory-neutral terms at the so-called "justification" stage of science, we will find that they still work their influences upon us.

Second, that we learn to metacommunicate more clearly about our metaphors — this so that we may overcome some of the ambiguities and paradoxes attendant upon their use. Social-scientific metaphors need to be labeled as such. Moreover, their users should indicate whether they are being employed playfully and/or seriously, and they should also comment on both the similarities and the dissimilarities in the comparisons which their metaphors imply.

Third, that communities of scholars subject metaphors and metacommunications about metaphor to careful analysis as part of a larger, ongoing project in rhetorical criticism of social-scientific discourse. Viewed broadly, rhetorical criticism involves much more than exposing the games social scientists play with metaphor. It may involve long and detailed justifications for the superiority of alternative metaphors.

Finally, that we compare and evaluate rival metaphors in terms of a variety of criteria — clarity, economy, provocativeness, etc. — usually settling for an optimal tradeoff among these values. Evidence, too, can be brought to bear upon metaphor, though never through a fully rule-bound, hypothetico-deductive logic. By experiment in the case of some metaphors, and by anecdote in the case of others, we may at least offer plausible arguments that our metaphors are useful conceptual strategies.

NOTES

1.   Bateson and his colleagues (Bateson, 1955; Bateson, Jackson, Haley & Weakland, 1956; Haley, 1976) have helped reinforce this distinction in maintaining that the metaphorical and the literal are "logical types" in the Russellian sense. As a form of linguistic play, metaphor is said to deny at a meta- or second-order level what it asserts at a first-order or literal level.

2.   See for example Mooij's attempt at differentiation. Mooij tells us that to qualify as a metaphor, the "foreign" term must continue to have some surprise or shock value; it must deviate in a special way from one or more other ways of using it that are considered to be primary or normal; and the deviation from primary or normal usage must be radical or major. These are hardly precise guidelines for differentiation.

3.   Nor, as Ricouer (1977) observes, does grammar provide any assistance. "For example, grammar makes no distinction between Churchill calling Mussolini 'That utensil!' and the use of the same phrase in a frying-pan advertisement" (p. 252).

4.   The problem of metaphoric ambiguity has led some traditionalists, particularly those reared in a logical positivist tradition, to conclude that metaphor has no place in science. Representative of the traditionalist view is this statement by Tedeschi, Schlenker, and Bonoma (1973):

> The words the poet uses may be quite ambiguous, and a free use of metaphor or simile allows the reader to decipher many different meanings from the same poem. Much of the profoundness discovered from literature is a function of symbolism and ambiguity of interpretation. The scientist's language does not permit ambiguity, since precise deduction of theories would become impossible , and then no empirical test of the theory could be made (p. 191).

5.   Kuhn (1970:207) notes for example that "in some respects, though by no means in all, Einstein's general theory of relativity is closer to Aristotle's than either of them is to Newton's." Newtonianism itself was roundly denounced in its time for relying on innate forces — metaphors associated with the Dark Ages (Kuhn, 1970:163).

6.   By the Batesonian Interactionists I include in particular Bateson, Haley, Jackson, Weakland and Watzlawick. The term should become clearer from the works that I cite. I recognize, of course, that my list is by no means exhaustive and that there are differences among the theorists cited. Still, they have shared an interest in theorizing about communication from Bateson's mix of cybernetic and Russellian perspectives.

7.   Less relevant for our purposes are the Batesonians' clinical applications of metaphor. As Haley (1976) makes clear in his essay on "Communication as Bits and Metaphor," the Batesonians listen carefully for their patients' metaphors, view their behavior in therapy as analogic to their relationships outside therapy, describe problems and prognoses in metaphoric terms, attempt to overcome resistance to change by the use of metaphors, and consider patients "cured" when they have substituted "appropriate" analogies for "inappropriate" ones.

8.   There are said to be levels of mathematics, levels of meaning, levels of communication, levels of language. The term is used in discussions of the content-relationship

distinction, definitions of self and others, logico-mathematical and pragmatic paradoxes, illusion of alternatives, games without end, and double-binds (Watzlawick et al., 1967:260).

9. I have taken some liberties in "translating" Bateson's treatment of *ethos* here, but I believe my reading is on target.

10. Examined too late for commentary in the text of this chapter is Bateson's (1979) latest volume. Bateson's manner of metaphorizing here and his comments about metaphors — his own and others included — are consistent with my descriptions of his earlier works. A great many terms and expressions are labeled as metaphors, including so-called "dead" metaphors (e.g., *triggering* a response, *inside* and *outside* as applied to the self). Bateson is critical of mechanistic and physical metaphors as applied to biological phenomena (e.g., p. 43, p. 101), in part because of their feeling-tone. More than most theorists, Bateson also metacommunicates about the limitations of his own metaphors — e.g., the concept of logical types as applied to causality (p. 59); the concept of self (p. 135). As in his earlier works, Bateson builds on structural metaphors. His method of extending and "testing" such metaphors is given a name — *abduction* — to distinguish it from induction and deduction.

11. The authors' applications of the change metaphors seems to be informed by a strong ideological bent. Given their conceptual framework, one might think that a shift from a capitalist system (from each according to his ability, to each according to his ability) to a socialist system (from each according to his ability, to each according to his need) would be viewed by the authors as second-order change. Not so. Disregarding the shift in logic between economic systems, they construe the change as a mere redistribution of wealth, and, having applied the rule that a combination of opposites yields an identity number, they conclude that there has only been first-order change.

This same rule is applied equivocally to the concept of renaming. When Watzlawick *et al.*, relabel they assume that second-order change has been produced since the patient's thinking has (presumably) been altered fundamentally. But, when the Red Guards of China relabeled street signs, this, according to the authors (p. 210), was only first-order change since the renaming of street signs goes back to Confucius.

The shift from math to morals is also evident in their chapters on how we "mishandle difficulties." Their aphorisms aside, I am still not at all sure, for example, why nothing can be done to narrow the generation gap or why people should not be encouraged to seek utopian solutions. Surely, these recommendations do not follow directly from the mathematical theories they present.

12. The history of drive theory in psychology corresponds well to Kuhn's (1970) account of paradigm development and shift within the physical sciences. More by its rhetorical appeal than by logical necessity, the drive theorists fastened on drive-as-mechanism, with its three ineliminable components. Rhetorical considerations were at work, too, in the stipulations by particular theorists of additional defining characteristics. An eclectic definition could be offered, for example, one designed to please all segments of the scientific community. Or the theorist could elect to stand with some single segment of the community — with the Hullians rather than the Skinnerians, for example. As reported by White, the thinking of most drive theorists eventually coalesced around the following core propositions: that biological drives arise from a tissue deficit; that the tissue deficit is painful and hence energizes the organism to reduce the drive; that drive-reduction is pleasurable or rewarding; that drive-reduction is accompanied by acquisition of secondary drives through a process of conditioning. Considerable evidence was brought to bear upon the theory, much of it supportive. But the

accumulated evidence on the "competence" motives proved anomalous, leading some theorists to attempt revisions of drive theory. If, for example, exploration, mastery and activity were biological rather than acquired and neurogenic rather than tissue-based, one could simply redefine their place in the scheme of things. It was only when the "competence" motives appeared not to conform to the ineliminable components of the drive metaphor that a sense of crisis developed. That White and others elected to switch rather than fight is testament in part to the availability of an alternative metaphor which might prove more promising as a conceptual strategy.

13. In Wheelright's (1962) terms, they move from a diaphoric status to an isophoric status.

Communication Theory in a New Key

W. Barnett Pearce
Linda M. Harris and Vernon E. Cronen

"Imitation," it is often said, "is the sincerest flattery." Not so — at least not in the Olympian culture of *academe*. In the development of thought, imitation rings hollow praise, and the sincerest compliment is that of allowing one's work to be shaped by the ideas of a person, and then extending those ideas and respectfully returning them to their source.

The "coordinated management of meaning" is a theory of human communication which we have developed during the past six years. As quite a few reproving reviewers for scholarly journals have insisted, this theory is in important respects unlike most others. One way in which it is atypical is that it purports both to be scientific, complete with measuring apparati and statistical tests of hypotheses, *and* to be based on a humanistic conceptualization of communication as the collective creation and management of social reality. Most people who take either of these orientations seriously assert that an integration of them is not possible without profaning one or both.

Perhaps they are right and we have produced a purile eclecticism, or maybe we have found a way around some of the obdurant obstacles which have plagued contemporary thought. Regardless of the success of our attempt to build a scientific theory of human communication, the *process* has been a prolonged, self-conscious tribute to many thinkers, chief among them Gregory Bateson, Arthur Koestler and Rom Harre. We have attempted to extend the ideas we have learned from these persons and to return the result to them: this is the highest praise that we can give.

All three of us have been trained in the history, philosophy and methodology of science, and we prize the "virtues" traditionally claimed for science: descriptive and explanatory power; predictability; intersubjectivity, or the ability to make knowledge public; and an established verification procedure which functions to "correct" erroneous thinking. However, as we argue elsewhere (Pearce *et al.*, 1981), scientists have seldom known exactly what they were doing and have described their "method" egregiously. As a result, when *social* scientists attempted to duplicate the spectacular successes of the 18th and 19th century *natural* scientists, they created a new and sterile form of inquiry based on, e.g., Newton's *description* of the scientific method rather than on what Newton actually *did* as a scientist.

The sterility of early efforts to apply science to human communication stems from a reversal of the relationship between form and function. The early natural scientists invented a form of inquiry — a "method" — which, somewhat to everyone's surprise, functioned by producing the "virtues" identified above. The 20th century social scientists — with reason — coveted those virtues, and decided to achieve them by reproducing what they *thought* was the original method. The upshot is a most unscientific imperialism and imperativism in which anything not meeting the criteria for "form" is declared "unscientific." For example, in his widely used text *Foundations of Behavioral Research*, Kerlinger reserves science for stable phenomena with "adequate empirical referents." Phenomena which do not meet these criteria are "out of bounds." Kerlinger cited the concept of "authoritarianism":

> Although many studies of authoritarianism have been done with considerable success, it is doubtful that we know what authoritarianism in the classroom means. For instance, an action of a teacher that is authoritarian in one classroom may not be authoritarian in another classroom. The alleged democratic behavior exhibited by one teacher may even be

called authoritarian if exhibited by another teacher. *Such elasticity is not the stuff of science* (Kerlinger, 1973:24. Emphasis added).

But such elasticity *is* the stuff of human communication. Bateson (1979:47) said that "Billiard balls do not respond to each other's responses, and that is the essential component of schismogenesis, armament races, the creation of tyrants and willing slaves, performers and spectators, and so on."

Can there be a form of inquiry which achieves the "virtues" of science without profanely trivializing the phenomena of communication?

In 1974, when the first author began exploring "coordinated management of meaning" as an ancestral term for communication, it was not at all clear that a scientific theory was possible. It was here that Bateson's example more than his preachments was our guide. During his intellectually peripatetic career, he developed novel concepts and research techniques to deal with the characteristics of Balinese culture, play among primates, European national cultures, and schizophrenia rather than selecting phenomena for study which fit his concepts and methods. Anticipating the epistemology of Richard McKeon, Bateson apparently sought out a diverse array of topics for study and assessed the validity of concepts by their power to explain and inform inquiry when "translated" across several topical domains. Following Bateson's example, we began by exploring the characteristics of communication, letting the ability to be "scientific" stand or fall on its own merits. Later, we learned that the "dominant paradigm" in social sciences, logical positivism, was not the only — or even the best — exemplar of science, and we found a way to do a scientific theory of communication. Reversing the actual chronology, we will describe the nature of science first, then explicate our concept of communication. The final sections report research which achieves the scientific "virtues" and which is based on a conceptualization of communication we believe to be compatible with the basic insights of Bateson and his colleagues.

ON "DOING SCIENCE"

The most crucial century for understanding intellectual history is the sixth B.C. Lao Tzu in China, the Buddha in India, and the Greek philosophers in Ionia developed systems of thought which have shaped the intellectual climates of continents for millenia.

Western thought has oriented around three characteristics of Ionian philosophy. First, the assumption that there is an underlying, eternal order beneath the flux of sensible experience. In classical Greek thought, this took the form of a differentiation between "appearances" and "reality," and a value judgment that only the latter was an important object for study. Second, the belief that reality is composed of irreducible atoms, and that the atomic units of each type of entity were identical. This form of atomism orients attention away from the nature of entities and toward "external" causes and effects. Third, the assumption that the existence or action of any entity comprises a problem which must and can be explained, and that the locus of the explanation is "outside" the entity itself.

The effect of these assumptions has been to dismiss communication from the center of attention in the human study of the human condition. Until this century, communication has been the primary concern of second rate minds and the secondary concern of first rate minds, and usually thought of under the headings of the devices of florid embellishment or the techniques of gaining personal prestige or influence. Further, these assumptions restricted the development of forms of inquiry. The history of the development of science may be read as the tortured emancipation from the limitations of thought imposed by these assumptions (cf. Whitehead, 1925).

Newtonian physics represented the limit to which one could go within the Ionian assumptions, and twentieth century social science — at least in the Anglo-American community — was an attempt to duplicate that procedure (Koestler, 1967). Carnap (1966:3,6) gave this definitive statement of scientific "method":

> The observations we make in everyday life as well as the more systematic observations of science reveal certain repetitions or regularities in the world. Day always follows night ... objects fall when we drop them; and so on. *The laws of science are nothing more than statements expressing these regularities as possible.*
>
> . . . . .
>
> ...science begins with direct observations of single facts. Nothing else is observable. Certainly a regularity is not directly observable. It is only when many observations are compared with one another that regularities are discovered. These regularities are

expressed by statements called "laws."

Rom Harre has inauguered what he describes as a new Copernican Revolution in the philosophy of science, the major points of which are these. First, the method described by Carnap never has been that used by scientists and would be sterile if it were. A closer reading of the history of science shows that scientists actually develop models of phenomena with which they work and do research which tests the implications of these models.

Second, the "irreducible and stubborn facts" demanded by Galileo and the "single facts" which Carnap believes are the sole observable phenomena simply do not exist. Reality consists not of "atoms" of behavior but of variously constructed entities which act in ways consistent with their natures.

> According to this view one may see the behavior of powerful particulars as flowing from their nature or constitutions, that is, as consequences of what they *are*. . . Being of a certain nature endows a thing or material with the power to manifest itself in certain ways, or to behave in certain ways, or to behave in certain ways in appropriate circumstances. In the extreme case of the pure agent, it is to do something, or to be capable of doing something, whatever the circumstances, i.e., to be the initiator of the act. A pure agent is that thing or material in which a causal chain terminates, be it resolute gardener or a radium atom (Harre & Madden, 1975:90-91).

We share Harre and Madden's doubts that there are any absolutely "pure agents," but obviously persons have some degree of "agentry" about them, and this creates a whole new method of doing science. If an entity is complex and/or "free," then its behavior should not be expected to have the characteristics of regularity on which Carnap would build all knowledge. The process of science is to construct a model of the entity which depicts its degree of "agentry," and to test the implications of that model. According to Harre, the key to his "new" Copernican Revolution is that of identifying models as the *substance* rather than as discretionary *luxury* of scientific theory.

THE COORDINATED MANAGEMENT OF MEANING
AND THE INTERACTIONAL VIEW:
SOME COMMON GROUND

The theory of "Coordinated Management of Meaning" has been developed over the course of recent years by the authors of this chapter and their students. (See: Pearce, 1976; Cronen & Pearce, 1978; Cronen, Pearce & Harris, 1979; Harris & Cronen, 1979; Harris, 1979). The comparison between the "Coordinated Management of Meaning" (hereafter CMM) and the "interactional view" is summarized in Figure 1.

The theory of Coordinated Management of Meaning and the Interactional View share a number of crucial premises. Both view human communication from the perspective of systems theory. Of course, commitment to a systems view requires both theorists to examine particular acts in light of the functions they perform within a communication system and to examine the interdependence of the conversants. But the move to a systems perspective involves even more fundamental changes.

Bateson's remarkably fertile descriptions of communication as elaborated into the "interactional view" (Wilder, 1979) comprise a refutation of the assumptions of the Ionian philosophers (cf. Watzlawick, 1976) fully as dramatic as and in content, compatible with Harre's Copernican Revolution in the philosophy of science. Bateson's early acquaintance with the life sciences — his father was a biologist prominent in the exploration of heredity — probably helped him see around the corners of the assumptions of atomic reductionism and of mechanistic causation. Biologists were well aware that entities were organized wholes, not irreducible atoms, and that the structure of entities was at least part of the explanation for why they acted as they did (Harre, 1972). Consistently preoccupied with *pattern* rather than with "atoms" of behavior, Bateson viewed *interactions* between persons as entities in themselves which had a structure which contextualized and thus explained the component parts of conversations. This was in direct contrast to the "scientific" procedure of reducing an interaction to the smallest components and looking for "regularities" among their frequency, sequence, etc. Further, Bateson side-stepped the assumption that entities must be "orderly": he began to look for the existence and implications of disorder. Over two decades ago, Bateson introduced himself at one of the "Macy" conferences as

Figure 1.   A Comparison of Two Communication Theories

The "Interactional View"	The "Coordinated Management of Meaning"
Nature of communication:	
hierarchically and temporally extended systems	hierarchically and temporally extended systems
pragmatic: creates a shared social reality context-dependent	pragmatic: creates a shared social reality context-dependent
hierarchial organization: two levels, fixed order	hierarchical organization: multileveled, some flexibility in number and sequence of levels
Structure of communication systems:	
transpersonal	holonic
Locus of explanation:	
social reality	social reality
Nature of social reality:	
disordered: lists of types of disorder	disordered: measurement model of the structure of disorder
Rules:	
behavioral redundancies	descriptions of the way person's process information
Method of discovery:	
observer defines transpersonal patterns	actors supply content; observers define structure at intrapersonal and interpersonal levels
Scientific power:	
description post-hoc explanation	description, explanation, prediction of relationships among patterns

...on the whole, an angry man, who believes that what happens to people oughtn't to happen to dogs...

I suppose the thing I hold sacred is something in the nature of patterns, and that which makes me angry is the violation of patterns in some form or another. So I find myself today studying schizophrenic subjects, trying to help them find valuable patterns in their lives; and, on the other side of the same picture, I find myself angry at the distortions of pattern that happens to them as children, and I try to study what in fact does happen to them as children. I also speculate about what sorts of violations of pattern in children would form the logical base for the later distortions which we call schizophrenia (Bateson, 1957:9).

In the capable hands of Don Jackson, John Weakland, Paul Watzlawick, Carlos Sluzki, and others, this search for patterns and for the implications of patterns has provided a rich description of communication. We have found the "interactional view" an important source of our understanding of communication, and have added to it the results of our own research and of other literatures.

The two theories also agree that communication events have the properties of hierarchial organization and temporal extension. Messages must be understood in terms of what they "do" to people (their relational level of meaning), not merely in terms of their content or referential meaning. Moreover, messages must be understood as constituting patterns punctuated by human actors. Both CMM and the Interactional View explain the logic by which human systems function as a set of "rules." The idea of systems organized by rules frees both theories from the false choice between describing communication as fully determined by fixed laws or throwing up one's hands and proclaiming communication to be capricious and chaotic — beyond the powers of social science. Finally, both CMM and the Interactional View endorse the assumption that persons live in a socially constructed reality that evolves through the process of talk. Watzlawick (1976) like Austin (1955) before him differentiates first order reality (e.g., brute facts, things-in-themselves) and second order reality (e.g., the significance of facts, and institutional facts which have no empirical referents but which are treated as real).

The commitment to (1) a general systems framework, (2) hierarchically and temporally extended analysis of messages, (3) the concept of "rule" organized action, and (4) socially constructed "second-order" reality provide important points of metatheoretical communality between the two views of human communication. When we shift perspective from metatheory to theory, however, a number of significant differences emerge. In the next section of this chapter we will discuss the central features of CMM. In the course of our discussion we will show how our own thinking led to departures from the Interactional View.

THE COORDINATED MANAGEMENT OF MEANING

The theory of the coordinated management of meaning is derived from a central metaphor; that of human actors attempting to achieve coordination through managing the ways messages take on significance. From this central image a more complete description of human communication has emerged. In this section we will present the essential features of CMM and compare our position to that of the interactional view.

The Concept of Coordinated Management of Meaning

In CMM research we aim to explore the fundamental principles that make social coordination possible. Our efforts have led us away from a locus on the communality of experience or the extent of shared meaning between persons in a communication system. Watzlawick (1976) defined communication as "creating a shared second order reality." We argue communication is the process by which persons cocreate, maintain, and alter patterns of social order (Cronen & Pearce, 1979; Harris, 1979), but that the coordination of talk through which patterns of order emerge is *not necessarily* based on mutual understanding or a shared social reality (Cronen & Pearce, 1978; Harris, Cronen, & McNamee, 1979). Because we believe that coordination is the more basic concept we focus on the means of coordination *per se* rather than on communality of meaning. Mutual understanding we see as one way of achieving coordination.

Very significant forms of coordination occur precisely because the conversants are *not* coordinated. Cultural anthropologists have observed that Eskimo *shamans* do not share the literal interpretation of rituals common among their celebrants. The *shamans* are aware of this difference and point to the social bonding that results from the celebrations. The coordinated performances of *shamans* and celebrants is not based on a shared social reality (Campbell, 1959). Cushman (1979), too, argues against overemphasis on shared social reality as the path to coordinated conversation. Cushman says that the modern fact of cultural and ideological diversity requires a rhetoric grounded in other means. In our own case studies we have observed close personal relationships in which different assignments of meaning to the same message, and different conceptions of the logic behind a pattern of talk *facilitated* coordination.

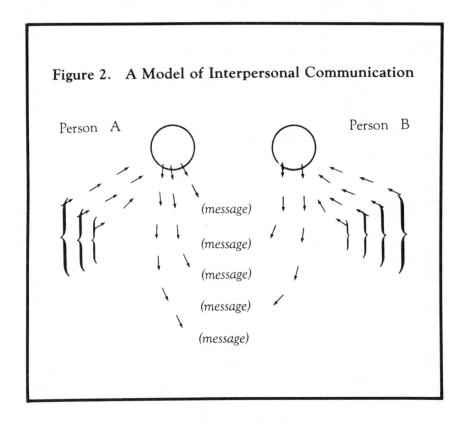

Figure 2.   A Model of Interpersonal Communication

Person A   Person B

(message)

(message)

(message)

(message)

(message)

If the most fundamental goal of talk is to generate coordination we must be specific about the minimal conditions that must be met to call a conversation "coordinated." First consider this analogy: Two motorists may successfully coordinate their driving behavior by avoiding each other on the road while inhabiting very different social realities. One may be dutifully obeying a rigid system of laws about speed, side-of-the-road, etc., while the other — the legendary Massachusetts drivers — may be spontaneously responding to the whim of the moment and the behaviors of others.

We conceptualize the process of communication as depicted in Figure 2, in which each person responds in turn to the messages/acts of the other and monitors the emerging sequence of messages, comparing it to what s/he expected and wanted. These terms seem useful in describing the conjoint construction of a communicative episode: *coherence*, or does the emerging sequence make sense to the actor; *valence*, or does the emerging sequence seem responsive to the actor's management. Obviously the actors may have quite different interpretations of the episode which they are creating. If *both* perceive the episode as coherent, we describe it as "coordinated," but note the array of patterns which may occur *within* coordinated communication: the actors may agree about the content of the episode, but disagree about valence and control; the actors may both think they know what they are collectively doing but have very different interpretations; etc. The research reported later in this chapter demonstrates that such complex patterns are not unusual

Of course we are not arguing that coordination, as we define it, is all that is important in communication. Rather, we contend that all other positive outcomes depend upon coordination. Mutual understanding, for example, may not be necessary for coordination. But mutual understanding is unlikely to develop when persons perceive the conversation they generate as lacking coherence or joint control. Coherence must of course be a precondition to the attainment of other purposes.

The Structure of Communication Systems

Every theory implies appropriate units of observation, and the appropriateness of a unit of observation depends upon the kind of order a theorist imposes on the system under study. Perhaps the most important difference between the theories lies in the concept of the structure of communication systems. Proponents of the "interactional view" explicitly deny the possibility of "getting into the heads" of individuals or the utility of knowing anything about any *individual* in the system. They describe systems "transpersonally," using only terms which denote relationships between two or more interacting persons. We fully agree that the transpersonal description of the communication system is necessary, but we do not believe that it is sufficient. Our alternative is based on Koestler's concept of the holon and on our claim that it is both possible and important to "get into the heads" of individuals.

A "holon" is an entity which is simultaneously a "whole" system and a component of a larger system.

> The concept of the holon is meant to supply the missing link between atomism and holism, and to supplant the dualistic way of thinking in terms of 'parts' and 'wholes,' which is so deeply engrained in our mental habits, by a multi-level, stratified approach. A hierarchically-organized whole cannot be 'reduced' to its elementary parts; but it can be 'dissected' into its constituent branches of holons (Koestler, 1967:197).

The term "holon" is a combination of the Greek *holos* ("whole") and the suffix -on ("part"). To think "holonically" is to view entities as "Janus-faced," simultaneously as parts and wholes. We conceptualize individuals as systems in and of themselves, with the properties of wholes. At the same time, individuals are component parts of interpersonal systems, and these systems have holistic properties not fully explainable by the characteristics of the parts. The two-leveled Janus-faced approach simultaneously uses both a transpersonal and intrapersonal level of analysis.

The "holonistic" conceptualization of communication systems has three values. First, it allows us to deal with individuals without committing the many foolishnesses of behaviorists and trait psychologists on the one hand, or losing them without a trace within larger systems as happens from the "interactional view." By modeling persons as systems, we retain Bateson's original concern for pattern, but see patterns embedded within patterns. By knowing the structure of *individuals'* information processing procedures, we can account for persons' ability to act and for the range of actions available to them in specified contexts, without trying to predict *what* act the individual will perform. By knowing the structure of *transpersonal* communication systems, we can specify the contexts within which persons act. The theory of the coordinated management of meaning consists of procedures for measuring/describing these structures, and for discovering the relationships between them.

Second, the holonic conceptualization of systems discloses that transpersonal systems are, in two ways, inherently structurally deficient. A "well-formed" cybernetic system has a superordinate monitor which extends over all parts of the system. The transactive system has no such superordinate monitor: there are multiple monitors within the system, but none has more than rudimentary access to the others. This is depicted in Figure 2: all each person knows of the other are the acts they perform. Further, the boundaries of the transpersonal system are not discrete. Each component is simultaneously a part of many other transpersonal systems, and most actions are contextualized by a poorly-defined array of relationships in which they may serve very different pragmatic functions. A demand for a raise, for example, may function quite differently in the relationship with one's employer; one's co-workers; and one's greedy spouse. We theorize that persons are variably enmeshed in any given transpersonal system, and that the extent to which they can control their enmeshment is an important consideration (cf. Harris & Cronen, 1979; Harris, 1979).

Third, the holonic conceptualization of transpersonal systems increases the ability to describe the disorder of social reality, and this provides a tie back into areas of substantive agreement between the theories.

As noted above, the Western intellectual tradition assumed that somewhere "out there," beyond the array of mere beliefs and appearances, lies an immutable order. Scientists and political reformers have frequently denounced the "contamination" of language, ideology, interpersonal communication and other foibles of humanity, which they perceive as obscuring the vision of the ultimate. In this century, however, a number of scholars have come to the conclusion that "reality" is "social," and is socially constructed. There is a reciprocal relationship between the forms of communication which occur and the concepts of reality which communicators hold, and one need not look beyond this relationship for the explanation of the contents of human knowledge or the institutions of human society. Humans seldom if ever deal with things-in-themselves; always it is with things-as-interpreted. Reflecting on the rituals and etiquette surrounding dining, Koestler (1978:74) quipped, "even while eating, man does not live by bread alone." This "second-order reality" as Watzlawick (1976) describes it, is itself both product and cause of human sociation.

Langer (1942) has called the discovery of "social reality" and the function of communication in forming and expressing it a "new key" in philosophy. It certainly inaugurs a new agenda for thought. Whitehead (1925:18) described the traditional Western view as "the trust that the ultimate natures of things live together in harmony which excludes mere arbitrariness. It is the faith that at the base of things we shall not find mere arbitrary mystery." Consider the plight of the proponents of this venerable assumption. First, the differentiation between appearances and reality was dismissed by the 16th and 17th century scientists, leaving the analyst to explain the appearances as really real. Second, communication was introduced by 20th century philosophers as the "causal force" of social reality, but communication occurs in structurally deficient systems which make communication inherently problematical. The startling conclusion: reality is more likely disordered than not, and the role of theory and research is to identify the forms and consequences of particular patterns of disorder rather than to discover the underlying calm, rational basis of the universe.

The literature of the "interactional view" is replete with nominalizations of disorder: double-binds; paradoxical injunctions; disinformation; confusion; etc. Our theory proposes the concept of "logical force," which provides a measurement model for the structure of social reality, and thus a basis for an empirically-grounded description of the varieties of disorder in social reality.

It should be noted that nothing we have said is intended to imply that a knowledge of individuals will suffice for an understanding of the interactional patterns they create. Our position is that analysis of the individuals is a meaningful *precondition* for the study of interpersonal systems and fully compatible with a general systems perspective. To us a theory of communication requires *both* individual and interpersonal levels of analysis. We fully recognize that the value of maintaining both levels must be established by its utility in both applied and basic research. While this decision must ultimately rest in the hands of the therapeutic and academic communities, our own commitment to a two-level form of analysis (individual and interpersonal) led to reexamination of both the problem of the organizing of meaning and the concept of "rules." We were impressed by the success of the constructivists following clinical psychologist George Kelly (1955) in developing ways of measuring the cognitive structures of individuals and deriving important findings from studies of the content and structure of individual differences.

Conversants' Meanings and Levels of Context

Both CMM and the Interactional View are informed by Bateson's analysis of the context-dependence of meaning. The classic statement is the analysis of the message "this is play" by monkeys at the Fleishhacker Zoo in San Francisco.

> I saw two young monkeys playing, i.e., engaged in an interactive sequence of which the unit actions or signals were similar to but not the same as those of combat. It was evident, even to the human observer, that the sequence as a whole was not combat, and evident to the human observer that to the participant monkeys this was 'not combat.'
> Now, this phenomenon, play, could only occur if the participant organism were capable of some degree of metacommunication, i.e., of exchanging signals which would carry the message 'this is play' . . . Expanded, the statement 'This is play' looks something like this: 'These actions in which we now engage do not denote that those actions *for which they stand* would denote' . . . The playful nip denotes the bite, but it does not denote what would be denoted by the bite (Bateson, 1972:179-180).

Bateson appealed to Russell's "Theory of Logical Types" to explain how this complex message could be communicated, and both theories are based on the assumption that the meaning and function of any message depends upon its location "under" more abstract meanings and before and after other messages at the same level of abstraction.

Bateson and his colleagues have described the hierarchical organization of interaction as having two levels, "content" and "relational," in which the order is fixed: relational meanings are "higher" than and thus contextualize "content" (cf. Watzlawick, Beavin & Jackson, 1967). Drawing from a variety of literatures, we argue that there are an indeterminant number of hierarchical levels and the relative order among them may vary (Pearce, Cronen & Conklin, 1980). Further, we believe that the number and relative order of these levels is an important aspect of the structure of particular individuals' interactive systems, and that this can be determined by appropriate research procedures. Figure 3 summarizes our model of hierarchical meanings in communication.

Level 1.   *Content* level meaning describes the referential function of verbal and nonverbal communication. This level of meaning was the preoccupation of the Western tradition until the later Wittgenstein (1953).

Level 2.   *Speech acts* are those things which one person does to another by saying something, such as "you are beautiful" counts as the speech act "compliment." There are many communicative events which are better understood as "performatives" rather than "declaratives," whose meanings are acts rather than referents. One of Watzlawick, Beavin and Jackson's (1967) "axioms" is that all messages invoke meaning on both "content" and "relationship" levels, with "relational" meanings comprising speech acts.

Level 3.   *Episodes* are "communicative routines which communicators view as distinct wholes, separate from other types of discourse, characterized by special rules of speech and nonverbal behavior and often distinguished by clearly recognizable opening or closing sequences." (Gumperz, 1972). They appear as patterned sequences of speech acts and establish the fields in which the rules governing speech acts exist.

Level 4.   *Relationships* are conversants' definitions of the bonds between themselves and others. The meaning of episodes differs if contexted by the relational meaning "equal partners in love" or "a real man and his obedient spouse."

Level 5.   *Life scripts* are clusters or patterns of episodes, comprising the person's expectations for the kinds of communicative events which can and probably will occur.

Level 6.   *Cultural patterns.* There are a number of archetypal patterns persons draw upon as they aggregate episodes into relationships, relationships into life scripts, etc. Hall (1977), for example, discusses the pattern of face-saving in oriental cultures and the organization of events by monochronic time in Western cultures, both of which are frames actors use to organize experience.

Our model of actors' meanings involves differences from the Interactional View that go beyond the identification of additional levels. In

Figure 3, levels 3, 4, and 5 are not assumed always to be in the same ordinal relationship to one another. Nor do we assume that levels 3, 4,
and 5 are always relevant for an actor. An actor may not, for example,
have to employ the context of life-script to interpret a prefunctory
greeting episode.

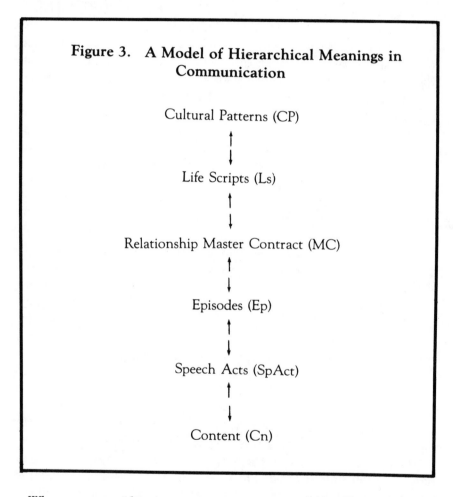

Figure 3.   A Model of Hierarchical Meanings in Communication

Cultural Patterns (CP)

Life Scripts (Ls)

Relationship Master Contract (MC)

Episodes (Ep)

Speech Acts (SpAct)

Content (Cn)

When one considers interpreting messages and forming meanings in
the *process* of temporally organized social action, certain fundamental
considerations emerge. First, it is clear that higher orders of meaning
must be inferred from lower orders; speech acts suggest what episodes
are underway, episodes suggest the kind of relationship two people are
establishing, etc. This does *not* mean that our relationship with another
is necessarily the simple sum of the episodes we perform together —

though this is sometimes the case. To have a higher-level context a social actor infers a higher-order conception such as "our relationship" from a pattern of episodes and then uses the superordinate concept to redefine and interpret the episodes themselves. This process of tacking back-and-forth between higher and lower orders of meaning has been documented by Rommetveit et al., (1971) and by Delia (1976). The interdependence of levels of meaning has profound implications for the development of relationships because it cannot always be assumed each individual has inferred a higher-order concept of relationship used to interpret episodes. In the earliest stages of a relationship particular episodes must fully define what the relationship is. Cronen and Lannamann (1979) argue that the development of a close personal relationship may be described as a movement from employing episodes as the context for defining the relationship to the evolution of relationship concept that forms the context for assigning meaning to episodes. The new relationship is a state where the question of what forms context and what is within the context is *innately* problematic. Perhaps this change in hierarchical relationships accounts for the ease with which new lovers can hurt one another by a single unexpected speech act — for the relationship is perceived through the context of unfolding action more than the other way around. When a relationship defined in specific ways assumes a position superordinate to episodes a "hurtful exchange" may be counted as evidence of fatigue or even a plea for compassion. Consider what may happen in an emerging relationship if one partner has developed a stable conception of the relationship and responds to a request for an expression of love by trying to invoke an episode of "kidding." This partner expects that the mutual commitment can be assumed, can be expressed in many different ways, and does not depend on any one particular episode. The other partner in this relationship, however, still perceives the definition of the relationship as yet indeterminant — to be inferred from this episode. The partner may be confused by the kidding or infer that theirs is not as "serious" a relationship as previously thought. A paradox may result if the recipient of the kidding cannot tell whether the unexpected episode should be interpreted in the context of what s/he believes about the relationship (e.g., the episode counts as a demonstration of the strength of our commitment — we can joke about it) or whether the relationship should be interpreted in the context of the episode (e.g., it's not a serious relationship). We suspect that developing relationships are particularly vulnerable to such confusions over logical typing.

We also suspect that people differ as to whether it is their life script that forms the context for understanding a particular relationship or whether it is a certain relationship that is the context for defining the self. Sartre first called attention to the problem when he differentiated playing the role of a waiter (which includes certain relationships and episodes) from "being" a waiter. In our research we note the possibility that some battered wives may find it difficult to terminate a dangerous relationship because they believe that crucial life-scripts are defined and infused with significance only through the husband-wife relationship. If a traditional community teaches that a woman counts as significant on-ly in the context of marriage, then the disruption of marriage poses a threat to the integration of the self concept.

One value in locating hierarchies of meanings in the heads of in-dividual actors is that it allows us to examine the juxtaposition of dif-ferent organizations of meaning in a relationship. Recent work on blue-collar communities suggests that males are taught to perceive their marital relationships through the context of life scripts that prescribe how to act like "a real man," while women are socialized to find their self concept largely through the context of the marital relationship.

Obviously, in any on-going relationship the situation is not simply which is superordinate: life script, relationship, or episodes. Some rela-tionships and episodes are more central to the life script than others. The analysis of a relationship should include efforts to find which episodes that have a *unique* function in defining the relationship — episodes which define the relationship in ways that no other episodes do. It is particularly interesting to observe how an episode that both partners perceive to be irrelevant or tangential to their relationship can later assume a position superordinate to the relationship. We have observed in new relationships how an episode like a chaotic disagree-ment over how to spend money can be passed off as reflecting the couples' individual life scripts but irrelevant to defining their relation-ship. After the couple makes a commitment to each other, however, the maintenance of economic solvency may become a larger issue and one or both partners may come to view their relationship differently because of this episode. Their relationship comes to be seen as a conflicted one between people with different values where earlier it was a very compati-ble relation between two people who happen to, on occasion, argue about money.

Our extended conception of meaning is thus thoroughly infused with the spirit of Bateson's original insights but differs in these ways: 1) Addi-tional levels of context are identified. 2) The organization of meaning is assumed to be flexible thus facilitating the juxtaposing of individual systems as a way of analyzing relationships. 3) The evolution of relationships is analyzed in terms of changes in position among elements in the hierarchy. 4) Paradox — confusions about logical typing — can occur at a variety of levels of meaning.

Rules and the Integration of Actors' Meanings

Both theories employ the concept of rules to account for the structure of social reality, but they mean quite different things by the term. For those in the "interactional view," rules are defined as "behavioral redundancies," or recurring sequences of actions, and they function by governing the homeostatic adjustments of the transpersonal system. We define rules as descriptions of the ways individuals process meanings. A system of rules comprises a "logic" of what things mean and what acts ought to follow what other acts. These rule systems represent each individual, but they are so structured that they are triggered by the acts of other people. When two or more persons exchange interactions, the "logic" of the interpersonal system consists of the interface of the logics of each person's intrapersonal system.

Requirements for a Structural Account of Communication Rules..   Theorists in a variety of disciplines have suggested "rule" as a descriptor of the facts that 1) social action exhibits regularities even though persons *can* behave in capricious or disruptive ways; 2) persons critique others and are held accountable for their actions in a way in which inanimate objects are not; and 3) persons perceive an "oughtness" or "expectedness" in their social actions, sometimes so strongly that they report — quite contrary to the fact — that they "could not" do other than they did, or that they had "no choice." A rule, unlike a "norm," may but need not to be socially shared. The theory of the coordinated management of meaning is unique in that it takes seriously the question of the structure of a rule. Other theorists have proffered declarative statements, imperative statements or grammatical re-write statements as instances of rules. These fail because the structure of language is so dissimilar to the structure of information-processing which humans perform as they communicate with each other. Rules are treated in CMM theory as organizations of a person's cognitions. The form chosen for representing rules was based upon our reading of a number of literatures all leading us to these requirements:

1) We cannot assume a simple isomorphism of meaning and action. While meaning and action are related, the experience of social psychologists working with the problem of predicting behavior suggests that the assignment of meaning to a situation does not fully entail the kind of action that is deemed appropriate nor the degree of obligation to act (Argyle, 1976).

2) As Koestler (1978) noted, acts are hierarchically contexted such that the meaning of the part is informed by the meaning of the whole. A number of studies have described the assignment of meaning to messages as a process of "tacking back and forth" between higher and lower level meanings (cf. Delia, 1976; Rommetveit et al., 1971).

3) Temporally antecedent conditions have been shown to contextualize — in this case, alter the probability of the occurrence of — subsequent conditions. Bales (1955), Stech (1975), Raush (1965, 1974) and Penman (1977) have found that certain types of messages tend to follow specified other types. Argyle (1976) found that situational factors consistently account for a greater percentage of the variance in behavior than personality traits, and clinical studies show that a failure to adjust messages according to antecedent conditions is a sign of psychological disorder (Moos, 1968).

4) Temporally consequent conditions — or the expectation that a given behavior will elicit a particular response — also contextualize sequences of behaviors. Bruner's (1975) analysis of mother-infant dyads, Pribram's (1976) studies of primate behavior, and Maier and Solem's (1962) small group process research all demonstrate the effect of desired or expected consequences on current behavior.

5) While human beings can act purposively, they often report that their own action was not predicated upon the strategic selection of action to achieve a particular purpose. Persons often claim that their behavior is "forced" or required by the nature of their situation — that they could not act otherwise. This kind of reaction-to-situation response is evident in Jones and Davis' (1969) studies of attribution.

Figure 4.   The Structural Model of a Cognitive Rule (cR)

Primitive form:

$$M_k$$
$$A \;) \; [M_i \quad M_j]$$

Where: A = Antecedent condition
) = Read "if ... then"
⌐ = Read "in the content of"
M = Actor's meaning
i,j.k = Level of abstraction
→ → → = Read "counts as"

Sample cR with some specified levels of abstraction:

$$Ep$$
$$A \;) \; [Cn \;\rightarrow\; SpAct]$$

Sample cR with specified content:

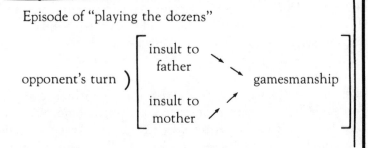

Episode of "playing the dozens"

opponent's turn) [insult to father / insult to mother] gamesmanship

With the foregoing requirements as guides, Cronen and Pearce (1978) developed structural models for individual actors' rules. The rules of two or more actors conjoin to form logics of conversation as we will show in a subsequent section. The careful reader will note that the operators used in these rules reflect our debt to the work of von Wright (1951), G. Spencer Brown (1972), Varela (1975) and Toulmin (1958).

Two types of rules are distinguished; constructive rules that define meanings within contexts, and regulative rules that assign degrees of appropriateness to action. This distinction follows Searle's (1969) work in linguistic philosophy and is consistent with our reading of the recent literature in social psychology. The primitive forms of regulative and constitutive rules are shown in Figures 4 and 5.

Constitutive Rules. Constitutive rules specify how meanings at one level of abstraction "count as " meaningful at the same or at a different level. For example, the statement "you are beautiful" counts as the speech act "compliment" — at least sometimes. Given the contextualization "dating," this constitutive rule may describe how persons process information. However, given the context of "argument," quite a different "speech act" or "relational" meaning may be invoked. Note that the various levels of the hierarchy model are linked by constitutive rules, and the interpretations of particular messages may be multiply contexted: in the episode "playing the dozens," a statement describing an improbable act with one's mother counts as the speech act "gamesmanship" and leads to a "retort"; outside that episode, the same statement counts as "grievous-insult" and leads to "retaliation."

The primitive form of a constitutive rule may be algebraicized as shown in Figure 4. This primitive form specifies that in a certain context, if specific antecedent conditions are satisfied, then meaning at one level of abstraction counts as meaning at another level of abstraction. For example, constitutive Rule 1 in Figure 4 should be read: In the context of the episode "playing the dozens," if it is the opponent's turn, then an insult to my mother and an insult to my father both count as 'gamesmanship.' " To "play the dozens" successfully, both players must share constitutive rules 1 and 2 among others.

Constitutive rules do not guide behavior. Rather, they identify the components of regulative rules and link meanings at different levels of abstraction.

Regulative Rules. The primitive form of a regulative rule may be algebraicized as shown in Figure 5. This form specifies that in the context of certain social action, if given antecedent conditions obtain, then there exists some degree of force for or against the performance of subse-

Figure 5.   The Structure Model of a Regulative Rule (rR)

Primitive form of a regulative rule:

$$\text{ACTN}_j$$

$$[\text{A} \,)\, (\text{Do}(\text{ACTN}_i))_{1\text{-}n}] \,)\, \text{C}_{1\text{-}n}$$

Where: rR   =   Regulative rule
A   =   Antecedent condition
ACTN   =   Action
i, j   =   Level of abstraction
Do   =   Deontic operator (obligatory, legitimate, prohibited, undetermined). The Do is not employed in the measurement model (Fig. 6) as it represents an ordinal measure of all forces operating on the action at level.
)   =   Read "if ... then"
¬   =   Read "in the context of"
C   =   Consequent conditions

Sample rR showing some specific levels of abstraction:

$$\text{MC}$$
$$\text{Ep}$$
$$[\text{A} \,)\, (\text{Do}(\text{SpAct}))_{1\text{-}n}] \,)\, \text{C}$$

rR with sample content:

Life Script of "A Brother"

| Young other initiates playing the dozens |) | (Legitimate (Engage in episode of playing the dozens)) (Legitimate (Scoff at that "kids game")) |) | Maintain Status in the group |

quent actions. The primitive form further indicates that within a context of social action if an antecedent condition is followed by specified action(s), then some consequences ought or ought not to follow. For example, regulative Rule 1 in Figure 5 should be read: In the episode of playing the dozens, if the opponent insults my parent, then it is obligatory to top his/her last insult in order to avoid the consequence of losing the game.

A Measurement Model for Rules

The various components of a rule are depicted as interrelated, but these primitive, algebraic formulas are merely place-makers for linkages which may vary widely in strength. In this sense, the formulas serve as measurement models, for we do not assume the entailments on acts within various rules to be similar. In fact, we expect the same speech act to be, e.g., obligatory for different persons but for very different reasons expressed as a different pattern of linkages within their rules. For example, some rules are non-specific as to the temporal antecedent of action. In initial interaction, there seems to be a consensual rule obligating equivalent speaking *at all times* during the episode. Similarly, the consequent may have a variable entailment to the act: some acts are "functionally autonomous" while others are "purposive," and these are differentiated by the strength of the act-to-consequent linkage. Finally, not all human actors link their acts to elaborated episodes and/or life-scripts. Like poor chess players, their acts are determined by the other's immediately preceding "move" rather than a temporally-durative strategy. These differences should appear in the relative strengths of the antecedent-to-act and episode-to-act linkages.

Figure 6 depicts the array of linkages the strength of which may be measured in any regulative rule. Not shown in the figure are the valences of each component, and the range of acts legitimated by a particular rule. The various configurations of these measurements depict different forms and strengths of logical force. For example, the linkage between the temporal antecedent and a particular act is measured by a Likert-type scale as shown below:

The situation/preceding message seemed to require me to respond with act _____ .

strongly agree__:__:__:__:__:__:__ strongly disagree

Figure 6.   A Measurement Model of Rule Structure

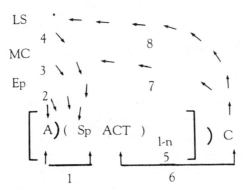

Prefigurative forces   *Practical forces*

1: Act — Antecedent linkage	6: Act — Consequent linkage
2: Episode — Sp Act linkage	(Function autonomy)
3: Master contract — Sp Act linkage	7: Consequent — Master contract
4: Life script — Sp Act linkage	(relationship) linkage
5: Range of alternate acts	8: Consequent — Life script linkage

The deontic operator is removed for purposes of measurement because it reflects the sum of prefigurative and practical forces influencing the choice of action.

This measure describes the extent to which a person perceives a given act as necessary given some preceding message or situation. The scale reflects degrees of obligation from very strong (obligatory) to weak (it doesn't matter). Another example is our Likert-type scale that measures the linkage of a speech act to intended consequent(s).

I would have to perform this act regardless of what the other person would say or do next.

strongly agree__:_:_:_:_:_ strongly disagree

This item measures the extent to which the choice of speech act is predicated upon its effects or functionally autonomous of consequents.

Similar scales are used to measure other relationships shown in Figure 6. Likert scales have also been developed to measure the desirability of responses and the predictability of responses. Some of our other protocols require that the researcher obtain a script of an episode. A set of scales reflecting linkage strengths for rules are then successively applied to each act in the episode. The conversants are of course interviewed separately for this procedure. The technique permits us to isolate what kind of forces seem to prefigure each conversant's action and to what degree they feel their choice of action to be "determined" by the pattern of action. One conversant may feel that his/her actions are "required" by the nature of the antecedent comments and by the requirements of their relationship, yet feel that it is their self concept that allows more latitude of action. We have also studied episodes in which one conversant's choice of action is contingent upon the consequents expected while the other reports their actions as prefigured — things they feel obligated to say regardless of what the other will do or say next.

The Logic of Conversation

The juxtaposition of rules having the form described above creates an array of potential lines of action because the rule-governed act of each person is interpreted (by the other's constitutive rules) as the antecedent condition of the other's regulative rules, which entails with some measurable amount of logical force a subsequent action, which the first interprets as the antecedent condition of one of his own regulative rules, etc. (see Figure 7).

Logics incorporate feedback when the speech act which one person performs is compared to the intended consequent in the rule governing the preceding act by the other. Unpredicted reponses may lead to a renegotiation of the contextualizing episode. For example, a teenage boy at dinner may make a request such as "may I have the car tonight?" The unexpected consequent "how's the soup?" indicates to him that his parent does not want to continue the episode of "who gets the car" because the unexpected statement about soup seems to have no place in that episode.

Figure 7.   A Logic of Conversation Formed by the Linking of Two Persons

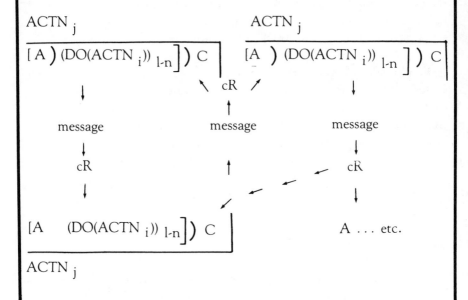

The arrows linking Others action back to one's own intended consequent (C) show feedback; the comparison of intended to observed outcomes.

Alterations in a logic are produced when individuals' rules change in content or structure. Such change may be occasioned when actors perceive (1) consequents that are undesired and (2) freedom of action to alter their communication behavior. Suppose an actor realizes that Other's use of profanity in a particular episode counts for Other as "informality" rather than "blasphemy." Taking the role of the Other — that is, reconstructing Other's rule system — the actor may develop new rules such as these:

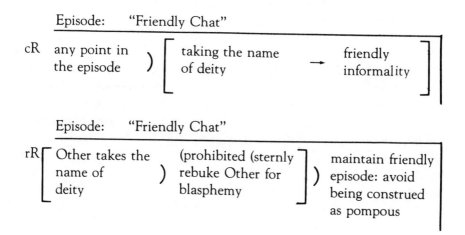

Episode: "Friendly Chat"

cR   any point in the episode) [taking the name of deity → friendly informality]

Episode: "Friendly Chat"

rR [Other takes the name of deity) (prohibited (sternly rebuke Other for blasphemy]) maintain friendly episode: avoid being construed as pompous

Suppose, however, that the actor in our example is a fundamentalist minister who uses these rules:

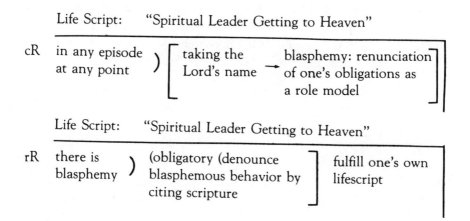

Life Script: "Spiritual Leader Getting to Heaven"

cR   in any episode at any point) [taking the Lord's name → blasphemy: renunciation of one's obligations as a role model]

Life Script: "Spiritual Leader Getting to Heaven"

rR   there is blasphemy) (obligatory (denounce blasphemous behavior by citing scripture] fulfill one's own lifescript

The existence of very strong linkage of the speech act "denounce blasphemy ..." to the minister's life script, plus the conviction that messages have obligatory, or "true" meanings which are not open to negotiation might lead the minister to continue following his regulative rule even if one outcome of its use is to prematurely terminate friendly conversations. Exploiting every possible stereotype of clinical and social psychologists, we invented a poorly coordinated conversation which illustrates the power of this logic to explain communication. Both persons relied on the "logic" of their rule systems to supply information which contextualized and interpreted the other's statement, and which guided their subsequent behavior. However, the "episodes which they drew upon as a description of what they were doing with each other differed enough to make each successive message *reduce* the extent to which they reciprocally understood each other. This hypothetical but not unrealistic conversation is analyzed in Figure 8.

The significance of this example lies in the fact that each person acted reasonably and consistently within his own rules and that these rules are not flagrantly pathological. However, the conjoint product of their sequential interaction was incoherent. Further, assuming that each person's rule system has a relatively stable structure, recurrent communication problems of this kind are attributable to the poor "fit" between the content and structure of their rule systems. Two social psychologists would have unproblematic, if somewhat brief, greeting episodes and two clinical psychologists would have unproblematic, if relatively long, pleasant conversations. In either case, the processes of conversation may be accounted for by citing the rule structure.

Types of Logical Force

Explanations of human action have traditionally been differentiated as "reasons" and "causes." "Reasons" stipulate cognitive, goal-oriented actions, and "causes" denote reactive responses to antecedent events. We follow this traditional differentiation but subsume both within the larger concept of "logical force."

Prefigurative logical force describes a cluster of linkages within the measurement model of rule structure in which the "act" is "prefigured" by the person's prior concept of who s/he is, the episode, the relationship, the antecedent act, and his/her range of options. For example, Philipsen's (1975) ethnography of "Teamsterville" indicates that "speak-

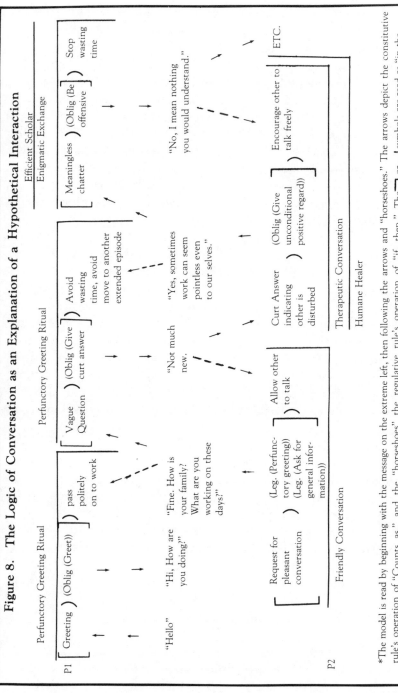

Figure 8. The Logic of Conversation as an Explanation of a Hypothetical Interaction

*The model is read by beginning with the message on the extreme left, then following the arrows and "horseshoes." The arrows depict the constitutive rule's operation of "Counts as," and the "horseshoes" the regulative rule's operation of "if, then." The ⌐ or ⌐ symbols are read as "in the context of."

**P1 is a social psychologist and P2 is a clinical psychologist.

ing like a man" involves strong prefigurative forces. Informants report that when one is *having an argument in a bar* (episode), and someone *insults your wife* (antecedent event), a *real man* (lifescript) has *no choice* (range of options) but to *fight* (act).

Practical logical force describes another cluster of linkages within the measurement model of rule structure in which the act itself "prefigures" subsequent definitions of self, episode, relationship and the consequent act. Continuing the example from Philipsen's study, fighting when one's wife has been insulted is a sure way to *establish respect* for one's manly prowess (consequent), *end the argument* (episode), *affirm my own identity* (life script) and *prove that my wife is respectable* (relationship).

In general, prefigurative force is synonymous with the general usage of "s/he did that *because of* . . .," and practical force with the general usage of "s/he did that *in order to* . . ." Given the rules for barroom behavior in Teamsterville, it is no wonder that fights are so frequent and/or insults to wives so rare: the logical force is so strong that the episode "fight" is easily triggered and then proceeds inexorably.

The symmetry of prefigurative and practical forces described in this example is probably very atypical. More often, the prefigurative and practical forces will differ in strength, and often there will be complex and confusing pattern making "simple" action impossible. For example, assume that a particular act has a strong direct linkage to a desired episode and an equally strong but *inverse* linkage to a desired relationship: that is, doing the act is certain to accomplish one goal while precluding another. It is possible to play with the various combinations of linkages in a manner reminiscent of the old "balance theories," and in the process describe "double binds," "triple binds," and other denizens of the bestiary of disordered social reality. In addition to providing a toy for twisted minds, the procedure suggests the beginnings of an algorithm of various sorts of binds, leading to a better description than ever before of the patterns and violations of patterns which Bateson (1957) announced as his concern. Further, it provides a way of utilizing the power of *quantitative* descriptions of pattern, in a way which Bateson (1979) apparently did not think possible.

Rule Structure and Episode Types

Episodes are jointly produced by persons acting in the context of the interpersonal system of rules resulting from the intermeshing of their intrapersonal rule systems. Since rules exhibit variable structural properties, expressed as different patterns of the strengths of the linkages among the components of the measurement model described above, we can deduce the proposition that differently structured rules will produce differently structured episodes. For theoretic purposes, we generated a preliminary taxonomy of episodes based on some of the rule structure variables which would be found in the interpersonal system of each, as shown in Figure 8.

The shape of the argument may be illustrated briefly. An *enigmatic episode* is one in which actors do not know how to act or what act will evoke specific consequences. In enigmatic episodes there should be very weak perceived linkages of life-script, antecedents or consequents to any speech act the actor may consider. The range of possible acts is unknown and valence of consequents tends to be negative as the actor's tentative efforts are followed by long pauses, puzzled expressions, irritation or outright rejection by those who know what is appropriate. Thus, as a whole, the enigmatic episode has a negative valence.

An *unwanted, repetitive pattern* is one in which the conversants feel enmeshed in a pattern beyond their control. Much attention has been given to the phenomenon of enmeshment — episodes that the participants cannot seem to break out of even though the conversants claim that they do not wish such episodes to occur. This phenomenon has been observed in families by Minuchin (1974) and in formal organizations by Walton (1969). Many subjects in our research program have little or no trouble identifying unwanted repetitive patterns in their own experience. From the perspective of CMM unwanted repetitive patterns represent an imbalance of certain prefigurative and practical forces shown in Figure 9. An episode we predict will feel out of control when the regulative rules underlying it possess these characteristics: strong antecedent-act linkage, narrow range of alternative speech acts, acts that tend to be functionally autonomous of consequents, strong act-life script linkage and undesirable consequent acts. As noted in Figure 9, episode is not a relevant level of context. Because the pattern created is simply the byproduct of other forces and not an orienting conception that conversants use to guide their actions.

Value expressive rituals are predicted to entail strong linkages of antecedents, life-scripts, and episode to speech acts at each talking turn. Unlike unwanted repetitive patterns, however, strong act-consequent linkages are predicted to exist. The episode itself is a purposely created entity, unlike the "unwanted repetitive pattern." In a religious ceremony that has great significance for a participant, the participant is predicted to feel that his/her acts are obligatory because of the antece-

Figure 9.   Analytic Schema

EPISODE TYPES

Structural Variables	Coordinated Management	Alienating Sequence	Positive Spiral	Unwanted Repetitive Pattern	Perfunctory Ritual	Value Expressive Ritual	Eigmatic Episode
Antecedent-Speech Act Linkage	Moderate to Strong	Moderate to Strong	Very Strong	Very Strong	Very Strong	Very Strong	Very Weak
Episode-Speech Act Linkage	Strong	Strong	None[a]	None[a]	Strong	Very Strong	Very Weak
Life-Script-Speech Act Linkage	Strong	Very Weak	Strong	Strong	Weak	Very Strong	Very Weak
Speech-Act-Consequent Linkage	Strong	Strong	Functional Autonomy	Functional Autonomy	Strong	Very Strong	Very Weak
Range of Alternative Speech Acts	High	Moderate	Narrow	Narrow	Very Narrow	Very Narrow	UNK
Consequent Valence	POS.	POS.	POS.	NEG.	NEUT.	POS.	NEG.
Episode Valence	POS.	NEG.	POS.	NEG.	NEUT.	Very POS.	NEG.

a = Actors do not intend the maintenance of episode and may only be aware of the episodic punctuation *post hoc* as in the gloss "Oh, Darn." "We did it again."

UNK = Unknown

dent condition (for example, the youngest child at a Passover Seder has asked the "four questions"), because of the consequent (the act of responding to the "four questions" is necessary to bring about the next part of the service), because of the episode (the actor strongly wishes to bring about a well-run service), and because of a life-script (the actor feels that his/her speech act in this episode is required by their self-concept — i.e., observant Jew). The consequent acts should be positively valenced and the valence of the whole episode very positive. On the other hand, if the celebrant regards the ceremony as a *prefunctory* rather than as a value expressive ritual, it is predicted that the linkage of act to life-script would be weak, and the valence of the episode and consequent acts less positive. In either type of ritual, the range of alternative acts is low or non-existent.

EXPLANATORY AND PREDICTIVE VALUE: RESEARCH

One of the scientific virtues which we have claimed for the theory of the Coordinated Management of Meaning is that it is amenable to empirical research. Granted that the quantity of research thus far conducted is modest, the array of projects we have completed demonstrates that the theory is in principle testable. We have developed an array of research protocols including simulation games and computer simulations of rule systems, case studies of families and formal organizations, and an interview protocol of rule structures in particular forms of episodes.

Simulations and Nomothetic Studies

Because our theory is derived from the philosophical position of Harre and Madden (1975) and systems theory, simulations are particularly appropriate forms of research since they provide demonstrations of the logical force within "interpersonal communication systems" which varied in predetermined ways in both content and structure. In order to demonstrate the operation of logical force, we programmed a computer to produce "conversations" by generating strings of acts in which each is a rule-following response to the previous act. This generated a quantitative value for the "amount" of logical force within each system: the *fewer* the number of *different* sequences, the stronger the logical force (Cronen et al., 1978). Further, we found that the logical force within the interpersonal system may be greater or smaller than that which each person has within his/her intrapersonal system. In some cases, a person is constrained from utilizing the flexibility apparent within his/her own rules system by interacting with particular others; in other cases, the individual is "liberated" by enmeshment in the interpersonal system. These findings have implications in two areas. First, continued work may derive specific relationships between various aspects of the form of rule structures and the amount of logical force. Second, we assume that persons communicating in rule systems having different properties will respond differently to each other and to the situation.

To test the latter assumption, our research group conducted two studies in which university students played a conversational simulation game using the same rules we had built into the computer (Pearce *et al.*, 1979; Johnson, 1979). Differences in logical force, manipulated by providing the subjects various rule systems, resulted in different perceptions of themselves, of their "conversational" partner, and of the way they collectively played the game. We were particularly interested to learn that the subject's perceptions of the other person's "competence" was highly related to perceptions of their own competence. This and other findings have important implications for understanding the development of social identities and relationships.

Recently our research group conducted a more traditional test of the concepts of prefigurative and practical forces and of participants' psychological reaction to episodes where prefigurative forces predominate (for a complete report see: Cronen, Pearce, & Snavely, 1979). We focused our attention on this dependent variable: to what extent do conversants feel themselves enmeshed in unwanted repetitive patterns beyond their control? Thirty-two subjects supplied dialogues of various types, one dialogue per subject. Each subject was interviewed and measures of rule structure and desirability of Other's responses were applied to each of the subject's own messages in the dialogue. Scaled values were averaged for all messages across the episode and cast into the following regression formula:

$$PE = \overline{X} \, ARF \, w_1 \; + \; \overline{X} \, Act\text{-}Ls \, w_2 \; + \; \overline{X} \, D \, w_3$$

where: PE = perceived enmeshment in the episode

$\overline{X}$ ARF = mean value of the products of act-antecedent linkage X range of alternative acts X degree of functional autonomy;

$\overline{X}$ Act-Ls = mean value of act-lifescript linkage;
$\overline{X}$ D = mean desirability of consequent acts;

w = empirically determined weights

This formula accounted for over 50 percent of the varience in subjects' perceived enmeshment in unwanted repetitive patterns of talk. All three factors made significant independent contributions to the model's predictive power, with the ARF variable accounting for the largest proportion of the varience.

The results of this study confirm the predictions made in one column of Figure 9. The rest of the figure may be interpreted as a series of testable hypotheses which potentially falsify the theory. The value of this line of reasoning goes beyond the formal apparatus of theory contruction, however; the systemic relationship between rule structures and types of episodes has great potential for therapeutic intervention and for assessing the potential of communications within particularly structured, e.g., business organizations.

Ray and Donna: A Case Study

The existence of convoluted logics of coordinated management of meaning is revealed in a case study of a normally functioning family (i.e., one which has not sought therapy or reported distress).

The purpose of this study was to describe the logic by which the family moves through their social reality and to observe the communication patterns by which they create and maintain this logic. The results confirmed the assumption of the mutually causal relation between communication and the social order and demonstrated the heuristic value of combining the two communication theories cited above. The logic discovered was curiously contorted in such a way that it perpetuated a form of communication which was simultaneously identified as the couple's greatest conflict and chief strength. This paradoxical logic is manifest in a mutually inconsistent premise at the "life-script" level of meaning. Other inconsistencies were exposed in a crucial "confrontation episode." One is akin in structure to the classic paradox:

All Statements In This Box Are False

A triangulated methodology, consisting of interview, written self reports, and role-playing, was used to elicit the couple's constitutive and regulative rules. Specifically, the analysis revealed paradoxical rules associated with restricted episodes in which the couple can not obtain their goal of eliminating conflict (see Harris, 1980 for a complete report of this study).

Individual and joint interviews revealed that the Flynn family (a pseudonym) are well-educated and have been influenced by college courses and social norms endorsing open communication, individualistic priorities, personal growth and rebellion against traditional middle class *mores*. This family was selected for study because they demonstrated exceptional communication skills in a screening interview.

Two episodes are described by the Flynns. A "conflict" episode is the classic "withdrawal-nag" mispunctuation described by Watzlawick, Beavin and Jackson (1967) in which Mr. Flynn attributes his lack of physical demonstrativeness to Mrs. Flynn's nagging, while Mrs. Flynn cites his withdrawal as the cause of her nagging. The "confrontation" episode features self-disclosure, validation and acceptance in which they try to eliminate the conflict episode. The energy expended during these confrontations is interpreted by the Flynns as an indication *of the strength* of their relationship.

Mr. and Mrs. Flynn agree that the life-script of their relationship consists of cyclical patterns of conflict followed by confrontation/resolution. They both maintain the contradictory beliefs that their personal characteristics which produce conflict are 1) inherent and unchangable; and 2) produced as a response to the other's behavior. The paradox produced by these beliefs is handled by dissociation: the "inherent" premise is affirmed during confrontation and leads to acceptance, while the "response" is affirmed during conflict and leads to tension. Their continued explicit validation of their unchangeable behaviors has solidified their belief that nagging and lack of physical affection are indeed personality flaws which must be tolerated. Consequently, they have institutionalized the belief that "we can't change." When the Flynns confront one another concerning the undesirability of their behaviors they punctuate the conflict episode such that one's behavior "causes" the unwanted behavior of the other. The agreed punctuation of the undesirable events has institutionalized a second belief that "we must change." Consequently, the Flynn's communication has produced a contradictory rule: *we can't change — we must change.*

The episode and life-script rules as perceived by the Flynns are illustrated in Figure 10. The contradiction between the simultaneous interpretation of behavior as "inherent" and as "responsive to other," coupled with a dissimilar sensitivity to "tension" on the life-script level, however, has produced a complication resulting in an unnoticed "negotiation" episode which institutionalizes the disliked "conflict" episode. The Flynns have different constitutive rules for the "tension" sufficient to invoke the life-script regulative rule which mandates that tension must be reduced by the confrontation episode. Specifically, Mrs. Flynn's constitutive rules have a lower threshold of what counts as intolerable tension than Mr. Flynn's. Consequently, she finds it impossible to follow the rule:

rR   "—if intolerable tension, then it is obligatory to enact 'confrontation' so that tension can be reduced"

because Mr. Flynn will not coordinate "confrontation" with her. Thus she acts as if she were following the rules:

rR   "—if intolerable tension, then it is permissable to nag so that confrontation will occur";

rR   "—if I nag and confrontation does not occur, then it is obligatory to increase nagging";

cR   "—if I nag and he withdraws, it is obligatory to construe withdrawal as increased tension";

cR   "—getting emotional counts as the ultimate in nagging."

These behaviors intermesh with Mr. Flynn's rules so as to force the cycle of increasing tension-conflict-confrontation. His rules are:

rR   "—if she nags, it is permissable for me to withdraw so that I can avoid tension";

rR   "—if she gets emotional, then we must have confrontation to reduce tension."

Conflict thus becomes a necessary strategic way of producing confrontation which is interpreted as a solution for inherent, unavoidable conflict. Further, they are unable to enact the mutually desired "confrontation" episode without first engaging in the "conflict" episode which they both identify as their primary relational problem. The Flynns perceive this pattern as an adaptive cycle rather than a vicious circle because they maintain disassociated affirmation of the contradictory beliefs "our behavior is inherent in our personalities" and "our behavior is in response to each other."

Further probing into the Flynns' analysis of their relationship revealed their own version of the problem of logical types, which prohibited them from reaching any three of their goals efficiently, frequently or to their satisfaction. The problem is exposed in these constitutive rules:

> Ray cR: In the context of conflict, Donna's attempts to confront the conflict count as nagging.

> Donna cR: In the context of conflict, Ray's refusals to confront the conflict count as withdrawing.

A joint life script rule emerges:

> In this relationship *attempts* to confront and *refusals* to confront count as hostile behaviors which obligate reciprocal hostile behaviors (i.e., nagging and withdrawing).

The two episodes being described here are not discrete. One, the conflict episode in which two recurrent behaviors obligate the enactment of each other creates an undesirable but unavoidable cycle with no beginning or end. The second episode is the confrontation in which the goal is to eliminate the conflict — a meta episode. A paradox exists at the episodic level where the conflict episode, which is cyclical and hostile in nature, is embedded in its meta confrontation episode, which is goal-oriented and friendly in nature. Specifically, the episode for eliminating the nagging and withdrawing cycle *contains* the nagging and withdrawing cycle. *This paradox, stated formally might be: All statements in this friendly episode are hostile.* It is usually impossible for either of them to know whether an act of initiating or refusing to initiate counts as undesirable behaviors which obligates the complementary undesirable behavior, or whether it counts as a signal that a tension threshold has

---

Figure 10. Model of the Flynn's Paradoxical Logic

	Life Script	— Donna — Intolerant — Ray — Undemonstrative We must change / we can't change We are committed to an open, loving relationship
Confounded	Management Episode	All acts in this friendly episode are hostile
	Episode	Must demonstrate undesirable behavior in order to demonstrate love
	Speech Acts	Nagging/withdraw

---

been reached. This is further confounded by the fact that Donna's lower tolerance level legitimates her efforts to confront sooner and more often, reinforcing her "bitchiness" and Ray's "lack of attention."

The Flynn's communication skills function to perpetuate this logic of conversation. Their metacommunication has allowed them to construe conflict, including simple punctuation problems, as inevitable given their personalities and as a sign of the health and vitality of their relationship. Ignoring the ethical questions about intervention, it seems obvious to us that change in this relationship would not likely be induced by skills training but would be effected if either or both acted in ways inconsistent with the rules of the relationship; for example, if Mr. Flynn violated the rule that Mrs. Flynn's emotionalism obligates confrontation. Specifically, the logic would be altered perhaps significantly if Mr. Flynn periodically initiated "confrontation" without the presence of intolerable tension.

Dave and Jan: A Case Study

Qualitative and quantitative methods were brought together in another case study, this one of a cohabiting couple we shall call Dave and Jan. This study not only illustrates the use of our rule structure measures for analyzing particular relationships but also illustrates the way couples can achieve coordination through other means than establishing a shared social reality. The researchers (for a full report see: Harris, Cronen & McNamee, 1979) focused on an episode that Dave and Jan both said was typical of their relationship: getting Jan to look for a job.

The couple believes that economic realities require her additional income so that they can continue to live together. They must pay rent, buy food, etc. Of course, Jan would need to have income if she and Dave split up, but the couple sees the economic situation as a relationship problem. The importance of the episode we have chosen goes beyond the particular problem of Jan's employment. Both see this episode as reflecting the fundamental problem in their relationship: Dave's search for a nondominant role, and Jan's life script which requires a dominant other to impel her to assertive action. Dave expressed the importance of the job-seeking episode when he told the interviewer, "What we're really fighting is the dependency thing" which is "a much bigger issue than finding a job."

This episode depicts a convoluted interpersonal logic. In essence, Jan's intrapersonal logic takes the simple form of an invitation to Dave: "Make me assertive." This invitation is similar in structure to the "be spontaneous" paradox Watzlawick (1976) has discussed. From Dave's perspective this invitation "forces" him to perform undesirable acts in order to achieve a desired goal. For example, the "ultimatum" is interpreted as a dominant act but a necessary one for "making her less dependent." Dave's logic then takes the simple form of a response to her invitation: "In order to make you my equal, I must be dominant."

This episode culminates in a message where Dave gives explicit instructions for what Jan should do. Jan says that this is for her an "ultimatum" — which in turn spurs her to action. This is just what Jan wants. Jan told the interviewer that she will reinitiate the episode later if she does not get what, in her constitutive rules, counts as an ultimatum. For Dave, however, the same message counts as a backing down. "I'm telling her everything will be okay, what's past doesn't matter, she can just start fresh tomorrow." Thus, Dave believes that he is acting to move out of the dominating position by this act; no longer holding Jan's inactivity over her head. The result of this particular enactment, we subsequently learned, was that Jan did in fact interview for a job the next day and was hired. The *lack* of agreement on the meaning of a particular message is precisely how this couple succeeds in spite of a convoluted logic.

The quantitative analysis indicated how different the structural features of the two persons were. The researchers employed the variables used in the nomothetic study of unwanted repetitive episodes plus two additional variables. A scale was included to measure episode-act linkage or the degree to which an act was felt to be required by the pattern of action conversants were in, and another to measure consequent-lifescript linkage or the degree to which a person felt that he/she had to obtain a certain response in order to create the desired self image. The Mann-Whitney U Test, a nonparametric test appropriate for very small samples, was used to compare Dave and Jan's responses to measures of rule structure using the .05 criterion for statistical significance.

Three significant differences emerged. Across the episode Dave's scores for act-consequent linkage were significantly lower than Jan's, (U = 12.5, p ◄ .05) while Jan's life-script-act linkages were significantly higher than Dave's (U = 10.5, p ◄ .025), and her life-script-desired consequents linkages were significantly lower than Dave's (U = 12, p ◄ .05).

These results support the conclusion that Jan was *incorrect* in her perception that Dave *purposively* gives her a "kick" into action when he knows she needs it. It is Jan who is operating more purposively adjusting her acts to a conception of the response she wants from Dave. Jan's speech acts, together with Dave's conception of the episode sets up a pattern of prefigurative forces that channelize his action. Indeed, Dave's *most* functionally autonomous acts are those which lead up to and include the "ultimatum" or "kick" Jan wants him to give her. Consistent with our qualitative data Dave's life-script-act linkages are significantly lower than Jan's. He wishes to avoid the dominant role while Jan's life script requires her to use Dave to correct her laziness. The quantitative findings are also consistent with Jan's claim that she is innately lazy and that nothing can change this. The desired consequent-life script linkages for Jan are much weaker than Dave's. Jan's life script entails certain actions, but the consequences she desires from those actions could not from her perspective alter her life-script.

In the job hunting episode, Jan acts purposively by acting lazy forcing Dave into a dominant position while Dave acts "passively" by doing what is required. The resulting episode is a jointly coordinated one in which each act logically follows the preceding one. These acts and the actors', compatible but different, interpretations fit into the coordinated episode of cross purposes. It is jointly controlled in that its enactment requires the cooperative effort of each participant to "misinterpret appropriately."

Because the episode is coordinated does not, however, mean that it is in all respects desirable. There is no resolution of Dave's confounded logic which we have stated as "I must make you assertive." Dave's actions must, of course, perpetuate Jan's system. He must take the dominant position because his sense of self and master contract require him to initiate these role dominant episodes and Jan deliberately creates conditions that entail Dave's initiation of these episodes. Dave wants a non-dominant, symmetrical relationship with Jan, but the logic created by the conjoining of their rules perpetuates the current situation.

We believe that these case studies show how CMM can be used to illuminate the ways couples *deal* with paradox. Both Watzlawick (1963) and Winston (1978) have observed that paradoxical situations are ubiquitous. The key to understanding their effects lies in how persons deal with paradox.

The studies we have briefly reported here are representative of the kinds of nomothetic and ideographic research that have been done within the framework of CMM. Other investigations by our research group include studies of formal organizations, persuasion in campus elections, prolonged separations in military families, and family violence.

IMPLICATIONS

The theory of the coordinated management of meaning has borrowed heavily from the "interactional view" in the description of communication. In the main, the differences between the two stem from their orienting assumptions. In addition, we have found Harre's Copernican Revolution in the philosophy of science and Koestler's history of science (1957) analysis of the creative act (1964) and description of the human condition (1967) powerful tools for the development of a scientific theory. Frankly, the ability to "do science" from a perspective compatible with the interactional view surprised and delighted us. When we began, we thought that there might be a way of measuring some of these concepts; now we have an embarrassment of riches.

The method of discovery|clearly differentiates the two approaches. In the "interactional view," the observer defines transpersonal patterns in ways comparable to that used by Bateson in his report of monkeys at play quoted above. From our perspective, the actors themselves supply the content of the rules under a variety of observational and interview protocols, which the observer then uses to calculate the structure of rule systems at both intrapersonal and interpersonal levels. We have begun to suspect that there are "laws of form" such that particular structural characteristics of individuals' rules and of interpersonal systems have a necessary relationship. Such "laws of form" are far different from the Ionian or the Newtonian concepts of an underlying order because they pertain to the *abilities* or "powers" rather than to the *behaviors* of entities. The laws of form do not describe regularities of occurrences but the extent to which particular entities are the *agents* of their behavior or behave in *response* to external events. This concept seems curiously similar to Bateson's (1957:9) speculation about "what sorts of violation of patterns ... form the logical base for the later distortions" and his later conviction of a universal Mind, in which ideas have consequences (Bateson, 1979). In any event, we believe that the conceptualizations and measurement techniques of our theory provide a useful set of tools with which to explore these issues.

Our motivation is not solely academic. We are social creatures and have a vested interest in the interpersonal relations and social structures in which we live. The theory of the coordinated management of meaning proffers at least a way of identifying some of the recurrent problems of social relationships. It may offer more: guidance in doing something about those problems. Maslow (1971) said that there are "only" two problems confronting social scientists: that of creating healthy individuals and that of creating a healthy society, and these problems are really two sides of the same one. Maslow had many perceptive but mainly anecdotal things to say about these problems. The concept of holonic systems with measureable logical forces suggests that it may be possible to describe social systems and situations with far greater precision than Maslow had available to him, and our sneaking suspicion that there are laws of form intimates that it may be possible to predict types of problems in specified systemic structures. For example, an interpersonal rule system which is "exclusive" — that is, which is based on the injunction "thou shalt have no other system before me" — whether in international religion, jingoistic patriotism, marriage, etc., will be characterized by predictable and different problems than a system which is "inclusive," premised on the injunction that "this is one system among many." At this point, we suspect that both types of systems have problems and that there may be some disagreement about which are the easiest to live with, but the point is that this is a powerful and useful way to frame those questions. It seems to us that there are some individuals whose logics of meaning and order are so contorted that they place anyone with whom they interact in "binds." Perhaps we can identify these people and warn others who do not handle binds well to avoid them. The modern version of the leper's cry "unclean" would be a small, neat label "Warning: the Surgeon General has determined that communicating with this person may be hazardous to your mental health."

The previous paragraph is a pleasant fantasy of the social relevance of our theory, of course. But the theory described here includes a set of procedures which have the "virtues" of science — descriptive and explanatory power, some predictability, intersubjectivity and a rigorous verification procedure — without compromising the concept of communication inherent in the "interactional view." We are confident that continued research based on this theory will enhance the understanding of human communication along lines initiated by Bateson and his colleagues.

Implications of the "Interactional View" for Communication Theory

B. Aubrey Fisher

During the past decade an increasing number of communication scholars have become enthralled with the work of the psychotherapists involved in the Mental Research Institute at Palo Alto. There are nearly as many devotees of Gregory Bateson, the conceptual founder of the interactional view, in the field of communication as there are in any other field. Consequently the 1979 Asilomar conference, offering an opportunity for cross-fertilization of communication and psychotherapy, was anticipated with great relish by many of us in communication. No one looked forward to this conference with greater anticipation than I.

The conference and the chapters included in this volume are, at once, exhiliarating and disappointing. In many ways, the anticipation of anything is greater than the realization; the potential is greater than the outcome. Too easily one becomes confused by the abstractions and the diversity, disoriented by the incongruities and even inconsistencies, and disappointed by the lack of concrete data or specific underlying principles. The purpose of this summary is not to clarify all the incongruity and complexity of the disparate contributions, but to appreciate them for just those qualities. To avoid being disappointed because of unrealistic expectations, the reader should peruse this volume keeping several assumptions in mind. With these assumptions one is more able to appreciate the implications which the interactional view holds for the advancement of communication theory.

PRELIMINARY ASSUMPTIONS

One should be aware of the fact that interaction is not the mainstream of communication theory or research. In fact, it is far from it. As a scientific community, the vast majority of communication scholars do not subscribe to and may even be only slightly aware of the existence of the interactional view. The participants in the Asilomar conference of 1979 who represented the field of communication, varied widely in the extent to which they believe in and employ, epistemologically or investigatively, the interactional view. The papers presented reflected that diversity.

One should also be aware that the interactional view does not represent the mainstream of psychotherapy. A recent book (Binder, Binder & Rimland, 1976), describing twelve different types of therapy, includes no discussion at all of the interactional view and no reference to any of the therapists associated with interactionism. In one sense, then, those (both therapists and communication scholars) who subscribe to the interactional view are mavericks in their own field. They may consider themselves to be in the vanguard, but in no way can they be considered representative of their respective fields of endeavor.

The Asilomar conference and this volume pay homage to the interactional view. This homage is due, in part, to the assumption that many communication scholars employ the interactional view in their research and theorizing. In a way, this assumption is unfair to members of the Palo Alto group. The interactional view may not even exist in communication. I have earlier (Fisher, 1978) described a "pragmatic perspective" of communication, which probably comes closest to the interactional view, but chose to use the term "pragmatic" (unabashedly stolen from the title of Watzlawick, Beavin, and Jackson's 1967 book) rather than the term, "interactional." The latter term, used in communication, is likely to be confused with symbolic interaction, a highly dissimilar view of the world. But the pragmatic perspective is clearly an adaptation of the interactional view and is, to some extent, independent of it.

In terms of theory, communication is in the used car business. We take in previously owned theories (often not one-owner theories) and modify them considerably. After "repairs" which are often extensive, we place the "theory" on the market and attempt to "sell" it to our colleagues as communication theory. We have usurped and adapted the therapeutic principles of the interactional view to "pure research," focused these adapted principles on a variety of communicative phenomena and, in the process, have modified them considerably. I suspect that the therapists from MRI would recognize their interactional view in our research projects only with extreme difficulty.

Compounding this problem is the fact that, as adapters and modifiers, we often resist relinquishing our own "pet theories." Consequently, we succumb to the seductive language of interactionism and system theory. The terms take on an aura of mysticism. We may talk, for example, of "analogic" and "digital" communication but mean no more than a distinction between verbal and nonverbal modes of message transmission. We may use the term "relational communication" to refer to a non-Batesonian form of individualized empathy. We talk of "punctuating" interaction sequences as merely differences in individual's perceptions. In other words, we may use the new phrases and language, but we place them within the old frames and, in so doing, have further confused the conceptual issues.

Reading the preceding discussion, one might conclude that it is possible to place some conceptual parameters around a set of clearly stated principles which may be known as the "interactional view." Such an assumption may be overly naive. One need not read far in the writings of Bateson, Watzlawick, Weakland, Jackson, Haley, etc., before coming to the conclusion that the interactional view, though highly provocative, is quite incomplete and even inconsistent upon occasion. The literature is composed of a series of innovative conceptualizations and descriptions of everyday phenomena with an overall gestalt based on an interactional (i.e., behavioral) focus. But the series is disjointed, unconnected, and certainly not incremental in the sense of providing a unifying body of theoretical principles.

Precisely what is the interactional view? Many have referred to it as a "theory," an "epistemology," a "research and therapy program," a "perspective." Taken as a whole, it is probably none of these. It is a viewpoint of therapy or research which provides a new way of looking at old problems. It does not include any operationalization of concepts so much as it recasts them within a different conceptual framework. Is the interactional view a theory? An epistemology? Probably not. We would find its greatest benefit if we considered the interactional view to be a state of mind, an attitude or framework which we can bring to the therapeutic or the research setting. Consequently, we should not expect the interactional view to provide answers or results but, rather, to provide a framework within which we can contemplate our old questions. In a sense, then, the contemplation of the problem is of more value than the solution.

IMPLICATIONS FOR COMMUNICATION THEORY

Given these preliminary assumptions, one should be more aware of what not to expect from the interactional view. It is not a panacea, a "new theory," which can be adopted as *the* theory of communication. It is not a set of new techniques for observing communicative phenomena or for gathering and analyzing communicative data. In fact, it provides no guidelines for determining what communicative data would look like. The researcher must provide the research techniques from an existing arsenal.

Although the interactional view does not provide a new epistemology, it does offer some important implications for communication theory. As implications, the following principles are presented as interpretations of the interactional view and must be adapted to communication in order to be of any practical benefit. The following list of implications is not intended to be comprehensive but suggestive. Each represents commonly held, frequently mentioned assumptions of the therapists who advocate and practice the interactional view. How they are employed in actual communication research or theorizing is a matter of each individual's operationalizing and adapting them for the purpose of addressing practical questions.

External Locus

The familiar phrase, "One cannot not communicate," is central to the locus of communication within the interactional view. Communication is behavior; and since behavior has no opposite (in the sense that "one cannot not behave"), then communication also has no opposite. Prior to the development of the interactional view, psychotherapists (despite their numerous approaches to therapeutic treatment) agreed on focusing treatment on a single person. They agreed further that any pathology was located *in* the person. Thus, behavior was considered to be a surface manifestation of that innate phenomenon. In terms of communication, "crazy" behavior was considered a form of nonbehavior, and schizophrenic speech ("word salad") was considered abnormal and therefore meaningless. It certainly was not communication. The interactional view, by considering communication to be behavior, brought a discordant view to the field of therapy.

Skeptics are quick to question the external locus of communication within the interactional view. They remain curious about the relation of behavior to intrapsychic phenomena. They wonder whether this locus of communication in behavior is arbitrarily chosen. These issues are not trivial. Nor are they particularly meaningful. The nature of the relation of behaviors to intrapsychic phenomena is an interesting question but rather extraneous to the interactional view or to communication. If the relation is close, then observing behaviors is tantamount to observing the intrapsychic phenomena (certainly as good as scored on a paper-and-pencil test). Observing the latter would only be redundant. If little relation can be found to exist, then intrapsychic phenomena are trivial and need not be observed.

But the external locus cannot be selected solely on an arbitrary basis. To do so would render it, too, trivial. The theorist always owes the consumer an explanation for the locus. When the interactional therapists departed from the axiomatized assumptions of psychotherapy, they also cast into doubt the focus on the single person as the subject for therapeutic treatment. Rather than seeking an intrapsychic "cause" for a pathology, the interactionally oriented therapist views instead the interaction of an entire social system (typically, in practice, the family) and devises intervention strategies into the functional pattern of interaction which characterizes the system (see Watzlawick, 1977).

The fundamental conceptual move, then, is from the intrapsychic to the interpersonal. Interaction (i.e., communication) goes on *between* people rather than *within* them. The focus is on the human system as a whole and not so much on the person within the system. It is impossible to understand the entire system *as a system* if one looks at only a part or even all parts of the system. Viewing the system from the vantage point of someone within the system is destined to be an incomplete and highly distorted view of the system. The eye cannot see itself. One understands the system as a system by looking for and at the *con-nectedness* of the parts, how each part relates to the other parts and to the system as a whole. The single person is but one part of the human system. To understand the human system is to understand interaction (connections) between persons and not extrainteractional phenomena within a single person.

And how does one person relate to another person and to a human system? The answer to this question is basic to the interactional view. One person *acts* toward another person and is, in return, acted toward by the other. The resulting pattern of actions is *inter* action. The pattern is not to be understood simply as a series of stimulus-reponse pairs but as actions occurring in a sequence and comprising a meaningful whole, the human system. But actions need not be considered meaningful in the sense of having some antecedent meaning endowed by the person and relative to some intrapsychic phenomenon (e.g., motivated, intentional, perceived). Indeed, understanding and meaningfulness often follows action. In acting, even without any meaning, one creates or enacts reality and is bound by the consequences of that reality (see Watzlawick, 1976). The interactionist thus looks for "reality" within the actions (the interpersonal) and not within the person.

Messages and Metamessages

One of the key elements in the conceptual framework of the interactional view concerns the interpretation of a message. No message is viewed in a "pure" or "meaningful" form. Rather, a message is always considered in terms of a metamessage. That is, a message is interpretable only within a context or frame. Isolated from its context, any message (i.e., action or behavior) is meaningless and incapable of being interpreted. The context or frame, then, is the metamessage which always exists and forms the basis of interpretation or deriving meaning from the interaction (and, hence, of the relationship or human system).

Appropriately, the next question should concern the delineation of the context. Precisely what is the frame within which one can interpret the message? What constitutes the metamessage? Some might answer that the interpretative context is within the communicator or the perceiver in the sense that "Words don't mean; people do" or that "Meaning is perception." But this context drives communication back into the intrapsychic phemonena of the single person and away from the interpersonal connections which bind together single persons within the relationship of the human system.

A second frame may be that of the connection between actions and goals. The person performs action A in order to achieve goal X because A is necessary or instrumental to achieving goal X. To the extent that interactants agree on these action-goal connections, then the context is effective. But such a view of context also focuses on single persons and views the relationship as an overlap or coincidence of intrapsychic phenomena of two or more single persons. The human system is thus rendered understandable as a summative consideration of single persons' internalizations. Such a context for interpreting actions also seems inappropriate to the interactional view.

This discussion is not merely an exercise in argumentative meandering. There is good reason to spend so much time on this issue of context. Even though this message-metamessage relation is vitally important to its conceptual framework, the literature representing the interactional view is unclear as to a precise description of context. Nor is the literature of communication any more helpful in determining the context of communication, even though it, too, places great importance on the importance of context (see Bochner & Krueger, 1979). In fact, both sets of literature often provide inconsistent definitions and examples of context. But rather than dwelling on the inconsistencies (which we know exist), the greater value probably lies in providing some guidelines for identifying the context of a message within an actual observational setting.

Watzlawick, Beavin, and Jackson (1967) provide some assistance in this quest for identifying the context (i.e., the metamessage) of a message:

> . . . context does not consist only of institutional, external (to the communicants) factors. The manifest messages exchanged become part of the particular interpersonal context and place their restrictions on subsequent interaction (p. 132).

From this statement, one can infer that the context of communication probably does include environmental or situational facts. But more important, perhaps, is the context of other messages. That is, a particular message exists within the context of other messages. And that context (the sequence of the interactional stream) restricts the future possibilities or outcomes of interaction. And what is meaning other than the restriction of alternative possible interpretations?

Writing within the spirit of the interactional view, Scheflen (1974) may be even more explicit on this point:

...we cannot think of any act as having a meaning of its own, for meaning is not a property of the behavior itself. The term 'meaning' applies instead to the relation of behavior and context. So when one is asked what a given behavior means, he must answer . . . by referring to broader and broader levels of context. He must proceed in some kind of systematic way to describe the immediate sequencing and framing of the act, its location in a relationship and in a program on an occasion, and so on (p. 179).

A truism within systems theory (specifically, hierarchy theory) is that a system, to be understood in context, must be viewed in relation to other systems. It seems reasonable, then, to expect that the context within which a behavior or message is interpretable is composed of other behaviors or messages. At the same time, the observer/interpreter needs to recognize the extrinsic factors of context, as well — the institutional, situational, and environmental elements of context. But the place to begin the interpretative process is to view a message within the context of other messages, the sequence of interaction. In this sense, actions make up *interaction*, and interaction (the connectedness of actions) is the context or metamessage for interpreting component actions.

I have not presented this definition of context as a definitive statement of how actions are to be interpreted within the interactional view. Nor is any methodological technique being advocated, implicitly or explicitly. Of course, some empirical techniques are more appropriate than others for the empirical purpose of message-metamessage relationships, but a number of techniques are quite appropriate even though they would ask different questions and generate different answers (e.g., conversation analysis, ethnomethodology, interaction analysis, hermeneutics, some forms of language analysis).

More to the point, this view of context is intended as a starting point, a place to begin observation in order to put into practice the conceptual framework of interactionism. Certainly other elements of context should be considered in order to provide the most comprehensive interpretation of any communicative relationship. Further, any attempt to interpret a message or action without employing the context of the interactional sequence is doomed to be incomplete. In this sense, then, the interactional sequence should be considered a necessary element of context (or frame of metamessage), but it is not sufficient (in the sense that no other elements of context exist).

Multidimensionality

In one respect at least, the literature of the interactional view reads like a manual of rhetoric written by Peter Ramus. The interactional therapists may be the greatest bifurcators of the twentieth century. Everything, it seems, is divisible into two parts. Language has both report and command aspects. Communication is analogic and digital. Relationships are symmetrical or complementary. And then there is the double bind. The important point, however, is not that the number "2" possesses any mystical significance, but that human interaction/communication is complex, it is composed of many dimensions. Paul Watzlawick summmarized succinctly the immensity of this multidimensionality in his address to the Asilomar conference when he stated, "a clear realization that the situation is hopeless, but not serious."

To recognize the multiple dimensions of human communication is to know that a complete understanding of it is impossible. In fact, such recognition carries with it the knowledge that any observation is destined to be incomplete and distorted. Communication simply cannot be reduced to a manageable number of elements or even dimensions without ignoring many other elements and many other dimensions. No conceptual framework, epistemology, or theory (the interactional view included) can even hope to prove itself; but it can explain the phenomena rather well. In this sense, the researcher who adopts the interactional view knows full well its incompleteness and its distortions but doesn't consider the futility of a comprehensive explanation a particularly serious flaw. The same futility exists, of course, for all researchers who employ any epistemology. Unfortunately, not all of them are aware of it.

The key to viewing communication as multidimensional phenomena is to view more than one dimension at the same time and in relation to one another. Communication is thus problematic when the two dimensions are not in concert with one another and uninteresting when they are. Such an attitude toward the phenomena of human interaction, at least with the goals of therapy in mind, led to the discovery of the double bind and interactional paradoxes in general. Research and theory in communication by scholars who are less involved in therapeutic treatment, have not reflected such an attitude. Our tendency has been to concentrate on one dimension of the communicative situation, reduce it to its component factors or variables, and look for less problematic resolution of research hypotheses. We observe relational control modes of interaction in isolation from the content dimension, and vice versa. We observe nonverbal communication without considering the relation to verbal communication, and vice versa. If we do observe both and find disparity between verbal and non-verbal messages, for example, our first tendency is to resolve the disparity to ask which is more accurate, rather than to find the problematic nature of the disparity a theoretically interesting discovery. We may be missing the point by failing to view the multidimensionality of communication as an object of investigation itself. We are more apt to consider multidimensionality as an empirical difficulty. We need to treat the complexity of communication directly and attempt to clarify it rather than simplify.

Time

One of the most significant consequences of the external locus of communication in behavior is the increased importance placed on the time dimension. The interactional view's focus on behavior automatically translates the data of communication into events. That is, the observable phenomena of communication are actions, events which occur in time. The data of communication are, thus, inherently time data. The data are then associated with other data on the basis of time relationships rather than spatial relationships characteristic of the traditional data of social science.

To understand the tension created by the interactional paradox, a metaphor, or a double bind is to be able to view data as occurrences. Furthermore, such data must be observed as occurring at the same time. Therefore, observing simultaneity (a time-related relation) of data is central to observing some of the concepts associated with the interactional view. To view an action (message) in the context of other actions is to view time relations of data. Events occur in sequences. Sequences are punctuated in order to interpret them. And punctuating events which recur in a continuous stream or sequence requires observing and analyzing the phenomena of communication as time data interpreted in the context of other time data in some time relation.

Communication researchers often pay lip service to the importance of the time dimension but often ignore it in actual research practices. When time becomes important to the research question, it is often conceptualized as subjects' perceptions of time. But such a conceptualization misses the point of the interactional view's notion of time. Time perception is an intrapsychic phenomenon inconsistent with the interactional view's external locus of communication in the interpersonal (between rather than within persons). Time is a quality of the data, the phenomena of communication, and not an object of perception. To treat data as time phenomena requires conceptualizing the nature of the data and employing techniques capable of analyzing the data in terms of time relations. Such conceptualizations explain, in part, the reason for the upsurge in the recent popularity of Markov statistics and conversation analysis in communication research.

Patterns

When the interactionists began to look at communication between rather than within persons, they were locked into interpreting meaning with a broader context. This decision led to a rejection of some linear model of explanation in which a particular behavior was the consequent of some primal operator or the stimulus for some form of predictable response. A particular behavior, then, became the enactment or creation of some reality rather than the manifestation of some nonbehavioral reality.

Sheflen (1974) capsulizes this approach when he inquires into "how behavior means" rather than asking what people mean by their behavior. In the first place, this statement emphasizes the shift in locus from the person to the behavior. But beyond that initial realization is the implication that the structure or form of communication (and, hence, of communication theory) is discernible in the behavior itself. Communication thus becomes structured as patterns of behavior. Sheflen (1969) then suggests that interactants enact or create structure in their communicative relationships, and that structures or patterns become identifiable in the form of "behavioral programs."

When structure becomes discernible as patterns rather than linear modelling, the questions asked by the researcher change considerably. Reductionism is discarded. One does not look for causes or conditions which enable one to predict some effect or consequent (such as behavior). One does not search for the essence or component elements of some phenomenon (such as through factor analysis). One seeks to discover some recognizable form or pattern in the phenomena themselves. And having found this pattern, one makes a decision (e.g., choosing a strategy of therapeutic intervention) on the basis of the earlier inquiry.

As theoretical questions change through conceptualizing communicative phenomena, the purpose and mode of inquiry also change. Researchers become relationists rather than reductionists. They forsake empirical control (Bateson called it "calibration") because they know they can have little control over the interaction and because they are interested in other questions. In this case, empirical control becomes of trivial importance. Research within the interactional view is thus often more descriptive (discovery of the patterns of interactional structure). Results are judged more on the basis of how interesting they are and less on their instrumentality. The context or metamessage, for example, does not always yield clearcut interpretations of meaning. Indeed, the context may be a highly confusing element. The relationist is interested in understanding the confusion and considers such a result potentially very interesting. The reductionist would consider the empirical result (confusion) a failure.

Explanation within the interactional view is based more on description than prediction. As a result, the nature of communication theory is less traditional and less recognizable as a theory. At least it is less understandable within the rubrics of philosophy of science. It is in this sense that the contribution of the interactional view to communication theory is most pronounced. It provides a different and less customary conceptualization of communicative phenomena. It offers primarily a different way of looking at the familiar phenomena of communication. It does not provide new research techniques and analytical devices. Therefore, it should be judged less on the basis of the answers it obtains and more on the different questions asked.

Reflexivity

The focus on behavior as the principal phenomena of communication endows the action with an existence almost independent of the actor. Once enacted, a behavior cannot be taken back. It exists as a past event and has consequences independent from any intention or antecedent meaning held by the original actor. Watzlawick, Beavin, and Jackson (1967:131-132) describe this phenomenon as the principle of limitation in which actions engender interactional involvement and serve to define the interpersonal relationship. Furthermore, such actions imply the interactional commitment which is inherent in every communicative event. Hence, interaction itself inevitably affects subsequent interaction. Communication is thus inherently reflexive; it affects itself.

Another sense of reflexivity is also inherent in communication theory and research. In order to understand communication, one is obligated to use the phenomena of communication. Compounding the complexity of the observed communication is the complexity of the communication used to talk about it. The researcher who observes interaction is, at once, engaged in interaction and in the act of observing and reporting interaction. The result is an inevitable, untenable, and perfectly natural infinite regress. Watzlawick and Beavin explain:

> . . . to communicate (or even to think) about communication itself is itself communication. In this sense both one's subjective experience of communicative processes with others as well as the study of communication as such has to employ concepts whose range includes themselves, and, thus, lead into Russellian paradoxes of self-reflexiveness, into an infinite regress of assertions about assertions, and into the problem of undecidability. . . (1967:66).

How is it possible to be able to understand the phenomena of communication if we must employ the phenomena of communication in order to understand the phenomena of communication? Perhaps the answer lies in the nature of communication itself. Watzlawick (1976:xi) points out that "communication creates what we call reality." As long as one keeps in mind the fact that many realities (equally true and valid, even though potentially contradictory) exist, then the research enterprise itself is (in its existence as communicative phenomena) one version of enacted reality. Of course, different research efforts may enact different realities and, in so doing, provide different explanations, understandings, and conceptualizations of commmunication. Knowledge and understanding are thus subject to the reflexivity of communication and are not a reflection of objective truth or reality. After all, what is objectivity in observation other than an attempt to discount itself and its own observation? Objectivity is, in one sense, a paradox — a logical contradiction.

The present discussion may sound like the author is indulging in hopeless relativism. Perhaps this is so, but the issue is more than that. Earlier in this chapter I suggested that the act of research within the interactional view is rather consummatory, in its goal of contemplating the question, and less instrumental toward a goal of being able to predict outcomes. If one views the phenomena of communication as inevitably reflexive and the act of observing communication as exerting a multiplier effect on this reflexivity, then one reconceptualizes and accepts the nature of reality as confused and paradoxical. If this is relitivism, so be it. More importantly, it treats the problematic as interesting. With the untraditional conceptualizations from the interactional view, the questions asked become more significant than the answers. More importantly, perhaps, the asking of the questions is more interesting than the answers obtained.

CONCLUSION

Upon encountering the interactional view, the newcomer is likely to find this perspective quite unsatisfying. The attitude may be similar to that of Redding's (1979) response to one of my earlier articles: "And, after reading Fisher's lucid essay, I cannot escape the queasy feeling of 'now you see it, now you don't.' " (p. 330) The interactional view is too abstract, too loaded with mystical generalities. It contains no set of easily recognized principles, no techniques, no manual setting for the theory. It contains no cohesive body of empirical results. In short, it has nothing into which one can sink his or her teeth. Worse, it is untraditional and flies in the face of our customary training and educational background. "What do we do with it?" we ask. The only possible response to such a question, "Whatever you want," doesn't help. One is tempted to discard the interactional view as not worth all the effort. The reaction is woefully shortsighted.

An equally inappropriate reaction is to play the "true believer" to the seductive language and mystical cliches which are evident throughout the literature of the therapists writing within the interactional view. Such converts tend to view the acquisition of this new conceptual framework as a spiritual undertaking, not unlike training in Zen. The initiate acquires the "koan" and eventually attains the state of enlightenment. Acquiring the koan, of course, requires long hours of contemplation and remains a mystical experience of a highly developed intuition. To the uninitiated and unbelievers, the convert is solicitous. Those who have not yet attained the state of enlightenment have simply not developed the intuitive ability and are trapped by the chains of their traditional experiences. Naturally, the true-believer reaction is woefully egotistical.

Attending the Asilomar conference or reading this volume need not be and should not be a conversion experience. No one needs to believe or understand everything that Watzlawick, Weakland, Bateson, etc., have to say. For those who are interested in understanding more about the interactional view in their own theorizing or research, the best advice is to use it. In other words, the value of the interactional view (or any other view) lies ultimately in the results of employing it, whether the purpose is empirical inquiry or therapeutic intervention. We forge ahead on the basis of incomplete theory and an inadequate understanding of connections between phenomena. If results are provocative and insightful, we have succeeded. If results are confusing and uninterpretable, we may discard the interactional view as unworthy of further attention in communication theory. Whatever the destination, the trip will be worthwhile.

RESEARCH

For years we sought funding to support the development of
research methodologies appropriate to the systemic nature of
an interactional approach to communication theory and
therapy. And, always, we were turned down with the question: "*But what is your methodology?*"

— Paul Watzlawick

*The literature of the interactional view, including more than three hundred
publications from MRI research associates alone, has been criticized for its
dearth of quantitative research. Research results are what count in social
science, and "count" is what social science research often does: subjects, self-
reported attitudes, codified utterances, and so forth.*

*Our vocabulary of the individual is replete with conceptual and operational
terms related to personality, drives, motives, needs, instincts, traits, forces, attitudes and behavior. But our research vocabulary for interaction is nearly
nonexistent.*

*What are the words for the communicative patterns which connect? What
are the forms of description adequate to an ecology of communication and
behavior? What are the ways of knowing, the methods, which do not "murder
to dissect"?*

*The essays in this section, with varying fidelity to Bateson's epistemology,
demonstrate the complex problem of doing systematic research from a systemic
point of view.*

*In "The Epistemology of Form," Donald Ellis suggests that thinking about
communication process has been dominated by a substance metaphor rather
than a form metaphor, but "the communicative processes which constitute
human interactive behavior have no substance." Ellis argues that "form determines the properties of its constituents rather than the other way around."
Form begins in organized distinctions or differences. These differences then
relate to one another in some way: such relationship is a connective principle or
rule which instructs, clarifies, and explains how two things stand toward one
another. A set of relationships is a pattern, and the sequentiality of communication is important because patterns are identified by redundancy over
time. These patterns of relationship and sequence are also defined by larger
patterns of hierarchies of context. "No research is complete until form and context are preserved and accounted for," Ellis writes. Finally, time-as-
experienced is an essential aspect of form. In sum, "the form analogy contains
the rudiments of some significant suggestions about how best to approach in-*

teractive behavior and the social world."

L. Edna Rogers, in *"Symmetry and Complementarity: Evolution and Evaluation of an Idea," presents a review of the conceptual and operational development of two of the few interactional constructs in the communication research vocabulary. Symmetry and complementary were terms coined by Bateson during his early anthropological field work. In the original usage, symmetrical differentiation referred to situations in which there was a similarity of response patterns between groups; complementary differentiation included situations in which response patterns were fundamentally different. Either pattern alone might lead to progressive differentiation, or schismogenesis. When response patterns alternate, the resulting reciprocal differentiation produces more stable symmetry over time. Symmetry and complementary were borrowed into the family therapy literature to describe behavior between individuals, and symmetrical interaction became characterized by the minimization of differences in message exchange, while complementary interaction became characterized by the maximization of difference. Since 1965, symmetry and complementarity have been operationalized in a variety of empirical studies. Rogers traces the development of relational coding schemes which have evolved from these ideas and resulted in a substantial body of research. Rogers offers a number of suggestions to guide future work along the lines of symmetry/complementarity, concluding that since these concepts are prototypes of the paradigmatic shift from single message to transactional level variables, "they are the beginning tools for moving toward the higher logical levels necessary to describe patterns of patterns."*

Kenneth N. Leone Cissna *and Evelyn Sieburg, writing on "Patterns of Interactional Confirmation and Disconfirmation," explicate the theoretical bases of these constructs, describe behaviors associated with confirming and disconfirming response patterns, review confirmation research, and consider implications for future study. Cissna and Sieburg suggest that confirming behavior expresses recognition of the other's existence, acknowledges a relationship of affiliation with the other, expresses awareness of the worth of the other, and accepts or endorses the other's self-experience. Disconfirming behavior denies the other's existence, relationship, self-experience, and/or worth. The authors present a review of confirmation literature and consider several aspects of this research, including measurement problems, the relationship between agreement/disagreement and confirmation/disconfirmation, and the possible "shapes" of a confirmation model. Cissna and Sieburg conclude that "while these findings are only exploratory and should be regarded tentatively, initial research seems to affirm the significance early theorists gave to the confirmation construct."*

In *"Pragmatics of Interpersonal Competence,"* John Wiemann and Clifford Kelly summarize the thinking that led to the concept of pragmatics as it is now used by communication scholars, review major conceptualizations of competence, and argue that a pragmatics of interpersonal competence provides *"a new and valuable approach to the study of interpersonal relationships."* Pragmatism is a philosophy of purposive action, rooted in the assumption that philosophy should address the nature and resolution of specific problems as they exist in personal and social context. Pragmatics in communication deals with the origins, uses, and effects of signs in relation to the behavior in which they occur. Pragmatics is concerned with sender-sender relations as mediated by communication, rather than with sign-sign, sender-sign, or receiver-sign relations. Wiemann and Kelly argue for *"a pragmatics of interpersonal competence with the notion of relational control at its core."* They outline the shortcomings of a *"social skills"* approach, suggesting instead that *"competence lies in the relational system."* Characteristics of interpersonal competence include control, empathy, affiliation and support, behavioral flexibility, social relaxation, and goal achievement. In sum, interpersonal competence is seen as a *"multifaceted, contextually defined concept in which successful individuals mutually define their goals for a relationship and then work together to carry out those goals."*

Robert Norton, in *"Soft Magic"* metaphorically connects components of magic to brief therapy techniques and argues that the soft magic of communication interventions is a function of establishing an interactional structure and securing premises for that structure. In both magic and therapy, the participant wants both to believe and not believe, the logistics are often over before the effect is realized, misdirection and patter are essential strategies, surprise and humor often appear, the person gets more than bargained for and often does not understand what has happened, the process is designed to guarantee success, and the event seems like an extra-normal experience. Norton summarizes the brief therapy approach, argues that *"the function of structure in brief therapy is to create an enthymematic process,"* and presents an illustrative case study. He suggests that future work should seek to develop new models of interpersonal logic, to understand the role of metaphor in interaction, and to explicate the interplay between content and style. *"In short,"* Norton concludes, *"communication interventions are pragmagic — soft pragmagic."*

C. W.-M.

The Epistemology of Form

Donald G. Ellis

Progress in any science is a matter of epistemology. That is, if the study of human communication is going to progress as a scientific discipline, theorists and researchers must come to grips with issues about the nature of knowledge within the discipline and how one comes to "know" something about communication. The epistemological domain is where the nature of knowledge, its origins, its limitations and possibilities, and the relation of the knowing subject to the known object become articulated. It is here where one can examine a researcher's perspective; what he studies, the methodological procedures utilized, and the nature of the results are a consequence of the researcher's epistemological stance. And epistemological issues are the central points of difference between divergent scientific activities. Even the most cursory glance at the social psychology literature reveals recent rumblings about which epistemological set might be most appropriate for the social sciences (Gergen, 1973; Schlenker, 1974). And, of course, communication is experiencing controversy with respect to the epistemological merits of covering law models (Miller, 1978; Berger, 1977; Miller & Berger, 1976) versus rule systems (Cushman & Whiting, 1972; Cronen & Davis, 1978), constructivism (Delia, 1977), logical empiricism (O'Keefe, 1975), the nature of data (Fisher, 1979), system theory (Fisher & Hawes, 1971; Monge, 1977; Fisher, Glover & Ellis, 1977), and phenomenology (Hawes, 1977; Lanigan, 1977).

Although I consider these excursions into entering assumptions invaluable to any discipline, there are two problems which typically accompany controversy over epistemology. First, proponents for particular belief systems emerge and become overly zealous about their position. This promotes competition for disciples which is motivated more by the egoism of power than by a legitimate claim to utility. Moreover; this competitiveness obstructs efforts to critically examine the premises of the warring belief systems and turns researchers into social activitists rather than social scientists. Since, in the end, it is extremely unlikely that any enduring empirical claim will result from a single perspective, such rigid polarization of perspectives seems unreasonable.

The second problem refers to the nature of the models we construct when researchers are dueling over epistemologies. These models tend to be detached and isolated from one another. The models and theories of advanced sciences are somewhat more integrated and more closely aligned with the conceptual properties of the discipline. The social sciences generate many models which are insular and associated with individuals rather than generic significance. For any discipline to advance there must be some minimal collective agreement on basic assumptions (Kuhn, 1970). Even though alternatives and variation from these basic assumptions are often insightful, progress is a matter of systematic research which is inextricably tied to a common conceptual framework.

I do not mention these problems by way of passing criticism, but to offer some pivotal point for the epistemological-procedural scheme I want to introduce; a scheme which emerges as compatible with the interactional view. I believe that the combination of certain assumptions can loosely be called the interactional view, and that these epistemological assumptions serve as an alternative to most current social scientific thinking. Moreover, these assumptions have research implications for the nature of human communication which can account for complexity and increase nomothetic significance. My intent is to further establish some conceptual groundwork for a perspective on how the study of human interaction might proceed. Hopefully, some of the issues discussed below will stimulate future researchers to seek out new research questions and develop precise operationalizations.

What follows should not be construed as a paean to the interactional view. Rather, I maintain that the research possibilities which result from epistemological assumptions associated with the interactional view have potential for the study of human communication in three areas. First, there is potential for efficiency and *integration*. By concentrating on a few encompassing conceptions which are logically related we can avoid the confusion of isolated models of human communication which are essentially incommensurate. Second, there is potential for *substantive insight*. Many of the ideas inherent in the interactional view direct attention to qualities of interaction which have been neglected in the past. And third there is potential for increased *relevance*. This stems largely from a holistic approach which accounts for change.

THE EPISTEMOLOGY OF FORM

A fundamental principle of the interactional view is the pre-eminence of form over substance and the attendant epistemology of form. Bateson's opinion was apparent when he said:

> It follows of course, that we must change our whole way of thinking about mental and communicational processes. The ordinary analogies of energy theory which people borrow from the hard sciences to provide a conceptual frame upon which they try to build theories about psychology and behavior — that entire procrustean structure — is non-sense. *It is in error.* (1972:452-453).

The social sciences borrowed numerous conceptions from the physical sciences and have been relatively uncritical of these borrowings. The result is a conception of social phenomena based on substantive properties which are believed to be the defining characteristics of the phenomenon. Substance refers to the essential nature of a thing which is not a modification or relation of anything else. The substance analogy implies that social processes (communication) can be conceptualized as material entities whose structures are discovered in terms of forces acting on one another. Traditional approaches to the study of communication have been characterized by this substance/energy analogy from the natural sciences. Analogies are mixed blessings. They may be useful conceptual devices which call attention to isomorphisms; but they can also be misleading and tempt researchers into reifying their properties. The substance/energy analogy is simply less descriptive of the communication process than a form/pattern analogy. And the adequacy of this description is the essential base on which other formulations rest — or at least should rest. For example, Fisher (1978:103-104) explains how the substance/energy analogy is responsible for how we think about a variety of issues in communication. Communication is often discussed as a material substance which moves in space. As a result we talk about communication "effects," "breakdowns," and "restrictions." Communication is something that "goes" from one place to another. Moreover, because communication is substantial it possesses spatial properties and can go "upward" or "downward." All of this is the language of the substance/energy analogy and has structured our thinking about communication.

The relationship between the analogy and the phenomenon is one reason the substance/energy analogy is less appropriate for understanding communication. Very simply, the communicative processes which constitute human interactive behavior have no substance. The proper study of these processes recognizes their symbolic nature and, therefore, that they possess no intrinsic meaning. Communication (talk) is part of the social world and acquires meaning through interpretive processes of the members of the social world. Talk is meaningful only in the context of an observer's attributions of meaning — otherwise talk is random noise from an organism. Moreover, the substance/energy analogy holds that communication is composed of invariant qualities. Communication is more accurately portrayed as functioning in time and context; and the meanings, qualities, and attributes of communication are alterable over time. A form analogy is better able to recover the communication process for the researcher.

To conduct research under the rubric of the interactional view requires the researcher to respect certain epistemological assumptions about the nature of the social world. One of these assumptions is the primacy of form. The form analogy means that structural and functional patterns are more fundamental than constituent parts. Form, rather than individual constituents, is what matters. *Form determines the properties of its constituents rather than the other way around.* The primacy of form is not a new idea. Classical philosophers made the same argument centuries ago. But until recent times the principles of form have not been treated very systematically and the hope for new achievements was an undeveloped intuition. However, I believe there are six principles which enter into the concept of form and must be seriously considered before conducting research within the conceptual confines of the interactional view. These principles are difference, relationship, pattern, sequence, context, and time.

Difference

Bateson (1972) and Brown (1972) address the importance of difference. The concept of difference is central to form. G. Spencer Brown, in his toilsome book, *Laws of Form*, presents the notion of "distinction" as the defining characteristic of form. Distinction, according to Brown, is continence or a restraining boundry. A form is indicated when a distinction is made and the spaces, states, and contents within the boundaries are apparent. Bateson complements Brown when he argues that understanding "differences" is the key to making sense of phenomena.

Form is organized distinctions. It is impossible to understand some phenomenal unit without referring to differences between the phenomenon and something else. Bateson has suggested that perception is based on comparison and is, therefore, a matter of difference between one thing and another. The difference between a thing and some "thing" else is what defines and clarifies the thing. To state that there is no difference between two things is, of course, to say that the two are the same. It follows, then, that researchers must articulate differences to fully identify the forms of particular interactions. Consider the following example:

(1)   A: Are you going to be home early tonight?
(2)   B: Why? Do you need me for something?
(3)   A: No, just wondering.
(4)   B: No, the regular time.

One can point to differences in the above example and show how the arrangement of differences (form) helps make the interaction sensible. Moreover, we will see below that these differences can be framed on various levels of abstraction. Imagine if person B in line (2) had inserted the communicative act, "God, you are always bothering me about when to come home," rather than the comment in the example. The *difference* between this comment and others changes the entire form of the interaction and therefore its meaning. If this had occurred, lines (3) and (4) would probably (but not necessarily) have been different.

The reframing strategies used by the Palo Alto group and the soft magic described by Norton in this volume are dependent on the principle of differences. To reframe is to change a conceptual viewpoint (Watzlawick, Weakland, & Fisch, 1974:91-109). A behavior acquires meaning because of its membership in a class of behaviors. When that same behavior is placed in the context of a new class of behaviors, its meaning changes. In other words, to reframe is to reorganize differences. Norton's attempt to help a student remember a speech is essentially an effort to make the student redefine the perceived differences between various acts. Norton, like Grinder and Bandler (1976), uses metaphor as a way of refocusing a problem. This refocusing changes one's perception of a situation because the individual can no longer make the same comparisons; Bateson makes the same argument. Therefore, Norton's subject begins with a fear that she will not remember her speech because of her nervousness. Norton then equates control with the subject's apparent ability to forget a speech. As the interaction unfolds, the subject discovers her own solution by realizing that purposely forgetting a speech was a type of control and if she has control she can also *remember* the speech. Difference is an important entering assumption for the epistemology of form, but the nature and type of difference is probably more important. Therefore, the relationship between and among constituents is the second dimension of form.

Relationship

The distinction or restraining boundaries between any set of constituents in a form relate in some way. That is, there are modes in which one thing stands to another. It may be possible to recognize differences, but capturing the nature of these differences or the relationship between constituents is more important. A relationship is a connective principle. It is a rule which instructs, clarifies, and explains how two things stand toward one another. The researcher, therefore, identifies relevant differences and then attempts to understand the relationship among the differences. Relationships are the primary ordering principles (Bateson, 1972). Until relationships are categorized, the researcher has nothing but unorganized distinction. Differences among component parts are meaningful because of their classification into relationships.

The above is consistent with Watzlawick, Beavin, and Jackson's (1967) discussion of relationship. Information and meta-information are analogous to difference and relationship. Two numbers, say 2 and 3, can be considered different units of information. By themselves the two numbers are merely different constituents; but if there is a stated relationship between the two numbers, we have a rudimentary form. The two numbers may stand toward each other in any number of ways, but when this relationship changes, the meaning of the unit (number) in the form changes. The effects of changing from an additive to a multiplicative relationship, for example, have obvious implications for the function of each constituent and the resultant outcome which is now part of the form.

If we return to our human communication example, we see the importance of relationship on a number of levels. Consider statement (1) by person A. Rather than the comment in its present form, what if the reader had encountered the following: "Going are be to early your tonight home." Obviously the relationship among the words (the constituents in this case) is central to understanding. Now this principle is common knowledge among linguists, but its importance is neglected for larger units of interpersonal behavior. If relationships classify parts, what if we take the communicative acts within turns at talking as constituents and interpret them according to the relationship between people. Given the relationship between A and B (and some other issues discussed below), the exchange in the example could be heard as simple and efficient coordination of daily activities or as threats and evidence of suspicion.

Although a number of researchers have turned their attention to the relational dimension of communication (e.g., Ellis & McCallister, 1980; Ellis, 1978; Fisher & Beach, 1979; Mark, 1971; Parks, 1977), the work by Edna Rogers and her associates has been the most consistent. Rogers has devoted her efforts to particular types of relationships; she has been concerned with complementarity and symmetry. Complementarity and symmetry are examples of connective principles discussed above. Rogers' work exemplifies how when interactants enact messages the relationship between the constituents (the messages) can be characterized as complementary or symmetrical. These relationship types "instruct" us as to how the message exchange is to be interpreted. This work is important because it represents efforts to move from the individual level of analysis (a by-product of the substance/energy analogy), to the relational level. A question-answer sequence or a family discussion are more than their content; these communicative exchanges are meaningful to the extent that some relationship principle (e.g., complementarity, symmetry, reciprocity, reflexivity, nonreflexivity, etc.) organizes them. A pattern of relationships, however, is equally important to the form analogy.

Pattern

A *set* of relationships among constituents is a pattern. Pattern comes about from the relationships which govern the constituent parts. Pattern identification is basic to any inquiry. Meaningful experience is not the result of the "booming, buzzing, confusion," but the regularities we detect. Also, explanation depends on recognizing regular relations between recurrent events. It is logically and mathematically impossible for there to be an absence of pattern. Randomness is in the eye of the beholder (Brown, 1957). The important question concerns our confidence in the validity of the patterns we posit to explain human interaction. The validity of these patterns is directly related to the relationship "rules" which are responsible for pattern development.

I stated above that a relationship was a connective rule which clarified how one thing stood toward another. And since relationships form patterns, rules of various types are integral to pattern development. The epistemological importance of the concept of *rule* is well documented in Toulmin (1969), Shimanoff (1980) Cushman and Whiting (1972), Cushman (1977), Cushman and Pearce (1976). However, the source of rules for many of these authors is limited and less amenable to the epistemology of form. Cushman (1977) cites the self-concept as the progenitor of rules and Pearce (1976) and Cushman and Pearce (1977) structure rules according to von Wright's (1971) practical syllogism. The rules reside in the subjective experience of the individuals and act as triggers for action. These conceptions of rules are certainly valuable; but there is a difference between a rule as a trigger or generative mechanism and a rule as a connective principle. The implicit assumption of rules as triggers or generative mechanisms is that communication is the product of an individual's intentional state. Rules as connective principles act as the other side of the circuit by directing attention to the patterned (rule governed) interaction which is the data an individual uses to create his subjective state in the first place.

Interestingly, researchers seem to forget that externalized symbolic behavior is largely responsible for shaping internalized cognitive structure. An individual's position in a web of communication and the patterns and metaphors of speech he is exposed to are compelling upon his psyche (Ruesch & Prestwood, 1950; Lee, 1950). Furthermore, the epistemology of form holds that connective rules operate as performance rules *in the interaction*; that is, talk organized by connective rules is responsible for patterns which emerge as meaningful for an individual. Adler (1978) explains how rules according to Cushman and Pearce influence the minor premise in the practical syllogism. The rule "explains" an individual's choice of action by referring the action to its plausibility within the practical syllogism. Performance rules, on the other hand, reside in the interaction. They make the interaction sensible and meaningful to an individual. Performance rules "connect" sequences of verbal behavior. They function pragmatically to instruct interactants on how to organize their communicative events. Performance rules are linked to the constraint inherent within the interaction. The nature of constraint leads to the next dimension for form —sequence.

Sequence

If relationships among communicative events develop into patterns and these relationships are governed by performance rules which connect these events, then the sequentiality of the communication is important to the epistemology of form. A sequence is a predictable movement from one event or occurrence to another. There is constraint between one event and another (a sequence) when the predictability of one event following another is understood. Ashby (1968) provides a well known discussion of this issue and I will not dwell on it here. Suffice it to say that a form implies constraint between two or more events (say communicative events). This constraint is measurable and usually indicative of the type of rule which is connecting events. Research which is consistent with an epistemology of form must explicate the nature of the sequences which characterize the parts of a form. Sutherland (1973) is helpful when he explains how the sequential qualities of a given form can be placed along a deterministic-indeterminate continuum. Although Sutherland is referring to systems in general, the issues are quite applicable to understanding the sequential and relational nature of phenomena. The table is composed of ideal types. I think an important assumption about human communication as a form, is that communication is *inherently* stochastic. Unlike Skinner who argues that human behavior is effectively stochastic at this point in time, Piaget suggests that no amount of research will make an inherently stochastic process a deterministic one.

TABLE 1		
Nature of Sequences	Relational Stability	Emergent Patterns
DETERMINISTIC: Only one event can follow another	No relational change	Automata; primitive social systems
MODERATELY STOCHASTIC: A limited number of events can follow another	Some important relational changes	Decision-making groups; most families
SEVERELY STOCHASTIC: A large number of different events can follow another	Many important relational changes	Human relations groups; some schizophrenic families
INDETERMINATE: No event can predictably follow another	Change is extreme; Independent variation	Creative exchange; Artistic activity

It makes little sense, then, to conduct research which is incompatible with the nature of the phenomenon. And some traditional research techniques are not very compatible with the process of communication; they have limited utility. A more appropriate research strategy will consider a *matrix* of interacting elements where sequences are a function of conditional probabilities. These conditional probabilities result from a rather complex sequence and arrangement of events. Moreover, there is no such thing as error *within the form*. That is, the probability of one event following or not following another is data. Assume that A has occurred and it can be followed by B, C, D, or E. If we find that B follows A with a probability of .95, the other .05 is not error, but data about the structure of the form. My understanding of sequences in the form may be in error; my predictions about what should occur may be error; my analytical techniques may produce error; but the interaction process does not err — it simply behaves.

A concentration on interaction sequences is central to all research that is consistent with the form analogy. For Norton to perform his soft magic he must express the logical sequences among the patient's interaction. In the essays which follow, Rogers, Cissna and Sieburg, and Wiemann and Kelly all spend time analyzing interaction sequences in some way. Communication exists *in* time and, therefore, moves through time. If communication is an event in time then there is some sequential structure as transitions are made from one communication event to another. Moreover, the interactional view holds that intrapsychic phenomena result from interaction between people. If a therapist or practitioner is interested in influencing some mental state, he must first intervene in the interaction. This principle governs the theory, research, and practice of interactional therapy.

Context

A form, by its very nature, exists in a context. Just as constituent parts are defined by relationships and sequences, they are also defined by context. A context is a particular spatial-temporal arrangement of people and objects. It defines and is defined by the forms within the context. Interactants will use information about the context to influence and interpret their communication and, in turn, their communication will influence and interpret the context. Research from this perspective requires some detail about the situation in which communication takes place. If this point had not been so neglected, it would be trivial. But the behavioral sciences still conceive of phenomena as a substance which functions invariably across situations and over time. Too many research contexts are artificial and prompt subjects to produce behaviors which may only be appropriate for the research context (see Rosenthal, 1966). Examples of how context affect forms of communication are abundant; moreover, there is considerable research which suggests that communicative forms are contextually dependent (Coulthard, 1977; Schenkein, 1978; Ellis, 1980).

The researcher investigating some communication form must understand context hierarchies. Again, this stipulation is grossly violated in most communication research. The relationship between form, its context, and other contextual levels can be approached by what has been termed "tensity" (Ellis, Werbel, Fisher, 1978). Tensity refers to the discrepancy (difference) between the state of a form and its context. This discrepancy accounts for the "transactional commerce of the environment" (Allport, 1960). Ellis, Werbel, and Fisher attempt to organize groups according to tensity classes. They succeed in reorganizing conceptualizations of groups according to interaction patterns. That is, the particular form of a group is characterized by the communication which is deemed appropriate for the contextual discrepancies. Typical problem-solving groups, for example, require a different relationship with their environment than typical T-groups. This difference accounts for the different communication patterns which characterize and define the groups.

The context of a form is also hierarchic. Part of the differences which make forms intelligible is the difference between environments. And when one environment is embedded in another a hierarchy is apparent. Hierarchical contexting, according to Koestler (1978), is a part-whole relationship which helps account for meaning. This is little more than stating that certain speech acts are adapted to a context and the context is part of a still larger context. A family member's communication, for example, is sensible in the context of the family; it may not be sensible in the context of another family. Meanings are also hierarchical. Watzlawick, Weakland, and Fisch (1974) turn to the theory of logical types and Gödel's theorem to make the point about level structures. In short, any statement about a system must come from outside the system. If these logical levels are not kept separate, the result can be either confusion and schizophrenic behavior (Laing, 1970), or creativity and humor (Fry, 1963).

Context is a key feature of communicative competence as discussed by Wiemann and Kelly. (Also see Bochner & Kelly, 1977) An individual is communicatively competent when he has knowledge of situations and can actualize this knowledge. Wiemann and Kelly discuss control and empathy as the central characteristics of competence. Competence implies a variety of skills such as behavioral flexibility, relaxation, affiliation, and goal achievement. *Contexting* is the essential cognitive activity of interactants. Communicators are continuously making decisions about people, situations, and talk. The necessary inclusion of contexts is an attractive aspect of the Wiemann and Kelly work. They recognize that naturalistic situations are not simply areas where interaction occurs, but *part of* the interaction. No research is complete, then, until form and context are preserved and accounted for.

Time

The implications of time for most social scientific research have yet to be realized; but time is prominent in the epistemology of form. Time is typically conceived as "clock" time; it is constantly moving forward and durational. But Fisher (1978, 219-222) discusses a pragmatic perspective of time which increases the complexity of time. Time is an essential aspect of form. It is experienced as *part of a form*. In other words, time can be equated with action (e.g. communicative behavior) and time can recur as action recurs (see Kolaja, 1969). If communicative actions are considered part of a larger communicative form, then these actions affect our subjective experience of time. Kolaja explains how the past layers onto the present when past action is relevant or similar to the present. Human action occurring at various points in durational time is continuously influencing our interpretations of the past, present, and future.

Interactive behavior plays an important role in the experience of time. If a fifty-year old father tells his fifteen-year old son that he must wait two years for a car, the interval is 4 percent of the father's life and 13 percent of the boy's life. It is possible that this variation in experience accounts for the increased sense of delay for the boy. Brody (1969) discusses a similar orientation to time when he writes about "information time," "time driving," and "time graining." Brody suggests that time is experienced according to information in the environment; therefore, a drive across the desert seems to take longer than a drive through a more scenic (i.e. informative) route.

A relationship is defined according to the organization of communicative behaviors the interactants exchange, and this relationship has formal qualities. It follows that research which seeks to understand the form must consider the temporal qualities of the form. The relational reality we call a form has elements which describe points in time, cyclic and phasic qualities, and an idiosyncratic rule set which structures time according to the relational reality. Interactants must orient in time; they must have a sense of past, present, and future in order to synchronize behavior. In turn, behaviors influence time. Understanding time and its implications for communication is a demanding task. Although the epistemology of form incorporates time as an essential ingredient in the research process, the heuristic potential of the concept remains unrealized.

SOME FINAL COMMENT

It takes little imagination to see that different epistemologies will lead to different appreciations of a phenomenon. Assumptions about how reality is organized and how we should investigate it will determine no less than what we study, how we study it, and what we claim to know. The epistemology of form is no different. The models generated from this perspective will act as allegories of reality and be either valuable or not. But what are some of the methodological and instrumental implications of the form analogy? Although this issue is beyond a detailed treatment, I would like to comment on it.

Those adhering to the form analogy might consider the following assumptions: (a) There should be an ontological commitment to the assumption that knowledge relates to empiricals; (b) communicative phenomena are moderately stochastic; (c) therefore, an unobserved portion of a form is somewhat attainable by a projection of that portion of the form which is accessible to observation. This is most true, however, for a given time interval since the form can alter its structure over longer periods of time; (d) finally, the primary research process should consist of the observation of entities in their natural environment and the ordering of these observations into a concatenative science. The value of controlled environments is not denied; however, their limitations (often severe) must be recognized.

One aim of this type of research is to reorder *social* logics. In other words, a logic emergent from observations of the entity in the question — not from a priori axioms or mathematics. However, since the fit between constructs and data is most central, any model which can usefully represent the phenomenon is valuable. Nevertheless, the human communication sciences have suffered more from the capricious application of models from other areas (telephones, Darwinian evolution, machines, human cells, thermodynamics) than from honest attempts to observe and organize. No researcher approaches his subject matter with a *tabula rasa*, but the epistemology of form requires greater emphasis on refining models according to observation rather than forcing observations into a priorily constructed models.

Therefore, models are produced inductively and are probabilistic to the extent that the model predicts how a phenomenon behaves according to certain empirically generated generalizations. The influence of data is strong, but models of forms also owe something to statistical and logical mediations. It is obvious that the quality of a model will depend on the quality of our observations. While this is always true, it is important to underscore the word "process" in research process. Since forms in the social world have "organic" properties which make the past, present, and future only moderately correlated, our observations are less valid as time elapses. And attempts to artificially constrain phenomenon by assuming away stochasticity simply invites error.

Inquiry into forms will benefit from qualitative analyses. This type of analysis emphasizes characteristics of a phenomenon — kinds, types, variations, etc. My point is not to make the popular call for descriptive research; rather that "how" questions have been overlooked in communication research and are integral to answering "why" questions. By identifying a form and examining its qualities, the researcher understands how a form is organized, what follows what, frequencies, durations, variations, types, properties, categories, etc. Qualitative analyses strengthen the link between empiricals and theoretical terms. Meaning, for example, is not in words or in people, but the product of conjoined individuals. The qualitative nature of observable interaction between individuals is indispensible to an accurate representation of the meaning of communication. Moreover, the plethora of intrapsychic states, traits, attitudes, and beliefs which currently plague the social sciences are often quite remote from the behaviors they claim to represent. A disciplined qualitative analysis can return these concepts to respectable theoretical constructs. As of now, most psychological traits have been reified and treated as energy forces which buffet people about in the social world.

The form analogy can certainly benefit from refinement. The six dimensions I have sketched above do not exhaust the principles of form. Nevertheless, I believe that the form analogy contains the rudiments of some significant suggestions about how best to approach interactive behavior and the social world. Human communication is a naturally developing form which is historical, temporally constrained, and embedded in other forms. Ultimately, the most stable conclusions about communication will come from research based on these premises. And the task is no small one. Communication, to quote the Bard, does nothing less than give "to airy nothing local habitation and a name."

Symmetry and Complementarity: Evolution and Evaluation of an Idea

L. Edna Rogers

INTRODUCTION

The conceptual insights of Gregory Bateson contributed many of the underpinnings of the interactional view, a view that has had a profound effect on the study of human communication. Among the seminal constructs formulated by Bateson are the patterns of symmetry and complementarity. This set of opposing, heuristic abstractions has been the seed for the unfolding study of relational communication.

Bateson was among the pioneers in the social sciences to push for a behavior-based, dynamic assessment of cultural patterns. His work on the differentiation of interaction patterns and the processes of schismogenesis offered beginning descriptions of the transactional aspects of behavior exchange. The decreasing resistance to conceptualizing communication as a social process is in part due to the work of Bateson. Yet, his early work went largely unknown by communication scholars until the formation of what has become known as the Palo Alto Research Group. Who among us were aware of *Naven* (Bateson, 1936) or even *Communication: The Social Matrix of Psychiatry* (Ruesch & Bateson, 1951) before the publication of *Pragmatics of Human Communication* (Watzlawick, Beavin & Jackson, 1967)?

Prior to the 1960s, communication researchers seemed unaware or uninterested in the more systemic properties of communication, even though a relatively rich heritage of process-oriented views of social behavior and structure existed in the sociological literature (e.g., Simmel, 1950; Small, 1905; Park & Burgess, 1921; Mead, 1934; Shibutani, 1961; Duncan, 1967; Blummer, 1969). The neglect of this work seems in part a result of psychological "blinders" that most communication researchers had been trained to wear. (The discipline is just beginning to recover from the psychological over-dose it experienced in its formative years.) Within this set of filters, the psychotherapeutic flavor of the systems approach of the Palo Alto group may have appeared more compatible with the psychological perspective, but in actuality, this approach fostered the beginning inroads to the existing epistomological barriers of change. If it had been commonly known that the writings of this group rested on the theoretical positions of a cultural anthropologist, I wonder if "communicologists" would have been as open to the encroaching acculturation.

Among the offshoots of the Palo Alto work is the developing area of research known as "relational communication" (Parks, 1977). The label and primary assumptions are rooted in Bateson's "report-command" (1951:179-180) *message* duality distinction. Bateson asserted that two types of meaning are transmitted in all messages, a referential (content) meaning which is simultaneously overlayed with a logically higher order of relational meaning.

Bateson as well as others have reminded us that in the long evolutionary history of language, the relational aspect of messages, though appearing in the literature as a "new" dimension, is the primordial element. It was later in the evolutionary process, after pre-hominids came down out of the trees, that words came to "fall out of the sentence" (Bronowski, 1978:38). Before there were words, i.e., representations, there was only or largely command, i.e., presentations (Danziger, 1976). The whole "sentence" was relational in nature. As Bateson states, preverbal mammalian discourse was "primarily about rules and the contingencies of relationship . . . . What was extraordinary — the great new thing — in the evolution of human language was not the discovery of abstraction or generalization, but the discovery of how to be specific about something other than relationship" (1972:367).

Relational communication builds upon this "rediscovered" duality. Its focus, however, is not within the single message, but rather within the exchange of messages, particularly at the relational level. Relational communication stresses the co-defining nature of relationships, the reciprocally defined rules of interdependence of system members. It attends to transactional level communication processes in searching for the "pattern which connects" (Bateson, 1978). Within this perspective, interaction process measures, rather than individual actor measures, become the basic data. Theoretical and empirical attention is directed toward the redundancies in interaction sequences, i.e., the patterns of relationships.

In the developing stages of delineating the focus of relational communication, it was often equated (and I played a part in this) with the control defining patterns of symmetry and complementarity. This initial view was too short-sighted. At present, complementarity and symmetry are the main patterns that have been operationalized and researched, but they tap only one of several aspects of relational dynamics. This essay will focus on the control dimension and control patterns, but hopefully with a clear understanding that relational communication is concerned with the conceptual development of other generic relational dimensions.[1]

In sum, the concepts of symmetry and complementarity, formulated by Bateson in 1935, have led the way in the empirical development of the relational approach to communication. These concepts capture a universal dimension of social relationships. They have been sufficiently delineated to facilitate the qualitative shift necessary for operationalization at the transactional level. They stand as models of the movement from the monadic to the relational level of conceptualization and measurement that is beginning to take place in communication research.

The purpose of this chapter is: to trace the development of symmetry and complementarity 1) conceptually, as they have evolved through the literature, 2) empirically, as they have been operationalized and utilized in accumulating research findings and 3) to project on future issues and potentials of these constructs.

CONCEPTUAL DEVELOPMENT

The Early Phase

The influence of Bateson's work on communication has come largely from the writings of his Palo Alto research colleagues. Awareness of Bateson's original work seems to have emerged only in the last several years. The publication of *Steps to an Ecology of Mind* (1972) facilitated this awareness, but Bateson is still probably more cited than read. This indirect influence is particularly the case with symmetry and complementarity. The lag time between Bateson's original formation of these constructs and any references to them by researchers in the discipline was approximately 35 years.

It is to the historical tracing of these constructs that we now turn. In "true anthropological spirit," Bateson's early career years were spent doing field work among primitive peoples, particularly the Iatmul and Balinese. From the beginning, however, he resisted many of the discipline's accepted methodologies and category systems. His writing of "Culture Contact and Schismogenisis" (1935) represents an interesting mixture of deference (a style soon abandoned, 1972:81) and resistance to the Social Science Research Council's approach to the study of culture contact and change. Bateson's ideas seemed reasonable. His suggestion was to look at the "problem" first and *then* attempt to "answer" the question (1935;178), i. e., to let conceptual schemes emerge from detailed behavioral observations rather than apply a predetermined framework onto behaviors. The use of *a priori* schemes was a predominant research strategy of the time, a strategy which missed the holistic, overlapping nature of cultural systems and promoted an overstructured, if not fallacious, set of conclusions. Bateson's recent statement that "all typologies are misleading" (1978:48) emerged as an early theme in his thinking as illustrated by the following comment:

> . . . . . our categories 'religious,' 'economic,' etc., are not real subdivisions which are present in the cultures which we study, but are merely abstractions which we make for our own convenience when we set out to describe cultures in words. They are not phenomena present in culture, but are labels for various points of view which we adopt in our studies. In handling such abstractions we must be careful to

avoid Whitehead's 'fallacy of misplaced concreteness'...
(1935:179)

Bateson's argument for a more dynamic analysis of cultural contact and change was to move away from a "given" set of classifications toward the study of relationships between groups of individuals with differentiating behavior patterns. In suggesting "the possibilities of differentiation of groups" (1935:181), Bateson first described his meaning of symmetrical and complementary relationships and the process of schismogenesis. In describing these types of differentiation, Bateson used both within and between group responses, but the basic distinction appeared to rest on the between group behaviors.

In the original formation, symmetrical differentiation referred to situations in which there was a similarity of response patterns within groups A and B and a similarity of response between the two groups, but the response patterns *between* groups were different from the *within* group patterns. Thus, if boasting was a between group response pattern, boasting by either group was replied to with boasting by the other, but it was not a response pattern within either group. Complementary differentiation included situations in which the within and between response patterns of group A and B were fundamentally different. These differentiated patterns, however, produce a mutual "fitting together." If one group exhibits assertiveness, it is responded to by the other with submissiveness. Either of these patterns might lead to progressive differentiation, i. e., schismogenisis.

A further distiction outlined by Bateson was reciprocal differentiation. It referred to situations in which members of group A and B responded to one another with different but alternating behavior patterns. Thus, an ongoing reciprocity of asymmetrical exchange produces a symmetry of relationship over time that does not tend toward schismogenesis. The reciprocal pattern is "compensated and balanced within itself" (1935:182). This pattern appears to be the basis of what Lederer and Jackson (1968) later termed the "parallel mode" of relationship.

The concept of reciprocity has been used by Fisher (1977) and Ellis (1977) in their descriptions of interaction patterns and by Rogers-Millar and Millar (1979) in developing measures of relational dominance. However, this pattern has received less attention in the literature than the other two patterns; and as such, we may be overlooking a way of expanding our conceptual vocabulary for talking about pattern of patterns. Reciprocity rests on symmetry and complementarity but is not of that class. And thus, is of a higher logical level.

With the publication of *Naven* (1936) the initial descriptions of symmetry and complementarity took on a more dynamic quality. Bateson's explications moved away from group differentiation toward a focus on "the reactions of individuals to the reactions of other individuals" (1936:175). The term schismogenesis was defined more fully as "a process of differentiation in norms of individual behavior resulting from cumulative interaction between individuals" (1936:175). This set the stage for Bateson's growing search for form and pattern within the communication processes. He stated that when attention is given to reactions of reactions, "it is at once apparent that many systems of relationship, either between individuals or groups of individuals, contain a tendency toward progressive change" (1936:176).

By combining form with tendencies toward progressive differentiation, Bateson described two basic process patterns: complementary schismogenesis and symmetrical schismogenesis. These distinctions were used in *Naven* to analyze Iatmul culture, but Bateson indicated their analytical potential for other cultural and relational settings as well, e.g., marital and parent-child interaction, neurotic and schizoid maladaptions, cultural contact, political and international relations. Although Bateson (at this time) was writing prior to the onset of the cybernetic "revolution" and the evolution of terms such as deviation counteraction, amplification, homeostasis and morphogenesis, he was beginning to capture their essence in his discussions of the process and control of schismogenesis. "The writing of *Naven*," Bateson stated, "had brought me to the very edge of what later became cybernetics, but I lacked the concept of negative feedback" (1972:x).

Bateson continued to use the symmetrical and complementary motifs in developing a conceptual frame for describing cultural patterns. Meanwhile, numerous developments were occurring in biology, mathematics, and communication engineering that expanded the concepts of ecology, system, information, self-regulation and feedback. Within these general influences, Bateson specifically cites the Macy Conferences on cybernetics as a strong influence on his subsequent thinking and writing (see Bateson & Mead, 1976). In his comparative analysis of the Balinese and the Iatmul system, in "Bali: The Value System of a Steady State" (1949), Bateson began to apply cybernetic concepts for describing the different interaction patterns by which the two systems maintained a steady state. Among the Balinese this was accomplished by avoiding cumulative interactions of maximization — a nonschismogenic pattern

— in contrast to the maximizing tendency of the Itamul schismogenic pattern.

The Later Phase

After the writing of "Bali," the concepts of symmetry and complementarity seemed to lay dormant, even for Bateson, until the forming of Bateson's Palo Alto research team in 1952 and Don D. Jackson's Mental Research Institute in 1958. From these interlinking groups, a literal "spill" of writings began to emerge in the literature from the mid 1950s on. Bateson's theoretical notions formed the foundation of the groups' thrust into therapy-oriented, family research. Symmetry and complementarity were reintroduced much as they had originally been defined, but with each additional "treatment" slight modifications emerged. One of the persistent problems noted in reviewing this literature is an inconsistency in the level of description of these concepts.

In one of the earlier articles, Haley described a symmetrical relationship as one characterized by an exchange of similar behaviors.

> This type of relationship tends to be competitive; if one person mentions that he has succeeded in some endeavor, the other person mentions that he has succeeded in some equally important endeavor. The people in such a relationship constantly emphasize their equality to, or symmetry with, the other person. (Haley, 1958:44)

A complementary relationship, on the other hand, involved one person giving and the other receiving. In this relationship, one individual was seen as being in a superior position and the other in an inferior one.

> A 'superior' position means that the person initiates action and the other follows that action; he offers criticism and the other accepts it, he offers advice and the other assumes he should, and so on. In such a relationship the two people tend to fit together or complement each other. (Haley, 1958:44)

These relational definitions were based not only on what was said, but how it was said. The qualification of *how* it was said, Haley referred to as maneuvers.

> Maneuvers consist of 1) requests, commands, or suggestions... and 2) comments on the other person's communicative behavior. Should A ask B to do something...B must either do what A says and accept A's definition of the relationship, or refuse to do it and thereby counter with a maneuver to define the relationship differently. He may as a third possibility, do what A says but qualify his doing it with a statement that he is 'permitting' A to get by with this and therefore he is doing it but not agreeing with A's definition of the relationship. (Haley, 1958:45)

This latter situation quoted above as a "third possibility," begins to cloud the definitions of symmetry and complementarity by the movement away from behavioral identification toward behavioral interpretation. Haley (1963) later referred to the situation of one person "letting or forcing" the other to be in charge as metacomplementarity. Pseudosymmetry was used to refer to the opposite where one lets or forces the other to be symmetrical. Sluzki and Beavin (1965) pointed out that when being "one-down" is really being "one-up,"intentions become confused with behavior and conceptual and subsequent measurement problems result. With this emphasis, "relational" concepts digress toward a monadic level of interpretation, and the accompanying indication that only one member defines the relationship. This translation was totally at odds with Bateson's conceptualization.

Jackson, Riskin and Satir (1961) suggested that symmetry and complementarity be identified by examining the statements made by dyadic participants, but continued the monadic digress by referring to *statements* as being symmetrical or complementary, rather than *relationships*. "A symmetrical statement is a comment on the equality of some aspect of a relationship" and is characterized by competitiveness. "A complementary statement is one that 'asks' or 'offers.' Arbitrarily, we call 'asking' the complementary one-down position and 'offering' the complementary one-up position" (1961:323). No standard specifications were given by these authors as to types of statements that would fit the suggested categories, other than a relatively intuitive interpretation of an interaction transcript.

In subsequent writings the terms "one-up" and "one-down," referring both to positions and/or maneuvers (Haley, 1963: Watzlawick, 1964), became the language for identifying "who was in control" and who was accepting control. This emphasis on "who" often resulted in these terms, especially "one-up," being erroneously used as if they were, by themselves, transactional terms.

Bateson and Jackson (1964) reinserted the original relational meaning of symmetry and complementarity by stressing that an interaction perspective shifts attention from individual response to contingency patterns within a relationship. They emphasized that there is "no such thing as a complementary [or symmetrical] piece of behavior" (p. 273). Later writings attempted a more consistent relational focus, with paired exchanges of contiguous messages being defined as the smallest unit of analysis (Watzlawick & Beavin, 1967). Symmetrical interaction became characterized by "the minimization of differences" in message exchange; complementary interaction was characterized by "the maximization of difference" (Watzlawick, et al., 1967:69). Complementarity was further categorized as "one-up" (↑ ↓) and "one-down" (↓ ↑). In a complementary transaction the interactor's behaviors are fully differential. The relational control definition offered by one interactor is accepted by the other. In a symmetrical transaction one interactor behaves toward the other, as the other behaves toward him. There is a similarity of control definition between the interactors.

The application of complementarity and symmetry to a psychotherapeutic context, however, accented a number of problems. Although the approach was oriented toward identifying self-reinforcing redundancies of interaction, there was a tendency to emphasize the pathological nature of the patterns, rather than develop a general theory of interaction patterns. There was a particular lack of emphasis on methodological issues. There appeared a "contentment" with intuitively defined concepts, validated by selective clinical examples. With the exception of the work by Sluzki and Beavin (1965), little effort was exerted toward specifying rigorous measurement procedures.

Pattern identification was sketched in terms of primary and secondary, equal and unequal status, superior and inferior, one-up and one-down positions (Jackson, 1959; Haley, 1963; Watzlawick, et al., 1967). It was cautioned that these terms should not be equated with good or bad, strong or weak. Despite these cautions, the terminology itself promoted a tendency to "talk" power positions, rather than control patterns — a situation which Sluzki and Beavin noted "can lead to the erroneous idea that *one* person defines the nature of the relationship . . . . ." (1965:323). The difficulty of moving to the transaction level of analysis, as illustrated in these writings, was cogently expressed by Jackson:

It is only when we attend to transactions between individuals as primary data that a qualitative shift in conceptual framework can be achieved. Yet our grasp of such data seem ephemeral; despite our best intentions, clear observations of interaction process fade into the old, individual vocabulary, there to be lost, indistinguishable and heuristically useless (1965:14).

The conceptual development of symmetry and complementarity is representative of the ebb and flow of which Jackson speaks. The earlier delineation of the constructs was perhaps the most robust of the species, representing a clear qualitative shift to the transactional level. Later elaborations frequently moved the two patterns of differentiation toward "the old, individual vocabulary." But over time, in spite of the level-slippage found in the literature, the transactional focus of these constructs has not been lost. The earlier developers of transactional concepts deserve less criticism for this monadic slippage than those of us who follow.

EMPIRICAL DEVELOPMENT

Measurement Procedures

In the process of operationalizing symmetry and complementarity, Sluzki and Beavin (1965) did the landmark work. Their work was the systematic attempt to put rigor into specific pattern identification. The three main subsequent relational coding systems all have a direct tie to their original scheme.

Sluzki and Beavin assumed that long-lasting dyads behave as homeostatic systems with a constant tendency towards equilibrium, both within the dyad and between the dyad and the environment. This equilibrium is created and maintained through interaction. The interaction is not random but follows some mutually established set of rules. If it were possible to achieve "....a comprehensive and mutually exclusive systematization of the field of interaction ... each dyad could be classified according to its main (more repetitive) type of interaction" (1965:323).

These authors build on the earlier assumption that every message in an interaction either defines, reinforces or redefines the nature of the dyad's relationship. Further, they contend that in every interactional sequence, even those of short duration, there will be key indicators that will allow the specification of the dyad's typical transactional pattern. Sluzki and Beavin operationally define symmetry as the structural similarity, and complementarity as the structural dissimilarity, in the dyad's reciprocal control defining behaviors. In their creative and well-reasoned approach, they posit that control is based on both the grammatical form (e.g., assertion, question) and the response style (e.g., agreeing, disagreeing) of each message. In their scheme contiguous message controls are linked to form transaction "scores" which represent the structural relation of paired messages. Examples of symmetrical and complementary transactions given by Sluzki and Beavin are:

- giving/taking instruction = complementary (giving = one-up/taking = one-down)
- asking/answering = complementary (asking = one-down/answering = one-up)
- asserting/agreeing = complementary (asserting = one-up/agreeing = one-down)
- referential statement/referential statement = symmetrical agreeing/agreeing = symmetrical
- giving/countering instructions = symmetrical (1965:326)

Disappointingly, Sluzki and Beavin convert transaction scores into individual speech scores. The scores are based on a comparison of paired speeches, but index a "member's definition of his interactional position" (1964:327). It is at this point that such a promising transactional scheme reverts to an interactional one, with dyadic typologies based on the patterning of each member's assigned speech scores, rather than transactional or system parameters. Nevertheless, this work provided a strong base for later developments.

In the first of these efforts, Mark (1971) borrowed heavily from Sluzki and Beavin's approach, but attempted to refine their work so that the dyad's relationship is the direct focus of analysis. He developed a three digit coding scheme to identify the speaker, the grammatical form and response style of each message in an ongoing verbal interaction. With a set of coding rules for translating messages into one-up, one-down and symmetrical codes, relational scores of paired messages are designated and are the basis for identifying a dyad's predominant communication pattern. The second digit code categories devised by Mark are as follows: (1) question, (2) assertion, (3) instruction, (4) orders, (5) talking over, (6) assertion and question, (7) question and assertion, (8) other, and (9) laughter. The third digit codes are: (1) agreement, (2) disagreement, (3) extension, (4) answer, (5) disconfirmation, (6) topic change, (7) agreement and extension, (8) disagreement and extension, (9) other, and (0) laughter.

A message coded as a 122 followed by a 213 indicates that the first speaker made an assertion in disagreement with the previous message and it is followed by the second speaker asking a question in extension. This is a relatively clear example. However, many of the code categories and coding rules are not this straightforward.

Mark's scheme expands on the message descriptions given by Sluzki and Beavin, by increasing the number of codes and the specificity of message identification. However, it includes double message categories in both the second and third digit codes, lacks an internally consistent distinction between those two types of codes, uses a confusing set of rules, and ignores level distinctions with the designation of "symmetry" as a message control code.

In designing the relational communication coding system, Erickson and Rogers (1973) and Rogers and Farace (1975) incorporated various aspects of the two previous methodologies while attempting to minimize some of the difficulties. An important consideration was to devise a relatively simple system, yet one capable of capturing significant structural aspects of ongoing message exchange. This revision included 1) the elimination of double message codes, 2) the reworking of grammatical (second digit) and response (third digit) codes to increase the internal consistency of these two sets of categories, 3) a clear set of message control code rules, 4) the addition of a leveling control code, and 5) the deletion of symmetry as a message control code.

Stemming from Sluzki and Beavin's design, Mark included "symmetrical" as one of the control code designations.[2] Rogers insisted that to use symmetry as a control code is to confuse levels and thereby deny the definition of symmetry as "structural similarity" in the dyad's relational pattern. In the relational communication coding system (Rogers, 1972) symmetry is only used to refer to transactional units. In the development and use of this system, a firm attempt was made to clearly distinguish between control maneuvers, based on message behavior, and co-defined relational control patterns, based on message-exchange. The latter is a dyadic variable, the former monadic.

Symmetry and complementarity based on one-up and one-down movements "catch" the ends of the control continuum of relational definitions. To expand and refine the control measure, Rogers included a leveling, one-across control direction for coding messages that minimize the one-upness or one-downness of control movements.[3] With the addition of a third control direction, a third transaction type was created (referred to as transitional since it represents a midrange between maximally different control patterns) as well as an additional type of symmetry.

The relational control coding system involves three progressive steps. First, each message in an ongoing interaction is assigned a three-digit code to indicate the speaker, the grammatical form of the message and the response mode relative to the previous message. The *grammatical codes* are: (1) assertion, (2) question, (3) talk-over, (4) noncomplete, and (5) other. The *response codes* are: (1) support, (2) nonsupport, (3) extension, (4) answer, (5) instruction, (6) order, (7) disconfirmation, (8) topic change, (9) initiation-termination, and (0) other. In this manner, communication exchanges are represented by a series of sequentially ordered numerical codes.

The next step translates the numerical codes, according to a set of rules, into control directions. Messages attempting to assert definitional rights are coded one-up (↑); requests or acceptances of the other's definition of the relationship, one-down (↓); and nondemanding, nonaccepting, leveling movements, one-across (→).

In the third step of the coding procedure, control directions of each pair of sequentially ordered messages are combined to form nine transactional types: one-up, one-down *complementarity* (↑ ↓, ↓ ↑); competitive, submissive and neutralized *symmetry* (↑ ↑ , ↓ ↓ , → →); one-up, one-down *transitory* (↑ →, → ↑, ↓ →, → ↓).

In a *complementary* transaction (e.g., ↑ ↓) the control directions are different and directionally opposite; the definition of the relationship offered by one interactor is accepted by the other. A *symmetrical* transaction (e.g., ↑ ↑ or → →) where the control directions are the same, involves one interactor behaving toward the other as the other has behaved toward him; there is a similarity in the control attempts offered by the two individuals. In a *transitional* transaction, where the paired directions are different but not opposite (e.g., → ↓ or ↑ →), one of the interactor's offers or responds with a neutralizing control attempt which minimizes the issue of control. Each of the transactional units provides a measure of the interactors' relationship (a pattern of connectedness) and their sequential grouping provides a "musical score" of the control dynamics (a pattern of patterns of connectedness).

The most recent of the major relational coding systems was devised by Ellis (1976) in his work with Fisher. Importantly, this system builds an intensity dimension into the message code. The scheme consists of five control categories which are designed to index "qualitatively different definitions of human relationships" (unpublished coding manual). The major coding distinction is based on the degree to which a message, in reference to a previous message, is an attempt to restrict or restrain the behavior options of others. The five categories are; 1) dominance, a strong one-up (↑ +), 2) structuring, a weak one-up (↑ -), 3) equivalence, a one-across (→), 4) deference, a weak one-down (↓ -), and 5) submissiveness, a strong one-down (↓ +).

Message intensity adds a needed expansion to relational control coding, but some previous problems reappear in the category system. For instance, the use of the relational term "dominance" as a label for a single message code, promotes the mixing of conceptual levels found in the literature. The implication of the "equivalence" label is less clear, but it is suggestive of a "symmetrical" message.

The multifunctional aspects of the code categories in Mark's system reappear with Ellis' scheme. For example, the codes for messages of "agreement" span three directional control modes. A message indicating "agreement with extension" is coded as a weak one-up (↑ -), an "agreement extended with personal experience" as a one-across (→), while "simple agreement" is coded as a weak one-down (↓ -). In contrast, messages of "disagreement" are coded only within one control direction, as either weak or strong one-up.

In reviewing the development of the major procedures for coding relational control[4] we find a common heritage, but each "branch" in the lineage has incorporated to some degree, different aspects and perspectives — and the evolutionary process goes on (Rogers, Courtright and Millar, 1980). In utilizing these control coding systems and accumulating research findings, the inter-coding distinctions must be recognized in order to make appropriate comparisons.

The comparability of the coding schemes is a current concern. A study by Ellis (1978), utilizing one-up and one-down statements, included only those messages that were classified as such by both the Ellis and Rogers coding schemes. Applying and comparing different coding schemes to the same interactional data is under way and hopefully will be a useful step toward methodological refinement and consensus(O'Donnell-Trujillo, 1980). An inital effort by Folger and Sillars (1977) concerning the validity issue of relational control coding has been extended in Folger and Poole's work (1980) and Ayers and Miura's (1979) comparison across major coding systems.

Research Summary

The empirical work on symmetry and complementarity stem from two main sources: a series of studies 1) by Fisher and his colleagues based on Markov analysis of small group interaction, and 2) by Rogers and her colleagues, based on the analysis of marital interaction.[5] The following will not be a comprehensive review but rather a brief account of the general thrust of the work on symmetry and complementarity by these two groups of researchers.

Fisher's earlier work on a four-phase model of small group decision-making (1970) and an interact system model (Fisher & Hawes, 1971) precipitated later studies on relational communication. In general these studies have focused on discovering, via Markov procedures, the transactional patterns that are associated with different phases of group interaction and relational development. Fisher's (1976) initial study was a comparison of relational rules in "emergent" small discussion groups and established family groups. Interactions of both types of groups were coded according to Mark's system and submitted to a Markov analysis. Virtually no difference was found between the interaction structure of the groups at the interact (paired messages) or double interact (three sequential messages) levels.

Ellis (1976) studied three small-group interactions over a three phase period in an attempt to discover the relational rules operating in decision-making groups. Using Mark's coding system and a Markov-type analysis, complementarity and "equivalent" symmetry ($\rightarrow \rightarrow$) were found to be the predominant patterns. Competitive ($\uparrow \uparrow$) and submissive ($\downarrow \downarrow$) symmetry were frequent sequences; but when they occured, they were more likely to be in the early phases of interaction. Later studies (Fisher & Beach, 1977, 1978), however, found the reverse for competitive symmetry, with its occurrence more likely to be in the later phases of group interaction.

In a following study, Ellis (1977) applied his coding scheme to interaction data collected from two decision-making groups and two consciousness-raising groups. Again, using Markov analysis, both types of groups were found to exhibit "equivalent" symmetry ($\rightarrow \rightarrow$) as a predominant pattern. With the decision-making group, a cyclical pattern was found "among the ($\uparrow$ - $\rightarrow$), ($\rightarrow$ $\rightarrow$) and ($\rightarrow$ $\uparrow$-) interacts" (1977:11). The consciousness-raising groups showed considerably less variation in interacts.

An exploratory investigation by Fisher and Beach (1977) attempted to combine both content and relational dimensions of interaction. Using Ellis' codes, interaction from a T-group meeting was analyzed by the Markov procedures. Again, "equivalent" symmetry and combinations of one-across and weak one-up interacts were predominant. One-up, one-down complementarity was more evident in the first half of the interaction than the second, while competitive symmetry was more frequent in the second half. Fisher and Beach hypothesize that idea-testing, goal-setting and task performance are correlated with competitive and equivalent symmetry and are most likely to occur in the later phases of the group's discussion.

Another study by Fisher and Beach (1978), based on longitudinal data, attempted to identify relational patterns in the formation and maintenance of dyads. The interaction of four dyads was studied over a ten-day period. A Markov analysis was done on each dyad's interaction broken into five phases of two-day periods. The study, which is a preliminary report of a larger research project, is one of the few in the relational communication area to analyze interaction data over an extended length of time. The results, as the authors point out, are tentative. But the relational patterns for three of the four dyads exhibited several common features. A slight fluctuating pattern of complementarity was evident across all five phases, with the lower frequencies occurring in phase three. The one-up and one-across interact combinations were fairly frequent in the first two phases; but phased out by phase five, while the frequency of competitive symmetry increased in phase five. Fisher and Beach suggest that competitive symmetry is an indication of a stabilizing relationship. They further posit that the back and forth variations found between competitive symmetry and reciprocal complementarity may be characteristic of relational maintenance patterns.

Turning to the work of the other group, Mark (1970) carried out the first of a series of exploratory studies on husband and wife communication patterns. The goals of these early efforts were to see first, if the devised coding schemes were workable; second, if any consistent patterns emerged from the data; and if so, were there any meaningful connections among the patterns.

In the initial application of his coding scheme, Mark analyzed the interaction of 30 married couples, varying by social class. His study focused more on methodological concerns than findings. However, he found the two patterns of differentiation, symmetry and complementarity, to be unequally utilized by husbands and wives of differing social classes. The "middle upper" group exhibited more symmetrical exchange than the "middle lower" group, while the latter group utilized more complementary exchange.

A sample of 65 marital dyads was the data base for the following three studies. Utilizing the revised relational communication coding system, Rogers (1972) compared the transaction patterns of couples varying by length of marriage and level of marital role discrepency. She found that symmetrical exchange, particularly neutralizing symmetry($\rightarrow$ $\rightarrow$), was associated with higher levels of discrepancy; especially for couples married for a shorter period of time. Higher discrepancy, which was assumed to index marital strain, was further associated with the transmission of more one-up messages; especially for wives. Correspondingly, one-down transitory ($\downarrow$ $\rightarrow$, $\rightarrow$ $\downarrow$) exchanges, especially with husband one-down, was associated with lower discrepancy. Dyadic strain appeared to be evident in the different relational communication behaviors.

Erickson (1972) utilized self-report "dominance" scores as predictors of transactional types. He found no relationship between the perceived dominance variable and complementary or symmetrical transactions. This result can be interpreted as supportive of an underlying assumption of the relational approach, i.e., the inability to predict communication patterns on the basis of intrapersonal (psychological)variables. Erickson did find differences in transactional patterns by topic. Controlling for social class, he found that marital dyads used fewer transaction types and thus, maintained a narrower range of communication behavior when discussing a family oriented topic than an emergency-oriented topic.

Millar (1973) developed two structural communication measures based on transactional data: a rigidity-flexibility dimension and a stability-instability dimension. Rigidity refers to a lack of alterations in the transactional pattern and stability to the predictability of the pattern. For the first time, relational communication variables were used as predictor variables with this set of data. Lower degrees of rigidity were related to competitive and submissive symmetry with higher rigidity related to neutralizing symmetry. Both higher degrees of rigidity and stability were related to transitory transactions.[6]

In the continuing search for pattern recognition, Markov analysis techniques were applied to this data (Park, Farace & Rogers, 1975; Park, Farace, Rogers, Albrecht & Abbott, 1976). While high levels of unpredictability were found to exist in the interaction, the most predominant relational communication pattern was the one-down transitory type exchange. One implication of this finding is the centrality of the minimizing, leveling control movements in the maintenance of long-term relational systems.

A more recent set of analyses in this ongoing research program has been the work on relational dominance and domineering behavior. Domineeringness refers to the transmission of one-up control maneuvers while dominance is based on the complementary transaction in which one-up maneuvers are accepted by one-down messages. In these studies, control patterns are indexed on the basis of interaction processes and are used as primary predictor variables.

The first study (Rogers-Millar & Millar, 1979) found wife domineeringness to be associated with lower levels of marital and communication satisfaction and higher levels of role strain, while husband dominance tended to be associated with higher satisfaction and lower role strain. A second study, (Courtright, Millar & Rogers-Millar, 1979) based on a sample of 86 couples, was supportive of the above findings. In addition, husband domineeringness, and dominance were found to relate to lower levels of dyadic understanding. The inverse relation between these control variables and understanding was supported by a third study (Millar, Rogers-Millar & Courtright, 1979). In this analysis it was found that the more clearly a dominance pattern was evident, the less each spouse understood the other. The results suggest the "functionality" of the reciprocal pattern of complementarity.

The investigations of relational control currently underway by this group include measures of submissive behavior and submission patterns, but more importantly, they include an expanded measure of message control intensity (Rogers, Courtright & Millar, 1980; and Courtright, Millar & Rogers, 1980a) and a new measure of pattern variation (Courtright, Millar & Rogers, 1980b). The intensity dimension, based on a distancing continuum implicit in the combined grammatical form and response mode control direction rules, increases the ability to map out the range of variation in the interaction data. In keeping with the musical score analogy that has been used for thinking about interaction patterns, the intensity measure indexes in greater detail, the pitch of the crescendos, the diminuendos, and middle range modulations. The recently developed measure of pattern variation represents the overall modulation in a dyad's musical score divided by the homeostatic set point of that score. This measure allows the indexing of interactional data at the pattern of patterns level. Two additional aspects are in process: 1) a time dimension of each message, so that not only the range of "notes" can be mapped out but also, the tempo or rhythm of the "notes," and 2) a content analysis of the interactions to be overlaid on the structural form of the interaction.

In summary, it is clear that the research in relational communication has a strong tie with Bateson's two major constructs of pattern differentiation, symmetry and complementarity. These constructs have stimulated and guided much of the work aimed at mapping out patterns of interaction which characterize ongoing interpersonal relationships. In these pursuits, the "branch" of relational communication research which has focused on small groups has been innovative in extending this analysis beyond the two-person group to larger sized groups; in combining content with relational dimensions; and including longitudinal data in the search for pattern description. The research "branch" which has focused on long-term dyads has particularly pushed for expanded measures of pattern recognition and distinction at different levels of conceptual abstraction. This push has been oriented toward more complete descriptions and analyses of relational form.

Future Issues

The adventure into relational communication analysis largely began with an exploration of the original symmetry-complementarity typology and the underlying assumptions. In presenting this evolutionary process, a number of conceptual issues were discussed and will not be reviewed in detail. The following comments will be limited to several broad concerns:

1. A clear recognition of logical types is necessary to further relational research. As Bateson has stressed, "Insofar as behavioral scientists still ignore the problem of *Principia Mathematica*, they can still claim approximately sixty years of obsolescence." (1972:279) The conceptual confusion of descriptive and analytical levels has been and is a persistent problem. An important advantage of a relational framework is that data can be treated at different logical levels, but this advantage is lost if these levels are not clearly distinguished.

2. There has been some verbal "applauding" of the fact that relational communication studies are expanding into a wider variety of interactional contexts, e.g., doctor-patient (Folger & Puck, 1976) male-female (Ellis & Skerchock, 1979), friend-friend (Orth, 1974). Simply carrying out studies in different settings, however, is not of particular value by itself. Hopefully, this area of research will avoid the morass of inconsis-

tent findings accrued across a hodge-podge of contexts as was the case in small-group research (resulting from the study of any "grouping" on which data could be collected). Accumulating noncomparable results seems to be a common problem and deters effective theory building.

A prime issue is the development of a unifying descriptive frame for classifying groups and social relationships on generic, relational dimensions. Working within such a conceptual framework, researchers could describe and compare interaction systems in terms of basic dimensional characteristics rather than by relatively meaningless and unending noun pairs, (e.g., doctor-patient, employer-employee, husband-wife, decision-making-consciousness-raising groups, etc.) Only in this manner, can the results of different investigations be compared, accumulated, and the directions of needed research more clearly identified. (See Fitzpatrick, 1977.)

3. A central operational issue concerning the comparability of findings, of course, resides in the compatibility of coding systems and measures utilized. At present, the main coding schemes share many similarities, but have some important differences as well. The suggestion is not that one technique be used over another, but that the comparable and noncomparable aspects be clearly recognized. This would increase the possibility of being able to "translate" from one study to another. This suggestion urges that the different coding systems be applied to the same sets of data as a way of clarifying the translation possibilities.

4. A number of suggestions have been made for expanding our knowledge of relational dynamics. For example, sampling interaction systems over time, matching the content of verbal exchange to the relational structure, adding message intensity and duration measures would all increase our "mapping" ability and potential relational insight. But most important in expanding our knowledge and understanding is the need to increase our ability to "talk" about the patterns of relational patterns. Movement to this higher level of analysis presents even more of a challenge than the previous issues. Bateson's concept of reciprocity and Millar's conceptualizations of rigidity and stability, are examples of movement toward this level. These patterns rest on transactional level concepts and, thus, are metatransactional. Analogies at this level are few, but in addition to the musical score analogy, perhaps a wave notion is useful. So far, in relational communication there has been some success in measuring the "particles" and segments of interaction waves. But as we focus on the smaller units, we lose sight of the larger patterns. We need to move toward indexing the wave of waves — the larger pattern-

ing of the combined heights of the crests and the distances between the crests.

Conclusion

Symmetry and complementarity are important notions. They are two of the few transactional constructs in our vocabulary; and two of the even fewer that have been operationalized. They appear to index a central dimension of relationships — the dimension of control. These conceptual distinctions are prototypes in the field of communication of the paradigmatic shift from single message to transactional level variables. As such, they are the beginning tools for moving toward the higher logical levels necessary to describe pattern of patterns. With symmetry and complementarity, it has been possible for message-exchange to become a primary source of behavioral data on which to build predictive models of behavior. The use of communication variables as predictors, rather than criterion variables, is a sign of "coming of age" in our discipline.

NOTES

1. Other key relational dimensions have been suggested and explicated from a communication point of view in previous work (Millar & Rogers, 1976; Millar, Rogers-Millar & Villard, 1978).

2. Mark (1970:46) erroneously gave Bateson "credit" for developing the three control categories of one-up, one-down and symmetrical. Fisher and Beach (1977:6) also erred in referring to "... Bateson's original control modes of ↑ , ↓ and → ."

3. Fisher (1965:7) incorrectly interpreted symmetry as being converted to a one-across code in the Rogers system.

4. Recent papers by Fisher (1978) and Fisher and Beach (1978) state that they have rejected Ellis' system but give no details. The five major categories that are reported are the same as Ellis'. Folger and Puck (1976) offer a question coding scheme but was not included in the above discussion because of its limiting nature.

5. A search of the "family process" literature revealed no formalized interactional schemes for measuring symmetry and complementarity that had developed much beyond the original, interpretive analysis of clinical transcripts. For instance, Hassan (1974) speaks of an "Interactional Positions Scale" but describes the scale only by giving the classic definitions of Watzlawick *et al.*, (1967) with no guidelines or standard criteria for coding decisions. Scoresby's (1975) "Relationship Styles Inventory" measures individual perceptions of complementary, symmetrical, and parallel interaction styles.

6. See Millar and Rogers (1976) for a more complete description of the analysis procedures and findings of these studies.

Patterns of Interactional Confirmation and Disconfirmation

Kenneth N. Leone Cissna
and Evelyn Sieburg

The "interactional view" of human communication can trace its roots at least to the publication of Ruesch and Bateson's *Communication: The Social Matrix of Psychiatry* in 1951. Bateson, Jackson, Haley, and Weakland's (1956) classic article, "Toward a Theory of Schizophrenia," provided impetus to further work utilizing this view. By 1967, the perspective had emerged further; Watzlawick, Beavin, and Jackson published *Pragmatics of Human Communication* and John Weakland edited a special issue of *The American Behavioral Scientist* devoted to the "new communication," a concise summary of the interactional view. In 1969, Evelyn Sieburg initiated speech communication research at the University of Denver to examine "interpersonal confirmation," a relational construct derived from the interactional view and discussed in a general way by Watzlawick *et al.*, (1967). During the decade since Sieburg's initial work, a body of research literature has grown up about the confirmation construct in an attempt to refine it conceptually and study it empirically in a variety of settings. Because current research in human communication reflects an increasing concern with relational communication (Parks, 1977) and the interactional view (Wilder, 1979), the concept of confirmation is receiving renewed attention from scholars in various disciplines. It is the purpose of this chapter to integrate what is known about confirmation by (a) explicating its theoretical bases, (b) describing specific observable behaviors associated with confirming/disconfirming response, and (c) reviewing confirmation research and considering implications for future study.

BACKGROUND

Until the last decade the term "confirmation," as it applies to human interaction, was too imprecise to form a basis for empirical study. Nevertheless it has long been regarded by many as a significant feature of human communication and has provided a useful perspective for examining social acts in terms of their impact upon other people.

The term "confirmation" was first used in an interpersonal sense by Martin Buber (1957), who attributed broad existential significance to confirmation, describing it as basic to humanness and as providing the test of the degree of humanity present in any society. Although Buber did not explicitly define confirmation, he consistently stressed its importance to human intercourse:

> The basis of man's life with man is twofold, and it is one —
> the wish of every man to be *confirmed* as what he is, even as
> what he can become, by men; and the innate capacity in man
> to confirm his fellow men in this way.... Actual humanity
> exists only where this capacity unfolds (p. 102).

R. D. Laing (1961) quoted extensively from Buber in his description of confirmation and disconfirmation as communicated qualities which exist in the relationship between two or more persons. Confirmation is the process through which individuals are "endorsed" by others, which, as Laing described it, implies recognition and acknowledgment of them. Though Laing developed confirmation at a conceptual level more thoroughly than anyone prior to him, his focus remained psychiatric: he was concerned with the effects of pervasive disconfirmation within the families of patients who had come to be diagnosed as schizophrenic. In such families, Laing noted, one child is frequently singled out as the recipient of especially destructive communicative acts by the other members. As Laing explained it, the behavior of the family "does not so much involve a child who has been subjected to outright neglect or even to obvious trauma, but a child who has been subjected to subtle but persistent *disconfirmation*, usually unwittingly" (1961:83). Laing further equated confirmation with a special kind of love, which "lets the other be, but with affection and concern," as contrasted with disconfirmation (or violence), which "attempts to constrain the other's freedom, to force him to act in the way we desire, but with ultimate lack of concern, with indifference to the other's own existence or destiny" (1967:58). This theme of showing concern while relinquishing control is common in psychiatric writing and is an important element in confirmation as we understand it. Although Laing stressed the significance of confirmation, he made no attempt to define it in terms of specific behaviors, noting only its variety of modes:

> Modes of confirmation or disconfirmation vary. Confirmation could be through a responsive smile (visual), a handshake (tactile), an expression of sympathy (auditory). A confirmatory response is *relevant* to the evocative action, it accords recognition to the evocatory act, and accepts its significance for the other, if not for the respondent. A confirmatory reaction is a direct response, it is "to the point," "on the same wavelength," as the initiatory or evocatory action (1961:82).

In 1967, Watzlawick, Beavin, and Jackson located confirmation within a more general framework of human communication and developed it as a necessary element of all human interaction, involving a subtle but powerful validation of the other's self-image. In addition to its content, they said each unit of interaction also contains relational information, offering first, a self-definition by a person (P) and then a response from the other (O) to that self-definition. According to Watzlawick *et al.*, this response may take any of three possible forms: it may confirm, it may reject, or it may disconfirm. The last, disconfirmation, implies the relational message, "You do not exist," and negates the other as a valid message source. Confirmation implies acceptance of the speaker's self-definition. "As far as we can see, this confirmation of *P's* view of himself by O is probably the greatest single factor ensuring mental development and stability that has so far emerged from our study of communication" (p. 84). The descriptive material provided by Watzlawick *et al.*, to illustrate disconfirmation includes instances of total unawareness of the other person, lack of accurate perception of the other's point of view, and deliberate distortion or denial of the other's self-attributes.

Sieburg (1969) used the structure provided by Watzlawick as well as the concept of confirmation/disconfirmation to begin distinguishing between human communication which is growthful, productive, effective, functional, or "therapeutic," and communication which is not. She developed measurement systems for systematically observing confirming and disconfirming communication (1969, 1972); she devised the first scale which allowed for measurement of an individual's feeling of being confirmed by another person (1973). She has continued to refine the basic theory of confirmation (1975), and has recently used the concepts to describe both organizational (1976) and family (in preparation) communication systems. During this time, a growing body of theoretical development and empirical research has attempted to explore these important concerns (cf. Cissna, 1976a, 1976b).

THEORETICAL FOUNDATIONS OF CONFIRMATION: RELATIONAL COMMUNICATION

Gregory Bateson (Ruesch & Bateson, 1951:179-181) first used the concepts of "report" and "command" to distinquish two different "sorts of meaning" in communication. Watzlawick *et al.*, (1967:51-54) interpreted these dimensions as equivalent in human communication to the "content" and "relationship" "levels of communication." The content is the "information," the "data," the "what is being talked about." The relationship level of communication provides information on what sort of message this is, how this communication is to be taken, which ultimately describes the nature of the relationship between the interactants. Both of these types of "information" are essential parts of human communication — perhaps even more than we need to know "what we're talking about," we need to know "who we're talking to" and "who the other believes us to be." The relationship level of communication involves communication about communication, and functions then as metacommunication. It provides people with information about the way in which messages are to be interpreted, and hence provides information about the current state of their relationship. Thus, the second axiom suggested by Watzlawick *et al.*, provides the beginning point of our analysis: "Every communication has a content and relationship aspect such that the latter classifies the former and is therefore a metacommunication" (p. 54, emphasis omitted), alternately phrased by Watzlawick and Beavin (1967), "there are many levels in every communication, and one always pertains to the *relationship* in which the communication occurs" (p. 5).

At any given point in a communication sequence it is possible to identify the relationship-oriented metacommunication of one communicator as implying "This is how I see myself (in relation to you in this situation)" (Watzlawick *et al.*, 1967:84). Human beings are always and everywhere offering self-definitions to others and responding to the self-definitions of others. These self-definitions which we offer to one another, as noted earlier, may be responded to in any of three different ways: confirmation, rejection, and disconfirmation. Confirmation communicates an acceptance of the other's definition of self. Rejection of the other's definition of self implies at least a limited recognition of the person being rejected. Disconfirmation involves negating the other as a valid source of any message.

The process of offering and responding metacommunicationally to self-definitions is apparently continuous (though there appears to be some disagreement on this issue), and occurs in both"pathological" and "normal" relationships. Perhaps, it is when these self-definitions are *not* accepted that most people become consciously aware of them — a process Carl Larson (Dance & Larson, 1976:78-79) describes as an "orientational shift" away from the content of communication and toward the relationship, especially toward the self-image which has been rejected (the term rejection as used by Larson seems to include both rejection and disconfirmation, as Watzlawick *et al.*, use these terms).

We must recall also that these relationship messages are only very rarely coded in the digital language of communication content. It is the *analogical* or metaphorical use of human language through which the self-definitions are both offered and responded to (Bateson, 1972). Seldom does one person say to another, "I see myself as dependent on you." And seldom, too, do human beings respond to one another by overtly saying "I agree with how you see yourself in relation to me," "I disagree with how you see yourself," or "You are not a valid message source." The behaviors which we have identified as confirming or disconfirming are those that call out in the other person, relational messages which "say" "You exist," "You do not exist," "We are relating," "We are not relating," and so on. These are the covert messages which seem to have implications for how the individual sees him or her self.

BEHAVIORAL INDICATORS OF CONFIRMATION/DISCONFIRMATION

Our work with confirmation was strongly influenced by John Weakland's (1967) discussion of the "new communication." Its chief feature is a concern with the study and understanding of communication as it evolves in naturally occurring human systems, rather than with some ideal of what communication *should* be. Its primary focus is on features that characterize the interaction of pairs or groups of persons, rather than on properties of single messages or single individuals. Further, this view emphasizes that communication is central in influencing individual behavior, that it is ubiquitous, and especially that research should focus on directly observable behavior, with little if any concern about intentionality. It was this view of communication that we followed in systematizing the confirmation concept in subsequent research. The following section will explain how particular behavioral indicators of confirmation and disconfirmation were selected and systematized.

Dimensions of Confirmation

In the few direct allusions in the literature to confirmation and disconfirmation, several different elements are suggested. Confirmation is, of course, tied by definition to self-experience; our first problem, therefore, was to identify the specific aspects of self-experience that could be influenced positively or negatively in interaction with others. Four such elements seemed significant for our purpose:

1. The element of existence (the individual sees self as existing)

2. The element of relating (the individual sees self as a being-in-relation with others)

3. The element of significance, or worth

4. The element of validity of experience

Thus, it was assumed that the behavior of one person toward another is confirming to the extent that it performs the following functions in regard to the other's self-experience:

1. It expresses recognition of the other's existence

2. It acknowledges a relationship of affiliation with the other

3. It expresses awareness of the significance or worth of the other

4. It accepts or "endorses" the other's self-experience (particularly emotional experience)

Each unit of response is assumed to evoke relational metamessages with regard to each of the above functions, which can identify it as either confirming or disconfirming:

Confirming	*Disconfirming*
"To me, you exist."	"To me, you do not exist."
"We are relating."	"We are not relating."
"To me, you are significant."	"To me, you are not significant."
"Your way of experiencing your world is valid."	"Your way of experiencing your world is invalid."

In attempting to find behavioral correlates of these functions, we acknowledge that it is not possible to point with certainty to particular behaviors that universally perform these confirming functions for all persons, since individuals differ in the way they interpret the same acts; that is, they interpret the stimuli and assign their own meaning to them. Despite this reservation about making firm causal connections between the behavior of one person and the internal experience of another, we have followed the symbolic interactionist view that certain symbolic cues *do* acquire consensual validation and therefore are consistently interpreted by most persons as reflecting certain attitudes toward them on the part of others.[1] Such cues thus have message value and are capable of arousing in the receiver feelings of being recognized or ignored, accepted or rejected, understood or misunderstood, humanized or "thingified," valued or devalued. This assumption was borne out in a very general way by our research to date (Sieburg & Larson, 1971).

Systematization of Behavioral Indicators

Although the psychiatric literature abounds with clinical illustrations of interaction that is damaging to the self-concept (especially as it occurs between parent and child), no systematization of particular forms of response according to their confirming or disconfirming power has heretofore been attempted. The primary question we set out to answer is: What specific, observable, behaviors influence others in such a way that they feel confirmed or disconfirmed? A second question (only partially answered) is: In real interaction, do these behaviors occur in recognizable clusters? A third question, not yet undertaken, must be: (a) Can these clusters be arranged along a continuum (or a hierarchy) from *most* to *least* confirmning, or (b) Does confirmation comprise a distinct dichotomy, or (c) Is this construct best defined by the three states described by Watzlawick *et al.?* The descriptive material used in systematization of confirmation and disconfirmation was derived from many sources, each of which seemed to relate to one or more of the four functional criteria noted earlier.

Although confirmation has long been identified as crucial in forming and maintaining any human relationship, it has received the most attention in clinical or psychotherapeutic settings, particularly family therapy, and such writings provided the bulk of our material. Of particular value were the contributions of the Bateson group in Palo Alto, of Boszormenyi-Nagy and Framo in Philadelphia, of the Wynne group in Bethesda, and of Laing in London. These clinical accounts of disturbed family interaction seemed at least potentially applicable to any human interaction. It was our hope that interpersonal confirmation would prove to be another aspect of human interaction where transfer of knowledge about a disturbed population could ultimately be made to a normal one.

Systematizing Disconfirming Behavior

It should be noted that the categories of "rejection" and "disconfirmation," as used by Watzlawick *et al.*, (1967) have both been included under our heading of "disconfirmation," thus forming a dichotomy of confirming-disconfirming acts. There are other possible "shapes" of confirmation, several of which have been used in empirical studies, as will be discussed more fully later in this chapter.

A variety of specific acts and omissions have been noted by clinicians and theoreticians as being damaging to some aspect of the receiver's self-view. We have arranged these behaviors into three general groupings, or clusters, each representing a somewhat different style of response:

1. Indifferent response (denying existence or relation)
2. Impervious response (denying self-experience of the other)
3. Disqualifying response (denying the other's significance)

These clusters include verbal/nonverbal and vocal/nonvocal behaviors. Since they encompass both content and process features of interaction, it meant that scorers must be trained to evaluate each scoring unit in terms of its manifest content, its transactional features, and its underlying structure. In either case, no single utterance stands alone since it is always in response to some behavior or another, and is so experienced by the other as having implications about his or her self. A summary outline of the disconfirming behavioral indicators is included in Appendix A.

Disconfirmation by Indifference. To deny another's existence is to deny the most fundamental aspect of self-experience. Indifference may be total, as when presence is denied; it may imply rejection of relatedness with the other; or it may only deny the other's attempt to communicate.

1. Denial of Presence

The absence of even a minimal show of recognition has been associated with alienation, self-destructiveness, violence against others, and with psychosis. Laing used the case of "Peter," a psychotic patient of 25 to illustrate the possible long-term effects of chronic indifference toward a child who may, as a consequence, come to believe that he has no presence at all — or to feel guilty that he *does*, feeling that he has no right even to occupy space.

Peter ... was a young man who was preoccupied with guilt *because* he occupied a place in the world, even in a physical sense. He could not realize ... that he had a right to have any presence for others... A peculiar aspect of his childhood was that his presence in the world was largely ignored. No weight was given to the fact that he was in the same room while his parents had intercourse. He had been physically cared for in that he had been well fed and kept warm, and underwent no physical separation from his parents during his earlier years. Yet he had been consistently treated as though he did not "really" exist. Perhaps worse than the experience of physical separation was to be in the same room as his parents and ignored, not malevolently, but through sheer indifference. (Laing, 1961:119)

That such extreme indifference is also devastating to an adult is evident in the following excerpt from a marriage counseling session (Sieburg, personal audiotape). It is perhaps significant that throughout his wife's outburst, the husband sat silent and remote:

Therapist: ...and is it okay to express emotion?

Wife: Not in my house.

Therapist: Has he [the husband] ever *said* it's not okay to talk about feelings?

Wife: But he never *says* anything!

Therapist: But he has ways of sending you messages?

Wife: [loudly] Yes! And the message is *shut out* — no matter what I say, no matter what I do, I get no response — zero — shut out!

Therapist: And does that somehow make you feel you are wrong?

Wife: Oh, of course not wrong — just *nothing*!

Therapist: Then what is it that makes you feel he disapproves of you?

Wife: Because I get nothing! [tears] If I feel discouraged — like looking for a job all day and being turned down — and I cry — zero! No touching, no patting, no "Maybe tomorrow" — just *shut out*. And if I get angry at him, instead of getting angry back, he just walks away — just nothing! All the time I'm feeling shut out and shut off!

Therapist: And what is it you want from him?

Wife: [quietly] Maybe sometimes just a pat on the back would be enough. But, no! — he just shrugs me off. Where am I supposed to go to feel real? [tears]

2. Avoiding Involvement

Extreme instances of indifference like those above are presumed to be rare because even the slightest attention at least confirms one's presence. Lesser shows of indifference, however, still create feelings of alienation, frustration, and lowered self-worth. Although recognition is a necessary first step in confirming another, it is not in itself sufficient unless accompanied by some further indication of a willingness to be involved.

The precise ways in which one person indicates to another that he or she is interested in relating (intimacy) are not fully known, but several clear indications of *unwillingness* to relate or to become more than minimally involved have emerged from research and have been included in our systemization of disconfirming behaviors. Of particular significance are the use of:

• Impersonal language — the avoidance of first person references (I, me, my, mine) in favor of a collective "we" or "one," or the tendency to begin sentences with "there" when making what amounts to a personal statement (as, "there seems to be . . .")

• Avoidance of eye contact

• Avoidance of physical contact except in ritualized situations such as hand-shaking

• Other nonverbal "distancing" cues

3. Rejecting Communication

A third way of suggesting indifference to another is to respond in a way that is unrelated, or only minimally related, to what he or she has just said, thus creating a break or disjunction in the flow of interaction.

Totally irrelevant response is, of course, much like denial of presence in that the person whose topic is repeatedly ignored may soon come to doubt his or her very existence, and at best will feel that he or she is not heard, attended to, or regarded as significant. Perhaps for this reason Laing called relevance the "crux of confirmation," noting that only by responding relevantly can one lend significance to another's communication and accord recognition (Laing, 1961:87).

The most extreme form of communication rejection is monologue, in which one speaker continues on and on, neither hearing nor acknowledging anything the other says. It reflects unawareness and lack of concern about the other person except as a socially acceptable audience for the speaker's own self-listening. A less severe communication rejection occurs when the responder makes a connection, however slight, with what the other has said, but immediately shifts into something quite different of his or her own choosing.

Disconfirming by Imperviousness. The term "imperviousness" as used here follows Laing's usage and refers to a lack of accurate awareness of another's perceptions (Watzlawick *et al.*, 1967:91). Imperviousness is disconfirming because it denies or distorts another's self-expression and fosters dehumanized relationships in which one person perceives another as a pseudo-image rather than as what that person really is. Behaviorally, the impervious responder engages in various tactics that tend to negate or discredit the other's feeling expression. These may take the form of a flat denial that the other *has* such a feeling ("You don't really mean that"), or it may be handled more indirectly by re-interpreting the feeling in a more acceptable way, ("You're only saying that because..."), substituting some experience or feeling of the *listener* ("What you're trying to say is..."), challenging the speaker's right to have such a feeling ("How can you *possibly* feel that way after all that's been done for you?"), or some similar device intended to alter the feeling expressed.

Some elements of what we are now calling imperviousness (including Laing's concept of mystification) are difficult to score empirically because they are socially approved behaviors and may be easily missed if one is attending to the content of the interchange rather than to its structure. For example, reassuring another or trying to minimize self-doubts is often thought to be useful, appropriate, and even helpful behavior, without recognizing that the self-experience of the other person is being questioned. Laing noted this problem and provided the following example of a conversation between a mother and her fourteen-year-old daughter:

Mother: You are evil.

Daughter: No, I'm not.

Mother: Yes, you are.

Daughter: Uncle Jack doesn't think so.

Mother: He doesn't love you as I do. Only a mother really knows the truth about her daughter, and only one who loves you as I do will ever tell you the truth about yourself no matter what it is. If you don't believe me, just look at yourself in the mirror carefully and you will see that I'm telling the truth.

The daughter did, and saw that her mother was right after all, and realized how wrong she had been not to be grateful for having a mother who so loved her that she would tell the truth about herself. Whatever it might be.

This example may appear somewhat disturbing, even sinister. Suppose we changed one word in it: replace "evil" by "pretty."

Mother: You are pretty.

Daughter: No, I'm not.

Mother: Yes you are.

Daughter: Uncle Jack doesn't think so.

Mother: He doesn't love you as I do. Only a mother really knows the truth about her daughter, and only the one who loves you as I do will ever tell you the truth about yourself no matter what it is. If you don't believe me, just look at yourself in the mirror carefully, and you will see that I'm telling you the truth.

> The *technique* is the same. Whether the attribution is pretty, good, beautiful, ugly, or evil, the *structure* is identical. The structure is *so* common that we hardly notice it unless the attribution jars. We all employ some recognizably similar version of this technique and may be prepared to justify it. I sug-

gest that we reflect upon the *structure* of the *induction* not only
the *content* thereof (Laing, 1969:121-123).

Many of us might identify the former as disconfirming and the latter
as helpful, even confirming; however, the *structure* of the interaction
process is a disconfirming one regardless of the content.

A slightly different form of imperviousness occurs when a responder
creates and bestows on another an inaccurate identity, and then confirms the false identity, although it is not a part of the other's self-
experience at all. Laing calls this pseudo-confirmation (1961:83). Thus a
mother who insists that her daughter is always obedient and "never any
trouble at all" may be able to interpret her daughter's most rebellious
aggression in a way that fits the placid image she holds of her daughter,
and the parents of even a murderous psychopath may be able to
describe their son as a "good boy." Such a false confirmation frequently
endorses the fiction of what the other is *wished* to be, without any real
recognition of what the other is or how he/she feels. As noted earlier,
this form of disconfirmation also appears as simply a well-meaning attempt to reassure another who is distressed, which too is usually
motivated by the speaker's need to reduce his or her own discomfort.

"Don't be silly — of course you're not afraid!"

"You may think you feel that way now, but I know better."

"Stop crying — there's nothing the matter with you!"

"How can you possibly worry about a little thing like that?"

"No matter what you say, I know you still love me."

Such responses constitute a rejection of the other person's expression
and often identity, raising doubts about the validity of his/her way of
experiencing by suggesting, "You don't really feel as you say you do; you
are only imagining that you do."

A subtle variation of the same tactic occurs when the speaker
responds in a selective way, rewarding the other with attention and relevant response *only* when he or she communicates in an approved
fashion, and becoming silent or indifferent if the other's speech or
behavior does not meet with the responder's approval. This may mean
that the speaker limits response to those topics initiated by self, ignoring

any topic initiated by the other person.

Imperviousness is considered disconfirming because it contributes to a feeling of uncertainty about self or uncertainty about the validity of personal experiencing. Imperviousness occurs when a person is told how he or she feels, regardless of how he or she experiences self, when a person's talents and abilities are described without any data to support such a description, when motives are ascribed to another without any reference to the other's own experience, or when one's own efforts at self-expression are ignored or discounted unless they match the false image held by some other person.

The consequences of imperviousness have received considerable attention in the literature under a variety of labels. Laing (1965) described "mystification," meaning the substitution of a speaker's motivation as a way of exploiting the other while expressing only benevolence. Boszormenyi-Nagy (1965) described disturbed family interaction in which the "autonomous otherness" of certain family members is ignored when another member speaks for them, interpreting their motives and describing their feelings. Buber (1957) expressed it somewhat more poetically when he said, "If we overlook the 'otherness' of the other person . . . we shall see him in our own image and not as he really is in his concrete uniqueness."

Disconfirmation by Disqualification. According to Watzlawick (1964) disqualification is a technique which enables one to say something without really saying it, to deny without really saying "no," and to disagree without really disagreeing. Certain messages, verbal and nonverbal, are included in this group because they (a) disqualify the other speaker, (b) disqualify another message, or (c) disqualify themselves.

1. Speaker Disqualification
This may include such direct disparagement of the other as name-calling, criticism, blame, and hostile attack, but may also take the indirect form of the sigh of martyrdom, the muttered expletive, addressing an adult in a tone of voice usually reserved for a backward child, joking "on the square," sarcasm, or any of the other numerous tactics to make the other appear and feel too incompetent or unreliable for his message to have validity. This creates a particularly unanswerable put-down by evoking strong metamessages of insignificance or worthlessness. The following examples are spouses' responses from conjoint counseling sessions:

- "Can't you ever do anything right?"

- "Here we go again!" [sigh]

- "We heard you the first time—why do you always keep repeating yourself?"

- "It's no wonder the rear axle broke, with you in the back seat!" [laughter]

- "Why do you always have to get your mouth open when you don't know what you're talking about?"

2. Message Disqualification

Without regard to their content, some messages tend to discredit the other person because of their irrelevance — that is, they do not "follow" the other's prior utterance in a transactional sense. (This is also a tactic of indifference and may serve a dual disconfirming purpose.) Such disjunctive responses were studied by Sluzki, Beavin, Tarnopolski, and Veron (1967) who used the term "transactional disqualification" to mean any incongruity in the response of the speaker in relation to the context of the previous message of the other. A relationship between two successive messages exists, they noted, on two possible levels: (a) continuity between the content of the two messages (are both persons talking about the same subject?), and (b) indication of reception of the prior message (what cues does the speaker give of receiving and understanding the previous message?). If a message is disjunctive at either of these levels, transactional disqualification of the prior message is said to have occurred.

A similar form of message disqualification occurs when a speaker reacts selectively to some incidental clue in another's speech, but ignores the primary theme. Thus the responder may acknowledge the other's attempt to communicate, but still appears to miss the point. This "tangential response" was identified and studied by Jurgen Ruesch (1958), who noted that a speaker often picks up on a topic presented, but then continues to spin a yarn in a different direction. The response is not totally irrelevant because it has made some connection, although perhaps slight, with the prior utterance. Because it causes the first speaker to question the value or importance of what he or she was trying to say, the tangential response is reported to affect adversely a speaker's feeling of self-significance, and is therefore included as a form of disconfirmation.

3. Message Disqualifying Itself

A third way in which a speaker can use disqualification to "say something without really saying it," is by sending messages that disqualify themselves. There are many ways in which this may be done, the commonest devices being lack of clarity, ambiguity, and incongruity of mode. These forms of response are grouped together here because they have all been interpreted as devices for avoiding involvement with another by generating the metamessage "I am not communicating," hence "We are not relating."

Systematizing Confirming Behaviors

Responses that confirm are less clearly defined than disconfirming behaviors because there has been less motivation to study them. In fact, identification of specific acts that are generally confirming is difficult unless we simply identify confirmation as the absence of disconfirming behaviors. More research in this area is clearly needed, but, in general, confirming behaviors are those which permit people to experience their own being and significance as well as their interconnectedness with others. Following Laing (1961), these have been arranged into three clusters: recognition, acknowledgment, and endorsement.

The Recognition Cluster. Recognition is expressed by looking at the other, making frequent eye contact, touching, speaking directly to the person, and allowing the other the opportunity to respond without being interrupted or having to force his or her way into an ongoing monologue. In the case of an infant, recognition means holding and cuddling beyond basic survival functions; in the case of an adult, it may still mean physical contact (touching), but it also means psychological contact in the form of personal language, clarity, congruence of mode, and authentic self-expression. In other words, confirmation requires that a person treat the other with respect, acknowledging his or her attempt to relate, and need to have a presence in the world.

The Acknowledgment Cluster. Acknowledgment of another is demonstrated by a relevant and direct response to his or her communication. This does not require praise or even agreement, but simple conjunction. Buber (Friedman, 1960) recognized this aspect when he wrote that mutually confirming partners can still "struggle together in direct opposition," and Laing (1961) made a similar point when he said that even rejection can be confirming if it is direct, not tangential, and if it grants significance and validity to what the other says. To hear, attend, and take note of the other and to acknowledge the other by responding directly is probably the most valued form of confirmation — and possibly the most rare. It means that the other's expression is furthered, facilitated, and encouraged.

The Endorsement Cluster. This cluster includes any responses that express acceptance of the other's feelings as being true, accurate, and "okay." In general, it means simply letting the other *be*, without blame, praise, analysis, justification, modification, or denial.

Confirming response is dialogic in structure; it is a reciprocal activity involving shared talk and sometimes shared silence. It is interactional in the broadest sense of the word. It is not a one-way flow of talk; it is not a trade-off in which each speaker pauses and appears to listen only in order to get a chance to speak again. It is a complex affair in which each participates as both subject and object, cause and effect, of the other's talk. In short, confirming response, like all communication, is not something one does, it is a process in which one shares.

Presented in this way, it seems inescapable that confirmation represents an idealized view of how communication "should be," rather than how it is, thus violating a principle tenet of the interactional view. Perhaps what we are discovering is that most *real* interaction involves one kind of disconfirmation or another (in varying degrees), and that confirming response exists only as an idealized counterpoint to disconfirmation.

IMPLICATIONS OF CONFIRMATION RESEARCH

In the decade since Evelyn Sieburg (1969) conducted the first "confirmation" research, we are aware of twenty empirical studies which have been reported utilizing the confirmation construct. Thirteen of these have appeared since Cissna's (1976b) review of the literature.[2]

This section will consider several aspects of confirmation research: measurement problems and implications, the relationship between agreement/disagreement and confirmation/disconfirmation, the possible "shapes" of a confirmation model (whether it is more accurately described as a continuum, a dichotomy, a trichotomy, or a hierarchy), and generalizations from the confirmation research.

Implications for Measurement

Two primary approaches to measuring interpersonal confirmation have been used. One approach involves determing the extent to which one individual exhibits confirming/disconfirming behaviors toward another individual; the second approach involves measuring the extent to which one person *feels* confirmed or disconfirmed by another individual. While other approaches have been used on occasion (especially experimental manipulation of confirming/disconfirming responses as an independent variable), we will, in this chapter, concentrate on the two major strategies. As many have noted, the interactional view contains constructs that are difficult to operationalize and measure (Wilder, 1979), and this has been especially true of confirmation research.

Observation of Behaviors

Consistent with Weakland's (1967) explication of the "new communication," confirmation research has frequently focused on observable behaviors in human interaction. The earliest such observational system was developed by Sieburg (1969) and was later refined (1972). This initial effort, called the "Interpersonal Responsiveness Category System," contained five "dysfunctional" categories and two "functional" categories of response. Using expert judges, she was able to achieve a high reliability after two four-hour training sessions (Sieburg, 1969; summarized in Cissna, 1976b). She then had the judges listen to audio recordings of actual group sessions, scoring frequency of occurrence of various response types.

Sundell (1972) employed a category system based on Sieburg and Larson's (1971) response forms using the behaviors that were described as typical of most preferred and least preferred partners (these were later identified as confirming and disconfirming behaviors). More recently,

Aveyard (1977) used only the seven "disconfirming" behaviors identified by Sieburg and Larson in an observational coding scheme. Mathews (1977) created and used a confirmation/disconfirmation observational system specific for librarian-patron interaction, and Hull (in progress) used a variation of Mathew's system, based on Sieburg's (1973) clusters.

Several measurement problems have been identified. Some behaviors, although noted frequently in psychiatric writings, simply did not occur often in these normal populations, especially those behaviors having to do with mystification, impersonal response, and self-disqualifying messages. Noting that these categories occurred so infrequently in the populations used, Sieburg (1969) speculated that these response forms may, in fact, be indicative of psychopathology.

Using the interactional view, the minimal unit of analysis is always the interaction — a statement and its response — which is usually operationalized as the relation of a verbalization to the immediately prior utterance. This is a useful restriction for most purposes, especially when the concern is with relevance of one utterance to the one just prior. For research purposes, it produces a simpler scoring system and increases reliability by making the unit of analysis and categories as narrow and specific as possible. However, confirming acts, and especially disconfirming ones, do not always come neatly packaged in such statement-response units. Like double-binds (Sluzki & Ransom, 1976), other kinds of disconfirming acts are not always evident in one sentence, and considerable expertise is required to recognize the often-lengthy patterns that comprise a disconfirming "act." Even if recognized, these patterns are difficult to score because scoring rules and unit of analysis often do not admit them. Further, some of the behaviors we identified above (e.g., messages which disqualify themselves or the speaker, monologue, or reliance on impersonal language, among disconfirming behaviors) do not require an "interact" for their observation at all. These can be and are observed from one person's utterance only. The interactional quality of these "messages" comes from the fact that they are *experienced* interactionally — participants *perceive* these behaviors as being related to their own behaviors and hence experience them as having something to do with their own identity. I perceive the other as responding to *me*, even if my utterances are not required for scoring the act as confirming/disconfirming.

An additional problem occurs because some individuals have difficulty recognizing forms of disconfirmation that are common in their own experience. An instance of this occurred in Sieburg's initial study in which one of her categories, "mystification," had to be dropped from the observational system because a coder could not agree with the others on what mystification was and when it happened. Several years later, Sieburg heard again from that rater, who had undergone a long period of personal psychotherapy. She reported that in the course of the therapy, she had come to realize that the mystifying response which she had been unable to identify earlier was a response form regularly employed in her childhood family — one that she had come to expect and see as "normal" interactional behavior. Similarly, some freshmen students in Jacobs' (1973) study reported being not in the least disturbed when confronted with professors who were role-playing indifferent behavior — commenting that it was about what they had come to expect from teachers!

Two additional issues regarding measurement emerge from the research. One concerns whether *all* communication events contain the power to confirm or disconfirm or whether confirming and disconfirming events occur only occasionally. That is, whether confirmation is continuous or discontinuous. Most studies have followed Sieburg (1969), assuming that all utterances contain a response to the other's definition of self and hence have confirming or disconfirming properties (Aveyard, 1977; Hull, 1979; Mathews, 1977; Sundell, 1972). Waxwood (1976), on the other hand, seems more consistent with Larson (Dance & Larson, 1976) in viewing human communication as opportunities for confirming and disconfirming events to occur — from time to time. This issue may be more a conceptual and theoretical one that can reasonably be resolved through reference to empirical research.

A second issue is whether the coding — the determination of whether any piece of behavior is confirming or disconfirming — should be done by an outside observer or by the participants themselves. Most of the confirmation research has followed the positivistic assumption of objective and external observers who have received extensive training to perform their rating task reliably. John Stewart[3] has suggested that the participants themselves may be the more appropriate ones to define these behaviors. Waxwood (1976) used simulated recall interviews, asking participants individually to view the videotapes of themselves interacting and to identify confirming and disconfirming behaviors as well as remark on behaviors the investigator suspected might be experienced as confirming or disconfirming. Stewart suggested that the genuinely relational way to proceed with measurement is to ask participants to discuss the interaction sequences together and to agree among themselves regarding which behaviors were confirming and which disconfirming.

Cushman[4] distinguished between measurement schemes which ask the participant (as in self-report scales), ones which rely on external observers, and ones which ask the participants to agree relationally on a definition of the phenomenon. While the latter seems consistent with the thrust of the interactional view, it has not yet been employed in confirmation research. It would also seem to raise the problem discussed above of (untrained) participants not recognizing certain forms of disconfirming behavior, which would not seem to lose their relational power merely because they are out of a person's awareness (Watzlawick *et al.*, 1967:37). Each of these types of systems may well rely on different definitions of the basic phenomenon under study, and/or may tap different aspects of it. As such, there is no necessary reason these should produce highly related results. Whether this is the case remains an empirical question, posing many interesting and perplexing problems.

The indicators of both confirming and disconfirming response include vocal and nonvocal as well as verbal and nonverbal behaviors and the research is weakened if observation does not include all modes. Sieburg (1969) as well as Hull (in progress) used audiotape recordings; Sundell (1972) and Mathews (1977) used live observation; and Aveyard (1977), Waxwood (1976), and apparently Litschutz (1979) used videotapes. Live observations allow for scoring both verbal/vocal and nonvocal behaviors, but have the disadvantages of not being available for reanalysis and are generally limited to interpretation and scoring by one observer. Videotape is clearly the method of choice, and as it becomes increasingly available to academic researchers, scoring procedures can be developed to take advantage of the video-plus-audio modes, with the greater reliability of multiple coders. Refinement of the nonverbal/nonvocal aspects of the indicators may be necessary, especially with regard to congruence of modes — as when spoken words do not "fit" with tone of voice or with accompanying body movement or gesture.

While we do have coding systems for observing confirming/disconfirming behaviors, these have for the most part been developed for sample specific purposes and/or have coded only limited aspects of confirming/disconfirming behaviors. Developments regarding the appropriate unit of analysis, the appropriate locus of observation, procedures for training observers all require continued attention. Ideally, a system should allow for systematically observing and coding both confirming and disconfirming behaviors at least in dyads and small groups, from videotapes or live interaction, with appropriate adjustments made when using audiotape or transcripts.

Measuring Feelings of Being Confirmed/Disconfirmed

Scholars interested in measuring the extent to which an individual feels confirmed by another have generally used the Perceived Confirmation Scale (PCS) developed by Sieburg (1973).[5] The PCS is a six-item Likert-type summated scale. Jacobs (1973) assessed construct validity for the PCS through finding high item-total correlations for each of the six items with three target persons, and by finding that subjects *do* distinguish between target persons in their PCS scores. The interesting findings the PCS yielded (Cissna, 1975, 1979; Clarke, 1973; Jacobs, 1973; Keating, 1977; Sutton, 1976) also support its validity. Though the PCS is rather brief, its reliability seems adequate. Clarke (1973) reported test-retest (three-week interval) reliability of $r = .70$ (married couples) and Cissna (1976b) found $r = .74$ and $.92$ for samples of day and adult evening students describing their parents (four-week interval), though this sample produced lower test-retest reliability coefficients for same sex friends ($r = .59$ and $.50$, for day and evening students respectively). The lower values for same sex friends can be accounted for in large measure because some students simply didn't remember which friend they used a month earlier. In addition, the phenomenon itself may be changed somewhat during this interval, as student friendships can change fairly rapidly. Internal reliability was assessed through the International Communication Association Committee on the Status of Women's 1978-1979 Research Project (see Cissna, 1979). They studied 980 students and non-students from a variety of sites around the country measuring (among other things) their feelings of being confirmed by three specific people in their lives: (a) a past or present work supervisor, (b) a lover or person with whom they were or had been involved in an intimate or dating relationship, and (c) a same sex friend. The Cronbach alpha statistics were $\alpha = .82$ (supervisors), $.78$ (lovers), and $.75$ (friends).

Serious philosophical questions can be raised, however, concerning our ability to measure perceived confirmation. Confirmation, as we have interpreted it, is derived jointly from immediately observable behaviors as well as from the existential and phenomenological reality of one's own experience. While behaviors are readily observable, confirmation as an internal experience is more difficult, deriving its validity from each individual's perceptions. Again, disconfirmation by "mystification" or imperviousness is a case in point. Laing's (1961) notions were derived from his work with the families of schizophrenic patients. He found his patients to be highly mystified (1965) and highly disconfirmed within their families (Laing & Esterson, 1964). However — and this is crucial — the very fact of mystification may cause the recipient's perceptions to become confused. *Because* they are mystified in a false self, they may experience disconfirmation as confirming (Laing, 1967). Since this kind of disconfirmation is schizogenic (Laing, 1961), it might well confound research findings since the observable behavior reported as disconfirming would not be expected to be congruent with the internal experience reported by the "victim." In other words, some forms of disconfirmation may not necessarily be available to phenomenological introspection. Further, if Laing is correct that mystification and alienation pervade our society, then perhaps many people would experience disconfirmation as confirming and would experience confirming behavior as threatening. The research problem is obvious: if disconfirmation is experienced as confirming, then measurement of the person's experience of feeling confirmed may only provide another echo of mystification.

Confirmation and Agreement/Disagreement

The confirmational effects of agreement and disagreement have been another source of confusion for researchers and theorists. Buber (1957) and Laing were clear that agreement was *not* necessary for confirmation. Laing (1969) wrote: "A partially confirmatory response need not be in agreement. . . . Rejection can be confirmatory if it is direct, not tangential, and recognizes the evoking action and grants it significance and validity" (p. 99). Watzlawick and his colleagues (1967) claim that disagreement at the *relationship* level (rather than disagreement about content) is disconfirming. The early research of Sieburg and Larson (1971) found that "agreement about content" was characteristic of their predominantly male subjects' descriptions of their "most preferred" persons, although "disagreement about content" was not part of the response pattern of "least preferred" targets. Further empirical investigation of agreement and confirmation has been limited and directed strictly to agreement and disagreement about the content of the discussion. Sundell (1972) found agreement about content to be the most frequent response of the more confirming teachers in his sample, and the response which best distinguished the confirming teachers from the disconfirming ones. Sutton (1976) trained interviewers either to agree or to self-disclose in response to students. Contrary to her hypothesis, self-disclosure was not experienced as more confirming by the females than by the males, and agreement was not experienced as more confirming by the males than by the females. Keating (1977; Cissna & Keating, 1979) studied frequency of agreement and disagreement in discussions between married couples and found a significant negative association between frequency of disagreement and his/her spouse's level of perceived confirmation. S. Leth (1977a), although purporting to measure confirmation and disconfirmation, actually appears to have been measuring various forms of agreement and disagreement.[6] We conclude from his findings that both clear direct agreement and clear direct disagreement are both appropriate and useful (perhaps even confirming) responses in same-sex friendships.

It may be that agreement about content is irrelevant to confirmation despite confused findings. Certainly it is pleasant to have another express agreement with our opinions. So, also, is confirmation usually experienced as pleasant. We should take care, however, that these separate findings do not lead us to create a faulty syllogism: Agreement is pleasant; Confirmation is pleasant; therefore Agreement is Confirmation. Until more data are available, we must conclude that agreement/disagreement *about content* is not related to confirmation/disconfirmation. Agreement or disagreement about another's *self-view* is quite another matter, and denial, rejection, or disagreement with regard to another's self-description must always be regarded as disconfirming. "You are wrong in the way you see yourself" is clearly an impervious responses.

Implications for the Nature of Interpersonal Confirmation

There are many different views of the appropriate shape of the confirmation construct. Sieburg at one time (1972) described the hierarchy of confirming responses, building on a base of recognition of the other's existence; Cissna (1976b; Cissna & Keating, 1979) explained confirmation as a continuum from highly confirming to highly disconfirming; Larson (Dance & Larson, 1976:73-90) described two states, acceptance and rejection, both of which had implicit as well as explicit forms, and a neutral area in which the orientational shift from content to relationship did not occur; Watzlawick, Beavin, and Jackson (1967) described three distinct response forms: confirmation, rejection, and disconfirmation. All of these views seem to have been offered somewhat prematurely. A confirmation-disconfirmation dichotomy seems now to over-simplify the phenomenon. For example, the troublesome "impervious response" is qualitatively different and is experienced differently from other disconfirming forms. To view confirmation/disconfirmation as a single continuum raises the problem of weights to assign to various forms of disconfirmation — a question that research has not yet even considered. There are, of course, behaviors that we can distinguish as confirming or disconfirming, and the extent to which individuals exposed to these forms actually *feel* confirmed may well range from high to low. The notion of a hierarchy, while reasonable, is still not verified with research data available. The "indifference" cluster of behaviors which totally denies the existence of the other person seems logically to be the most disconfirming; however, *imperviousness* is more frequently associated with severe pathology. Although we elected to use a dichotomous model of confirmation-disconfirmation, it may be that the three response forms described by Watzlawick *et al.*, confirmation, rejection, and disconfirmation, come as close as any other system to representing the phenomenon as it exists. We still believe that there are distinguishible levels of interpersonal confirmation, but caution that available evidence has not identified them precisely.

Generalizations from Confirmation Research

Confirmation and disconfirmation have been studied in several ways using a variety of different measurement procedures. In spite of a lack of an essential operational definition of confirmation/disconfirmation, the findings are provocative. These findings, from the speech communication discipline concerning "ordinary" interpersonal relationships, should be considered along side the considerable body of evidence from psychiatric studies of pathological communication processes (summarized by Sieburg, 1969, 1973, 1975).

The degree of presence or absence of confirming behaviors seems to make a difference in various kinds of human relationships — small groups (Sieburg, 1969), supervisor-subordinate (Jablin, 1977), teacher-student (P. Leth. 1977; Sundell, 1972), and friendships (S. Leth, 1977). The degree to which an individual feels confirmed as a person also is related to success in various relationships — marriage (Clarke, 1973; Cissna, 1975), health professions (Dangott, Thornton & Page, 1979), and teaching (P. Leth, 1977). Confirming communication is experienced as pleasant and is preferred by individuals over disconfirming communication (Sieburg & Larson, 1971). Patterns of confirming and disconfirming communication are reciprocated — individuals seeming to receive what they send (Sundell, 1972). Confirming and disconfirming behaviors are identifiable by interactants (Waxwood, 1976), and experienced differently by them (Jacobs, 1973). Predominantly confirming individuals have different values than individuals who are less confirming (Mathews, 1977). Confirmation/disconfirmation is the only pattern common to participants' perceptions of their own and others' communication in marriage, father-son, supervisor-subordinate, and counselor-juvenile delinquent relationships (Ross, 1973). Confirming communication patterns may be related to development of high self-concepts (Leth, 1977).

While these findings are only exploratory and should be regarded tentatively, initial research seems to affirm the significance early theorists gave to the confirmation construct.

CONCLUSION

This chapter has examined the theoretical foundations of interpersonal confirmation as an aspect of relational communication. Specific behavioral indicators of confirming and disconfirming communication have been proposed, completed research has been reviewed and conclusions have been drawn regarding the confirmation construct and the interactional view on which it is based.

It has been said that one's answers are generally limited by the horizon of one's questions. The behaviors and processes with which we have been concerned here are vital ones. Our goal now is to ask even better questions.

APPENDIX A

SUMMARY OF DISCONFIRMING
BEHAVIORAL INDICATORS

I. Disconfirmation by Indifference

    A. Denial of Presence

        1. Silence when reply is expected; refusal to respond
        2. Looks away while other is speaking
        3. Withdraws physically; leaves the scene
        4. Engages in unrelated activities while other is speaking

    B. Denial of Involvement (relation)

        1. Avoids eye-contact
        2. Avoids touch, uses nonverbal "distancing" behaviors
        3. Impersonal language; avoids "self" data, feeling statements or disclosure of any kind

    C. Rejection of Communication

        1. Monologue, repeated interruption, "talking over" other
        2. Interjects irrelevant comments

II. Disconfirmation by Imperviousness

    A. Denial, distortion, reinterpretation of other's self-expression

    B. Pseudo-confirmation

C.   Mystification

D.   Selective response

III.   Disconfirmation by Disqualification

A.   Messages that disqualify the other person

   1.   Direct disparagement: insult, name-calling
   2.   Indirect disparagement: verbal or nonverbal

B.   Messages that disqualify another message

   1.   Transactional disqualification
   2.   Tangential response

C.   Messages that are self-disqualifying

   1.   Unclear, incomplete, messages
   2.   Ambiguous messages
   3.   Incongruity of verbal-nonverbal modes

NOTES

1.   We believe that the interactional view addressed by this volume and symbolic interactionism are complementary, and both have influenced the development of this work. Though symbolic interactionism will not be explicitly identified in the remainder of this chapter, the informed reader will notice its influence at several points. See Sieburg (1973) and Leth (1977).

2.   The first author will provide a current chronological review and summary of this literature to the interested reader.

3.   Stewart made this recommendation in remarks for a "Lunch Panel" on confirmation and disconfirmation at the Asilomar Conference from which this volume originated, February 17, 1979. The authors of this chapter also participated in this panel, chaired by Phil Salem.

4. Cushman's comments were made during the ensuing discussion at the Lunch Panel mentioned above.

5. P. Leth (1977) also seems to us to have assessed perceived confirmation, though in a very different way. She asked students in an introductory speech communication class to react to their instructors' written critiques of their speeches according to five pairs of bipolar adjectives (unclear-clear, irrelevant-relevant, unrealistic-realistic, atypical-typical, and unhelpful-helpful) and one Likert-type question ("In general this critique agrees with my perception of myself as a public speaker") to which they could indicate the extent of their agreement/disagreement. These six items were summed to produce a score on the "Interpersonal Perception Scale." While the PCS asks subjects to indicate the extent to which they feel confirmed by another in general, Leth appears to have asked subjects to indicate the extent to which they feel confirmed by one specific message of the other.

6. The issue centers around the definition of confirming and rejecting behaviors. S. Leth's (1977) study involved two separate designs, both of which share common definitions of confirmation, rejection, and disconfirmation. In the experimental design one individual is asked to self-disclose regarding a particular attribute of self and the other is taught to respond with clear, relevant agreement (called confirmation), clear, relevant, disagreement (called rejection), or a response which is neither clear, relevant, nor agreeing/disagreeing (called disconfirmation). In the descriptive, field study design, subjects are asked to indicate how they think their friend would respond to a self-disclosure by them regarding various aspects of their self-concepts using the same categories and definitions used in the experimental study. We do not believe the concepts of confirmation and rejection have been defined and operationalized in ways consistent with the definitions given by Watzlawick, Beavin, and Jackson (1967). For Watzlawick *et al.*, as well as ourselves, the self-definitions and subsequent confirming, rejecting, and disconfirming responses are implicit metamessages, rarely explicitly coded in the digital language. In fact, it is precisely their subtle and out-of-awareness nature that gives these messages their power. S. Leth has tried to take responses to the self-concept out of the fuzzy territory of the analogic and into the clear-cut domain of the digital. His subjects have overtly disclosed an aspect of their self-concept which the other has overtly responded to. Rather than measuring confirmation and rejection as he had intended, we believe that agreement and disagreement have been measured (the operationalization of disconfirmation makes more sense to us as it is in the implicit analogic language of metacommunication). That it is the individual's self-concept which is being agreed and disagreed with is interesting and perhaps important but not sufficient to make the study into one of confirmation and rejection. When one reconceptualizes his interpersonal responses as we have done here, and regards both clear, relevant agreement and clear, relevant disagreement as confirming in contrast to the responses which lack these and are classified as disconfirming, we make different predictions than S. Leth on nine of his twenty-six hypotheses. As it turns out, all nine of these are ones in which S. Leth's predictions were not upheld. We have no difficulty whatsoever seeing rejection (as operationalized in this study as disagreement) as a valid and appropriate form of interpersonal response (cf. Leth 1978:26).

Pragmatics of Interpersonal Competence

John M. Wiemann
and Clifford W. Kelly

Two important recent developments in the study of interpersonal communication are the emphasis placed upon identifying components of communicative competence and the emergence of the pragmatic perspective. While these heuristic frameworks have generated considerable interest and excitement within our discipline, they have not been used to enlighten one another in any systematic, integrated way. In this essay we briefly summarize the thinking that led to the concept of pragmatics as it is currently being used by communication scholars, review major conceptualizations of competence, and demonstrate that a *pragmatics of interpersonal competence* provides a new and valuable approach to the study of interpersonal relationships.

PRAGMATICS

In order to fully appreciate current views of pragmatics, it is necessary to trace it to its origins in American pragmatic philosophy. Although American pragmatism typically brings to mind the names of James and Dewey, it had its origins in Charles Peirce's article, "How to Make Our Ideas Clear" published in the *Popular Science Monthly* in 1878. Twenty years later, it was James who revived Peirce's ideas in a lecture delivered before the Philosophical Union of the University of California, a lecture that spurred the movement in American thought known as pragmatism (Moore, 1961). The term "pragmatism" was used by Peirce who adapted it from Kant's *Critique of Pure Reason* in which Kant employed the term *pragmatisch* to express a "relation to some purpose" (Morris, 1970:9). Characteristic of the pragmatists was the central assumption that philosophy ought to inquire into the solution of some specific problems under specific personal and social conditions. A second theme underlying this philosophy is that problems emerge in situations, many features of which are unproblematic in nature. That is, problems can be solved only within the context in which some objects and meanings and beliefs are accepted without question (Morris, 1970).

Morris (1938, 1946) linked James' philosophy with the study of communication when he proposed a scientific empiricism in which semiotics provides for the study of three types of relations sustained by signs and which defines three dimensions of meaning. *Syntactics* is viewed as dealing with combinations of signs without regard for their specific significations or their relation to the behavior in which they occur. *Semantics* is concerned with the signification of signs in all modes of signifying. And *pragmatics* deals with the origin, uses, and effects of signs within the behavior in which they occur. In an extension of these dimensions established by Morris (1938) and, later, Carnap (1942), Watzlawick, Beavin, and Jackson (1967) point out that syntactics treats problems of transmitting information and is thus suitable for study by the information theorist. Semantics refers to the study of meaning and the accompanying role of social agreement upon the significance of shared information. Finally, pragmatics describes that which deals with the effects that communication has on other individuals. It is at this point that we wish, with Watzlawick *et al.*, (1967), to depart from the tradition of syntactics and semantics, and concern ourselves with the notion of pragmatics as it has evolved from this historical and epistemological perspective.

As Hardy (1978) suggests, the pragmatic dimension of semiosis is perhaps easiest to understand. It has, over the years, evolved from a highly philosophical abstraction through the writings of Peirce, James, Dewey, Mead and Morris to the distinct behavioral definition offered by Watzlawick *et al.,*:

> For the data of pragmatics are not only words, their configurations, and meanings, which are the data of syntatics and semantics, but their nonverbal concomitants and body language as well. Even more, we would add to personal behavioral actions the communication clues inherent in the *context* in which communication occurs. Thus, from this perspective of pragmatics, all behavior, not only speech, is communication, and all communication — even the communicational clues in an impersonal context — affects behavior (1967:22).

Watzlawick and his colleagues go on to point out that they are less concerned with sender-sign or receiver-sign relations than they are with *the sender-receiver relation, as mediated by communication.*

Thus, great importance is placed upon behavioral effects which serve as criteria by which an individual may assess the relative impact, and therefore the relative efficacy that a message has with respect to its recipient. Additionally, the nature of an ongoing, long term interaction suggests a dynamic model of reciprocal attempts to assess these effects as individuals work toward some (assumed) common definition of their relationship. While historical treatments of the pragmatic stressed the importance of the meanings of the term, current conceptualization views the essence of the search for meanings as that dealing with the natures and effects of relationships. It has been posited that the explanatory principle underlying this process of relational definition is the reduction of uncertainty (Berger & Calabrese, 1975). If we accept this relational perspective and the view advanced by Kelly (1955) that individuals seek this uncertainty reduction as a means of anticipating future events, we may conclude that this process heightens one's ability to make accurate predictions about the world and thereby structure one's behavior accordingly. Based on this reasoning, we are compelled to argue for a pragmatics of interpersonal competence with the notion of relational *control* as its core. Since pragmatism was originally conceived as a philosophy of purposive action, we believe that our thinking articulates well with earlier conceptualizations.

Before developing a pragmatics of interpersonal competence, it is necessary to place this approach to interpersonal communication in perspective of previous conceptualizations of competence.

INTERPERSONAL COMPETENCE

The notion of competence has been with communication scholars since Artistotle set forth the components of ethos. Over time the concept has been broadened in several directions, but for the most part has not significantly changed from its classical inception. As a consequence, scholarly inquiry into communicative[1] competence has not proceeded much beyond a static or linear conception of interactants affecting each other. That is, the more persuasive or more skilled interactants get their way. Viewing competence from an interactional perspective, however, allows for the legitimate introduction of the concept of *interpersonal* competence, and permits a significant break from mechanistic thinking about social communication. A brief review of recent theorizing and research focused on communicative competence will set the stage for the introduction of a pragmatic approach.

Conceptualizations of communicative competence can be dichotomized into cognitive and behavioral (social) categories. The former category includes definitions of competence which are primarily mentalistic and are *not* concerned with actual behavior. Behavioral definitions, on the other hand, focus on interactants' performances, how others evaluate those performances, and the practical outcomes of specific types of performances.

Competence as a cognitive process. The definitions that fall into this category conceive competence as being a mental phenomenon distinct and separate from behavior, as characterized by the linguistic distinction between competence and performance (cf. Chomsky, 1965). Competence is indicative only of potential performance or capability. By avoiding behavioral concerns, cognitive theorists attempt to describe the type of knowledge the "ideal" interactant possesses in order to communicate adequately within his/her social system. The goal of cognitive theories of competence is not the explanation of events, but the discovery of the cognitive structure and mental representations that underlie events. Linguistic competence, for example, is generally defined as the individual's knowledge of the structure of the language. Broadening the concept to include more than language behavior, Habermas (1970:138) states that "communicative competence means the mastery of an ideal speech situation."

The representation of competence as knowledge does not capture the full spectrum of cognitive approaches, however. Competence has also been characterized as a drive or trait. For example, White (1959:297) defined competence as "an organism's capacity to interact effectively with its environment." He discusses competence as both "diagnosis" and "effectuation" — that is, the predisposition to act on, manipulate or adapt the environment. This type of conceptualization is important from our perspective because it underscores that knowledge alone is an insufficient criterion for competence when a person must live with the consequences of his or her behavior. Competence as trait differs from behavioral conceptualizations in that traits are seen primarily as enduring predispositions of an organism — that is, cognitive processes or, in White's term, motivations.[2]

Competence as effective performance. Several scholars have attempted to expand the concept of competence to include behavior as a central concern. Hymes' (1971:16) definition illustrates this expansion:

> ... the most general term for the speaking and hearing capabilities of a person. Competence is understood to be dependent on two things: (tacit) knowledge and (ability for) use.

The focus, of course, is on the ability for use. The eventfulness of specific classes of performances has attracted most attention; as a consequence, performance effectiveness has been the focus of much theorizing and research.

The bulk of this work has been accomplished from a "social skill" orientation. Following Argyle (1969; Argyle & Kendon, 1967), social behavior is conceived in much the same way as are motor skills. In terms of communicative behavior, an individual can be taught specific message strategies with the consequence that he/she will become more competent as mastery of these skills increases. Using the motor skill analogy, learning to communicate is much like learning to drive an automobile. At first, each action is under the constant conscious control of the novice driver. But with experience the process slips into the unconscious; we might say that driving becomes overlearned or a habit. Few of us with more than a couple years of driving experience could describe the discrete actions we employ in driving around the block!

The social skill perspective leads us to characterize competence as specific behavioral routines which people "carry around" with them. This conceptualization is not far removed from that trait of psychology. Both conceptualizations treat competence as a property of individuals, with social skills researchers emphasizing performance rather than cognitive processes. Foote and Cottrell (1955:36) still provide the best summary of the social skill perspective:

> Competence is a synonym for ability. It means a satisfactory degree of ability for performing certain implied kinds of tasks .... As with virtually all human abilities by practice and purposeful training wide differences result. In this sense, interpersonal competence although based upon inherited potentialities, and directly contributing to self-conceptions, may be compared to acquired skills.

Scholars working from within the social skill perspective have seemed to arrive at a consensus that communicative competence should be defined as effectiveness in terms of appropriate adaptions to communicative contexts (see, for example, Bochner & Kelly, 1974; Heath, 1977; O'Malley, 1977; Wiemann, 1977a). While the consensus emphasis on effectiveness is striking, the criteria by which effectiveness is to be judged are still being debated.

One product of viewing competence as a collection of skills is the conceptualization of a performance continuum. A person can be said to be more or less competent — that is, have some quantity of adaptiveness, a smaller or larger behavioral repertoire, etc. Within the social skill context, such a continuum is a valuable and logical way of categorizing individuals. A close analysis reveals, however, that this conceptualization does not allow the prediction of effective interactions or relationships engaged in by any given individual.

An example should make this deficiency in the social skill perspective clear. Let us consider the case of a hypothetical professor who happens to be an excellent lecturer. In the context of the classroom he is without peer and would be judged effective (competent). This professor, however, continues to lecture[3] to students wherever he meets them — at lunch, at parties, in theater lobbies.Since our professor is apparently insensitive to social context and since he appears to have only one communicative strategy (lecturing), he would be judged relatively incompetent if our criterion is *quantity* (range) of adaptiveness across context or breadth of behavioral repertoire. Our decision would be reinforced if we found that our hypothetical professor lectured to his wife, colleagues and basset hound as well.

This determination of relative incompetence is unfortunate and misleading for at least two reasons. First, the professor's competence as a lecturer is not accounted for by this description. Second, and more importantly, the communicational demands placed on the professor by his fellow interactants are not taken into account. That is, students, colleagues, and wife may all tacitly "call for" or demand lecturing across situations and may find such a communication strategy on the part of our professor quite rewarding for them.

A view of communicative competence which is interactional and pragmatic provides an alternate framework which more closely fits interpersonal communication realities.

Beyond social skills: Relational competence. From this perspective, competence lies in the relational system. Consequently, judgments of competence can only validly be made in terms of systemic effectiveness, appropriateness and satisfaction. We will use the term *interpersonal competence* to emphasize that communicative competence from an interactional perspective involves more than one actor.

By conceptualizing competence as interpersonal, we have not abandoned the notion of social skill, nor do we change the focus of competence from enacting appropriate behavior. The interpersonally competent communicator is seen as responsible not only for being able to perform appropriately, but also for choosing relationship partners who will find satisfaction (i.e., have their own goals accomplished) with the performance options the individual has in his or her repertoire. In addition, the concept is removed from the realm of the ideal and placed squarely in the world of everyday experience. Interpersonal competence then becomes more a matter of avoiding errors or traps that lead to relational distress (or impasse) than of getting things just right communicationally. Competence is manifest in the endless developings and workings-out, as is implied in the emphasis we place on goal achievement. The general, cross-contextual goals against which interpersonal competence is evaluated are the initiation and maintenance of desired relationships and the termination of undesired ones. The relationship is the context in which communication takes place (and in which meaning emerges).

In terms of the example we presented earlier, the professor would be judged competent or incompetent based not solely on his repertoire of social skills, but rather on the matching of those social skills to relational partners who found them satisfying. Further, the relational partners would be considered at least partially responsible for the professor's performances (i.e., using a lecturing style of speaking across situations) in that they place communicative demands on him (have expectations of how he should behave) which it would be incompetent for him to ignore.[4]

Conclusions. The cognitive-behavioral dichotomy in the study of communicative competence is spurious. It is just as inappropriate to focus only on behavior with no concern for how the person "got that way" as it is to study only "ideal" communication structure with no regard for the fact that the real world in which humans interact is far from ideal. An alternative is to treat competence as both cognitive and behavioral.[5]

It is equally crucial to consider the person interacting in the context of a relational system. The on-going product, the relationship as indicated by behavior, is of paramount importance. But the working-out of relationships is partially dependent on the communicative predispositions and skills a person brings into them. It is at this point that we see an interactional perspective on competence reconciling social skill and cognitive approaches.

Interpersonal competence is intimately bound to the maintenance of mutually satisfying, effective relational systems. Quantity of "skill" alone does not make a person competent. In fact, from an interactional perspective, it makes no sense to talk about a person being competent apart from a specific relationship or set of relationships, i.e., the context. A large behavioral repertoire may facilitate competence, in that a person with such a repertoire will be able to more easily enact rewarding episodes with others. But a person with a relatively small repertoire upon which to draw may still be interpersonally competent; the probabilities of such competence are reduced because of the limited repertoire, however.

From this perspective, interpersonal competence is the appropriate actualization of knowledge and social skill in a relationship. Knowledge without skill is socially useless, and skill cannot be obtained without the cognitive ability to diagnose situational demands and constraints.

We now turn our attention to the characteristics or components of interpersonal competence.

COMPETENCE IN RELATIONSHIPS

We have argued that a pragmatic approach to communicative competence is necessary if the process of interpersonal communication is to be adequately captured. If our (or anyone else's) conceptualization of interpersonal competence is to be useful, we must be able to identify the characteristics of competence in relationships. Further, the characteristics must be general enough so that they are pertinent to several large classes of relationships (e.g., close friendships, marriages, manager-employee dyads, etc.), and at the same time delineate interpersonal competence with enough specificity so that it can be operationalized and measured.

Based on the philosophy of pragmatism reviewed above, we have identified *control* as a central characteristic of interpersonal competence. A second characteristic, *empathy*, emerges from both cognitive and social skill perspectives as crucial to satisfying, effective relationships. Each of these characteristics will be developed as both general and specific components of interpersonal competence. We will, however, pay special attention to their generalizability across relationships.

Control. We are using the term control to mean the constraints interactants place on one another which limit behavioral options appropriately available to each relational partner and to the system as a whole. In cybernetic terms, control is characterized as the reduction of the necessary number of possible alternative courses of action in order to produce optimum decision-making. This view of interpersonal competence-as-control grows out of the information theoretic conception that "information about an effect, if properly fed back to the effector, will ensure the latter's stability and adaptation to environmental change" (Watzlawick *et al.*, 1967:29-30). Here we have a framework which treats interacting individuals as social units mutually attempting to maximize their ability to understand and influence their world. The vehicle of this process is, of course, verbal and nonverbal communication.

Support for this conception of control of interpersonal relationships is considerable, and is reflected in many literatures. Ruesch and Bateson (1968), for example, view the communication process as not only the intentional transmission of messages, but all those processes by which people inflence one another. Thayer (1968) and Miller and Steinberg (1975) similarly argue that communication essence is realized in the ability to control or adapt to the environment so as to realize certain physical, economic, or social rewards from it. White's (1959) concept of effectance motivation presumes that from birth, human beings are engaged in the process of mastering the environment. The importance of control is also reflected in the vast literature on persuasion and attitude change, the underlying theme of which assumes that human beings are vitally concerned with strategies for controlling the attitudes and/or actions of others (Cohen, 1964; Insko, 1967). Bowers, Elliott and Desmond (1977) characterized communication events as game-like, and suggested that what distinguishes better players from worse ones is the ability to apply a set of implicit rules for success — i. e., pragmatic rules.

In a practical sense, control is often considered to be equated with *power*. Certainly the pervasiveness of research on this variable evident in social science literature is testimony to its importance (cf. Etzioni, 1961; Franch & Raven, 1960; Jacobson, 1972). Power frequently has been considered central to relational definition. The view of control as a power-related phenomenon also appears in Lederer and Jackson's (1968) definition of three kinds of relationships — complementary, symmetrical, and parallel — in which power is distributed in a one-up, one-down, or in a relatively flexible manner, respectively. In all these contributions, the notions of power, inflence and control are central to an understanding of human effectiveness.

The question "power to do what?" must be addressed in order to explicate fully the pragmatics of interpersonal competence. In a review of conceptualizations of interpersonal competence, Bochner and Kelly (1974) described the central role of *goal-achievement* in virtually all of human endeavor. In a more detailed treatment of this issue, Parks (1977) compared the concept of goal specification to that of Weinstein's (1969) definition of "interpersonal task," and generated six general phases of the control process: goal specification, information acquisition, prediction-making, strategy selection, strategy implementation, and environmental testing. In an empirical application of the interpersonal competence paradigm proposed by Bochner and Kelly (1974), Kelly and Chase (1978) determined a four factor solution for the construct of competence, one of which was labeled "Task Completion" and another "Need for Achievement."

It is clear to us that interpersonal competence essentially is found in relational contexts in which individuals have sufficient power over their own actions and the actions of others that they may set, pursue and achieve the interpersonal objectives deemed necessary for a mutually satisfying exchange with their social environment.[6]

At the level of specific behaviors, control can be operationalized in several ways (e.g., giving verbal commands, unilateral decision-making, position in a status hierarchy), but one measure which clearly meets both our criteria is interaction management (Wiemann, 1977a). Interaction management is necessary in all types of encounters and management behaviors can be precisely specified to facilitate measurement of control in relationships. Interaction management is concerned with the "procedural" aspects of interaction — those elements which serve to structure and maintain it as an interaction, including such behaviors as initiation and termination of conversation, the allocation of speaking turns and selection of topic. It is through the mastery of interaction management rules (cognitive competence) and skills (competence as a social skill) that a person is capable of participating in relationships as a rewarding (and rewarded) partner.

The rules that govern social encounters are generally concerned with how persons comport themselves; that is, they specify what is "proper" behavior in a given situation. Underlying all other forms of proper behavior is the responsibility of each person to support the face and line presented by other relational participants whenever possible — that is, to confirm their presented selves. The way the interaction is managed implicity defines the relationship of the participants, especially in terms of control.

Although working from within the social skill paradigm, Argyle (1969:321-322) nonetheless provides two general goals of interaction management which translate easily into the pragmatic perspective: (1) a "smooth and easy pattern of interaction" must be sustained and (2) each interactant must maintain control of the interaction without dominating (parallel symmetry) — "responding in accordance with an internal plan, rather than simply reacting to the other's behavior." Following this line of thought, interaction management has been operationalized in terms of idealized cultural conversation rules, e.g., interruptions of the speaker are not permitted; one person talks at a time; speaker turns must interchange; lengthy pauses should be avoided; and a person in an encounter must be perceived as devoting full attention to the encounter. Patterns of deviations from these idealized rules indicate the distribution of control in a relationship.

The second of the interaction management goals taken from Argyle — the ability to maintain control of the interaction — is particularly relevant to the notion of goal achievement discussed above. This facet of management has been operationalized as topic control.[7]

Empathy. While we are arguing that the ultimate criterion for communicative success lies in a desired behavioral outcome of some type, we are no less concerned with the importance of viewing behavioral outcomes in dynamic relationships along with cognitive processes. According to a constructionist perspective, human beings are, by nature, constantly structuring, ordering and interpreting their world through what Kelly (1955) refers to as a complex system of personal constructs. The individual is thus conceived as an active information processor who "invents" his social environment, based on communicative experience since physical or social reality can never be directly observed (Cassirer, 1944; Johnson, 1972). Central to the constructivist argument is the idea that control cannot exist without an understanding by an individual of the contextual rules for interaction, role of self and other, and the intentions of the other. Control and understanding are complementary facets of the goal-achievement process.

The concept which best subsumes diagnosis (White, 1959), role-taking, perspective-taking, and the like is *empathy*. While the concept has been variously defined, empathy generally means to put oneself in the place of the other cognitively and emotionally (or, at least, to grasp the other's position) in an encounter.

But to take the role of the other is not enough. In order to be considered competent, an interactant must communicate this empathic stance to the other — or, minimally, to appear to the other to have assumed such a stance. Bochner and Kelly (1974:289-290) describe the empathic person as one who "forms accurate impressions of the other people and communicates by the content and tone of his messages that the other's feelings and thoughts are correctly perceived and accepted." In other words, empathy can be viewed as both psychophysiological response (I yawn when you yawn) and social perception skill (I know when you're unhappy). An interactional view of empathy is more than either of these, however. Not only does the empathic partner know and understand the feelings of the other, but acts in a way appropriate to those feelings within the context of the relationship (since you're unhappy, I'll try to cheer you up).

Empathy can be operationalized at two levels: a "microscopic" level of discrete behaviors and a more general level termed feedback. On the microscopic level, behaviors such as other-directed gaze, active listening cues (e.g., headnods, smiles), temporal and spatial immediacy, and owning statements have been identified as indicants of empathy (Wiemann, 1977b). The empathy as feedback relationship has been expressed in various ways; in most cases it is compatible with Watzlawick *et al.*'s (1967) notion of the role of feedback in relationships mentioned earlier in this chapter. Empathy-as-feedback can best be described in terms of *responsiveness* to others in a relationship or encounter. Goffman (1967) suggests that it is each interactant's duty to support the line of fellow interactants whenever possible. Argyris (1965) deals with feedback in terms of how ready and able a person is to receive incoming information — "openness" in his terms. We hasten to add that appropriate action in response to feedback is necessary if empathic responsiveness is to be meaningful in a relationship.[8]

Control and empathy are thus seen as primary characteristics of interpersonal competence; furthermore, behavior and cognition are viewed as functionally related to essential communication process, and cannot be realistically separated.

Secondary characteristics of interpersonal competence. While control and empathy emerge as the central characteristics of interpersonal competence, not only from theoretical and philosophical inquiry, but also from empirical research into effective interpersonal communication, several secondary characteristics have also been identified.

Affiliation and support have been shown to play a role in perceptions of competence (Wiemann, 1977a), although at the operational level it is virtually impossible to separate these constructs from empathy. The similarity between empathy and affiliation/support is interesting because it suggests a yet-to-be-explored relationship between interpersonal competence and the several generations of factor analytic studies of effective communication in small groups. The predominant findings of this body of research are that power and affiliation are major functions of communication (see Carson, 1969, for a review of this literature).

Behavioral flexibility (Bochner & Kelly, 1974; Feingold, 1977; Ruben, 1976; Rushing, 1976; Wiemann, 1977a, b) has also emerged as important to competence. It is not clear, however, if this is a prerequisite for competence across contexts, or if flexibility is a product of participation in many relationships which make varying types of control demands on an individual.

Social relaxation (Wiemann, 1977a) also may be an important characteristic of interpersonal competence in that it serves as a signal of self control. For example, a person in control of self can be counted on not to embarass the relationship. Relaxation in this sense could be related to the general notion of control which we advanced earlier.

Goal achievement (Kelly & Chase, 1977), as mentioned earlier, is an outcome of control, and as such contributes to a pragmatic conceptualization of competence.

CONCLUSION

We have attempted to articulate a pragmatics of communicative competence, which we have designated *interpersonal competence*. This conceptualization differs from other perspectives on communicative competence in that it focuses on performance-in-relationships as opposed to individualistic, psychological variables. At the same time, we have tried to incorporate both cognitive and social skill aspects of competence into our pragmatic one, in order to account for the fact that individuals bring both predispositions to action and varying abilities into relationships.

Control and empathy are central characteristics of a pragmatics of interpersonal communication. The ability of relational partners to meet their collective goals — especially relationship maintenance — is dependent on each partner being able to act (rather than react) in anticipation of environmental contingencies. Since the major environmental contingency is likely to be the feelings, needs, etc., of other relational partners, empathy is a necessary ingredient of successful relationships. Hence, control and empathy appear to be equally necessary and sufficient characteristics of interpersonal competence.

Interpersonal competence is thus seen as a multifaceted, contextually defined concept in which successful individuals mutually define their goals for the relationship and then work together to carry out those goals.

NOTES

1. As applied to competence, the adjectives "communicative," "social" and "interpersonal" have at times been used interchangeably, and at others to differentiate among "types" of competence. While we believe taxonomic considerations are important, they are not appropriate here. For clarity we will use *communicative* competence to denote the general concept developed in this section and *interpersonal* competence as a subset of that concept.

2. Recent empirical work which treats communicative competence as a trait or collection of traits includes Hart, Eadie and Carlson's (1975) rhetorical sensitivity construct and Norton's (1978) communicator style construct.

3. Here we use "lecture" to denote a generic speaking style.

4. There are ethical and social values implicit in naming some communicative performances competent, and others incompetent, and these should be confronted. In one sense, the term "interpersonal competence" is value-free. Mutual satisfaction with a relationship does not necessarily mean that the relationship is moral or positive or happy (by "normal" standards). In this non-evaluative sense, a relationship is effective if the systemic goals are achieved in a manner that is at least minimally satisfying to the participants in the system. System maintenance is one obvious measure of competence, one which indicates that relational goals are being met. Therefore, a relationship between two mutually antagonistic people would be considered "competent" as long as both were sufficiently satisfied with the relationship to remain in it.

We are not quite satisfied with this value-free interpretation of interpersonal competence, although we find that the kinds of values we would like the concept to carry are very ambiguous and difficult to specify. It is our feeling that individuals who find themselves in the type of negative relationship just described are often not really satisfied, but merely lack the resources to withdraw. Hence, we equate competent relationships with *healthy* ones. But we can specify "healthy" only in terms of the usual cultural norms that surround that concept. In the long run, such a vague definition will prove insufficient, but for now it provides a touchstone for ethical/value considerations.

There is one sense in which competence is used that is, from our perspective, unacceptable. We reject out of hand the notion that people are competent only to the extent that they are successfully manipulative without regard for other system members.

5. This is not a novel thought. Thayer (1968) discussed two types of competence, strategic and tactical, which closely parallel the cognitive and behavioral perspectives discussed here. Few people would disagree that either cognition or behavior should be studied to the exclusion of the other. But this is seldom actualized in research; it seems worthwhile to us to repeat what may seem obvious.

6. Power and control are being used in a non-perjorative, value-free sense. Power, like anything else having to do with strategic interaction, is used and that fact remains unobscured by arguments concerning its inherent morality (or immorality). In this sense it is competent to accept control (as well as to control) depending on relational goals, environmental contingencies, etc.

7. Interaction management as a communicational indicant of either power or general responsiveness to others has received empirical support from several studies (Harris, 1977; Ruben, 1976; Rushing, 1976; and Wiemann, 1977a, b).

8. The importance of empathy to interpersonal competence has been supported by the work of Backlund (1977), Feingold (1977), Kelly and Chase (1977), Norton (1978), Ruben (1976) and Wiemann (1977a, b).

Soft Magic

Robert Norton

Magic, illusion, humor, orgasm, ventriloquism, therapy, drugs, play, hypnosis, fantasy, metaphor, dreams, schizophrenia, synergy, freaks, and art arrest attention for many of the same reasons. They violate expectations, sometimes gently, sometimes roughly. They capitalize on juxtapositions. They exploit ambiguities; sometimes emphasizing them, sometimes uncovering them. They let "the same" interpenetrate "not the same."

In this chapter, the phrase "soft magic" metaphorically connects components of magic to brief therapy techniques. The qualifier "soft" — analyzed in the next section — highlights the pragmatic impact of this orientation. In this second section, it is argued that the "soft magic" of communication interventions is a function of establishing an interactional structure and securing premises for that structure. A case study relating to fear of giving a speech will be examined.

MAGIC AND THERAPY

In both magic and therapy, *the participant wants to believe and not believe in the phenomenon at the same time.* If the phenomenon exists, some reality images have to be altered. In magic, the range of perceptions are expanded; in therapy, change occurs. If the phenomenon does not exist, the initial "one-up" attitude is preserved. Whatever the outcome, the dual tension that the person brings primes the participant for something to happen.

In both interactions, *the logistics of the trick/therapy are often over before the impact of the effect is realized.* Bandler and Grinder double bind a patient whose symptom was that she could not say "no" by instructing her to say "no" about something to every member of the group. She refused quickly and strongly.[1] The magician lets a spectator pick a card from a deck composed of only the ten of spades. The logistics of the trick are over before the selection. The magician merely has to "sell an effect"after the selection.

Misdirection is an essential element in both magic and brief therapy. Harry Blackstone, Jr., one of the best professional magicians in the country says, "If I let you check something about the trick, it's probably not worth checking."[2] Typically, the patient has already carefully directed attention to where something is expected to occur. The brief therapist redirects the person's attention concerning the symptom or the anticipated cure. Erickson instructs the bedwetter *to wet* the bed, tells the sexually inhibited woman *to keep* her symptom of choking and gasping, and urges his son *not to obey* him.[3]

Patter is an essential component for both the magician and therapist. It is used to address the verbal part, the left hemisphere. It provides the audience a pseudoexplanation to latch onto logically and analytically. In addition, the patter with its cadence and tone serve to misdirect. While the person is listening and processing, the magician/therapist works toward an analogic impact. For the therapist, the imparting of information through patter can operate as a curative component.[4] In skilled practitioners, it is an art. From the brief therapy perspective, patter is marked by (1) speaking the patient's language, (2) utilizing the patient's resistance, and (3) preempting.[5]

Both phenomena happen quickly, unexpectedly, sometimes humorously, and often delightfully. In magic, the elephant disappears, the man walks through a wall, the woman is fragmented into three parts.[6] In brief therapy the sexual dysfunction disappears, the paralyzed Prussian German commander walks again after a year, and the catatonic state is broken.[7] The effects happen faster than expected.[8] The person is often told to do the very thing that is being avoided: The shy person is given a diverting task which requires that he or she meet people, intentionally or serendipitously.

In some ways, the quickness of effective reframing techniques reminds me of a sketch done by Carol Burnett, Harvey Corman, and Tim Conway. In the sketch, Burnett plays the Queen of England, Corman, the King, and Conway a guard at Buckingham Palace who will not let the royal couple pass. The Queen reports to the King that the guard told her to shove the medal of honor up her nose. The King, very concerned, looks her in the eye and says, *"Well, don't do it!"* To which she replies, *"I shan't!"*

Typically, in brief therapy, a patient comes to a therapist and says, *"I'm afraid of people."* The brief therapist, very concerned, looks the patient in the eye and says, *"Well, be more afraid of people!"* To which the patient replies, *"I shan't!"*

Brief therapy is often marked by the unexpected injunction to do "A" which is the very thing the patient anticipates being told not to do. As a result, the injunction or the effect from the injunction is often startling; and, as such, it delights and has the capacity to elicit humor by forcing the person to function both as object of observation and observer.

In both magic and brief therapy, *the participant frequently gets more than bargained for.* The participant expects X and often experiences not only X, but X + Y. The person might expect the magician to produce a card, but not to have the card fly out of the deck. The patient might expect Erickson to provide some nice therapeutic advice, but not to the extent that it radically changes his life patterns.[9]

Furthermore, like magic, *the patient is often likely not to know how the trick was done or even be aware that a trick/therapeutic intervention was done.* Weakland reports a case in which a pilot could not turn his head to a normal position. He had been to many physicians and therapists who failed. Weakland told him that since others before him had failed, there probably was no reason to expect help now. In fact, nobody could help him; he would probably be like that the rest of his life. The pilot stormed out of the office. A little later, Weakland received a letter from the pilot saying that he was cured and that Weakland was wrong.[10] This illustrates the hidden power of reframing. The patient expected X and got X + Y without his awareness.

Both the magician and therapist set themselves up so that there will be success no matter what. The good card manipulator has multiple ways of producing the same effect. If one way fails, the other way works. The good brief therapist has many ways to produce positive change because he or she is going to capitalize on the patient's resistance, utilize the patient's expectations, and orchestrate an effect grounded in the patient's framework. No matter what the patient does, leverage will be provided by the patient.

Finally, magic and brief therapy appear to be "extra-normal" life events. The effects may be perceived as acts of wizardry. Something extra-ordinary is conjured from the ordinary. This perception is not surprising. The magician/therapist presents a persona "bigger than life," a person who can do things when others cannot. Of course, this posturing can be the curative component in and of itself. Certainly, it regulates and filters the process that happens. The props, rituals, and patter complement the impression.

In summary, the following parallels between magic and brief therapy have been suggested:

- The participant wants both to believe and not believe the phenomenon.

- The logistics are often over before the impact of the effect is realized.

- Misdirection [reframing] is an essential element.

- Patter is an essential element.

- The phenomenon happens unexpectedly, sometimes humorously, and often delightfully.

- The person gets more than bargained for.

- The person is often likely not to know how the effect was done or even be aware that it happened.

- The process is designed to guarantee success.

- The phenomenon seems like, and indeed is for many, an "extra-normal" life experience.

These metaphorical connections while not definitive or rigorous help to shed light on the primary task of this chapter — namely, to identify what has to be done to understand the magic of brief therapy. Or, to ask the question in a less mystical way, *what are the critical foci that a communication scholar must examine to understand the workings of brief therapy?*.[11] To the degree that this question can be answered, brief therapy techniques become increasingly teachable.

THE MAGIC IN INTERVENTION

The magician is always reluctant to reveal the mechanics of a trick. Almost always the reaction has a condescending edge to it: *"Oh, so that's how it is done."* The explanation veils the wide-eyed, incredulous enthusiasm shown seconds earlier. In like manner, explicating the magic of intervention hides the dramatic quality of the actual interaction. Nevertheless, an explanation has the potential of improving the quality of future magic by stimulating the practitioners to greater challenges.

In the remainder of this chapter, it is argued that the relationship of two components needs to be understood to learn about the dynamics which make brief therapy work. First, the function of structure in the interaction must be identified. Second, the means of securing premises for the structure must be realized. Both the structure of interaction and securing premises for the structure occur simultaneously, synergistically, and inextricably.

Before specifically discussing the function of structure and the means of securing premises, consider what the brief therapy perspective looks like. The following section condenses a standard procedure outlined by Fisch, Weakland, Watzlawick, Segal, Hoebel, and Deardorff (1975) in *Learning Brief Therapy: An Introductory Manual* and by Weakland, Fisch, Watzlawick, and Bodin (1974) in an article, "Brief Therapy: Focused Problem Resolution."

The Brief Therapy Perspective

The general format of brief therapy at the Mental Research Institute (MRI) in Palo Alto, California, entails six steps: (1) Introduction to the treatment set-up; (2) Inquiry and definition of the problem; (3) Estimation of behavior maintaining the problem; (4) Setting goals of treatment; (5) Selecting and making behavioral interventions; (6) Termination. At each step, therapeutic "work" is being done.

Even in the introduction to the set-up, expectations are created which provide some leverage for an intervention. For example, the therapist informs the person that a maximum of ten meetings, and often fewer, constitute the length of the therapy. This information in itself signals that some kind of rapid change is likely.

Even though much of the first meeting is devoted to information seeking, a lot of groundwork is being laid for the future structures and interactions. Fisch *et al.*, (1975) claim that the initial interview "constitutes the base for all subsequent interviews, precisely because the various steps are interrelated, and sets the tone for the whole treatment relations" (p. 13).

In the first interview, three critical questions are asked:

> 1. *What is the problem that brings you here?* An acceptable answer identifies the particular problem that has led the client to seek treatment, uncovers in what way the problem involves a day-to-day difficulty enough to justify seeking help, finds out how it came about that this step was taken now, and discovers how the Brief Therapy Center was chosen.

> 2. *How have you been attempting to handle or resolve this problem?* The information here is often crucial. If the person has been repeatedly trying X to solve the problem, the brief therapist should not recommend X as a solution.

> 3. *At minimum, what would you hope to see happen or be different as a result of coming here about this problem?* Here a behavioral goal is preferred.

One of the most esoteric steps in the brief therapy perspective is estimating the behavior maintaining the problem. Weakland *et al.*, (1974) offer the following guide:

> Our view . . . is that problem behavior persists only when it is repeatedly reinforced in the course of social interaction between the patient and other significant people. Usually, moreover, it is just what the patient and these others are do-

ing in their attempts to help that appear most "logical" or un-
questionably right — that is most important in maintaining
or exacerbating it (p. 153).

Setting a minimal goal serves two purposes: (1) it signals that positive
change is feasible given a particular time period, and (2) it provides a
way to judge therapeutic accomplishment for both the therapist and patient. At MRI's Brief Therapy Center, the aim is to establish a goal by
the second session, although there is flexibility here.

Step five represents the "largest, most varied, and probably most
unusual part of our treatment" (Fisch *et al.*, 1974). Here the brief
therapist will use such things as (1) redefining, relabeling, or reinterpreting dysfunctional behavior, contexts or situations, (2) appealing to
idiosyncratic characteristics and motivation, (3) directing behavioral
change, (4) giving paradoxical instruction, and (5) incorporating interpersonal influence. Watzlawick's *Language of Change* (1978) provides
the reader with more detailed strategies.

Finally, termination processes are designed to keep any leverage gained by reminding the person about future improvement and pointing out
that the treatment was not intended to achieve final solutions, "but an
initial breakthrough on which they themselves can build further"
(Fisch *et al.*, 1974). If the patient is particularly negativistic, an opposite
termination tack may be taken: Positive results of the treatment may be
minimized and skepticism may be expressed about any progress in the
future. In both cases, the aim is to extend the therapeutic influence
beyond the period of actual contact.

This section represents only the most sketchy outline of the brief
therapy perspective and the reader is encouraged to examine some of
the related texts mentioned throughout this chapter. The reader can
find a more lengthy discussion of the theoretical basis for this work in
Change: Principles of Problem Formation and Problem Resolution by
Watzlawick, Weakland and Fisch (1974). The explications offered in the
next sections are not found in the brief therapy literature, but represent
my viewpoint regarding some of the dynamics of the brief therapy process.

Function of Structure

*The function of structure in brief therapy is to create an enthymematic pro-
cess.* The enthymeme is a truncated syllogism. The conclusion, minor

premise, or major premise is unspoken by the sender, and, as a result, there is pressure on the receiver to supply, overtly or covertly, the missing part or parts which would make the form of the argument reasonable.[12]

The connection between rhetoric and therapy is natural — both involve persuasion. What Aristotle says about persuasion is surprisingly appropriate advice for a modern therapist, especially one who is trying to understand what is working in the change process.

The good therapist or good rhetor controls the enthymematic process by first shaping the *structure* of the enthymeme. Aristotle reminds us that since the enthymeme is a kind of syllogism:

> ... the person with the clearest insight into the nature of syllogisms, who knows from what premises and in what modes they may be constructed, will also be the most expert in regard to enthymemes, once he has mastered their special province [of things contingent and uncertain such as human actions and their consequences], and has learnt the differences between enthymemes and logical syllogisms. [The latter are complete, and yield an absolute demonstration]. (Aristotle, 1355a)

The enthymematic process works because the receiver brings something to the process; the receiver supplies critical premises. The enthymematic process works because the sender and receiver *interact*.

A person entering therapy may be completely or partially oblivious to the structure of the enthymeme. At the entry level, the patient may not care whether an "If Y, then X" strategy permeates the interaction. But, for the therapist, the form of the enthymeme is important, primarily because it provides a way to get extra leverage communicatively.

For example, if a patient's problem revolves around holding onto a "not-X" (i.e., being not-assertive), the therapist could work on getting the patient to accept "X." The work may take the form of cajoling, exhorting, tricking, or demanding.

In traditional logic, validity is determined by the form of the deductive agruments, not by the content of the statements comprising them.[13] However, the "hard" validity of traditional logic by itself does not serve the communication scholar well in analyzing brief therapy interventions. The notion of "validity" need not be reserved for and dominated by traditional logicians. Furthermore, brief therapy scholars must ask, "*What constitutes 'validity' in communicative interventions?*"

Traditionally, the soundness of the argument or the relationship of the statements to one another is judged in light of the appropriate distribution of terms in the premises of categorical, hypothetical, and disjunctive syllogisms. *In brief therapy interventions, the soundness of the interaction or the relationship of the points of intervention to one another should be judged in light of the pragmatic outcome.*

The assumption embedded in this notion of "validity" is that the information of the interaction not only includes the content of the premises, but also can have an agenda setting function in terms of structure. If the blend between "validity" and "truth" is fuzzy and vague, I call the process "soft." If it works, I call it "magic."

What makes it possible to judge validity in pragmatic terms is that the brief therapist in collaboration with the patient trys to stipulate what is considered positive change. Because the brief therapist is guided by teleological commitments, he or she will be directive, active, pragmatic, and somewhat daring in moving toward outcomes which are clear indicants of successful intervention.

Consider the following situation. A client comes to the therapist and says, "I'm too shy to meet people." The enthymeme is: If I am too shy, then I will not meet people. Symbolically stated, the enthymeme is: If s [shy], then not-p [not meet people]. The therapeutic goal could be to get the person to meet people.[14] The goal of the intervention is to secure a "p" — meet people.

One brief therapist might tell the person "Go talk to some strangers and tell them you are too shy to meet them." Namely, do "p." This intervention denies the consequent and a valid hypothetical syllogism can be recovered. Another brief therapist might tell the person "You are not shy enough! Try to be deliberately more shy around five people today." Namely, be more "s." The antecedent is affirmed even stronger to get the patient to pragmatically deny the consequent. If a "p" is secured, the interaction will be considered valid no matter what the strategy of the intervention is. Of course, if the goal of the intervention is something other than "p," the validity will be judged accordingly.

The fact that both valid and invalid syllogisms, in terms of traditional logic, might be recovered highlights an essential feature of brief therapy. Where much of psychiatry spends time trying to unravel the correct, clear cause of the problem with a crystalline analysis devoid of inconsistencies and pure in its structural flow, the brief therapist will settle for a dirty little solution that works. The flow of the structure can be marred, illogical, and inconsistent as long as the solution works.

A Case Study

A person with a problem like the one described in the above example came to me. She was afraid that she would be so nervous that she would forget her speech. In the course of the first meeting, she had mentioned that she was on the cross country running team. The overall strategy for this case developed around the following structure:

Verbally Stated	Symbolically Stated
If you remember the racing course, you will remember the speech.	If r, then s. [r = remember racing course; s = remember speech]
You will remember racing course.	
Therefore, you will remember speech.	Therefore, s.

A lot of therapeutic help would center on denying the nervousness or asserting that the speech will be remembered. The brief therapist, on the other hand, tries to secure any of the following premises: (1) n: "Be more nervous!" (2) not-s: "Deliberately forget your speech!" and/or (3) r: "You will remember the racing course." In each instance, it is hoped that the patient will supply enthymematically either of the following conclusions: (1) not-n: "I am not too nervous." "I am not so nervous that I can't get through the speech." "It does not matter whether I am nervous." "I will be nervous and get through the speech." and/or (2) s: "I will not forget the speech." "I will not forget the speech if I am familiar enough with it."

The brief therapist will settle for a logically valid or invalid syllogism in terms of traditional logic as long as it is functionally operative. In actuality, the brief therapist weaves both processes to move toward a positive change in a reasonably short time. The following table summarizes the structural flow of this case study. In the next section, the actual dialogue and the work of securing the premises are identified.

TABLE 1

Flow of Interaction Symbolically Stated

Patient's Structure of Problem	If n, then not s.	n = too nervous s = remember speech
Therapist's Structure of Overall Strategy	If r, then s.	r = remember racing course
The Work of the Intervention: Securing Premises	(1) Propose "n" to move the patient to "not-n." (2) Propose "not-s" to move the patient to s. (3) Impose "r" to move the patien to s.	

*In every instance, the brief therapist should be able to identify the overall structural strategy he or she will be using.

Securing Premises for Structure

In addition to establishing the overall structure, essentially controll-ing the form of the interaction, the enthymematic process entails secur-ing the premises in such a manner that the pragmatic outcome is pro-bable. Sometimes the process is straightforward and obvious in securing premises. Other times it is circuitous, complex, or illogical. Securing the premises, given the structure, is the magic of communicative therapy.

Watzlawick, in *The Language of Change*, elegantly explains many of the steps needed to secure premises which are going to be used to gain leverage to do the work of intervention. Grinder and Bandler in *The Structure of Magic* offer similar explanations. Securing premises in each instance entails dealing with strategies grounded in both digital and analogic processes; it entails addressing both the right and left hemispheres of the person; it involves both valid and invalid logical pro-cesses; and, it involves understanding the function of content and style in working toward successful intervention.

The following sections report the dialogue from the case study and the communicative work. The analysis is not definitive, but illustrates the direction of an explanation grounded in the enthymematic process.

I.

T: Do you think you could honestly forget the course? (1)

P: Well, if you are not familiar with it enough. (2)

T: You could forget where the course was? (3)

P: Yeh. (4)

T: r. (1) (r = remember racing course)

P: If not f, then not -r. (2) (f = familiar enough)

T: r. (3)

P: not-r. (4)

The work of the interaction shows two things. First, the tacit structure guiding the overall strategy — "If you remember the racing course, you will remember the speech" — is not challenged. Second, the issue of nervousness has the potential of shifting to an issue of familiarity. If this happens, leverage is gained because the strategies for dealing with familiarity are more tangible.

II.

T: So, then, do you think you could deliberately forget your speech, or the main points of your speech? (5)

P: I'm getting confused. (6)

T: Not-s. (5)

P: + + + (6)

A reframing attempt is made here by suggesting that she deliberately forget her speech. The suggestion functions two ways. It commands her analytic attention suggesting to her to think about the problem in an unusual way. It is a misdirection. Second, it "softly" links remembering the speech to remembering the race course.

III.

T: Well, you say, that ... okay, I agree   T: + + + (7)
with you .... (7) I'm saying perhaps   not-r. (8)
you could deliberately forget a course.   + + + (9)
(8) Now the reason you're giving is
because ... (9)

P: (interrupting) How about   P: not-r (10)
"undeliberately?" (10) You know, what   If b, then not-r. (11)
if you just ... your mind goes blank   (b = mind goes blank)
and you forget it? (11) Does it have to
be deliberate? (12)   not-r. (12)

The person attempts to control a critical qualifier in this exchange which would shift the responsibility to something beyond her control. If she can *accidently* forget, then the locus of control is beyond her power.

IV.

T: Well ... let's take that analogy in   T: If r, then s. (13)
running. (13) Could you
"undeliberately" forget a course? (14)   r. (14)

Instead of taking issue with the person, the situation is set up so that she must analyze it. In the process of analyzing "How one could 'undeliberately' forget a course," she simultaneously and metaphorically analyzes how she could accidentally forget a speech.

V.

P: Yeh! (15) What if you're ... never   P: not-r. (15)
... not sure of the course ... and
you're ... don't know it good enough   If not f, then not-r (16)
T: And, you accidently forget? (17)   T: not-r. (17)
P: Yeh, or ... you're tired, you just ... P: If t, then not-r. (18)
(18)   (t = tired)

T: Can you control that (19) On   T: If c, then r. (19, 20)
running? (20)   (c = control)

P: Well, they usually have people standing around telling you where to go
too . . . (21) and they have signs, and
. . . (22)

P: If o, then c. (21)
(o = others telling)
If sg, then c. (22)
(sg = signs telling)

P: Run the course a couple of times. (24)
T: How would you . . . yeh, run the
course (25)
P: Walk the course . . . (26) make sure
you know it. (27)
T: Walk the course. (28)

P: c. (24)
T: c. (25)

P: c. (26) c. (27)

T: c. (28)

VI.

T: *Do you think there is anything in your
whole life you could not control?* (29) I
mean you could . . . don't you think
you can set yourself up to forget this
speech? (30)
P: Yeh, by not working on it. (31), by
not going over it enough. (32)
T: Well, do you want to do that or not?
(33)
P: No-o-oo. (34)
T: *You know exactly how to control this.*
(35) Just as you know exactly how to
remember where the course is. (36)
P: I know exactly how to control it (37
If I work on it. (38) Right? (39)

T: I don't know what you want though.
(40) What do you want out of this?
(41) I'm saying you might as well
stand up there . . . (42)

P: Yeh, but . . . (43)
T: . . . and really forget it. (44)

T: C. (29)

Not-s. (30)

P: Not-f. (31)
not-f. (32)
T: Either f or not-f. (33)

P: f.   (34)

r. (36)

P: c. (37)
If f, then c. (38)
If f, then c. (39
T: Either c or not-c. (40)
Either c or not-c. (41)
not-s. (42)

P: s. (43)
T: not-s. (44)

The notion that she can control it, whether referring to remembering the course, remembering the speech, or getting familiar with something, is now asserted. The transition from racing to speaking is overtly suggested. She is put into the position of deciding whether she wants it now. A brief therapy solution might be that she does not want the solution *now*, but with the realization that she can have it whenever she wants it. In statements 37, 38, and 39, she repeats, almost trancelike, the main points of the enthymematic process.

VII.

P: . . . well, what if you . . . what if somebody does all the work, and remember it, and they forget it? (45)

P: If f, then not-s. (45)

T: Well, let me ask you this: Suppose somebody really works out, primes themselves to run . . . ah, six miles in an incredible time, and they forget where the course is? (46) What do you say to that? (47)

T: If f, then not-r. (46)

f. (47)

P: (cognizant laughter) *Impossible!* (48)

P: f. (48)

She tries one last time to test the intervention, but when the critical premises are identified, she capitulates and accepts the analysis. With the acceptance, the enthymematic process is completed for this exchange.

Summary

Three critical enthymematic links occur in the flow of interaction: (1) If r, then s; (2) If c, then r; and (3) If f, then c. When the "f" was obtained, the premises of the remaining structures were also obtained such that the antecedent in the first major premise is affirmed which yields the consequent "s." As the interaction unfolds, the person introduced her own solution, namely, if one was familiar enough with the speech, one would remember the speech. The issue of nervousness magically disappeared.

Future Directions

Understanding the enthymematic flow should enhance the power of the therapist using mainly communicative tools. The task is twofold. First, more about the dynamics of structure in interaction must be learned. In this chapter, a crude framework was introduced and no attempt was made to explore precisely and definitely what constitutes "pragmatic validity."

If the enthymematic approach is going to contribute to the understanding of structure in communicative interaction, then systems of logic beyond the traditional perspective need to be integrated into the study. We should learn about the *logic* of giving counsel or advice, of upbraiding or reproaching, of denouncing, of imploring aid or requesting cooperation, of supplicating, and of making purely factual assertions. Rescher offers a good starting point in his book, *The Logic of Commands* (1966). For example, he argues that to understand the function of commands a careful and explicit account of temporal considerations needs to be developed. How do chronological propositions operate in brief therapy interventions? In the logic of commands, we need to know how the "conclusion command is tacitly or implicity contained in the 'set of instructions' presented by the command premises."[15] A lot of the brief therapist's magic is found in the set of instructions presented in early premises.

Also, we should study more about the form of structures. For instance, the theorems of completeness and consistency, the theorems of procedural contractions, and the theorems of connection from Brown's book, *Laws of Form*, might be used to identify the most basic flow of interaction.[16] In the case study, "r" was asserted four times and "not-r" was asserted six times. Even though the same premise is being asserted or denied, the assertions carry different pragmatic impact depending upon where they are operating in the interaction. It is possible that a series of rules, such as Brown's condensation and cancellation, could be developed to identify the basic, pragmatic form of the assertions.

Finally, attention should be paid to systems of many-valued logic. The two orthodox truth-values (truth and falsity) found in traditional logic are too restrictive for the communication scholar who needs to consider indeterminate, neuter, alethic, and probabilistic modalities.[17] Every statement in an interaction is not necessarily true or false. For example, the injunction, not-s, "Deliberately forget the speech," pragmatically may entail simultaneously multiple communications as a function of content, context, time, sequence patterns, and style. The person might pragmatically react to the not-s injunction in the following ways:

1 ."He wants me to really forget the speech, but I won't do it."

2 ."He doesn't really want me to forget the speech. He is just using reverse psychology. I'll try to remember the speech."

3 ."I don't know how in the world or why in the world he would want me to forget the speech. I don't think I can do it."

4 ."I don't want to forget the speech, but I will try."

5 ."What is he really saying to me?"

The not-s injunction is not simply a one-valued stimulus in an interaction; it has the capacity to function in a multivalued modality. This point is explored further below. If more than one modality operates, then some systems of many-valued logic will provide viable ways to analyze the pragmatic impact of brief therapy intervention.

The second part of the twofold task is understanding more about securing premises. Two areas in particular need to be extended: (1) understanding metaphor in interaction, and (2) understanding the interplay/interpenetration/interaction of content and style.

The metaphor helps secure not only premises, but also structures. It makes connections which can use attributes of other objects, actions, or people without formally embracing the full impact of rules governing the thing/action/person alluded to. Because the metaphorical connection is a partial equation, it functions "softly."

In the case study, the racing course was never formally equated to giving a speech until later in the exchange. As a result, the real problem could be discussed directly. The metaphor provided a way for the person to analyze the problem; it never allowed a means to refocus on the issue of familiarity rather than the nervousness. Erickson was especially creative in his use of the metaphor.

In the spirit of Grindler and Bandler, Gordon explores the metaphor as a pragmatic tool in *Therapeutic Metaphors*. He states that "what makes it possible for a metaphor to be influential is that it is isomorphic with the client's actual situation."[18] The metaphor works because it creates the enthymematic process: "By intentionally refraining from specifying particular information, actions, and experiences of the characters within the metaphor, we force its audience to derive and employ their own interpretations of what is 'really going on.' "[19] More work like this is needed to learn about metaphor.

In addition, content and style work to secure premises.[20] In a computer system, the content is the information and style is the signal concerning what to do with the information. In human communicaion this analogy is partially useful, but breaks down at critical points. In human communication, for example, the content can operate stylistically, but in a computer system this is not the case. The numbers or data never simultaneously function as messages indicating what to do about the numbers or data — report and command never fuzz together. In human communication, the two components always fuzz together — "softly."

I like the analogy which relates content and style to mind and body. The mind is to body as style is to content. Just as the identity of the individual is the inextricable combination of mind and body, the communicative act is the inextricable combination of style and content. The mind serves to direct the body; it regulates, guides, focuses, controls the body. Similarly, style serves to direct content; it regulates, guides, focuses, controls content. The mind generates priorities for the body; style generates priorities for content. The mind can destroy, divert, or dilute the impact of the body; style can do the same to content.

Conversely, the body can influence the mind, and content can affect style. A sick body can make the mind seem confused, ineffectual, and numb. The analogue to a sick body would be "sick content." What would "sick content" be? Content which is not functioning the way it is supposed to. Consider the following sentence: "When you deny your feelings for me I really hurt inside." If every pair of words in the sentence were reversed, the content of the sentence could not function the way it is supposed to.[21] It would read: "You when your deny for feelings me for really I inside hurt."

Any style, given "sick content," would seem confused, ineffectual, and numbing. "Sick content" contaminates any stylistic impact. It does not make a difference how the style is manifested. No matter how a person says the above sentence, whether forcefully or softly, lovingly or vindictively, subtly or crudely, the content of the sentence, as such, has contaminated the impact of style. For this reason, paradox can be considered "sick content." The converse is true, also. "Sick style" can contaminate content.

The interplay between content and style provides four basic interactive tools to help secure premises. The following table is a simplification of the four interactions:

TABLE 2

Content and Style Combinations

	Style Redundant to Content	*Style Not Redundant to Content*
Unambiguous Content	Straightforward, direct, denotative communication.	Ambiguous message; more to communication than referents in sentence indicate.
	"Deliberately forget your speech" indicates that the person should actively try not to remember the speech.	*"Deliberately forget your speech"* invites a reaction which makes person wonder whether the denotative referents are real message.
	Trust content to mean what it says.	Maybe trust the content to mean what it says, or really trust it more intensely.
Ambiguous Content	Ambiguous message; connotative communication. More referents than sentence indicates.	Disorienting messages; maybe humor, playing, manipulating, random, disconfirming, or crazy message.
	"Deliberately forget your speech" [communicated in such a way that either a written speech or the actual speaking could be the referent] invites the person to decide which referent is primary. Trust style to help decide primary referent.	*"Deliberately forget your speech"* is communicated in such a way that the person searches beyond content and style for the real message. Trust neither content or style primarily.

In each instance, the not-s injunction, "Deliberately forget your speech," can have a different pragmatic impact. Depending on how the therapist wants to secure the premises for the structure, content and style will interact differently. For example, in Erickson's confusion technique, the content tends to be ambiguous and the style is not redundant to the content. The technique is used to gain leverage in cases where the person is intellectualizing too much.[22] The style and content combinations probably need to be indexed in order to appreciate the work they do in securing premises within a structure.

Conclusion

Part of the communicative magic occurs because the process is "pre-structured" in two ways. The very fact the person comes to the therapist predisposes the patient and the therapist to expect something to happen. It is as though the patient is operating from the following major premise: If I come to you, I am granting you permission to grant me permission to change. To this extent, the logistics of the trick/therapy are often over before the impact of the effect is realized; to this extent, the process is designed to guarantee success.

The second way that the process is "pre-structured" is that, *a priori*, the brief therapist will go with the flow of the patient; reframe, use beliefs and behavior from the patient, employ the patient's resistance, and capitalize on information provided regardless of its quality. Because of the extraordinary flexibility of the brief therapist, the person is often likely not to know how the effect was done or even be aware that it happened.

Part of the communicative magic occurs because of the way the brief therapist secures premises bringing to bear a subtle combination of content and style components, working with metaphor, pacing, preempting, and gaining leverage in counterintuitive ways. Misdirection and patter aid the process. The phenomenon happen unexpectedly, sometimes humorously, and often delightfully. Many times the therapist seemingly reverses the roles such that the patient sounds progressively more like the therapist and vice versa. The patient ends up making a case for what he or she was initially prepared to resist. As such, the person often gets more than bargained for.

Finally, change is so sudden that the phenomenon seems like an "extra normal" life experience. Many times the person realizes for the first time in his or her life that control can be had whenever they want it. Many times the person learns how to function like a schizoid so that he or she can be healthy — that is, the person learns how to operate both as observer and object of observation. In short, communication interventions are pragmagic — soft pragmagic.

NOTES

1. Bandler, Richard & Grinder, John. *The structure of magic, I. A book about language and therapy*. Palo Alto: Science and Behavior Books, 1975:170-171. Cf. also *The structure of Magic, II. A book about communication and change*. Palo Alto, Science and Behavior Books, 1976. Cited and analyzed by Paul Watzlawick, *The language of change: Elements of therapeutic communication*. New York: Basic Books, 1978:104-105.

2. Paraphrase from Harry Blackstone, Jr. when he appeared on *Good Morning America*, ABC, December 18, 1978. Interestingly, I have found misdirection for children is different than for adults. Card tricks which work for kids do not work for adults always, and conversely. In addition, the audience determines whether patter will be linear or mosaic.

3. Haley, Jay. *Uncommon therapy. The psychiatric techniques of Milton Erickson, m.d.* New York: W.W. Norton, 1973. Cited and analyzed by Paul Watzlawick, *The language of change*.

4. Yalom, Irvin. *The theory and practice of group psychotherapy*. New York: Basic Books, 1970. Yalom lists imparting of information as one of the ten curative components which cut across all group therapies. This curative component functions to transfer information, structure the group, and explain the process of illness. Patter operates similarly as a curative component in that it structures the patient's expectations about the therapeutic process, provides information which may in itself be therapeutic, and presents a vehicle for the interaction.

5. Watzlawick, Paul. *The language of change*. pp. 138-154.

6. Harry Houdini specialized in the first two tricks. Harry Blackstone, Jr. developed the third trick.

7. Haley, Jay. *Uncommon therapy*. p. 311.

8. I had a graduate student in horticulture come to me at the urging of her husband. The complaint was that she was very nervous when she gave a speech. I asked her why she thought that her professors' criticism was more valid than her evaluations. She stopped talking, smiled, thanked me, and left.

9. Haley, Jay. *Uncommon therapy*. The case of Harold is especially to the point, p. 120.

10. John Weakland reported this case in a brief therapy workshop given by him and Richard Fisch in Palo Alto during June, 1979.

11. I am not saying what makes brief therapy work, yet. I am saying what do we need to look at to understand its working. Then, and only then, can the first question be answered.

12. *The rhetoric of aristotle*, translated and with introduction by Lane Cooper. New York, 1932. For Aristotle there are two types of emthymemes: "By the demonstrative enthymeme we draw a conclusion from inconsistent propositions. [p. 158]" He identifies both genuine and spurious enthymemes. The enthymematic process is not a function of whether a valid syllogism can be recovered.

13. Salmon, Wesley. *Logic*. Englewood Cliffs: Prentice-Hall, 1963.

14. Of course, there are other therapeutic goals which would be acceptable. For instance, a goal might be to stop caring about meeting people. Another goal might be to get the person to the point that he or she realized that the problem could be solved whenever the person wanted, but it need not be solved at this point in time if the person did not want to solve it.

15. Rescher, Nicholas. *The logic of commands*. New York: Dover Publications, 1966:123-124.

16. Brown, G.S. *Laws of form*. New York: Bantam Books, 1973. For example, assuming that each "r" which was asserted was equivalent, Brown's rules of condensation and cancellation might be used to reduce the series of "r's" to the following basic form:

$$\text{Let } r = \quad \neg \quad \neg\neg\neg \quad \neg \quad = \quad \neg$$

17. Rescher, Nicholas. *Many-valued logic*. New York: McGraw-Hill, 1969. The notion of the many-valued logic was not foreign to Aristotle. He pointed out that "enthymemes are derived from four sources: these are: (1) probabilities, (2) examples, (3) infallible signs, (4) ordinary signs. [p. 178]."

18. Gordon, David. *Therapeutic metaphors*. Cupertino, California: Meta Publications, 1978:51. What Gordon is essentially discussing is the enthymematic process.

19. *Ibid.*, p. 50.

20. In *Pragmatics of human communication*, by Paul Watzlawick, Janet Beavin, and Don Jackson, the term "command" refers to "what sort of a message it [the content] is to be taken as, and therefore, ultimately to the *relationship* between the communicants. [pp. 51-52] Later, the terms "relationship" and "relation" become increasingly interchanged when a clear distinction is useful. Consequently, I prefer the term "style" to mean "the way one verbally and paraverbally interacts to signal how literal meaning should be taken, interpreted, filtered, or understood. [See Robert Norton, "Foundation of a communicator style construct," *Human Communication Research*, 1978, 4(2):99-112.] Given this definitional move, one can say every communication has a content and style component which defines the relationship between people.

21. Here the unit of analysis is *sentence* content. If just the words were considered the units of analysis, then we have an instance of style not doing what is expected.

PROVOCATIONS

Nothing is true except our conviction that the world we are asked to accept is false.

— Greil Marcus

Begin with the assumption of Cartesian dualism, setting man against nature in a quest to conquer matter with mind.

Add to this a metaphysics of scientific absolutism proposing that there are finite determinants of all things, independent from our values.

Propel these inclinations with the force of the inherent need of industrial economics to be infinitely expansionist.

Frame this view within a two-valued Aristotelian logic and Christian eschatology, both of which imply that since propositions and beliefs are either true or false, then some people, and not others, will be in possession of those which are True.

Reward the members of this alienated, absolutist, expansionist, righteous civilization with the products of their premises — nuclear weaponry, for one — and the peril of these ways becomes evident.

Gregory Bateson wrote, in the late 1960s, "it is clear now to many people that there are many catastrophic dangers which have grown out of the Occidental errors of epistemology." Later, in 1978, he wrote that still "there is really something deeply wrong, and I am not convinced that what is wrong is a necessary tribulation about which nothing can be done."

The following essays by Paul Watzlawick, Kenneth Burke, and Gregory Bateson provoke us to transform our vision from first to second sight.

C. W.-M.

Riddles of
Self-Reflexiveness

Paul Watzlawick

I have chosen the somewhat strange title: "The Riddles of Self-Reflexiveness." The advantage in talking about riddles is that you do not have to provide solutions. The questions that I want to deal with ought to be dealt with by somebody of a different training than I. What I can present to you are only some considerations of somebody who came into contact with these questions merely as a result of being a psychotherapist, not as a result of any particular training.

In the field of psychopathology, it is customary to talk about normalcy or illness purely on the basis of what appears to be a very simple criterion: the reality-adaptation of a person. If somebody had a view of reality that differed from the way reality really is, he was considered disturbed, and this is still the basis of most psychiatric thinking. Very often it is naively assumed that there is such a thing as a "real reality" of which sane people are more aware than madmen.

The reason why we are all — even outside psychiatry — so concerned about the question of reality is, in itself, quite a riddle. I do not think it is exaggerated to say that the quest for certainty — the quest for an adequate view of the world — is a basic theme of Western philosophy, or perhaps of mankind in general. The reason is not immediately clear. We know, for instance, that it is not only a human problem. If we observe animals we can see that they, too, behave with anxiety, react in a rather dramatic fashion, to anything that apparently does not fit into their view of reality. A puppy barks at a shiny can standing in the corner because he sees some movement in the reflection. He does not know the object, and he behaves — *mutatis mutandis* — the way a human being would behave in a comparable situation.

I think it is obvious that people, in order to function adequately in different life situations, need a view of reality that is more or less adequate and non-contradictory. We need certainty to be able to make decisions, and there is no fonder dream than to have total certainty and never to be wrong, never to make a wrong decision. These are commonplace remarks, and they still do not explain why we observe in ourselves a quest for certainty even when the particular question is of minor importance; when it would not threaten our survival to live with doubt or with uncertainty in that particular situation. But even here, there is this rather anxious quest for a solution or an answer — for certainty. For instance, the Polish philosopher Kolakowski mentions the high school student who for the first time understands Euclid's proof that the number of primes is infinite, and has a feeling of elation, of having somehow achieved an insight into the inner workings of the world, even though the fact that the number of primes is infinite does not help very much as far as any concrete life problems are concerned. But there is a feeling of somehow having grasped an aspect of the otherwise mysterious nature of things, of having arrived at some degree of certainty, that, after all, there is an order. And — he may think — if he has been able to do this, that he will probably be able to go on to other forms of certainty, and eventually arrive at a point where most of his uncertainties are relieved.

I have already mentioned a basic motif of Western thought, the idea that here am I, the recognizing subject, the observer, the theory builder, and there, outside of my skin, is the world. And the world is that which I have to recognize. Out there is the world of objects, and now I have to try and find the order that I (naively) assume has to be there. The moment we do this, we run into that which I would like briefly to consider here: the problems of self-reflexiveness, or of recursiveness.

The recognizing subject — the "I" — is, at the same time, also the object of his attempts at recognition, of cognition. That is to say, I not only want to understand the world, but, inevitably, in trying to understand the world I also include myself in these attempts at understanding. Therefore, I am not only my own subject, but I am also the object of my quest, of my search. And the solution that is quite seriously attempted in psychiatry and psychology is too often based on the rather touching assumption that there is a little man in my head who represents my consciousness. And then, of course, the question arises, "Yes, but how about the fact that I am conscious of my consciousness?" So one must assume that in the head of the little man there is another little man who has consciousness of consciousness, and then the question arises, "Yes, but what about *his* consciousness?" And we get into an infinite regress, and it gets nowhere, as infinite regresses tend to go.

But these are really philosophical questions that I am quite incompetent to solve, so let me try and approach the problem in a much more concrete, more simplistic way. Let me suggest to you that there are really two possibilities: First, there is a real reality, which is what most of us believe even though intellectually we may make different noises; an idea of reality into which I think most of us — ultimately, when the chips are down — retreat. Within the framework of this rather naive belief that there is a real reality, we proceed with the assumption that we must somehow find out what it is. The moment we do this, we are then in the universe of Aristotelian discourse — and out of this very quickly grows the problem of paradoxes. It then turns out that there are certain things which are true only if they are false, and false if they are true, and this, in essence, is the structure of paradox.

There is another great disadvantage connected with this idea, and this is a much more immediate, much more painful disadvantage, because most people can live even with the existence of paradoxes; but we cannot so easily live with the fact that once the idea prevails that the world can be divided into true and false propositions, we will perforce encounter those who hold convictions and claims of being in possession of the truth. With the idea that there are true and false propositions it becomes equally inevitable — equally true — that there will arise very definite claims of having discovered *the* truth. People then come and tell us that they have found out what is really the case, and they are usually animated by some kind of messianic fervor, and try to tell us what *they* can see so clearly. They are usually willing to give us a little time, a little probation period to catch on to their eternal truth, but if we do not they are eventually quite likely to send us to the gas chambers, or to some modern equivalent. I think if we look over the history of Western civilization (and we do not have to go very far back, we can begin at the Spanish Inquisition) we find that up to the very, very immediate present, the most terrible crimes were committed in the service of some kind of eternal truth that somebody had discovered and had tried to force upon the rest of us. So be they old Utopias, or be they modern ideas about how mankind can be turned into a joyful ant heap, as Dostoevsky once referred to this social order, it does not really matter: Whatever the ideology is, the structure remains the same, and the outcome is the same: camps, barbed wire, mass graves, and so on.

Now, the common denominator of what I have said so far about this first possibility is that the transmission of this particular view of reality which is believed to be eternally, and finally, and inevitably true, is, of course, a process of communication. It is somehow transmitted, and people are required to let themselves be brainwashed into believing it, and brainwashing is a form of communication.

The second possibility, the alternative to the first idea of a real reality, is the idea that there is *no* reality, or rather the assumption that there may be a reality, but it is not accessible to us. It is not accessible because whatever is inside a particular frame, cannot at the same time also be outside it, which means that if you are inside a system, you can never have full cognizance of that entire system. This basic fact has been expressed already by the Zen Buddhists when they said that life is like a sword that cannot hurt itself, like an eye that cannot see itself, because the eye, as the perceiving organ, cannot have an awareness of the entire body since it is part of the body itself. Gregory Bateson has written about this. Also, Kenneth Boulding and a number of other people have pointed out over and over again that at best we may have *images* of the world, and some of those images are better than others *only* in the sense that they are more viable, that they contain fewer contradictions than others. But this is about all we can say, and yet this has very far-reaching consequences for science, as well as our personal lives.

For many people, the idea that there should be no clear perception of reality — in fact, no perceivable reality — is very frightening. Apart from this, the idea that we only have images of a reality, has itself rather unpleasant and difficult consequences because the question then is, "Where do these images come from?" We are all blind to the realization, at least from moment to moment, that those images are created by ourselves in ways that may remain totally outside our awareness. They are again the result of communication; of what my parents told me; the kind of culture I grew up in; of my experiences under various conditions and in multiple contexts. In any case, we are, by and large, blissfully unaware that we are the architects of the world that we believe we are seeing "out there," and we are trying to interpret it and discover its order.

Philosophically, we are approaching the idea of constructivism: realities are constructed; or, as Saint Exupery said, "truth is not what we discover, but what we create." Schopenhauer talked about it in his *Will in Nature:*

> This is the meaning of Kant's great doctrine, that teleology (the study of evidences of design and purpose in nature) is brought into nature only by the intellect, who thus marvels at the miracle that it has created itself in the first place. It is (if I may explain so sublime a matter by a trivial simile) the same as if the intellect were astonished at finding that all multiples of nine again yield nine when their single figures are added together, or else to a number whose single figures again add up to nine; and yet, it has itself prepared this miracle in the decimal system.

So the thought is not exactly new. Behind this thought, there emerges very clearly the venerable archetypical image of the Ouroboros, the snake that swallows its own tail, or if you want a less poetic image, the dog who chases its tail — namely, the problem of recursiveness, of self-reflexiveness. What is supposedly discovered turns out to be determined by itself, turns out to be its own cause.

The amazing thing, however, about any self-reflexive proposition is that while it *produces* itself, it can never *prove* itself. It can never provide proof of its own consistence, provability, freedom from contradiction, etc. In fact, it mysteriously seems to *have* to stand in contradiction to its own basic premise, to itself. Take determinism. Determinism, as you know, is the assumption that the world is strictly determined by cause-effect relationships. One may embrace this view of the world, and it does a great deal to explain many things. It may, indeed — if you can put up with it emotionally — explain everything. Except it cannot explain itself. In order to subscribe to the idea of determinism, one has to make a totally indeterministic assumption, i.e., that everything is determined. By the same token, Kierkegaard calls rationalism an irrational belief in reason. The same goes for the quest for certainty or meaning.

Nowadays many people are engaged in quests for all sorts of things, but mostly for meaning.

There was a period in Central European thinking — the era of Romanticism — when the *goal* of the quest was the Blue Flower. The Blue Flower had to be found; it was somewhere. The Romanticists sought it everywhere. The trouble when you seek is that if you do not find, your failure to find *only* means that you may not have looked in the right place yet. Thus the search, the quest, may become interminable. For it could be that there is no such thing as the Blue Flower, and this would explain the fact that you have not found it yet. But this is not as easy to realize as it was for the King of Hearts in *Alice in Wonderland*, who said about the nonsense poem of the White Rabbit, "Well you know, if there is no sense in it, then it saves us a lot of trouble, then we don't have to look for one." But very few of us can take this rather philosophical attitude in the face of uncertainty.

The British logician Lucas puts it this way:

> The Marxist who says that all ideologies have no independent validity and merely reflect the class interests of those who hold them, can be told that in that case his Marxist views merely express the economic interest of his class and have no more claim to be judged true or valid than any other views. So too the Freudian, if he makes out that everybody else's philosophy is merely the consequence of childhood experiences, he is by parity of reasoning, revealing merely his delayed response to what happened to him when he was a child.

We get into this problem over and over again; and much more painful is the question, "How does democracy defend itself against undemocratic procedures?" What does democracy do in the face of terrorism? There is — to the best of my knowledge — no answer. Or to give you an example from literature: the Beckett expert, Breuer, says about Beckett's novel, *Watt*:

> The novel thus resembles the attempt of the schizophrenic to say nothing, and, at the same time, to avoid that his silence is taken as a message; the attempt of the mathematician, who attempts to prove his logic by this very same logic, because he does not want to fall into an infinite regress; the attempt of a

person who feels prompted to reinforce a promise, whose reliability is questioned, by promising to keep his promise; the dilemma of the politician who wants to attain noble goals through bad means — for instance, to wage war in order to abolish war — and is doomed to failure; or else, the simple problem of the near-sighted person who is groping for his glasses.

I would suggest to you that any search for the truth, certainty, provability, consistency, runs into riddles and traps of recursiveness, or self-reflexiveness. And in this sense, as you know, even Gödel's theorem is paradoxical because it proves — Spencer Brown notwithstanding — that undecidability can be decided. As I said, people get extremely rattled, the charge of nihilism is quickly raised — and yet, if we look at human problems, we find very quickly that Nietzsche was right when he said that people will bear any "how" as long as they have a "why." That is to say, we can put up with many, many things in life — in fact, human resistance in the face of the most adverse conditions is fantastic — as long as there is some kind of a viable idea in our head that explains this adversity. The study of concentration camp victims has shown that people who succumbed were the ones who had given up. The people who survived even the most horrible conditions were the ones who somehow had a "why" in their minds.

Let me change gears, and simply ask what remains. What remains is the undeniable fact that in spite of everything that I have said, it is an everyday phenomenon that people, social systems and so forth, are capable of somehow transcending the very traps and knots that I have tried to exemplify here. There is no question that there is such a thing as spontaneous change. Archimedes already thought he knew how this can be brought about when he said, "Give me a point outside the universe from which I can unhinge the world." Peter Weiss in his *Marat/Sade* says, "The important thing is to pull yourself up by your own hair, to turn yourself inside out and see the whole world with fresh eyes." I have a suspicion that Peter Weiss took this from the stories of Baron Munchhausen, because this is exactly what he did when he jumped and fell into a quagmire, and then pulled himself and his horse out by his own pigtail. We find a similar thought in Wittgenstein at the end of the *Tractatus*. He says, "My propositions serve as elucidations in the following way: Anyone who understands me eventually recognizes them as nonsensical, when he has used them — as steps — to climb up beyond them." Wittgenstein had already foreseen that which, in our days, is beginning to take a more and more concrete shape; namely, the fact that we have reached the limits of a scientific universe in which the opposite stand of observer and observed can still be maintained. It has served us well; it has gotten us very, very far, but we have definitely reached the limit. If we were to continue to believe in the need to create a subject-free universe, so that the universe we observe is uncontaminated by the subjectivity of the observer, and even if this were technically possible, it would still be impossible for a much more important reason: An observer-free, a subject-free universe is no longer perceivable. And Heinz Von Foerster, referring to this problem, says:

> After this, we are now in possession of the truism that the description of the universe implies one who describes it or observes it. What we need now is a description of the describer, or, in other words, we need a theory of the observer. Since to the best of available knowledge it is only living organisms which would qualify as being observers, it appears that this task falls to the biologist. But he himself is a living being, which means that in his theory he has not only to account for himself, but also for his writing his theory.

And so, after this *tour de force* — we arrive at the realization that we have to entertain a different world image, one in which observer and observed somehow fuse. To quote the Polish philosopher Kolakowski again: "Certainty can only be achieved in the immediacy." By this Kolakowski means the identity of subject and object. But this identity remains incommunicable. It cannot enter into the linguistic and scientific discourse of man without ceasing to be certainty. Certainty expressed in words is no longer certainty. So we are really arriving at something that one might almost call a mystical view of the universe, in which, precisely, the difference between the observer and the observed falls away.

The Interactive Bind

Kenneth Burke

There is a range within "perspectivism" well worth the exercising that goes with it. A tangle of individual organisms can be so interrelated that the lot can be viewed as an individual organism. The invader in a body can become so incorporated in that body's processes as to become in effect a physiological function of that body. Genes can be considered as the units of survival which, in their cooperation and competition with one another, in effect "use" their hosts as dwelling places designed for their survival. Mandeville's *Fable of the Bees* is an ironic account of transactional ambitions which Adam Smith presented to the world in a rationale of quite favorable sentiments the same year as our Declaration of Independence. Though Darwin lamented his loss of an ability to enjoy poetry, he did indeed give us the makings of it when explaining how "it is quite credible that the presence of a feline animal in large numbers in a district might determine, through the intervention, first of mice, and then of bees, the frequency of certain flowers in that district." Amusingly, such thinking moved Samuel Butler to delightful satire when, in *Erewhon*, his chapters on "The Book of the Machine" depicted machinery as using human beings to help in the generation of higher mechanical orders by supplying a link in the reproductive chain not possible to the nonbiological nature of the machines themselves. And in the *Hints Towards the Formation of a More Comprehensive Theory of Life*, feeling moved to "indulge a Darwinian flight . . . from sober judgment," Coleridge suggests, "we might imagine the life of insects an apotheosis of the petals, stamina, and nectarines, round which they flutter, or of the stems and pedicles, to which they adhere." A graver plausibility, he says, "is given to this fancy of a flying blossom, when we reflect how many plants depend upon insects for their fructification."

In his *Steps To an Ecology of Mind*, Gregory Bateson opts for such "flexibility" in ways of his own thus:

> Darwin proposed a theory of natural selection and evolution in which the unit of survival was either the family line or the species or subspecies or something of the sort. But today it is quite obvious that this is not the unit of survival in the real biological world. The unit of survival is *organism* plus *environment*. We are learning by bitter experience that the organism which destroys its environment destroys itself.
>
> If now we correct the Darwinian unit of survival to include the environment and the interaction between organism and environment, a very strange and surprising identity emerges: *the unit of evolutionary survival turns out to be identical with the unit of mind.*

The step from organism-and-environment to mind leads to such statements as these with relation to the polluted condition of Lake Erie:

> You decide that you want to get rid of the by-products of human life and that Lake Erie will be a good place to put them. You forget that the eco-mental system called Lake Erie is a part of *your* wider eco-mental system — and that if Lake Erie is driven insane, its insanity is incorporated in the larger system of *your* thought and experience.

He then quickly reviews ideas of "self," totemism, metaphors borrowing from nature the terms for a social order, animism (a personifying that was "not a bad idea in many ways"), gods, partly useful, partly error — up to the situation now:

Struggle may be good for your soul up to the moment when to win the battle is easy. When you have an effective technology so that you can really act upon your epistemological errors and can create havoc in the world in which you live, then the error is lethal. Epistemological error is all right, it's fine, up to the point at which you create around yourself a universe in which the error becomes immanent in monstrous changes of the universe that you have created and now try to live in.

Yes indeed, technology is so great a coefficient of power that its mistakes, its misuse, can be horrendous. I'd want to call the "universe" that it is producing a realm of "Counter-Nature," since technology has critically altered the way of life that was "natural" to our primitive ancestors, and that would still be with us had not the human animal manifested a peculiar kind of inventiveness not developed by any other biological organism on this planet. And Bateson's statement of the case has in its favor the fact that his stress upon the environment as a necessary condition of our existence as biological organisms helps reinforce the cause of Environmentalist criticism now so badly needed. (I would call it "Technology's Self-Criticism," since the Environmentalist rationale bases its arguments upon the material which the records and instruments of technology itself have provided for such a diagnosis.)

When trying to figure out just where Bateson and I differ (if we do differ!), I'd propose to start with Horne Tooke's reference to the fact that language *abbreviates*. Thus, Bateson "from a system-theoretic point of view" bears down hard on the guy who "says, 'I cut down the tree' and he even believes that there is a delimited agent, the 'self,' which performs a delimited 'purposive' action upon a delimited object." I would agree with him — yet somehow things turn out differently.

In the first place, when Bateson says there is an "ecology of ideas" and an "ecology of weeds" I'd have to translate that thus: I'd put "ideas" in the realm of "symbolic action"; and "weeds" (like stones or any other purely physical things or processes) would be in the realm of "nonsymbolic motion." Also, my body would be classed in the realm of nonsymbolic motion. From the days of parturition (at birth) until my death, this biological organism would be a separate entity in the sense that, owing to the centrality of the nervous system, my pleasures and pains would be experienced as immediately mine and no one else's. In that sense, my purely physiological nature (in the realm of motion) would embody a "principle of individuation." And each different kind of organism would have a correspondingly different kind of environment, as a dog would be a menacing aspect of a rabbit's environment, but home sweet home for the dog's fleas.

Also, in contrast with other kinds of biological organism (to our knowledge) the human physiological organism is genetically endowed with the ability to learn the kind of behavior that constitutes an arbitrary conventional symbol-system such as a tribal language. Or, if you would abbreviate that a bit: such bodies are "naturally" endowed with the ability to learn verbal behavior (for which my term, borrowed from the anthropologist Malinowski, is "symbolic action").

Here arise all the notions right and wrong that constitute the ideas of reality I acquire through the use of such a medium (ranging from gossip to history, philosophy, the sciences). Here also develops my social "Identity," or "Self," or "Personality," which dissolves into all sorts of *contextual* relationships (a situation which, in my *Grammar of Motives*, I called the "paradox of substance," citing Locke's observation that the very etymology of the term betrays its embarrassment, since it names *what is* in a term that means *"stands beneath,"* a *contextual* implication whereby the "man of substance" is defined by his holdings and the like, which are what he is *not*, so he can never feel sure that he is truly loved "for himself"). And on various occasions I have applied the concept to characters of a drama, where role ("personality") depends upon the roles that the other characters contribute, when the whole is considered "from a system-theoretic point of view."

The given individual's *name* is the first "abbreviation" visited upon him. Think of all the varying relationships the name contains as thus summed up, a trick of abbreviation further perfected by the summarizing of his role in the kinship system, and then further moved in that direction (or dissolving of direction!) when the most *personalizing* devices of all, the pronouns, enable him to say "I" whereas De Gaulle would have more administratively said "De Gaulle did it."

But just where are we? Bateson and I are in agreement about the fact that the defining of Self or Identity gets lost in the systems of social interrelationship, and that the dependence of human organisms upon their environment must be emphasized, and all the more so owing to the critical changes of environment which technology makes possible (or might we not even say "makes inevitable"?). And his distinction between the "ecology of ideas" and the "ecology of weeds" fits quite comfortably with my distinction between the realms of "symbolic action" and "non-symbolic motion." But within the organism-environment relationship as seen "from a system-theoretic point of view," what about my need to hold out for a "principle of individuation" somewhere along the line? And what comes of the fact that I put it where I do?

To begin with, a *principium individuationis* of some sort is needed to take account of the fact that a high degree of technological development (so far at least) has led to fantastic disparities within the apportioning of its rewards. Even though, as environmentally considered, if things go on as they are, the favored will be like those who got the best berths on a sinking ship, many of such favored individuals will have flourished and gone on their way if what's sinking happens to be the Ship of State. Also, although the nature of the *individual Person* dissolves into the complexities of *contextual* systems, each such separate body serves as *ground* for a *unique* set of *personal equations* ("ideas" of desirable and undesirable, promising and threatening, admirable and loathesome, etc., "ideas" of *what equals what*, as such judgments become associated with *particulars* whereby the mere *things* of the environment become rather like a kind of *pageantry* in which we play our parts). And above all, I need this grounding in a purely physiological organism, in the realm of sheer motion, generated wordlessly and born wordless, but genetically endowed with the ability to learn words via its steps out of "infancy." For thereby I define *our* kind of animal in terms of that step from nonsymbolic motion to symbolic action — and thence we get to the ingenuities and abbreviations of words whereby the kinds of attention and communication that the medium of symbolic action made possible, in turn made for the kinds of interaction between verbal guidance and non-verbal tools, each realm "enriching" the other, now confronting us as our "objective" kind of self-portraiture, plus the vexing fact that every instrument has a nature of its own, over and above its nature as an instrument put to use for our purposes, hence leading to unforeseen consequences some of which can inspire a Bateson, ingeniously manipulating *his* terms, to make it convincingly clear why, within the proprieties of his sytematic nomenclature, Lake Erie is ecomentally insane.

I need that one difference: We are the kind of organism that, born as individual speechless bodies, learn language (a *collective* medium of expression and communication), which in turn assisted the development of technology (with "creative" responses back and forth), until we now confront ourselves thus "writ large," even possibly (as thus "translated") self-aggrandized beyond the limits of self-control — but in any case, with symbol-guided technologically "perfected" Counter-Nature as our (take your choice) ultimate Freedom or Compulsion. (Regarding a choice here, I plead the rights of Flexibility.)

So far, then, we have been quite close, except that (let's admit it!) my theory of Logology led me to *secularize* the Thomistic principle of individuation, by substituting my term "nonsymbolic motion" plus "centrality of the nervous system" for his idea of "matter" as the *principium individuationis.* (In the same style, Logology secularizes the idea of God by substituting "god-terms" for any such high level of generalization whereby "dialectical materialism" would be classed as a "god-term" in the *Marxist* "system" of nomenclature. In working thus, I don't feel that Logology is trying to sneak in the notion of "mind" as a vestige of a theology's God. Rather, Logology studies Theology in keeping with the fact that over the centuries Theologists, in their ponderings on The Word and with the word, got to the depths of these matters.)

Saint Paul tells us that Faith comes from hearing. And why not? For Faith involves Doctrine. And how "indoctrinate" sans words? So I take it that Theology is an Ideal (that is, Thorough) tracking down of the implications inherent in the nature of the medium in which the dogmas are being propounded. But in saying that Theology, by being a "perfect" fulfillment of linguistic possibilities, reveals profound things about the resources of language, we are not necessarily making a statement about its truth or falsity.

But that brings us to a further consideration. When trying to help myself make clear, in hopes of making clear to you, just how these things line up (where do we deviate if deviate we must), I encountered this angle: In the light of things as being said these days, I was surprised that in Bateson's pages there was no talk at all of "dialectic." So I began tossing out a few of such "transformations" that I had found likely to recur (or liable to recurrence). Borrowing from Bateson, I'd call them "differences that make a difference," to which I'd add "and in a big way."

The first one on my list of such shifts was lifted from a book by Charles M. Perry, *Toward a Dimensional Realism.* (I refer to it on pp. 53-4 of my *Grammar.*) Etymologically, this dialectical delicacy shows as the difference between being "a part of" something and being "apart from" it. I was there applying it to the shift whereby something viewed as "a part of" God could become treated as "apart from" God. Thus, the susceptibilities of dialectic being what they are, any *part of* a whole may become *apart from* the rest, any distinction may become a contrast.

Whereat I moved on to the word "against," which accurately translates the Latin word *contra,* from which (as per the "paradox of substance") we get our word "country." Then I got into twists whereby teams in competition cooperate to make it a good game. And I wondered whether an animal that grows heavier fur in the fall is preparing *against* winter or going along *with* the aftermath of summer.

Thereupon I got so demoralized that I got into a different groove. I thought of how yeast, in fermenting, finally produces the percentage of alcohol that kills it. And I wondered whether, if yeast knew what its inevitable production of alcohol would do to it in the natural course of what it thought of as a good life, it would get into a double bind that drove it crazy, in the way that Bateson's schizophrenics do, not like his Lake Erie, which has but the *eco* side of the *mentalism*.

Whereupon, of a sudden, a new light dawned upon me; namely: The overall design *is* The Dialectic. What Bentham might call its "neutral" appellation would be "system." Its corresponding "censorial" terms would be eulogistically "interaction" (when it's working well); and the most thorough example of the dyslogistic would be in cases of "double bind," where a "balance of powers" becomes rather a *conflict*, as sometimes happens with the qualitative turn from cooperation to competition among the legislature, judicial, and executive branches of our government.

Once I was among several who were asked to approve or disapprove of an application for a grant to make a documentary kind of film showing how confinement in our prisons turned out badly for the prisoners. I was all for it. But I also suggested that, if possible, the film could also give some inkling of just how it is that, occasionally, a prisoner in the worst of such demoralizing outfits comes out even far more reformed than the system was supposedly designed for, becoming an evangelist of one sort or another, inspirited with a life-work against the experience in one way or another.

Bateson's resonant term, "double bind," will surely and rightly earn him a permanent place in our civilization's archives (including of course his ingenious speculations and observations that go along with it). But the more I think of it, the greater area of our lives it seems to cover. Certain weeds, for instance, seem to thrive best when they are walked on (thrive best in the sense that they can take over more of a given territory than their competitors). If, for "heuristic" purposes, I endow them with personality and critical awareness, I'd not assume that they like to be walked on any more than you would. But in their prayers they give thanks to their Maker for having distributed their seeds precisely on such a path, since they could take the punishment better than their rivals could, and thus comparatively flourished.

And in *Coriolanus* there is the passage where Brutus refers to "dogs that are often beat for barking / As Therefore kept to do so." In effect they don't go as crazy as Lake Erie because after their fashion they would say to themselves, "Along with the reward of getting fed for doing my job as a dog there 'naturally' goes the need to get beaten by the guys who feed me."

And double-boundly systematized, I even offered a tune in Gregory Bateson's honor: "Why not try to be a something / Exactly like a something else./ When it begins to freeze hard, it also melts./ Flying down while it flies up and / goes in while coming out the door./ Outside is as in as inside / and when less, it's all the more." I have also claimed that, in principle, it's an ideal formula for how to be a good President of the United States.

Put two weights on a seesaw, equidistant from the middle. Neither side goes down. When that's all to the good, it's a balance (equals Interaction). But when it's not, it's an opposition, a conflict (equals Double Bind).

So we perforce fare forth, continually.

While that goes on all the time continuing, maybe the only real disagreement is only what stems from my insisting upon the wordless body, in the realm of wordless motion, as a principle of individuation for animals of our kind, within the organism-environment systems and randomnesses as a whole.

The dual realms of motivation (the conditions of the body as a physiological object in the realm of nonsymbolic motion, and the responsiveness to the symbolic structures which serve in their own way to define, rightly or wrongly, the nature of "reality") come to a focus in the character, "personal equations" of the individual symbol-using body (the unique unit of which each social security number is an abbreviated designation). Here is an unstable but not random complexity of tendencies, attitudes, dispositions which differentiates one such motivated locus from another.

I began my speculations of this sort by asking about the different characters of particular books — and though any book's use of the public medium shades off into symbolic and nonsymbolic contexts such that it can be viewed rather as a "result" of such contexts than as an independent act of its own, there still remains the fact that it does have a relatively stable set of internal relationships (equations and successive developments) which single it out as a character, properly designated by a title.

I confess, I end up with a notion that each of us is "like a book," a "book of human nature," in that sense, except that, so long as we exist, the personal equations and developments are to an extent unstable, whereas the "personality" of a book is relatively fixed, despite the fact that its survival as a "score to be performed" by readers in different "contexts of situation" can be to a large extent transformed in the "performing" by readers whose own differences of experience in effect suggest "new readings." Similarly the "character" or "personality" or "self" of each symbolizing body may be interpreted quite differently by other persons differently related to it, the "perspective" in terms of which they interpret it being shaped in part by a different point of view determined by different notions of "reality."

I take it that each such "book" brings to a focus in its "readers" some aspect of the "reflexive" principle intrinsic to the symbolic medium, the general ability of the medium to in some way set up the conditions for a second level of motives, as with words about words and tools for making tools.

In the realm of what Aristotle would call "politics," what we generally would call "social science," and what I would ascribe to a special aspect of social science I'd call a "dramatistic" brand of "logology," I'd want to hold that the over-all situation of organism-and-environment takes form in the *individual's* involvement in the motivational tangle whereby human prowess with symbol-systems has led to a high development of technology, with the symbolizing and the tool-using reinforcing each other and so giving rise to an ecology of Counter-Nature quite at odds with the kind of experience, with corresponding conditions of selectivity, which the human body, an incredibly "conservative" organism, was adapted to survive in.

Starting with the individual work, trying to develop a theory of literary form-in-general that would involve different casuistry as applied to individual cases, I found my speculations dissolving more and more into observations about situational matters that got me to moving from the analysis of poetic action to the theory of symbolic action in general. But I still find the need to keep going back and viewing individual cases in a way whereby I must think of the *individual human body* as the "unit of survival," now caught in a vast complexity of interactions and double binds (where does one end and the other take over?) coming to a focus in the tangle of personal equations that characterize particular psychic economies, while the "tracking down of implications" that the mutuality of symbolism and symbol-guided technics now makes possible, with every special nomenclature supplying in effect a local "vision" of its own, towards our highly problematic dealings with the Counter-

Natural realm now so much an anthropomorphized version of reality, our "second nature," that it has become self-perpetuating, since any *solution* of technology's problems is possible only insofar as we develop a still more effective technology with corresponding symbolic contributions towards the forming of political structures best adapted to its adequate control.

Addendum on Bateson

Kenneth Burke

After finishing my previous essay on "The Interactive Bind," I have read Stephen Toulmin's comprehensive characterization of Bateson that this collection of essays ends on. And I'd like to add some comments in the light of his highly suggestive observations.

In keeping with "the fact that scientists have run up against the limits of the Cartesian methodology at a dozen different points," Toulmin says, "We can no longer view the world as Descartes and Laplace would have us do, as 'rational onlookers,' from outside ... and whatever scientific understanding we achieve must be a kind of understanding that is available for participants within the process of nature, i.e., from inside."

Toulmin makes many related statements, such as references sometimes to "postmodern" *science*, sometimes to a needed *philosophical* "reorientation" (with sociobiology as indicative of such efforts), and a new "methodology" aimed at the "overall integration of the human sciences with the sciences of nature" (while praising Bateson for his pioneering efforts in this direction). But the handiest approach for our purposes is to single out the distinction between the view of the world as onlookers "from outside" and as participants "from inside."

My *Grammar of Motives* reminds me that I borrowed (from *Toward a Dimensional Realism*, by Charles M. Perry) that unassuming miracle-worker, that humble dialectical device, a shifting between "a part of" and "apart from." It can so readily function as a tiny difference that can make a world of difference. In the present case, its susceptibilities admonish us to recall that while we are all "a part of" our natural environment, there is also a notable respect in which each of us is "apart from" it, and even apart from the others of our own kind. I refer to the fact that, owing to the centrality of the nervous system, your sensations and feelings are *immediately* yours and no one else's. It "makes a world of difference" whether *you* are experiencing any given pleasures and pains or *I* am, though we are probably right in assuming that such experiences are largely analogous. Thus there is a "principle of individuation" in the human physiological organism (sheerly as a body) which, at parturition, makes each of us a separate entity "apart from" the environmental context which, at the same time, we are "a part of," and so integrally so that we could not exist without the external grounding of our internality.

Insofar as any such physiological organism becomes familiar with so stimulatively social, public, collective medium of expression and communication as a tribal language (with the experiencing of corresponding institutions that human groups so motivated develop) there arises a complexity of implicit and explicit judgments about the nature of "reality," all adding up in our time to quite a clutter of both fragmentary and would-be summational projects for variously putting together what goes on in us as bodies, along with the store of symbols that such bodies learn to "think by," or at least to "behave verbally" by.

As I see it, Toulmin uses his expressions, "postmodern science" and "philosophical reorientation," as though they were convertible terms. But with regard to the underlying "ontological," "epistemological," and "methodological" considerations here, I could quickly indicate the drift of my comments on Toulmin's comments on Bateson by proposing that we look skeptically at Toulmin's *equating* of "science" and "philosophy," instead allowing for the possibility that where the exceptional precisions of technological *science* leave off is precisely where the most momentous precisions of philosophy begin. By the sheer nature of the case, we could not expect that any one particular *specialized* science (not even so comprehensive a discipline as a brand of sociology) might serve as a "science of the lot" (a *scientia scientiarum*). Here, for better or worse, enter considerations of a *philosophical* nature, involving issues such that "science" and "philosophy" could not be used as convertible terms. If there are readers to whom this methodological statement of the case does not seem reasonable on its face, I might refer to my comments on the matter in my essay on "Dramatism" (*International Encyclopedia of the Social Sciences*).

When Bateson says, "Objects are my creation, and my experience of them is subjective, not objective," Toulmin observes: "This dichotomy of 'internal image' as against 'external event' is a piece of undigested Cartesian doctrine which Russell himself inherited from T. H. Huxley and J. S. Mill, and which goes back directly to the seventeenth century epistemological debate." Yet there is a sense in which a "philosophical orientation," as distinguished from what Toulmin would seem to include in an "epistemology of science," offers a much needed sophistication with regard to our notions about terms for separate "objects," whereat we'd have correspondingly good words for Bateson's slant. We might get at the issue roundabout thus:

There is an "objective triad," comprising a thing, its image, and its name. This ingenious linguistic invention enables us to single out for attention and communication countless such parts of nature, and to deal with each as a "substance," defined as "that which is conceived by itself" (*id quod per se concipitur*). But, as Spinoza points out (and I am quoting the definition from his *Ethics*), there are actually no such separate "substances" that meet this conceptual test. No existent *part of* nature can really be found *apart from* a context (or, in current cant, a "surround") that *per se*, denies any such substance the possibility of meeting the conditions specified in the definition. (In Spinoza's terministic accountancy, nothing less than Everything in its totality could pass the test.)

As I take it, Bateson's doubts about the "objectivity" of an "object" are in line with the style, the kind of pliancy exemplified by his unedged recipe for the "unit of survival." And both are quite in line with the kind of speculation that comes to a focus when one asks, as systematically as possible, what such elements that tradition has treated *psychologically*, as "mental" ("subjective") yield better *logologically* as "verbal" (along with the proposition that *verbal* discernments are "real"). In this regard, let us consider how we can fully recognize the exceptional ingenuity of the "objective triad" (which gives us thing, image, word — and thus is a basic terministic resource that made the high development of technology possible), while we retain the kind of admonitions that follow from the concept of such (often artifical) "objects" as in reality merged with (become "a part of") their *natural* context.

In T. S. Eliot's early doctoral thesis "Knowledge and Experience in the Philosophy of F. H. Bradley," there is a passage much to our purpose, since it proclaims the all-importance of *words*, or *names*, in shaping the objects of attention. "Without words, no objects," he asserts. And he questions whether "the explicit recognition of an object as such can take place without the beginnings of speech." (The passage is discussed at greater length in my article on "Terministic Screens," republished in *Language as Symbolic Action*, and serves well to buttress my position in "Definition of Man," also in that volume.)

While this peculiarly human resource (the objective triad) makes possible the fantastic efficiencies of innovation, production, distribution, and consumption that add up to the ever-expanding (at an exponential rate of increase) developments of technology, we should note another aspect of nomenclature, a mode of placement at least *in the direction of* the Spinozistic thought-style. That is: Our vocabularies of *things* are matched by our vocabularies of *situations, processes, relationships,* terms on the slope of the "contextual," "global," "holistic."

Note one radical difference between these two kinds of "signifiers" for the nonlinguistic "signified": If I were asking you what the name for a given object might be in some particular language, I could point to it, or to a picture of it, and say, "What is that?" And your answers would follow from the simple, direct act of pointing. But what could I point to if I wanted to ask you the Japanese words for capitalism, autumn, situations, processes, relationships?

If you think of the "signified" as the "thing to be defined," the *definiendum*, and of the name, the signifier, as a shorthand word for the definition, note the important difference between these two kinds of nomenclature. With the objective triad the thing, the *definiendum*, in effect "calls forth" the word, the signifier. On the other hand, consider the kind of hypothetical process which Freud calls the "unconscious." Here things are in effect reversed, and the *definiendum* is brought into the universe of discourse as a function of the definition. And it is, by sheer definition, a kind of *definiendum* outside the realm of such terms as go with the objective triad. It can't be pointed to.

The "heuristic" potentialities of terms for situations, processes, interrelationships are exemplified, for instance, in cases of comparative sociology, where a process that is quite *explicitly* present in one social order is shown, by analogical extension, to be *implicitly* present in another. And this kind of speculative pliancy, which seems to me typical of Bateson's adventurous improvisings, rather than a mere hang-over from an earlier usage, seems closer to the spirit behind such obser-vations as "Objects are my creation."

However, I may seem to have entangled myself in a contradiction when saying that the concept of separate "objects" (as "apart from" a context) is an ingenious *verbal* invention, and deceptive if not properly discounted along Spinozistic lines. For I have laid major stress upon an empirical, physiological "principle of individuation" that is typical of human bodies after parturition (a consideration that our typical theories of "culture" and "identity" seem in some way or another to leave out of account as a central point to build around with regard to the analysis of human relations). But there is no contradiction. No such body is "apart from" its natural environment in the sense that it can be empirically located in isolation, "by itself," *apart from* the local environ-ment upon which it depends and with which it integrally communes. Yet the "immediacy" of the sensations in any one such physiological organism gives it an internality as real as the surroundings both natural and cultural with which it merges.

However, we should note this ironic duality of effects that the localiz-ing kind of attention indigenous to the objective triad has had upon the course of our cultural development. Along with the kind of concentra-tion, or "efficiency," that "objectively" directed experiment con-tributed to the great rise of conditions alien (counter) to the state of nature out of which our current kinds of human societies evolved, there has also been the evaluating of a technical device's "success" by such tests of trial and error as attain their most "scientific" embodiment in the methodologically *narrowed* confinement of tests to controlled laboratory conditions.

Concepts of "success," as thus efficiently evaluated, owe technology's success (particularly if rationalized by a second such efficiency, sheerly monetary profit) to such narrowing of the criteria. But by the same token technology's "success" gives rise to unforeseen (and often un-foreseeable) consequences when let loose in the *wider* "context of situa-tion" comprising human relations as a whole. The indices of "success" in this wider sense simply are not present (though the beginnings of such are to be seen in so-called "impact statements" about the possible effect of a new project upon the surrounding area, considerations that often are reduced to questions as to how a new market might affect the structure of markets already there).

Every instrument or method has a "nature" not reducible to the purpose (however rational and benign) for which it may have been designed. This situation gives rise to a vexing "instrumentalist predicament," as man-made innovations that are imposed upon the conditions of primitive nature add up to a realm of "Counter-Nature," presenting tests of survival quite different from those which our ancestors proved themselves equipped to survive. All told, again and again one finds cause to recall Veblen's version of a highly enterprising proverb, as ironically distorted thus: "Invention is the mother of necessity." I never tire of repeating that witty act of mayhem.

Paradigmatic Conservatism

Gregory Bateson

I should apologize, perhaps, that I have not been here at Asilomar for your whole four days of deliberation. I was down in Los Angeles with the Regents of the University of California. We had a public meeting for students and members of the university faculty in one of the big auditoria in the convention hall in Los Angeles. This was a meeting to allow the public to tell us what they thought about the fact that the University of California runs the nation's principal labs for the devising and testing of atomic weaponry. About a thousand people turned out.

The Regents gave every speaker five minutes. So, in about three hours, we listened to about thirty people talk for five minutes each. As one of the Regents said afterwards, "That was democracy at work."

It was all surprising. Mostly, at such public meetings, those who speak are the very angry, the slightly paranoid, and so on. But this was a very thoughtful meeting. There were several people, god bless them, in whom affect (I never liked the word) and thought, or intellect, or something, were well integrated — people who were able to talk sanely of the tragedy and monstrosity of a culture devoting this much effort to the arts of destruction.

Others talked more wildly. But the comment that I want to bring you is that it seemed to me that the entire spectrum of those people speaking was all, in a sense, our creation. We Regents — twenty-five not very special human beings — were in a position of rather special responsibility not only to those who had a sane view of the tragedy but also to those who viewed it through paranoid lenses. It's very easy, you know, to listen to speeches of this kind and to notice that they are a little bit paranoid, and then not to listen any more. Whereas the correct perception was that they were — the sane and the insane — all a product of what we had met to discuss.

I was impelled the following day in a smaller committee to state that I thought what we were doing, proposing to do, and had been doing for some years was *evil*. And "evil" is not, I suppose, a technical term among communication theorists. It's possible that it should be. When we reach the final anguish we shall not, I think, need to repeat the ancient cry, "My god, why hast thou forsaken me?" Because I think the reasons for being foresaken will be amply clear by then.

Here I want to talk a little about those reasons. I believe that a large part of the deep underpinning of what is going wrong and what has been going wrong for a long time is very closely related to matters you have been discussing for the last three days. The epistemological underpinning of this whole mess is an important part of it. There are people in this room — and not a few — who know that epistemological errors are part of the machinery of the descent to hell.

I had a conversation, a long time ago now, in Princeton with Robert Oppenheimer. It was just after World War II and the physicists were feeling guilty about the bomb. And the Think Tank of Princeton, with Oppenheimer's blessing, had organized seminars and got in visiting speakers, one after another, to talk to the physicists about the social sciences. The physicists wanted to know (sweet optimistic creatures they were) whether the social sciences perhaps had any balm, any comfort for them, any hope. I was one of those speakers, and was Oppenheimer's house guest that night. Next morning it was wet, and the children had lost their rubbers. Mrs. Oppenheimer was going slightly crazy. It was the typical breakfast scene of the American family on a wet winter's morning. The still small voice of Oppenheimer cut through this. "You know, if anyone asked me why I left Cal Tech and came to Princeton, I suppose the answer would be that there were 500 students in Cal Tech who wanted to know the answers." I said I thought the answers to those questions were probably rather bitter. He said, "Well, as I see it, the world is moving in the direction of hell with a high velocity, a positive acceleration, and possibly a positive rate of change of acceleration, and will perhaps only *not* arrive at its destination upon the condition that we and the Russians *are willing to let it.* Every move we make in anxiety trying to put off the crash is, in fact, a move which speeds the system on the way to hell." I have not heard anything intelligent said about the international scene since. And I don't know if even that is very intelligent. But it's at least the beginnings of an intelligence.

I want to try to go a step further than that, if I can. We can take Oppenheimer's utterance as sort of prime permission to think whatever thoughts we want to think. Having accepted Oppenheimer's statement, you see, we can set free our fantasy to roam without responsibility in the roaming, always knowing that we have to come back from fantasy to a more concrete world.

There are three subjects I want to address from this point of view. They're very closely related and they're all epistemological. First I want to talk about the contrast between quantity and quality. Then later, in the light of this, I want to talk about the nature of cultural change. And finally I want to mention a particular sort of *responsibility* — the responsibility or duty of the social scientist to know what is going on.

First the question of quantity *versus* pattern. If you pull on a string, or on a chain, you quantitatively increase a variable called *tension.* At a certain point, predictably, the chain will break, provided you have enough quantity available to add to that tension. It is not possible in principle to say *which* link will break, only that *a* link will ultimately break. If the links are fairly equal, we can have approximate knowledge — always approximate — of the amount of tension required to break the chain.

(Notice, by the way, that quantities are alway approximate. It's in the nature of quantities. They're not numbers. You can have five eggs; you cannot not have five gallons of water. You get five gallons, plus or minus something. All quantities are approximate. And numbers, especially the smaller numbers, are of the nature of discontinuities, click-click-click, and therefore are patterns rather than quantities in many ways.)

I am talking about the contrast between quantity and pattern. You can build up the quantity of tension on the chain and at a certain tension the chain breaks at a link which we could not predict, at what is called the weakest link. That is, what the change in quantity did was to make evident a pre-existing pattern: the difference between this link and other links.

Now, in this whole business, let us look at how our Occidental society works. First of all, you will observe that we are preoccupied with quantity. Sir Francis Bacon was one of the people responsible for the emphasis on quantification in science. And this emphasis permeated from the physical sciences where, you know, it had magnificent history and great achievements and ended up making our friend, the atom bomb — the most wonderful thing. But quantification has become, as you all know, an orthodoxy in the psychology labs. It's not very clear that mental operations are at all suitably reduced in that way. On the whole, redundancy, pattern, and so on, seem to be right in the center of communication theory, with quantity related to them about as the tension of the chain is related to the underlying pattern that makes it break. If you grow up, as we do, with a worship of the quantitative aspect and a minimal attention to the qualitative aspect, I believe you inevitably land yourself in the dilemmas of our civilization. This is a very important component in the pathway that has brought us here.

Consider the business of government. The government has control over *quantities*. They can alter the tax rates and they can manipulate quantities in various ways, but the trouble for government is that the weakest link is never predictable. You can impose quantitative change upon the system but you can never tell what the outcome will be. This is the Achilles heel of government. Almost every decision that can be made at the Sacramento level or the Washington level is a *quantitative* decision. But that upon which the decision must act — the social organization, the education, or the foreign policy of the nation, is *qualitative*, and obeys qualitative laws which we very imperfectly understand. Decision becomes very difficult.

Similarly, the Regents know all about fussing with Scholastic Apptitude Tests to decide what percentage of high school graduates should be allowed to enter the university. And at the other end, on the exit from the university, they have grades and all that stuff which again is quantification imposed upon a patterned, biological world. We cannot discuss, at the regental level, the teaching of qualitative thought versus the teaching of quantitative thought. You know, "that's not the Regent's business." And yet every quantitative change we impose upon the system is in the end putting stress on the qualitative patterns whose breaking strains and whose evolutions and transformations we do not understand. We don't understand them, you know, because this meeting couldn't have happened ten years ago. We are only now begin-ning to discover how to think in any formal way about the sort of things that seem to matter more than anything else.

Of course it was known before this that such things mattered. There is, for example, the Tolstoyian and Marxian theory of history which asserted that the great men of history are irrelevant. That, for example, if Darwin had not published *On the Origin of the Species* in 1859, somebody else would have done so within two years, *plus* or *minus*. That the social "forces" (and I object to the metaphor with its presuppositions of quantity and physical analogy) would have determined this at that time. The *pattern* of evolution was visible and Darwin was actually preceded in the discovery of "Natural Selection" by both Alfred Russel Wallace and Patrick Matthew. There were a dozen people right on the edge of evolutionary theory at that moment. And the edition of *On the Origin of Species* was sold out before it hit the stands, so it wasn't that new.

But it would have made a very great difference if Wallace had written *On the Origin of Species* instead of Darwin. The theory of evolution would then have had a cybernetic model in it already at that moment. Wallace discovered natural selection under a psychedelic experience which followed a delirious attack of malaria. He wrote to Darwin. And in that long letter, he saw that natural selection was a difficult idea. He said: "The action of this principle is exactly like that of the centrifugal governor of the steam engine ..."

So here we are. And we are faced, I think, with a probability of major pattern changes in the next very few years. We can't do much about that, except keep our fingers crossed and not be damned fools — and hope there aren't too many of those around.

But as for the precipitation of change, we might be able to think about that. Do we want it to be military? Accidental? Economic? A matter of starvation, perhaps? Would we prefer to have the sea level rise a couple hundred feet? That would make a great big difference. Any one of these different things could precipitate profound change but each would have a different outcome. But I get back to the fact that the way we are going about things with this enormous emphasis upon the quantitative view and the minimal emphasis upon the patterned view is, I believe, the easiest way of descent into hell. The surest.

But on the patterned side, what can be said? And how do the two sides relate? I have made one statement about that, namely that they relate as in the breaking chain.

But here is another thing which we discussed long, long ago in the

Palo Alto project. I once wrote a small paper on it but I've never really touched it since. The idea came from Horst Mittelstaedt of the Max Planck Institute, who was working with praying mantises. The mantis has a claw which folds on itself and with this claw he catches flies on the wing. Mittelstaedt wanted to know how he aims and times his action.

There are two main ways in which he might do this. One is the way of the shotgun, and the other is the way of the rifle. In handling a rifle, you look along it; you sight; you observe that there is a difference between where the rifle should point and where the sights are pointing. And you correct that error, and you correct it again, and so on, until finally you pull the trigger. The error correction is in the act of aiming the rifle and in each single act of using the rifle, you have error correction.

Whereas, with a shotgun or a pistol the procedure is different. Let us suppose I want to shoot my enemy under the table. He is sitting over on that side of the table and I'm on this side of the table, and I've got a pistol under the table. I've got to shoot him. I cannot, obviously, aim that pistol. I could practice by putting dolls or something over on the other side of the table and firing at them. Bang, bang, one after the other. That is, I could have feedback over the *class* of events of shooting, but not within the single event. With the rifle I must *aim* each single shot; with the pistol or shotgun I must *practice*. Let us call the improvement by practice "calibration." I arrange my neurons, and muscles, and such things as if with a screwdriver, or similar instrument. I take in the slug of information. I then act upon computing that slug of information and shoot. This is how I was taught to shoot during World War II. They had me stand in front of a large oak tree with an automatic pistol, standing with my back to the oak tree. I was to jump in the air, draw the gun, turning as I jumped, and loose a bullet into the oak tree before I landed on the ground facing in the other direction. (I don't think I ever hit the oak tree.)

To mark the contrast, let's call the improvement which I achieve by aiming *error correction*.

Now let's take a look at any simple cybernetic system, say a house with a thermostat. You have wobbling quantity, the temperature of the house. And a sense organ which measures that temperature; it's called a thermometer. The thermometer controls a switch which turns the furnace *on* when the temperature falls below the lower threshold and *off* when the temperature rises above the upper threshold. This is already a simple control system at one level but this system is itself controlled by a calibration called the *bias*. This is on the wall of the dining room. You go and you set it to respond in a certain way. This now makes two feedback systems, one which controls the furnace and one which controls the bias. Between them is a calibration, the setting of the bias. But why do you alter the bias? Well, you alter the bias because the temperature here had an effect on you, the resident. You said, "The house is too damn cold; it's been cold for a week." Then you go and you change the bias. But your threshold, you see, was determined in you by feedback processes. You went up to Alaska for five years and you lived in an igloo. You are inclined, then, to think that the house is normally too hot. Or you went to the tropics, *et cetera.* Your bias gets fixed by changes which occur in you.

The total system is a sort of ladder, interlocking settings which are calibrations, which are qualitative, discontinuous, fixed, structural sort of things. And events which are usually quantitative.

The tendency of our thinking today, is to think almost entirely on the quantitative side of the picture, and to argue about quantities.

We are very impatient, you see, of the idea that there are patterns, that the patterns have rigidities and rigors which have to be respected. The nature of pattern is not something that you can fool around with. It's among eternal verities. *Two* is different from *three*, and the difference between *two* and *three* will concern all matters of symmetry, *et cetera, et cetera, et cetera.* I don't have to tell you about the enormous tyranny of patterns; what I do have to tell you perhaps is that their tyranny is something you have to accept. The mush of quantity you may have a certain amount of freedom to fool around with. I'm not sure. But the tyranny of pattern you have to accept. And I gave this talk the title "Paradigmatic Conservatism" because we are today at that place where we have to ask about change of patterns, change of very fundamental settings in our society. And we approach that at this moment in a state of mind totally unequipped to deal with it, namely a state of mind which is thinking all the time on the quantitative side of the diagram, in quantities, in SAT's, letter grades, words-per-page-per-dissertation, and things of this kind, which become quite monstrous at this moment in history when we face changes in pattern and calibration.

When we face the change from thinking about quantities to thinking about patterns — that's a change in itself and it is one that we're facing. For instance, we face this very peculiar business called women's lib. Obviously the value and liberation and beauty which are what women's lib should give are not related to some characteristic of the sexes which can be handled in a quantitative measurement. But there is a strong tendency to think that women's lib is to be achieved by quantitative changes in the role of women, thus we dispute about equal wages and so on. And we dispute about how equal they are with men, but not how equally valuable, equally patterned, but not similarly patterned. They tell me there are qualitative differences.

At this moment we have a double zig-zag, a double hook, between us and getting to where we want to get. We are hooked on thinking about quantities, and our whole economic theory is so hooked. Our whole theory of internal satisfactions, our pursuit of happiness and all that, our obsession with property, our measurement of time, and our obsession with money. Money is, you know, a pseudo-biological goal. True biological goals are always limited. Always what you want is an optimum quantity — of oxygen, calcium, protein, psychotherapy, love, whatever it is. We think about money as if it would be nice to maximize our supply of it, and hence also to maximize our supply of oxygen, calcium, protein, psychotherapy, and what have you.

Maximizing these things always makes them toxic. In the real biological world, every desirable object becomes toxic beyond a certain point, *except money*. Money is in this sense a fake. It is an imposed value structure, an imposed metaphor which does not fit that which we are talking about. It's a quantitative metaphor which does not fit the world of pattern. It is an epistemological blunder.

And then we have another set of metaphors which do not fit the world of pattern. These are the metaphors which we take from Newtonian physics. The metaphor of "energy." The metaphor of "power." We use "power" in political science to mean god knows what. Possibly capacity to bribe, capacity to harm, a complicated component in relationship — a characteristic of one end of a relationship. We say that "A" has power. What we mean is that there is something in the *relationship* between "A" and "B," something in the *interactive pattern*; I don't have to tell you about all that. That is the rubric under which you are met, after all.

We have this massive addiction to physical metaphors which, as far as I know, are completely inapplicable to the life and epistemology of real organisms living in a real world.

I am using "epistemology" now as a word in natural history. See, that's the hell of it. That there is a world of abstract epistemology and there is a world of epistemology of actual organisms interacting. The way in which they think they know, and the way in which thinking and knowing have to be done, are not necessarily the same.

Now the extraodinary thing is that this can now be said; that it can be said to as many people as there are in this room. I'm sure quite a large fraction of you heard what I was trying to say.

We are not where we were 20 years ago. One of the most moving things said at the atom meeting that I was talking about was a quote from one of the Nazis at Nuremberg. They asked him, "Did you know what was happening in the death camps?" And he was said to have said, "No, I did not know, but I *could* have known." And that is the critical point. We have now reached a moment at which we can begin to know something of the processes of this phony and crooked disease in the pathway we are following. We can know what is evil in the pathway we are following. At present, I don't think there are very many of us. A few thousand, maybe. But this is a very extraordinary epoch in which this knowledge is now becoming a part of the thinking of quite a lot of people. Thank god.

Afterword

The Charm of the Scout

Stephen Toulmin

In the literature and movies of the American Frontier the scout is usually depicted as a roughly clad eccentric who leaves the safety of the settlement and reappears unpredictably, bringing a mixture of firsthand reports, rumors, and warnings about the wilderness ahead — together with a tantalizing collection of plant specimens, animal skins, and rock samples, not all of which are fool's gold. At first the settlers find the scout's help indispensable; but once their community begins to consolidate he becomes a figure of fun; and finally, after respectability has set in, he is a positive embarrassment. Yet their premature respectability is vulnerable. When the settlement is struck by drought, the scout's nature lore leads the settlers to hidden springs of underground water, but once the crisis is past, respectability re-emerges, and the scout is ridden out to the town line.

Within the world of the American behavioral sciences, Gregory Bateson always had the scout's ambiguous status. He himself was never an orthodox academic, either in his position or in his activities. With grants from the National Institute of Mental Health and other agencies, he pursued his research in a Veterans Administration hospital in California, at the Oceanographic Institute in Hawaii where he studied the behavior and communication of dolphins, and toward the end of his life as a benevolent presence on the University of California campus at Santa Cruz and at Esalen Institute in Big Sur. The disciplinary respectabilities of the academic world meant little to him. For more than fifty years, he published books and papers on any subject to which he had something to contribute.

He wrote with equal fluency about animal behavior and anthropology, communication theory and evolution, paralinguistics and schizophrenia. His achievements have challenged the professional ambitions of academic behavioral scientists in this country to establish self-contained "disciplines" within the human sciences as autonomous and well defined as those in the physical and biological sciences. Again and again, just when the professionals began to get themselves nicely settled, Gregory Bateson reappeared in their midst, with arguments to demonstrate that their theoretical and methodological certainties were uncertain. No wonder many of them have found his work exasperating as well as admirable.

Born in 1904, Gregory Bateson came from the aristocracy of British intellectual life that Francis Galton described in such books as *Hereditary Genius*. His father, William Bateson, was a major figure in the revival of Mendelian genetics after 1900, and the Batesons moved among the Huxleys, the Darwins, and the other luminaries of English (particulary, of Cambridge) natural science. Gregory's own imagination quickly drew him beyond the boundaries of biology into anthropology; yet he preserved a first-rate understanding of the biological sciences, which play a significant part in his final book, *Mind and Nature: A Necessary Unity*. On a field trip to New Guinea in 1936 he met Margaret Mead, and from that time his life was centered in the United States. (Mary Catherine Bateson, their daughter, is herself an anthropological linguist.) Meanwhile his intellectual curiosity and fertility led him to build up for himself a circle of friends who formed a kind of American counterpart to Galton's intellectual constellation in England.

Gregory Bateson's background also did much to shape the problems that were at the center of his thought. He was born at a crucial moment in the scientific debate about Darwinism. During much of its first hundred years, the Darwinian theory drew its main scientific strength from its power to account for the anatomical and physiological forms of living things. From the start, the most convincing physical evidence of evolution took the form of fossils: notably, the sequence of fossil forms by which the discoveries of paleontology were shown to correspond with historical geology. So much so that many people came to think of Darwinism as concerned, above all, with explaining such things as the giraffe's legs, the hummingbird's beak, and the coloration of moths.

Yet from the start it was clear that there were two missing elements in the theory as it stood in 1859; the full case for Darwinism must include, also, a convincing theory of genetics and heredity, and an account of the significance of behavior in evolution — that is, an account of mental or psychological evolution. Darwin's own theory of "pangenes" as the bearer of hereditary features left him, in certain crucial respects, a Lamarckian in his explanation: and it was not until the rediscovery of Mendel's work that the material was at hand for making serious progress in genetics. Meanwhile, though much of the early debate about evolution focused on behavioral issues (e.g., the evolution of instincts) and though Darwin himself published a book on *The Expression of the Emotions in Man and Animals* whose full importance is only just being appreciated today, psychological evolution remained largely obscure.

Obscure it might be, but it was also crucial. In a thousand ways, the behavior of living things can make all the difference in their success or failure in the evolutionary selection process. The food that is effectively available to a species in any habitat depends largely on its feeding habits; the giraffe outruns its predators in the wild only because it is biologically equipped to take fright, as well as flight; and their propensities to build webs, dams, and honeycombs are clearly as relevant to the historical fate of spiders, beavers, and bees as the shapes of their legs, tails, and stings. So once the solid foundations for a modern science of genetics had been laid by William Bateson, the outstanding weakness in the Darwinian scheme lay in the realm of behavior. In the long run, the Darwinian "natural philosophy" would carry conviction only if its categories could be expanded to embrace the mental as well as the physical, the psychological as well as the physiological aspects of human and animal nature; showing, for instance, how intelligence, communication, and symbolic expression, quite as much as drives, reflexes, and instincts, can be understood as "advantageous" products of evolution, and explaining all these different mental functions in both healthy and pathological modes of operation.

That has been Gregory Bateson's central mission. In one way or another, all of his notable contributions to science have sprung from his habit of viewing the mental life and behavior of creatures as functional, adaptive activities that need to be intelligently related to their evolutionary history and habitat. So, in one phase of his work, he concentrated on animal communication, particularly the "language" of the dolphins. In another, he studied the ways in which living creatures improve their adaptation by learning; he was one of the first to point out the special power that comes with the evolution of a capacity for "learning to learn" — what he called "deuterolearning."

Elsewhere, Bateson played a pioneering part in the development of paralinguistics and kinesics: i.e., the study of the behavioral adjuncts and contexts of the use of language — including all those different ways in which our use or understanding of words and sentences cues in with our ability to "read" postures and gestures, facial expressions and hand movements, tones and inflections, emphases and hesitations. He was involved in a well-known collaborative project at the Stanford Behavioral Sciences Center on "The Natural History of an Interview" in the mid-1950s, which led to an elaborate system resembling musical staves, to display all the complex signaling modalities involved in the simplest exchanges.

Bateson's attempt to bring the concepts of semantics and semiotics to bear on the interpretation of behavior paralleled the program of contemporay structuralism and avoided some of its theoretical rigidities. It also served Bateson well in two fields. In psychiatry he invented the "double bind" theory to explain how failures in family communication can provoke mental illness: if a patient's words and nonverbal messages are sufficiently inconsistent and contradictory, a child can be put into a "no win" situation from which the only available exit is into psychopathology. (This theory is now an accepted element in the conceptual repertory of much family and other psychiatric therapy.) In Bateson's anthropological work, again, he never remained content with labeling a customary dance or ceremony, initiation procedure or mode of dress as "functional," just because it fitted in with the overall pattern or "structure" of the culture. Like a good evolutionist, he always demanded to know, also, *how* it was functional — what message it communicated, what skills it transmitted, or how else it contributed to the viability of the culture, regarded as a successful, well-adapted *Lebensform*. For Bateson, that is to say, it was always essential that culture and nature should each make sense from the viewpoint of the other. But he was no reductionist; he was as quick to find "cultural" elements in nature as he was to point out "natural" elements in culture.

To list Gregory Bateson's achievements in this fragmentary way is, however, misleading. For it distracts our attention from the integrating themes of his work, and makes it appear scrappy. Yet how else can one convey these themes? There is no Bateson's Law or Bateson's Theory, no formula to represent his unique thought, as $E = mc^2$ does for Einstein. What linked all Bateson's innovations together, and what his younger associates were drawn to in his work, was not so much a comprehensive theory about the phenomena of mental evolution as a systemic approach to its problems. In all our thought about human questions — whether about psychology or social science, politics or mental illness, education or language — we should (he insisted) never ignore the evolutionary significance of who we are and where we are. We should never forget, that is, to ask how our modes of living and thinking, talking and acting contribute to our success or failures as members of populations of natural beings, or fail to consider in what ways other natural beings, too, may share in the same mental heritage of intelligence, communication, and social organization.

In *Mind and Nature* as in its predecessor, *Steps to an Ecology of Mind* (1972), Bateson attempted to redirect our ways of dealing with human problems in an evolutionary direction. Centuries of formal logic and metaphysics developed in the service of an essentially ahistorical cosmology have (in his view) set our ways of thinking and talking into fixed molds and patterns of kinds that make it hard for us to adopt such an evolutionary approach. In his first few essays, therefore, he seeks to discredit and dismantle the rigid forms of thought generated by that earlier alliance of Aristotelian logic and ontology, Biblical history and pre-Darwinian taxonomy: forms of thought that encourage us to assume that all basic processes of nature lend themselves readily to unambiguous description, permanent classification, and scientific analysis according to a "linear" conception of causality.

In a chapter called "Every Schoolboy Knows," he attempts to formulate a view that is better "geared to . . . the biological world," offering a series of homely examples to show the fallacies of a scientific view based on coding, conventional description, and quantitative measure divorced from the object or phenomenon that is being measured. Thus every schoolboy knows, or should know, that science "never proves," but merely "probes" — and probes only as accurately as available instruments permit; like the microscope and telescope, all "improved devices of perception will disclose what was utterly unpredictable from the levels of perception that we could achieve before that discovery." Moreover, "there are large classes of phenomena where prediction and control are simply impossible":

Under tension, a chain will break at its weakest link. That

much is predictable. What is difficult is to identify the weakest link before it breaks. The generic we can know, but the specific eludes us.

Or to take another typical example, in defiance of the apparently logical notion that "nothing comes of nothing," successful evolution can depend on the meaning of zero:

> The letter you do not write, the apology you do not offer, the food that you do not put out for the cat — all these can be sufficient and effective messages because zero, *in context*, can be meaningful; and it is the recipient of the message who creates the context. This power to create *context* is the recipient's skill. . . . He or she must acquire that skill by learning or by lucky mutation, that is, by a successful raid on the random. The recipient must be, in some sense, ready for the appropriate discovery when it comes.

Bateson explains very well how Aristotle's commitment to a static ontology and taxonomy enabled him to harness his newly invented syllogistic process to his scientific world view, and so make formal logic the prime instrument of scientific explanation. So it was no wonder that Aristotle's philosophical successors fell into the habit of construing causal connections as though they were logical connections, thus confusing the physically necessary with the logically entailed. With an evolutionary world picture, by contrast, no descriptions can be trusted to hold good indefinitely, classification systems are all in shorter- or longer-term flux, and our deductive conclusions can be trusted only to the extent that natural events have in fact the character of "convergent" rather than "divergent" sequences.

Bateson's constructive counterprogram, as set out in the central essays of *Mind and Nature*, is built around three notions — the necessity for "multiple descriptions" of all natural processes, a "circular" conception of causal interconnections, and the role of "stochastic processes" such as natural selection in generating new modes of adaptation. All of these notions he expounds here with a kaleidoscopic procession of illustrations and allusions. (Many of these are indebted — ironically, as I shall argue later — to the ideas and arguments of Bertrand Russell: notably, Russell's causal theory of perception and his logical "theory of types.")

A properly evolutionary way of dealing with experience obliges us to recognize that no event or process has any single unambiguous description: we describe any event in different terms, and view it as an element in a different network of relations, depending on the standpoint from which — and the purposes for which — we are considering it. Nor shall we usually be able to distinguish the "causes" among phenomena from their "effects": within the organic world, especially in ecological and evolutionary processes, chains of objects and processes are commonly linked together in circles or spirals, so that each of them is implicated in the causal fate of all the others.

The best we can do in such a case is to understand all the interlinked chains within which our affairs are caught up, and consider how they might be modified so as to operate more advantageously as wholes: that is to say, in a way that these entire systems could become better adapted. During much of the twentieth century, from Durkheim and Parsons on, the central conceptions of social and behavioral science have been modeled on those of physiology: *system, structure, function.* The time has now come, in Bateson's view — and it is hard to disregard his argument — to look for those central conceptions rather in evolutionary theory: *variability, selective pressures, adaptedness.*

If that is so, Bateson argues, we must take more seriously the significance of "stochastic" processes: those dual processes, familiar in a whole range of fields from Darwinian theory to economics, in which randomly generated variations combine with external selection procedures to establish new patterns of adaptiveness and "optimization." In this respect, it is helpful to contrast Gregory Bateson's position with its direct opposite, as presented most recently in Arthur Koestler's *Janus.* Koestler finds repugnant the notion that creative innovations and worthwhile novelties could spring from a series of essentially "random" variations: he denounces this idea wherever it appears — in behaviorist psychology or quantum physics, in neo-Darwinism or the historians' acceptance of contingency. Great new achievements cannot simply appear out of the blue! New forms of value (Koestler insists) must surely have been provided for beforehand: either by conscious foresight, or by selective imagination, or by some form of neo-Lamarckian causality. Yet that is just what Bateson denied. Evolutionary ways of thinking, he argues, accustom one to the idea that true originality simply *cannot* be the outcome of straightforward planning or simple causality alone. Truly novel achievements can be recognized for what they are only after they appear. We then see that they have proved adaptive in ways that had not been "provided for beforehand," either conceptually, or causally. And the road to wisdom in the future must begin with the acceptance of that kind of unpredictability in historical events — with the encouragement of innovation, on the one hand, and the better understanding of "adaptation" and "adaptedness" on the other.

To point out that Gregory Bateson did not give us anything approaching a comprehensive theory of mental evolution is not really to criticize his work. For Darwin's failure to deal fully with the psychological aspects of evolution was no accidental lacuna. Quite apart from the lack of any direct evidence about the behavior of living creatures in earlier epochs, there were some more serious obstacles to any extension of evolutionary ideas into the realm of mind. Darwin's own teacher, Adam Sedgwick, was only the first of many who feared the consequences of bringing the mental and moral aspects of human nature within the scope of the new evolutionary theory: and even today attempts to move in this direction meet with stiff philosophical resistance. (Sociobiology is only one example.) Before we can reach the stage of developing specific theories of mental evolution, as a result, we need some kind of philosophical reorientation: setting aside the unscrutinized habits of mind that stand in the way of any such extension.

In that respect, the issues Gregory Bateson was concerned with are central to the development of twentieth-century scientific thought and method. The program that generated what we paradoxically call "modern" science, from the time of Descartes and Newton on, began with an act of abstraction whose consequences it has been hard to escape. What Descartes required us to do was not just to divide mind from matter: more importantly he set humanity aside from nature, and established criteria of "rational objectivity" for natural science that placed the scientist himself in the position of a pure spectator. The classic expression was Laplace's image of the ideal scientist as an omniscient calculator who, knowing the initial positions and velocities of all the atoms in the universe at the moment of its creation, would be able to predict, and give a running commentary on, the entire subsequent history of the universe — but only from outside it. Such a posture is open to us in practice, however, only when the "coupling" between the scientist and his objects of study goes only one way — when he can observe how those objects are behaving without influencing that behavior in the process.

The most significant novelty in twentieth-century science, generally, has been the fact that scientists have run up against the limits of that Cartesian methodology at a dozen different points. As Werner Heisenberg showed us, the required conditions do not fully hold even at the finest level of physical analysis: there, our acts of observation alter the states of the particles we observe. The emergence of psychology as a self-sufficient science (or family of sciences) has equally threatened the traditional claims of Cartesian detachment and objectivity. Most of all — and this is where Bateson's work comes in — the development of ecology has made it clear just how far, and in how many ways, human life — not least, the life and activities of scientists themselves — is lived within the world of nature that the scientist is seeking to understand. We can no longer view the world as Descartes and Laplace would have us do, as "rational onlookers," from outside. Our place is within the same world that we are studying, and whatever scientific understanding we achieve must be a kind of understanding that is available to participants within the process of nature, i.e., from inside.

Some contemporary commentators have, accordingly, concluded that the age of so-called "modern science" is past, and that we are now moving into a period of "postmodern science." (This phrase was coined by Frederick Ferré.) The point from which any "postmodern" science must start is the need to reinsert humanity into nature. Seen from that standpoint, many of Bateson's own claims (e.g., that "biological evolution is a mental process") seem less startling. Once we set ourselves seriously to the task of rebuilding the scientific world picture in a way that accommodates human beings — including scientists — along with all the other inhabitants of the natural world, the need to reintegrate matter and mind follows immediately: indeed, the supposed distinction between "material" and "mental" processes ceases to be terribly useful or fundamental for science.

What makes Gregory Bateson's work so significant is the fact that he has acted as a prophet of "postmodern" science, in this sense. The shortcomings he has seen in traditional behaviorist psychology and learning theory, in shallow interpretations of biological evolution, formal linguistics, in mechanical approaches to psychiatry, and so on, have all of them sprung from his basic insight into the weaknesses of the Cartesian methodology as a program for future science. And this same insight explains, also, why he saw the first step toward the necessary philosophical reorientation of the human sciences as calling for a new epistemology.

While the agenda for *Mind and Nature*, like the agenda for his whole scientific career, has great merits — not least, philosophical merits — its execution is, all the same, flawed and incomplete. Some of the flaws are in his style and manner. While he could write wisely and thoughtfully, too much of his argument is shrill and scolding in tone. (In this, he shows some of the less admirable features of a prophet.) By now, the sheer novelty of his program has surely worn off. What we need from a "postmodern" natural philosopher today is not more exhortations to change our ways: rather, we need a careful and detailed examination of what the new methodology implies, both for the separate sciences affected by this transformation, and for the overall integration of the human sciences with the sciences of nature. In this respect, *Mind and Nature* falls short of its proper objectives. Indeed, at many points the book seems unsure of its intended audience. Given the crucial character of its central themes, one might wish that Bateson had argued his case on a consistently higher plane. Too many of the essays (often with titles like "Every Schoolboy Knows . . .") are aimed at elementary, not to say sophomoric readers; and the tags that he chooses to expound ("Sometimes Small is Beautiful," "Nothing Will Come of Nothing" and the like) come across as exaggerated or trivial.

Why does he write in this tone? It may reflect the comparative isolation in which Bateson has lived and worked. Somehow, his background seems to have reinforced his sense that he did not need to "prove himself" as his colleagues all along have not been his contemporaries but his great precursors down the ages. As a result, he has cared too little about other people's opinions of his work; he may have left a clearer mark, and done more good, by engaging his opponents more closely. As things stand, *Mind and Nature* will strike some of his colleagues as shallow and patronizing; and there is a danger that he will, once again, provoke impatience rather than admiration from those who could most usefully listen to what he says. For those of us who respect his approach to natural philosophy, and who find many of his ideas congenial and appealing, that is a matter for particular regret.

There are also some very real difficulties in the content of his argument in *Mind and Nature*. Early in the book, he sketches out the main lines of an epistemology whose neo-idealist themes ("Science Never Proves Anything," "There is No Objective Experience") will be familiar to readers of such books as Thomas Kuhn's *The Structure of Scientific Revolutions*, Peter Berger and Thomas Luckman's *The Social Construction of Reality*, and Paul Feyerabend's *Against Method*. He backs up this "anti-objectivist" argument with considerations of two kinds. Some of them rely on the causal interpretation of perception that was made popular in the 1910s and 1920s by Bertrand Russell's *Our Knowledge of the External World* and *The Analysis of Matter*. For instance, Bateson writes:

> When somebody steps on my toe, what I experience is, not
> his stepping on my toe, but my *image* of his stepping on my

toe reconstructed from neutral reports reaching my brain
somewhat after his foot has landed on mine . . . To that extent, objects are my creation, and my experience of them is
subjective, not objective. . . Our civilization is deeply based
on this illusion [of perceptual objectivity].

Oddly enough, this dichotomy of "internal images" as against "external
events" is a piece of undigested Cartesian doctrine which Russell himself
inherited from T.H. Huxley and J.S. Mill, and which goes back directly
to the seventeenth-century epistemological debate. Most of those
philosophers and scientists who take evolutionary theory seriously in
thinking about perception — J.T. Lettvin and J.J. Gibson are two whose
names come to mind — have long since rejected that dichotomy, along
with the whole causal theory of perception, in favor of a functional and
adaptive interpretation of entire perceptual systems and processes; and
Bateson would have been truer to his own central insights if he had
followed their example.

In many ways, indeed, Bertrand Russell is the last philosopher one
would have expected Bateson to choose as an ally. (C.S. Peirce would
have been a happier choice.) Neither in his epistemology nor in his logic
did Russell ever show much sensitivity toward the significance of evolutionary ways of thought. His logic may be different from Aristotle's, but
in his own ways it is just as ahistorical; and certainly, in its original context, his "theory of types" had no relevance to the problems of multiple
description within an evolutionary world picture. As an epistemologist,
also, Russell never strove to carry the debate about sensation and
perception beyond Darwin; rather, he was concerned to take it back to
where it was before Kant. And, in any event, his causal analysis of
perception is, surely, prime illustration of just that kind of "linear causal
thinking" that Bateson's own argument justifiably attacks.

Elsewhere Bateson follows through his critique of "objectivism" to the
point of concluding that

epistemology is always and inevitably *personal*. The point of
the probe is always in the heart of the explorer. What is *my*
answer to the question of the nature of knowing?

Yet this conclusion is opposed not merely to a physicalist and formalist
epistemology and method, such as the Cartesian ideal of "rational objectivity through detachment" that he is right to reject. It is opposed
also to any kind of critical procedure for science — if epistemology is "in-

evitably *personal*," why not biology, too? — and it lands Bateson, at least in words, in the same kind of extreme romantic individualism as that of Paul Feyerabend. The difference is clear that, in Bateson's case, this conclusion is arrived at only through the exaggeration of a basically sound position. For what he was most concerned to emphasize, in *Mind and Nature* as elsewhere, is the nonexistence of any uniquely correct scientific point of view or mode of description: natural events and processes always lend themselves to a variety and multiplicity of descriptions, depending on one's point of view.

But what differentiates one legitimate scientific point of view or mode of description from another is not anything personal; e.g., the fact that this is *my* point of view and that is *yours*. Rather it is the fact that scientists are always free to approach any set of natural events and processes with a variety of legitimate purposes; and each of these alternative approaches generates, as a byproduct, its own distinct modes of description and styles of explanation, which — for methodological, not for personal reasons — are never in direct contradiction with one another.

Still, these criticisms do not affect the main course of Gregory Bateson's argument; and the sorts of adventurous forays into the intellectual wilderness that were his personal specialty make some exaggeration and fragmentariness in the final product almost inevitable. Like the keen-eyed scout he was, he has discovered terrain that future scientists will be exploring and settling for decades ahead, and he has brought back for our contemplation some fascinating and intriguing specimens. It is not always clear exactly what we should make of them. Some of them, no doubt, may even turn out to be fool's gold. But his work still gives us a tantalizing glimpse of what, in the new era of "postmodern science," an overall vision of humanity's place in nature will have to become.

Asilomar Conference

Program

THURSDAY, 15 FEBRUARY 1979

3 — 6 pm	CHECK-IN — Asilomar Administration Building
4 — 6 pm	RECEPTION — Nautilus
6 pm	DINNER — Crocker Hall
7:30 pm	OPENING SESSION — Nautilus

"ICA Welcome," Frederick Williams, ICA President
"SCA Welcome," Anita Taylor, SCA Second-Vice-President
"One Thing Leads to Another," Carol Wilder, San Francisco State University

KEYNOTE ADDRESS: "On the History of the Interactional View: A Personal Account," John H. Weakland, Mental Research Institute and Stanford University.

FRIDAY, 16 FEBRUARY   9 — NOON

MORNING SESSION   NAUTILUS

LANGUAGE, BEHAVIOR, AND CONTEXT

Chair: Dorothy Lenk-Kreuger, University of California, Santa Barbara

Presentations: "Toward a Cosmology of Communication," Dean C. Barnlund, San Francisco State University

"Toward a Logic of Interactional Rules," W. Barnett Pearce and Vernon E. Cronen, University of Massachusetts

"The Management of Metaphor," Herbert W. Simons, Temple University

Respondent   Paul Watzlawick, Mental Research Institute and Stanford University

FRIDAY, 16 FEBRUARY   1:30 — 4:30

AFTERNOON SESSION I   NAUTILUS EAST

RESEARCH

Chair: Lawrence Chase, California State University, Sacramento

Presentations: "Research and the Interactional View: The Epistemology of Form," Donald G. Ellis, Purdue University

"Interactional Foundations of Interpersonal Confirmation," Kenneth N. Leone Cissna, Saint Louis University, and Evelyn Sieburg, Pepperdine University and Chapman College

"Symmetry and Complementarity: Evolution and Evaluation of an Idea," L. Edna Rogers-Millar, Cleveland State University

Respondent   Carlos E. Sluzki, University of California Medical Center and Mental Research Institute

FRIDAY, 16 FEBRUARY   1:30 — 4:40

AFTERNOON SESSION II   NAUTILUS WEST

APPLICATION

Chair: Nancy Harper, University of Iowa

Presentations: "Soft Magic: Communication Interventions," Robert W. Norton, Purdue University

"An Analysis of Paradoxical Logic: A Case Study," Linda Harris, University of Massachusetts

"Pragmatics of Interpersonal Competence," John Wiemann, University of California, Santa Barbara, and Clifford Kelly, University of the Pacific

Respondents: Lynn Segal and John Weakland, Mental Research Institute

FRIDAY, 16 FEBRUARY   8:00 pm

EVENING SESSION   NAUTILUS

Chair: Arthur Bochner, Temple University

Presentations: "The Riddles of Self-Reflexiveness," Paul Watzlawick, Mental Research Institute and Stanford University

"Frontiers in the Philosophy of Science," Heinz Von Foerster, University of Illinois, Emeritus

Discussion following

SATURDAY, 17 FEBRUARY   8:30 — NOON

MORNING SESSION   NAUTILUS

EPISTEMOLOGY: IN SEARCH OF THE "PATTERN WHICH CONNECTS"

Chair: Thomas Scheidel, University of Washington

Presentations: "Implications of an Open Systems Cybernetic Analysis of Paradoxical Communication for the Development of a Contemporary Rhetorical Theory," Donald P. Cushman and Philip K. Tompkins, State University of New York, Albany

"On the Critical Terminology of Communication Theory," C. David Mortensen, University of Wisconsin, Madison

"Conversational Analysis and the Interactional View," Leonard C. Hawes, University of Utah

"Implications of the Interactional View for a Science of Communication," Arthur Bochner, Temple University

Respondent: Heinz Von Foerster, University of Illinois, Emeritus

SATURDAY, 17 FEBRUARY   **CONTRIBUTED SESSIONS**

I.   *Confirmation/Disconfirmation Panel and Discussion*

                          2 — 4 pm --- Deer Lodge Living Room

Participants: Ken Cissna, Saint Louis University
                    Phil Salem, Southwest Texas State University (organizer)
                    Evelyn Sieburg, Consultant in private practice
                    John Stewart, University of Washington

II.   *Research Reports*   *2 — 4 pm*   *Nautilus East*

                    "Marking Communication Boundaries with the
                    Metalanguage of Bateson and Korsybski: An Initial
                    Attempt," Patrick Hunt, San Francisco State University

                    "Paradoxical Communication in Organizational En-
                    vironments," Linda Putnam, Purdue University

                    "Relational Control in Marital Dyads: Research in
                    Progress," Don Emery, Purdue University

                    "Form, Function, and Process: The Concept of Command
                    from the Interpersonal View," Barbara Montgomery, Pur-
                    due University

SATURDAY, 17 FEBRUARY

  LATE AFTERNOON AND EVENING

4 — 6 pm   Reception for Gregory Bateson in Nautilus

6 pm   Banquet in Seascape

8 pm   EVENING SESSION — Nautilus

              "San Francisco State University Welcome," Lawrence Ian-
              ni, Provost, San Francisco State University

              "Paradigmatic Conservatism," Gregory Bateson, University
              of California and Esalen Institute

              "Response to Mr. Bateson," Kenneth Burke

SUNDAY, 18 FEBRUARY   **MORNING SESSIONS**

9 — 10 am   SYNTHESIS DISCUSSIONS
                 "Implications for Theory," B. Aubrey Fisher, University of
                 Utah, in Nautilus East

                 "Implications for Research," Peter Andersen, West Virginia
                 University, in Nautilus West

                 "Implications for Application," Carol Wilder, San Fran-
                 cisco State University, in Deer Lodge Living Room

10:30—11:30am   Synthesis reports to full conference by Fisher, Andersen, and
                 Wilder, in Nautilus

11:30 am   Closing Remarks: "On the Future of the Field of Com-
                 munication," Frederick Williams, Annenberg School of
                 Communications — University of Southern California, and
                 ICA President

NOON   Lunch and Check-out

Participants

JANIS ANDERSEN
West Virginia University

PETER ANDERSEN
West Virginia University

SHOKO ARAKI
San Francisco State University

DEAN BARNLUND
San Francisco State University

GREGORY BATESON
University of California

WAYNE BEACH
University of Nebraska

JANET BENNETT
Marylhurst College

MILTON BENNETT
Portland State University

ARTHUR BOCHNER
Temple University

EDMUND G. BROWN, JR.
State of California

KENNETH BURKE
Andover N.J.

KAY CAMPBELL
Children's Hospital, SF

JOHN CAPUTO
Chaffee College

FRANCIS CARTIER
Pacific Grove, CA

LAWRENCE CHASE
California State University,
Sacramento

KENNETH CISSNA
Saint Louis University

PETER CLARKE
University of Michigan

BECKY CLINE
Temple University

TIM CLINE
Temple University

JOHN COGGINS
University of Oregon

BEVERLEE COX
University of Western Ontario

VERNON CRONEN
University of Massachusetts

DONALD CUSHMAN
State University of New York,
Albany

DENNIS DAY
San Francisco State University

KATHRYN DINDIA-WEBB
University of Washington

WILLIAM EDWARDS
Columbus College

GILLIAN ELLENBY
Shoestring Designs

JOHN ELLENBY
Xerox Corporation

DONALD ELLIS
Purdue University

DON EMERY
Purdue University

B AUBREY FISHER
University of Utah

EDIE FOLB
San Francisco State University

JOYCE FROST
University of Montana

JOHN GARRISON
Auburn University

SALLY GEARHART
San Francisco State University

GEORGE GUM
Temple University

JANE GURKO
San Francisco State University

NANCY HARPER
University of Iowa

LINDA HARRIS
University of Massachusetts

LEONARD HAWES
University of Utah

BECKY HAYDEN
Wadsworth Publishing

JOHN HERR
Mental Research Institute

PATRICK HUNT
San Francisco State University

LAWRENCE IANNI
San Francisco State University

CLIFFORD KELLY
University of the Pacific

YOUNG KIM
Governors State University

SANDRA KNAUB
Sharp Hospital, San Diego

ANA KONG
Governors State University

DOROTHY LENK-KREUGER
University of California,
Santa Barbara

BEVERLY LANE
Mental Research Institute

LINDA HALL
Olanie, Hurst & Hemrich

BILL LEE
San Jose, CA

ELAINE LITTON-HAWES
University of Utah

ANNIE LEE
San Francisco State University

EDIE MCCOY
University of Nevada

NANCY MCDERMID
San Francisco State University

HANK MCGUCKIN
San Francisco State University

BETTY MECHLIN
California State University,
Fresno

FARIDEH MOHAJER
Los Angeles, CA

VINCENT MOLEY
Mental Research Institute

BARBARA MONTGOMERY
Purdue University

JOHN MORAN
Temple University

C. DAVID MORTENSEN
University of Wisconsin,
Madison

TIMOTHY MOTT
Xerox Corporation

GAIL MEYERS
Trinity University

MICHELE MYERS
Trinity University

LELAND NICHOLS
California State University,
Sacramento

NAOKI NOMURA
San Francisco State University

ROBERT NORTON
Purdue University

JOHN NUSSBAUM
Purdue University

W. BARNETT PEARCE
University of Massachusetts

GERRY PHILIPSEN
University of Washington

LINDA PUTNAM
Purdue University

WILLIAM RAWLINS
Temple University

STEPHEN RENDAHL
University of North Dakota

GRIFF RICHARDS
San Francisco State University

L. EDNA ROGERS-MILLAR
Cleveland State University

NORMA RHODE
Brigham Young University

MICHEL ROUBLEV
Wright Institute

PHILIP SALEM
Southwest Texas State
University

GABRIEL SALOMON
Stanford University

VALDA SALOMON
Mental Research Institute

JUDITH SCHUSTER
Purdue University

RUSSELL SCHWEICKART
State of California

LYNN SEGAL
Mental Research Institute

SUSAN SHIMANOFF
California State University,
Stanislaus

EVELYN SIEBURG
Communication Consultant

HERBERT W. SIMONS
Temple University

DENNIS SMITH
Temple University

THOMAS SCHEIDEL
University of Washington

CARLOS SLUZKI
University of California

THOMAS STEINFATT
Temple University

JOHN STEWART
University of Washington

ANITA TAYLOR
St. Louis Community College

STANLEY TAYLOR
Cal Poly — Pomona

BARBARA THORNTON
University of Nevada

HEINZ VON FOERSTER
University of Illinois,
Emeritus

ELLEN WATZLAWICK
Piedmont HS

PAUL WATZLAWICK
Mental Research Institute

CATHY WAXMAN
San Francisco State University

JOHN WEAKLAND
Mental Research Institute

JANET WEATHERS
University of Southern
California

TRACEY WEISS
University of New Hampshire

JOHN WIEMANN
University of California,
Santa Barbara

CAROL WILDER
San Francisco State University

FREDERICK WILLIAMS
University of Southern
California

VICTORIA WILLIAMS
University of Southern
California

WILLIAM WILMOT
University of Montana

CONFERENCE STAFF:

Coordination:	Carol Wilder
Registration:	Keiko Yamamoto
Travel:	Randi Nydish
Hospitality:	Mike Griffin
	Rosie Kontur

Documentation: Cynthia Hartley
Herb Ferrette
K.C. Schillhahn
Garth O'Donnell
Ann Nova Young

Design Consultant

Shoestring Designs
1032 Harker Avenue
Palo Alto, CA 94301

CONFERENCE FUNDING PROVIDED BY:

San Francisco State University

Office of the President
(Paul Romberg, President)
School of Humanities
(Leo Young, Dean)
Forensics Union
(Lawrence Medcalf, Director)
Speech Communication Graduate Students
(Randi Nydish, Organizer)

International Communication Association

Division II
Executive Committee

Speech Communication Association

Legislative Council

Special and varied thanks to Bill Work, Nancy McDermid, Hank McGuckin, Griff Richards, Cathy Waxman, Frank Moakley, Bob Norton, Don Ellis, Art Bochner, Herb Simons, Don Cushman, Lynn Segal, and Barnett Pearce.

Photographs

Kenneth Burke, Gregory Bateson

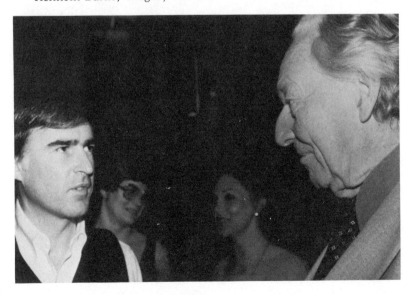

Jerry Brown, Gregory Bateson

Photography: Cynthia Hartley

Robert Norton, Donald Ellis, Linda Putnam

Barnett Pearce, Dean Barnlund

Clifford Kelly, Dorothy Krueger, William Rawlins

Donald Ellis, Aubrey Fisher

Herbert Simons, Lee Nichols, Leonard Hawes

David Mortensen, Arthur Bochner

Carlos Sluzki, John Weakland

John Coggins, Edna Rogers

Paul Watzlawick, Kenneth Burke

Lois Bateson, Heinz Von Foerster

Jerry Brown, Gregory Bateson, Carol Wilder

Gregory Bateson

Bibliography

ABELES, G. Researching the unresearchable: Experimentation on the double bind. In C.E. Sluzki & D.C. Ransom (Eds.), *Double bind: The foundation of the communicational approach to the family.* New York: Grune & Stratton, 1976:113-149.

ADLER, K. On the falsification of rules theories. *Quarterly Journal of Speech.* 1978, 64:427-438.

AGNELLI, V. *Documenta: Conceptual art exhibition.* Kassel, Germany, 1972.

ALLPORT, G.W. The open system in personality theory. *Journal of Abnormal and Social Psychology.* 1960:301-311.

ARENDT, H. *The human condition.* New York: Doubleday, 1959.

ARGYLE, M. *Social interaction.* Chicago: Aldine Atherton, 1969.

ARGYLE, M. Personality and social behaviour. In R. Harre (Ed.), *Personality.* Totowa, N.J.: Rowan and Littlefield, 1976.

ARGYLE, M. & KENDON, A. The experimental analysis of social performance. *Advances in Experimental Social Psychology.* 1967, 3:55-98.

ARGYRIS, C. Explorations in interpersonal competence — I. *Journal of Applied Behavioral Science.* 1965, 1:58-83.

ASHBY, R.W. *An introduction to cybernetics.* New York: Wiley, 1956.

ASHBY, R.W. Variety, constraint, and the law of requisite variety. In W. Buckley (Ed.), *Modern systems research for the behavioral scientist.* Chicago: Aldine, 1968:129-136.

AUSTIN, J.L. *How to do things with words.* Oxford University Press, 1955.

AVEYARD, B.C. The relationships between communication apprehension, self-acceptance, acceptance of others, the FIRO-B scales and disconfirming responses. Bachelor of Letters dissertation, University of New England, Australia, 1977.

AYRES, J. & MIURA, S. Relational communication instrumentation: Validity. Paper presented at the Speech Communication Association convention, San Antonio, 1979.

BACKLUND, P.M. *Speech communication correlates of perceived communication competence.* Unpublished Ph.D. dissertation, University of Denver, 1977.

BALES, R.F. Communication in small groups. In G.A. Miller (Ed.), *Psychology and communication.* Washington D.C.: Voice of America Forum Series, 1974.

BALES, R.F. The equilibrium problem in small group. In A.P. Hare, E.F. Burgatta, & R.F. Bales (Eds.), *Small groups.* New York: Knopf, 1955.

BANDLER, R. & GRINDLER, J. *The structure of magic I: A book about language and therapy.* Palo Alto: Science and Behavior Books, 1975.

BARKER, R. *The stream of consciousness.* New York: Meredith, 1963.

BARKER, R. *Ecological psychology.* Stanford: Stanford University Press, 1968.

BARKER, R. & WRIGHT, H.F. *One boy's day.* New York: Harper and Row, 1951.

BARNARD, C.I. *The functions of the executive.* Cambridge: Harvard University Press, 1938.

BARNLUND, D.C. *Interpersonal communication: Survey and studies.* Boston: Houghton Mifflin, 1968.

BARNLUND, D.C. *Public and private self in japan and the united states.* Tokyo: The Simul Press, 1975.

BATESON, G. Culture contact and schismogenisis. *Man.* 1935, 35: 178-183.

BATESON, G. *Naven.* Cambridge: Cambridge University Press, 1937. (Second edition, Stanford: Stanford University Press, 1958.)

BATESON, G. Experiments in thinking about observed ethnological material. *Philosophy of Science.* 1941, 8:53-68. Reprinted in *Steps to an ecology of mind.* New York: Ballentine Books, 1972.

BATESON, G. Bali: The value system of a steady state. In M. Fortes (Ed.), *Social structure: Studies presented to A.R. Radcliffe-Brown.* Oxford: Clarendon Press, 1949:35-53. Reprinted in *Steps.*

BATESON, G. Information and codification: A philosophical approach. In J. Ruesch & G. Bateson, *Communication: The social matrix of psychiatry.* New York: Norton, 1951:168-211.

BATESON, G. A theory of play and fantasy. *A.P.A. Psychiatric Research Reports, II.* 1955. Reprinted in *Steps.*

BATESON, G. Introductory comments. In B. Schaffner (Ed.), *Group Processes.* Madison, N.J.: Madison Printing Co., 1957.

BATESON, G. Form, substance and difference. *General Semantics Bulletin.* 1970:37. Reprinted in *Steps.* 1972:448-465.

BATESON, G. From versailles to cybernetics. In G. Bateson, *Steps to an ecology of mind.* 1972:469-477.

BATESON, G. Introduction: The science of mind and order. In G. Bateson, *Steps to an ecology of mind.* 1972:xv-xxvi.

BATESON, G. *Steps to an ecology of mind.* New York: Ballantine Books, 1972.

BATESON, G. Style, grace, and information in primtive art. In G. Bateson, *Steps to an ecology of mind.* 1972:128-152.

BATESON, G. Comments on J. Haley's "History." In C.E. Sluzki & D.C. Ransom (Eds.), *Double bind: The foundation of the communicational approach to the family.* New York: Grune & Stratton, 1976:105-106.

BATESON, G. Afterword. In J. Brockman (Ed.), *About Bateson.* New York: Dutton, 1977:235-247.

BATESON, G. The pattern which connects. *Coevolution Quarterly.* 1978, *18*:4-15.

BATESON, G. *Mind and nature: A necessary unity.* New York: Dutton, 1979.

BATESON, G. Personal communication. 1978.

BATESON, G. & GOLDMAN, D. *Breaking out of the double bind. Psychology Today.* 1978, *12*:43-51.

BATESON, G. & JACKSON, D.D. Some varieties of pathogenic organization. In D. Rioch and E. Weinstein (Eds.), *Disorders of Communication.* 1964, *42*:270-290.

BATESON, G., JACKSON, D.D., HALEY, J. & WEAKLAND, J.H. Toward a theory of schizophrenia. *Behavioral Science.* 1956, *1*:251-264.

BATESON, G., JACKSON, D.D., HALEY, J. & WEAKLAND, J.H. A note on the double bind. *Family Process.* 1963, *2*:154-161.

BATESON, G. & MEAD, M. For god's sake, Margaret. *Coevolution Quarterly.* 1976, *10*:32-44.

BATESON, M.C. *Our own metaphor.* New York: Knopf, 1972.

BAVELAS, J.B. Models that help; Models that hinder. Paper presented at the annual meeting of the International Communication Association, Acapulco, May 1980.

BEARDSLEY, M.C. The metaphorical twist. *Philosophy and Phenomenological Research.* 1962, 22:293-307.

BERGER, C.R. The covering law perspective as a theoretical basis for the study of human communication. *Communication Quarterly,* 1977, 25:7-18.

BERGER, C.R. & CALABRESE, R.J. Some explorations in initial interaction and beyond: Toward a developmental theory of interpersonal communication. *Human Communication Research,* 1975, 1:99-112.

BERGER, M.M. (Ed.) *Beyond the double bind.* New York: Brunner/Mazel, 1978.

BERGER, P.L. & LUCKMAN, T. *The social construction of reality.* New York: Doubleday, 1966.

BEVER, T.G. Language and perspective. In G. Miller (Ed.), *Psychology and Communication.* Washington, D.C.: Forum Series: Voice of America, 1974.

BINDER, V., BINDER, A., & RIMLAND, B. (Eds.), *Modern therapies.* Englewood Cliffs: Prentice-Hall, 1976.

BIRDWHISTELL, R.L. Some discussion of ethnography, theory, and method. In J. Brockman (Ed.), *About Bateson.* New York: E.P. Dutton, 1977:103-141.

BITZER, L.F. & BLACK, E. *The prospect of rhetoric: Report of the national developmental project.* Englewood Cliffs: Prentice-Hall, 1971.

BLACK, M. *Models and metaphors.* Ithaca: Cornell, 1962.

BLUMER, H. *Symbolic interactionism, perspective and method.* Englewood Cliffs: Prentice-Hall, 1969.

BOCHNER, A.P. Whither communication theory and research? *Quarterly Journal of Speech,* 1977, 63:324-332.

BOCHNER, A.P. Interpersonal bonding. In C. Arnold & J. Bowers (Eds.), *Handbook of rhetoric and communication.* Allyn & Bacon, 1981.

BOCHNER, A.P. & KELLY, C.W. Interpersonal competence: rationale, philosophy, and implementation of a conceptual framework. *Speech Teacher,* 1974, 23:279-301.

BOCHNER, A.P. & KRUEGER, D.L. Interpersonal communication theory and research: An overview of inscrutable epistemologies and muddled concepts. In D. Nimmo (Ed.), *Communication yearbook 3: An annual review published by the International Communication Association.* New Brunswick: Transaction Books, 1979:197-211.

BODIN, A.M. The interactional view: Family therapy approaches of the Mental Research Institute. In A. Guerin & D. Kniskern (Eds.), *The handbook of family therapy.* New York: Brunner/Mazel, 1980.

BOOTH, W. Metaphor as rhetoric: The problem of evaluation. *Critical Inquiry.* 1978, 5:49-72.

BOSZORMENYI-NAGY, I. A theory of relationships: Experience and transaction. In I. Boszormenyi-Nagy & J.L. Framo (Eds.), *Intensive Family Therapy.* New York: Harper and Row, 1965.

BOWERS, J.W. & OCHS, D. *The rhetoric of agitation and control.* Reading, Mass.: Addison-Wesley, 1970.

BOWERS, J.W., ELLIOTT, N.D. & DESMOND, R.J. Exploiting pragmatic rules: Devious messages. *Human Communication Research.* 1977, 3:235-242.

BRAND, S. *II cybernetic frontiers.* New York: Random House, 1974.

BRAND, S. Introduction to G. Bateson's "The pattern which connects." *CoEvolution Quarterly,* Summer 1978, 18:4.

BRAND, S. (Ed.), *The next whole earth catalogue.* New York: Random House, 1980.

BRAQUE, G. Quoted in A. Lieberman, *The artist in his studio.* New York: Viking Press, 1960.

BROCKMAN, J. (Ed.), *About Bateson.* New York: E.P. Dutton, 1977.

BRODEY, W.M. Information exchange in the time domain. In W. Gray, F.J. Kuhl & N.D. Rizzo (Eds.), *General systems theory and psychiatry.* Boston: Little, Brown & Co., pp. 229-243.

BRONOWSKI, J. *The origins of knowledge and imagination.* New Haven: Yale University Press, 1978.

BROWN, G.S. *Probability and scientific inference.* New York: Longmans, Green, 1957.

BROWN, G.S. *Laws of form.* New York: Bantam, 1972.

BRUYN, S.T. *The human perspective in sociology.* Englewood Cliffs: Prentice-Hall, 1966.

BUBER, M. Distance and relation. *Psychiatry.* 1957, 20:97-104.

BURKE, K. *Permanence and change.* Indianapolis: Bobbs-Merrill, 1965.

BURKE, K. *A grammar of motives.* Berkeley: University of California Press, 1969.

BURKE, K.   Personal communication, 1979.

BUTLER, S.   *The notebooks.* New York: E.P. Dutton, 1917.

CAMPBELL, J.   *The masks of god: Primitive mythology.* New York: Viking Press, 1959.

CAMPBELL, K.K.   *Critiques of contemporary rhetoric.* Belmont, Cal.: Wadsworth, 1972.

CAMUS, A.   *The myth of sisyphus.* New York: Random House, 1966.

CARNAP, R.   *Introduction to semantics.* Cambridge: Harvard University Press, 1942.

CARNAP, R.   *An introduction to the philosophy of science.* New York: Basic Books, 1966.

CARSON, R.C.   *Interaction concepts of personality.* Chicago: Aldine, 1969.

CASSIRER, E.   *Essay on man.* New Haven: Yale University Press, 1944.

CHERRY, C.   *On human communication.* Cambridge: MIT Press, 1957.

CHERRY, C.   *World communication: Threat or promise?* New York: Wiley, 1971.

CHESEBRO, J.W.   The small group technique of the radical revolutionary: A synthetic study of consciousness raising. *Speech Monographs.* 1973:136-146.

CHESEBRO, J.W. & HAMSHER, C.D.   Contemporary rhetorical theory and criticism: Dimensions of the new rhetoric. *Speech Monographs.* 1975, *42*:311-334.

CHIEN, I.   *Science of behavior and the image of man.* New York: Basic Books, 1972.

CHOMSKY, N.   Review of Skinner's *Verbal behavior. Language.* 1958, *35*:26-58.

CHOMSKY, N.   *Aspects of a theory of syntax.* Cambridge: MIT Press, 1965.

CIARDI, J.   Manner of speaking. *The Saturday Review.* March 14, 1964.

CISSNA, K.N.L.   Facilitative communication and interpersonal relationships: An empirical test of a theory of interpersonal communication. Doctoral dissertation, University of Denver, 1975.

CISSNA, K.N.L.   Interpersonal confirmation: A review of current/ recent theory and research. Paper presented at the Central States

Speech Association Convention, Chicago, 1976, and the International Communication Association Convention, Portland, Oregon, 1976a.

CISSNA, K.N.L. *Interpersonal confirmation: A review of current theory, measurement, and research.* Saint Louis: Saint Louis University, 1976b.

CISSNA, K.N.L. Gender, sex type, and perceived confirmation: A response from the perspective of interpersonal confirmation. Presented at the International Communication Association Convention, Philadelphia, 1979.

CISSNA, K.N.L. & KEATING, S. Speech communication antecedents of perceived confirmation. *Western Journal of Speech Communication.* 1979, 43:48-60.

CLARKE, F.P. Interpersonal communication variables as predictors of marital satisfaction-attraction. Doctoral dissertation, University of Denver, 1973.

COHEN, A.R. *Attitude change and social influence.* New York: Basic Books, 1964.

COOPER, L. (Trans.), *The rhetoric of aristotle.* New York: Appleton-Century-Crofts, 1932.

COULTHARD, M. *Introduction to discourse analysis.* New York: Longmans, Green, 1977.

COURTRIGHT, J., MILLAR, F. & ROGERS-MILLAR, E. Domineeringness and dominance: Replication and Expansion. *Communication Monographs.* 1979, 46:177-192.

COURTRIGHT, J., MILLAR, F. & ROGERS, E. Message control intensity as a predictor of transactional redundancy. In D. Nimmo (Ed.), *Communication yearbook 4.* New Brunswick: Transaction Books, 1980a:199-216.

COURTRIGHT, J., MILLAR, F. & ROGERS, E. The form of relational communication: A new measure of interactional patterns. Paper presented at the Speech Communication Association convention, New York City, 1980b.

CRONEN, V.E. & DAVIS L. Alternative approaches for the communication theorist: Problems in the laws-rules-systems trichotomy. *Human Communication Research.* 1978, 4:120-128.

CRONEN, V.E. & LANNAMANN, J.W. The hierarchy principle in the emergence of close personal relationships. Working paper, University of Massachusetts, 1979.

CRONEN, V.E. & PEARCE, W.B. The logic of the coordinated management of meanings: An open systems model of interpersonal communication. Paper presented at the ICA Annual Convention, 1978b.

CRONEN, V.E., PEARCE, W.B. & HARRIS, L.M. The logic of the coordinated management of meaning: A rules-based approach to the first course in interpersonal communication. *Communication Education.* 1979b, 28:22-38.

CRONEN, V.E., PEARCE, W.B. & SNAVELY, L. A theory of rule-structure and types of episodes, and a study of perceived enmeshment in undesired repetitive patterns (URP's). In D. Nimmo (ed.), *Communication Yearbook 3.* New Brunswick: Transaction Books, 1979c.

CUSHMAN, D.P. The rules perspective as a theoretical basis for the study of human communication. *Communication Quarterly.* 1977, 25:30-45.

CUSHMAN, D.P. Toward a rhetoric of negotiation. Paper presented at the Conference on Human Communication from the Interactional View, Asilomar, Cal., 1979.

CUSHMAN. D.P. & PEARCE, W.B. Generality and necessity in three types of human communication theory — special attention to rules theory. In B.D. Ruben (Ed.), *Communication Yearbook I.* New Brunswick: Transaction Books, 1977:173-182.

CUSHMAN, D.P. & WHITING, G. An approach to communication theory: Toward consensus on rules. *Journal of Communication.* 1972, 22:217-238.

DANCE, F.E.X. & LARSON, C.E. *The functions of human communication.* New York: Holt, Rinehart, and Winston, 1976.

DANGOTT, L., THORNTON, B.C. & PAGE, P. Communication and pain. *Journal of Communication.* 1978, 28(1):30-35.

DANZIGER, K. *Interpersonal communication.* New York: Pergamon Press, 1976.

DAVIS, G. *Art international,* 1971, 1:39.

DELIA, J.G. Change of meaning process in impression formation. *Communication Monographs.* 1976, 43:142-157.

DELIA, J.G. Constructivism and the study of human communication. *Quarterly Journal of Speech.* 1977, 63:66-83.

DE MAN, P. The epistemology of metaphor. *Critical Inquiry,* 1978, 5:13-30.

DEWEY, J. Quoted in W. Barrett, *Irrational man: A study in existential philosophy.* Garden City, New York: Doubleday, 1962.

DOGEN. *Shobogenzo.* (Translation by Naoki Nomura). Tokyo: Iwanami-Shoten, 1955, 1:83-84.

DUNCAN, H. The search for a social theory of communication in american sociology. In F. Dance (Ed.), *Human Communication Theory*. New York: Holt, Rinehart and Winston, 1967:236-263.

DUNCAN, H. *Symbols in Society*. London: Oxford University Press, 1968.

ECO, U. *The role of the reader*. Bloomington: Indiana University Press, 1979.

EDELMAN, M. *Politics as symbolic action*. Chicago: Markham, 1971.

ELIOT, T.S. *Four quartets*. New York: Harcourt Brace Jovanovich, 1971.

ELLIS, D.G. An analysis of relational communication in ongoing group systems. Unpublished Pd.D. dissertation, University of Utah, 1976a.

ELLIS, D.G. Relational interaction in decision-making groups. Paper presented at International Communication Association convention, Portland, Oregon, 1976b.

ELLIS, D.G. A social system model of relational control in two ongoing group systems. Paper presented at Speech Communication Association convention, Washington, D.C., 1977.

ELLIS, D.G. Trait predictors of relational control. In B. Ruben (Ed.), *Communication Yearbook 2*. New Brunswick: Transaction Books, 1978a:185-192.

ELLIS, D.G. Initial interaction: Some ethnographic considerations. *Western Journal of Speech Communication*. 1980, *44*:104-107.

ELLIS, D.G., WERBEL, W.S. & FISHER, B.A. Toward a systemic organization of groups. *Small Group Behavior*. 1978, *9*:451-469.

ELLIS, D.G. & MCCALLISTER, L. Relational control sequences in sex-typed and androgynous groups. *Western Journal of Speech Communication*. 1980, *44*:35-49.

ELSTER, J. *Logic and society: Contradictions and possible worlds*. New York: Wiley, 1978.

ERICKSON, M. The confusion technique in hypnosis. *American Journal of Clinical Hypnosis*. 1964, *6*:183-207.

ERICSON, P. Relational communication: Complementarity and symmetry and their relation to dominance-submission. Unpublished Ph.D. dissertation, Michigan State University, 1972.

ERICSON, P. & ROGERS, E. New procedures for analyzing relational communication. *Family Process*. 1973, *12*:245-267.

ETZIONI, A. *A comparative analysis of complex organizations*. New York: Free Press, 1961.

FEINGOLD, P.C. Toward a paradigm of effective communication: An empirical study of perceived communicative effectiveness. Unpublished Ph.D. dissertation, Purdue University, 1976.

FERNANDEZ, J. The mission of metaphor in expressive culture. *Current Anthropology.* 1974, *15*:119-145.

FESTINGER, L. *A theory of cognitive dissonance.* Stanford: Stanford University Press, 1957.

FEYERABEND, P. *Against method.* New York: Schocken Books, 1975.

FlAVELL, J.H. *The developmental psychology of Jean Piaget.* Princeton: Van Nostrand, 1963.

FISCH, R., WEAKLAND, J., WATZLAWICK, P., SEGAL, L., HOEBEL, F. & DEARDORFF, M. *Learning brief therapy: An introductory manual.* Palo Alto: Mental Research Institute, 1975.

FISHER, B.A. Decision emergence: Phases in group decision making. *Speech Monographs.* 1970, *37*:53-66.

FISHER, B.A. Relational rules: Still another step towards communication theory. Paper presented at the International Communication Association convention, Portland, Oregon, 1976.

FISHER, B.A. Evidence varies with theoretical perspective. *Western Journal of Speech Communication.* 1977a, *41*:9-19.

FISHER, B.A. An interaction analysis of dyadic relationship. Paper presented at the Speech Communication Association convention, Washington, D.C., 1977b.

FISHER, B.A. Current status of interaction analysis research. Paper presented at the Speech Communication Association convention, Minneapolis, 1978.

FISHER, B.A. & BEACH, W. Relational development in dyads: A preliminary report. Paper presented at the International Communication Association convention, Chicago, 1978.

FISHER, B.A. & BEACH, W. Content and relationship dimensions of communicative behavior: An exploratory study. *Western Journal of Speech Communication.* 1979, *43*:201-211.

FISHER, B.A. & HAWES, L. An interact system model: Generating a grounded theory of small groups. *Quarterly Journal of Speech.* 1971, *57*:444-453.

FISHER, B.A., GLOVER, T.W. & ELLIS, D.G. The nature of complex communication systems. *Communication Monographs.* 1977, *44*:231-240.

FITZPATRICK, M. A typological approach to communication in relationships. In B. Ruben (Ed.), *Communication Yearbook 1.* New Brunswick: Transaction Books, 1977:263-275.

FOLGER, J. & POOLE, M. On validating interaction coding schemes. Paper presented at the International Communication Association convention, Acapulco, 1980.

FOLGER, J. & PUCK, S. Coding relational communication: A question approach. Paper presented at the International Communication Association convention, Portland, Oregon, 1976.

FOLGER, J. & SILLARS, A. Relational coding and perceptions of dominance. Paper presented at the Speech Communication Association convention. Washington, D.C., 1977.

FOOTE, N.N. & COTRELL, L.S. *Identity and interpersonal competency.* Chicago: University of Chicago Press, 1955.

FRENCH, R.P. & RAVEN, B. The bases of social power. In D. Cartwright (Ed.), *Studies in social power.* Ann Arbor: Institute for Social Research, 1959:150-167.

FRIEDMAN, M.S. Dialogue and the "essential we": The bases of values in the philosophy of Martin Buber. *American Journal of Psychoanalysis.* 1960, *20*:26-34.

FRY, W.G. *Sweet madness: A study of humor.* Palo Alto: Pacific Books, 1963.

GEERTZ, C. *The interpretation of cultures.* New York: Basic Books, 1973.

GERGEN, K.J. Social psychology as history. *Journal of Personality and Social Psychology.* 1973, *26*:309-320.

GLUCKSBERG, S. & KRAUS, R. Referential communication in nursery school children: A method and some preliminary findings. *Journal of Experimental Child Psychology.* 1966, *3*:333-342.

GOFFMAN, E. *Interaction ritual.* Garden City, N.Y.: Doubleday, 1967.

GOFFMAN, E. *Frame analysis.* New York: Harper and Row, 1974.

GORDEN, W.I. Experiential training: A comparison of t-groups, tavistock, and est. *Communication Education.* 1979, *28*:39-48.

GORDON, D. *Therapeutic metaphors.* Cupertino, Cal.: META Publications, 1978.

GREENBERG, G.S. The family interactional perspective: A study and examination of the work of Don D. Jackson. *Family Process.* 1977, *16*:385-412.

GRINDER, J. & BANDLER, R. *The structure of magic II: A book about communication and change.* Palo Alto: Science and Behavior Books, 1976.

GUERIN, P.J., Jr., (Ed.), *Family therapy: Theory and practice.* New York: Gardner Press, 1976.

GUMPERZ, J.J. Introduction. In J.J. Gumperz and D. Hymes *Directions in sociolinguistics:. The ethnography of communication.* New York: Holt, Rinehart and Winston, 1972.

GUSFIELD, J. The literary rhetoric of social science. *American Sociological Review.* 1976, 41:16-34.

HABERMAS, J. Toward a theory of communicative competence. In H.P. Dreitzel (Ed.), *Recent sociology (No. 2).* New York: Macmillan, 1970:114-148.

HALEY, J. An interactional explanation of hypnosis. *The American Journal of Clinical Hypnosis.* 1958, 1:45-57.

HALEY, J. *Strategies of psychotherapy.* New York: Grune & Stratton, 1963.

HALEY, J. *Uncommon therapy: The psychiatric techniques of Milton H. Erickson, M.D.* New York: Norton, 1973.

HALEY, J. Development of a theory: A history of a research project. In C.E. Sluzki & D.C. Ransom (Eds.), *Double bind: The foundation of the communicational approach to the family.* New York: Grune & Stratton, 1976a:59-104.

HALEY, J. *Problem solving therapy.* San Francisco: Jossey-Bass, 1976b.

HALEY, J. Toward a theory of pathological systems. In P. Watzlawick & J. Weakland (Eds.), *The interactional view.* New York: Norton, 1977.

HALEY, J. Personal communication. 1980.

HALL, E. *Beyond culture.* Garden City, N.Y.: Doubleday, 1977.

HARDY, W.G. *Language, thought, and experience.* Baltimore: University Park Press, 1978.

HARPER, N.L. *Human communication theory: The history of a paradigm.* Rochelle Park, N.J.: Hayden, 1979.

HARRE, R. *The philosophies of science.* Oxford: Oxford University Press, 1972.

HARRE, R.& MADDEN, E.H. *Causal powers.* Oxford: Basic Blackwell, 1975.

HARRIES, K. Metaphor and transcendence. *Critical Quarterly.* 1978, 5:73-90.

HARRIS, L.M. The effects of interaction management and background similarity on perceived communication competence and attraction during initial interactions. Unpublished M.S. thesis, University of Kentucky, 1977.

HARRIS, L.M. Communication competence: An argument for a systemic view. Paper presented at the annual convention of the International Communication Association, Chicago, 1979.

HARRIS, L.M. The maintenance of a social reality: A case study of a paradoxical logic. *Family Process*. March 1980, *19*:19-34.

HARRIS, L.M. & Cronen V. A rules-based approach to the analysis and evaluation of formal organizations. *Communication Quarterly*. 1979.

HARRIS, L.M., CRONEN, V.E. & MCNAMEE, S. An empirical case study of communication episodes. Paper presented at the annual convention of the National Council on Family Relations, 1979.

HART, R.P., EADIE, W.F., & CARLSON, R.E. Rhetorical sensitivity and communication competence. A paper presented at the annual convention of the Speech Communication Association, Houston, December 1975.

HASSAN, S. Transactional and contextual invalidation between the parents of disturbed families: A comparative study. *Family Process*. 1974, *13*:53-70.

HAWES, L.C. Alternative theoretical bases: Toward a presuppositional critique. *Communication Quarterly*. 1977, *25*:63-68.

HAWKES, T. *Structuralism and semiotics*. Berkeley: University of California Press, 1977.

HEATH, D.H. *Maturity and competence*. New York: Gardner Press, 1977.

HENRY, J. A fragment from *Pathways to madness* (1973). In C.E. Sluzki & D.C. Ransom (Eds.), *Double Bind: The foundation of the communicational approach to the family*. New York: Grune & Stratton, 1976.

HERBERT, L. *A new language for environmental design*. New York: University Press, 1972.

HERON, W. The pathology of boredom. *Scientific American*. 1957, Vol. 196, *1*:52-56.

HOVLAND, C., JANIS, I., & KELLY H. *Communication and persuasion*. New Haven: Yale University Press, 1953.

HULL, J. The relationship of self-esteem, confirming communication behavior and emotional satisfaction. Doctoral dissertation, University of Denver, in progress.

HYDE, M. Understanding paradox: A communicative rhetorical approach. Paper presented at the annual convention of the Speech Communication Association, San Francisco, 1976.

HYMES, D. Competence and performance in linguistic theory. In R. Huxley & E. Ingram (Eds.), *Language acquisition: Models and methods*. New York: Academic Press, 1971.

INSKO, C.A. *Theories of attitude change*. New York: Appleton-Century-Crofts, 1967.

JABLIN, F.M. An experimental study of message-response in superior-subordinate communication. Doctoral dissertation, Purdue University, 1977.

JACKSON, D.D. The question of family homeostasis. *Psychiatric Quarterly Supplement*. 1957, 31:79-90.

JACKSON, D.D. Family interaction, family homeostasis and some implications for conjoint family psychotherapy. In J.H. Masserman (Ed.), *Individual and family dynamics*. New York: Grune & Stratton, 1959:122-141.

JACKSON, D.D. The study of the family. *Family Process*. 1965, 4:1-20.

JACKSON, D.D. Schizophrenia: The nosological nexus. In *The origins of schizophrenia*. Proceedings of the First Rochester International Conference, March 1967. Reprinted in P. Watzlawick and J. Weakland (Eds.), *The interactional view: Studies at the Mental Research Institute, Palo Alto, 1965-1974*. New York: Norton, 1977:193-227.

JACKSON, D.D., RISKIN, J., & SATIR, V. A method of analysis of a family interview. *AMA Archives of General Psychiatry*. 1961, 5:321-339.

JACOBS, M. Levels of confirmation and disconfirmation in interpersonal communication. Doctoral dissertation, University of Denver, 1973.

JACOBS, S. The practical management of conversational meanings: Notes on the dynamics of social understanding and interactional emergence. Paper presented at the annual convention of the Speech Communication Association, Washington, D.C., 1977.

JACOBSON, W.D. *Power and interpersonal relations*. Belmont, Cal.: Wadsworth, 1972.

JENKINS, J. Remember that old theory of memory? Well, forget it! *American Psychologist*. 1974:785-795.

JOHNSON, D.M. *Systematic introduction to the psychology of thinking*. New York: Harper and Row, 1972.

JOHNSON, K. The effects of the structure of communication rules on persons' simulated conversations. Paper presented at the annual convention of the International Communication Association, Philadelphia, 1979.

JONES, E.E. & DAVIS, K.E. From acts to dispositions: The attribution process in person perception. In L. Berkowitz (Ed.), *Advances in experimental social psychology*. (Vol. 2) New York: Academic Press, 1969.

KATZ, E. & LAZARSFELD, P. *Personal influence*. Glencoe, Ill.: The Free Press, 1955.

KEATING, S. The effects of agreement, disagreement, facilitative communication, and self-disclosure on the perceived confirmation of males and females. Master's final research project, Saint Louis University, 1977.

KELLY, G.A. *The psychology of personal constructs*. New York: Norton, 1955.

KELLY, G. Man's construction of his alternatives. In G. Lindzey (Ed.), *Assessment in human motives*. New York: Rinehart & Company, 1958.

KELLY, C.W. & CHASE, L.J. The California interpersonal competence questionnaire — I: An exploratory search for factor structure. A paper presentvd at the annual convention of the International Communication Association, Chicago, April 1978.

KERLINGER, N. *Foundations of behavioral research*. New York: Holt, Rinehart and Winston, 1973.

KIBLER, R.J. & BARKER, L.L. *Conceptual frontiers in speech-communication: Report of the New Orleans conference on research and instructional development*. New York: Speech Association of America, 1969.

KOCH, S. Psychology and emerging conceptions of knowledge as unitary. In T.W. Wann (Ed.), *Behaviorism and Phenomonology*. Chicago: Phoenix, 1964:1-41.

KOESTLER, A. *The act of creation*. New York: Macmillan, 1957.

KOESTLER, A. *The sleepwalkers*. New York: Macmillan, 1959.

KOESTLER, A. *The ghost in the machine*. New York: Macmillan, 1967.

KOESTLER, A. *Janus: A summing up*. New York: Random House, 1978.

KOLAJA, J. *Social system and time and space: An introduction to the theory of recurrent behavior*. Pittsburgh: Duquesne University Press, 1969.

KORZYBSKI, A. *Science and sanity*, Third Edition. Lakeville, Conn.:

The International Non-Aristotelian Library Publishing Co., 1948.

KUHN, T.S. *The structure of scientific revolutions.* Chicago: University of Chicago Press, 1970.

LABOV, W. & FANSHEL, D. *Therapeutic discourse and psychotherapy as conversation.* New York: Academic Press, 1977.

LAING, R.D. *The self and others.* New York: Pantheon, 1961.

LAING, R.D. Mystification, confusion and conflict. In I. Boszormenyi-Nagy & J.L. Framo (Eds.), *Intensive family therapy.* New York: Harper and Row, 1965.

LAING, R.D. *The politics of experience.* New York: Ballantine, 1967.

LAING, R.D. *The self and others.* (Second Edition) Baltimore: Penguin, 1969.

LAING, R.D. *Knots.* New York: Vintage Books, 1970.

LAING, R.D. & ESTERSON, A. *Sanity, madness, and the family.* Baltimore: Penquin, 1964.

LAKATIS, I. Falsification and the methodology of scientific research. In I. Lakatos & A.E. Musgrave (Eds.), *Criticism and the growth of knowledge.* London: Cambridge University Press, 1970:91-196.

LANGER, S.K. *Philosophy in a new key.* Cambridge: Harvard University Press, 1942.

LANIGAN, R.L. *Speech act phenomenology.* The Hague: Martinos Nijhoff: N.Y. Humanities Press, 1977.

LEDERER, W.J. & JACKSON, D.D. *Mirages of marriage.* New York: Norton, 1968.

LEE, D. Lineal and non-lineal codification of reality. *Psychosomatic Medicine.* 1950, *12*:89-97.

LETH, P. Self concept and interpersonal response in a classroom: An exploratory study. Doctoral dissertation, Purdue University, 1977.

LETH, S.A. Interpersonal response: Confirmation, rejection, and disconfirmation in established friendships. Doctoral dissertation, Purdue University, 1977a.

LETH, S.A. Toward a conceptual synthesis and empirical investigation of patterned interpersonal responses. Paper presented at the annual convention of the Southern States Speech Association, Knoxville, Tennessee, 1977b.

LETH, S.A. Interpersonal response: Confirmation, rejection, and disconfirmation in established friendships. Paper presented at the annual convention of the International Communication Association, Chicago, 1978.

LIPSET, D. Gregory Bateson: Early biography. In J. Brockman (Ed.), *About Bateson*. New York: Dutton, 1977:21-54.

LIPSET, D. *Gregory Bateson: The legacy of a scientist*. Englewood Cliffs: Prentice-Hall, 1980.

LITSCHUTZ, W. An experimental study of the effects of similarity /dissimilarity and cooperation/competition on reciprocity and compensation in confirmation and disconfirmation. Doctoral dissertation, Wayne State University, 1979.

MACORMAC, E. *Metaphor and myth in science and religion*. Durham: Duke University Press, 1976.

MAIER, R.N.F & SOLEM, A.R. Improving solutions by turning choice situations into problems. *Personnel Psychology*. 1962, 15:151-157.

MASLOW, A.H. *The farther reaches of human nature*. New York: Viking Press, 1971.

MATHEWS, A.J. Confirming and disconfirming behaviors, self-acceptance, and personal values: A descriptive study of librarian-user interactions. Doctoral dissertation, University of Denver, 1977.

MAY, R. *Love and will*. New York: Norton, 1969.

MCGUIRE, W.J. The nature of attitudes and attitude change. In G. Lindzey & E. Aronson (Eds.), *Handbook of social psychology, Vol. III*. Reading, Mass.: Addison-Wesley, 1969:136-314.

MCHUGH, P. *Defining the situation*. New York: Bobbs-Merrill, 1968.

MCREYNOLDS, P. Anxiety as related to incongruities between values and feelings. *The Psychological Record*. 1958, 8:57-66.

MEAD, G. *Mind, self and society*. Chicago: University of Chicago Press, 1934.

MEAD, M. End linkage: A tool for cross-cultural analysis. In J. Brockman (Ed.), *About Bateson*. New York: Dutton, 1977:171-231.

MERLEAU-PONTY, J. Quoted in R. May, *Love and will*. New York: Norton, 1969.

MILLAR, F. A transactional analysis of marital communication patterns: An exploratory study. Unpublished Ph.D. dissertation, Michigan State University, 1973.

MILLAR, F. & ROGERS, E. A relational approach to interpersonal communication. In G. Miller (Ed.), *Explorations in interpersonal communication*. Beverly Hills: Sage, 1976:87-103.

MILLAR, F., ROGERS-MILLAR, E. & COURTRIGHT, J. Relational control and dyadic understanding: An exploratory predictive regression model. In D. Nimmo (Ed.), *Communication Yearbook 3*. New Brunswick: Transaction Books, 1979:213-224.

MILLAR, F., ROGERS-MILLAR, E. & VILLARD, K. A proposed model of relational communication and family functioning. Paper presented at the annual convention of the Central States Speech Communication Association, Chicago, 1978.

MILLER, G.A. *Language and communication*. New York: McGraw-Hill, 1951.

MILLER, G.R. The pervasiveness and marvelous complexity of human communication: A note of skepticism. Keynote address presented at the 4th annual Conference on Communication, California State University at Fresno, 1977.

MILLER, G.R. The current status of theory and research in interpersonal communication. *Human Communication Research*. 1978a, 4:164-178.

MILLER, G.R. & BERGER, C.R. On keeping the faith in matters scientific. *Western Journal of Speech Communication*. 1978b, 42:44-57.

MILLER, G.R. & STEINBERG, M. *Between people*. Chicago: Science Research Associates, 1975.

MINUCHIN, S. *Families and family therapy*. Harvard: Harvard University Press, 1974.

MOOIJ, J.A. *A study of metaphor*. Amsterdam: North-Holland, 1976.

MOOS, H.R. Situational analysis of a therapeutic community milieu. *Journal of Abnormal Psychology*. 1968, 73:49-61.

MONGE, P.R. The systems perspective as a theoretical basis for the study of human communication. *Communication Quarterly*. 1977, 25:19-29.

MOORE, E.C. *American pragmatism: Pierce, James, and Dewey*. New York: Columbia University Press, 1961.

MORRIS, C. Foundations of the theory of signs. *International encyclopedia of unified science*. Vol.1, No. 2. Chicago: University of Chicago Press, 1938.

MORRIS, C. *Signs, language and behavior*. New York: Prentice-Hall, 1946.

MORRIS, C. *The pragmatic movement in American philosophy*. New

York: George Braziller, 1970.

NICHOLS, M.H. *Rhetoric and criticism.* Baton Rouge: Louisiana State University Press, 1963.

NIETZSCHE, F. Quoted in W. Kaufman (Ed.), *The portable Nietzsche.* New York: Viking Press, 1954.

NORTON, R.W. Foundation of a communicator style construct. *Human Communication Research.* 1978, 4:99-112.

O'DONNELL-TRUJILLO, N. On the validity of relational communication coding systems. Paper presented at the annual convention of the Western Speech Communication Association, Portland, 1980.

O'KEEFE, D.J. Logical empiricism and the study of human communication. *Speech Monographs.* 1975, 42:169-183.

O'MALLEY, J.M. Research perspective on social competence. *Merrill-Palmer Quarterly*, 1977, 23:29-44.

ORTH, A. Relational communication and perceptual discrepencies in dyads with-a-history. Unpublished M.A. thesis, University of Vermont, 1974.

OSGOOD, C., SUCI, G. & TANNENBAUM, P. *The measurement of meaning.* Urbana: University of Illinois Press, 1958.

PARK, R. & BURGESS, E. *Introduction to the science of sociology.* Chicago: University of Chicago Press, 1921.

PARKS, M. Relational communication: Theory and research. *Human Communication Research.* 1977a, 3:372-381.

PARKS, M. Issues in the explication of communication competency. A paper presented at the annual convention of the Western Speech Communication Association, Phoenix, November 1977b.

PARKS, M., FARACE, R. & ROGERS, E. A stochastic description of relational communication systems. Paper presented at the annual convention of the Speech Communication Association, Houston, 1975.

PARKS, M., FARACE, R., ROGERS, E., ALBRECHT, T. & ABBOTT, R. Markov process analysis of relational communication in marital dyads. Paper presented at the annual convention of the International Communication Association, Portland, Oregon, 1976.

PASCAL, B. Quoted in W. Barrett, *Irrational man: A study in existential philosophy.* Garden City, N.Y.: Doubleday, 1962.

PEARCE, W.B. The coordinated management of meaning: A rules-based theory of interpersonal communication. In G. Miller (Ed.), *Explorations in interpersonal communication.* Beverly Hills: Sage, 1976a: 17-36.

PEARCE, W,B. Coordination and enactment of conversational episodes: A perspective on interpersonal communication. Paper presented at the annual convention of the Speech Communication Association, San Francisco, 1976b.

PEARCE, W.B. Teaching interpersonal communication as a humane science: A comparative analysis. *Communication Education.* 1977, 26:104-112.

PEARCE, W.B., CRONEN, V. & CONKLIN, F. A hierarchical model of interpersonal communication. *Communication.* 1979.

PEARCE, W.B., CRONEN, V.E. & HARRIS, L.M. Methodological consideration in communication theory. In F. Dance (Ed.), *Comparative communication theory: An introduction.* (In press).

PEARCE, W.B., CRONEN, V.E., JOHNSON, K., JONES, G & RAYMOND, R. The structure of communication rules and the form of conversation: An experimental simulation. *Western Journal of Speech Communication.* 1979.

PECKHAM, M. *Man's rage for disorder.* New York: Schocken, 1973.

PENFIELD, W. The permanent record of the stream of consciousness. *Proceedings of the 14th International Congress of Psychology.* 1954, 6:67-68.

PEPPER, S.C. *World hypotheses: A study in evidence.* Berkeley: University of California Press, 1942.

PHILIPSEN, G. Speaking "like a man" in teamsterville: Cultural patterns of role enactment in an urban neighboorhood. *Quarterly Journal of Speech.* 1975, 61:13-22.

PITTENGER, R., HOCKETT, C. & DAHEHY, J. *The first five minutes: A sample of microscopic interview analysis.* Ithaca: Parul Martineau, 1960.

PRIBRAM, K. Self consciousness and intentionality. In G. E. Schwartz & D. Shapiro (Eds.), *Consciousness and self regulation, Vol. I.* New York: Plenum, 1976:51-100.

RABKIN, R. Critique of the clinical use of the double-bind hypothesis. In C.E. Sluzki and D.C. Ransom (Eds.), *Double bind: The foundation of the communicational approach to the family.* New York: Grune & Stratton, 1976.

RAUSCH, H.L. Interaction sequences. *Journal of Personality and Social Psychology.* 1975, 2:487-499.

RAUSCH, H.L., BARRY, W., HERTZEL, R. & SWAIN, M. *Communication, conflict and marriage.* San Francisco: Jossey-Bass, 1974.

REDDING, W.C. Organizational communication theory and ideology: An interview. In D. Nimmo (Ed.), *Communication yearbook 3.* New

Brunswick: Transaction Books, 1979:309-341.

RESCHER, N. *The logic of commands.* New York: Dover Publications, 1966.

RESCHER, N. *Many-valued logic.* New York: McGraw-Hill, 1969.

RICHARDS, I.A. *The philosophy of rhetoric.* New York: Oxford, 1965.

RICHARDS, M. *Centering in poetry, and the person.* Middleton, Conn.: Wesleyan University, 1964.

RICOUER, P. *The rule of metaphor.* Toronto: University of Toronto Press, 1977.

ROGERS, E. Dyadic systems and transactional communication in a family context. Unpublished Ph.D. dissertation, Michigan State University, 1972.

ROGERS, E., COURTRIGHT, J. & MILLAR, F. Message control intensity: Rationale and preliminary findings. *Communication Monographs.* 1980, 47:201-219.

ROGERS, E. & FARACE, R. Analysis of relational communication in dyads: New measurement procedures. *Human Communication Reseacrh.* 1975, 1:222-239.

ROGERS-MILLAR, E. & MILLAR, F. Domineeringness and dominance: A transactional view. *Human Communication Research.* 1979, 5:238-246.

ROMMETVEIT, R. *et al.,* Processing utterances in context. In R. Rommetveit & E.A. Carswell (Eds.), New York: Academic Press, 1971.

ROSEN, N. *Direct analysis.* New York: Grune & Stratton, 1953.

ROSENTHAL, R. *Experimenter effects in behavioral research.* New York: Appleton-Century-Crofts, 1966.

ROSS, R.F (Ed.), Perceived communication patterns and predictive accuracy of supervisor-subordinate dyads. Doctoral dissertation, University of Denver, 1973.

RUBEN, B.D. Assessing communication competency for intercultural adaptation. *Group & Organization Studies.* 1976, 1:334-354.

RUESCH, J. The tangential response. In P.H. Toch & J. Zuben (Eds.), *Psychopathology of communication.* New York: Grune & Stratton, 1958.

RUESCH, J. & BATESON, G. *Communication: The social matrix of psychiatry.* New York: Norton, 1951.

RUESCH, J. & PRESTWOOD, A.R. Interaction processes and personal codification. *Journal of Personality*. 1950, *18*:391-430.

RUSHING, J. Impression management as communicative action: A non-verbal strategy in interpersonal encounters. Paper presented at the annual convention of the Western Speech Communication Association, San Francisco, November 1976.

SALMON, W. *Logic*. Englewood Cliffs: Prentice—Hall, 1963.

SCHEFFLER, I. *Science and subjectivity*. Indianapolis: Bobbs-Merrill, 1967.

SCHEFLEN, A.E. Behavioral programs in human communication. In W. Gray, F.J. Duhl & N.D. Rizzo (Eds.), *General systems theory and psychiatry*. Boston: Little, Brwon, 1969:209-228.

SCHEFLEN, A.E. *How behavior means*. Garden City, N.Y.: Doubleday, 1974.

SCHENKEIN, J. (Ed.), *Studies in the organization of conversational interaction*. New York: Academic Press, 1978.

SCHENKER, B.R. Social psychology and science. *Journal of Personality and Social Psychology*. 1974, *29*:1-15.

SCHUTZ, W. *F.I.R.O.: A three dimensional theory of interpersonal behavior*. New York: Holt, Rinehart and Winston, 1960.

SCORESBY, A. *Relationship styles inventory*. Provo: Brigham Young University, 1975.

SEARLE, J. *Speech acts*. Cambridge: Cambridge University Press, 1969.

SELVINI-PALAZZOLI, M., BOSCOLO, L., CHECCHIN, C. & PRATA, G. *Paradox and counter-paradox*. New York: Brunner/Mazel, 1978.

SHANDS, H.C. Crystallized conflict: Semiotic aspects of neurosis and science. In C.E. Larson & F. Dance (Eds.), *Colloquium proceedings — Perspectives on communication*. Speech Communication Center, The University of Wisconsin-Milwaukke, 1968.

SHATTUCK, R. *The banquet years*. New York: Random House, 1968.

SHIBUTANI, T. *Society and personality*. Englewood Cliffs: Prentice-Hall, 1961.

SHIMANOFF, S.B. *Communication rules: Theory and research*. Beverly Hills: Sage, 1980.

SIEBURG, E. Dysfunctional communication and interpersonal responsiveness in small groups. Doctoral dissertation, University of Denver, 1969.

SIEBURG, E. Toward a theory of interpersonal confirmation. Unpublished manuscript, University of Denver, 1972.

SIEBURG, E. *Interpersonal confirmation: A paradigm for conceptualization and measurement.* San Diego: United States International University, 1975.

SIEBURG, E. Confirming and disconfirming organizational communication. In J.L. Owen, P.A. Page & G.I. Zimmerman (Eds.), *Communication in organizations.* St. Paul: West Publishing, 1976.

SIEBURG, E. *Family communication systems.* (in preparation).

SIEBURG, E. & LARSON, C.E. Dimensions of interpersonal response. Paper presented at the annual convention of the International Communication Association, Phoenix, 1971.

SIMMEL, G. *The sociology of Georg Simmel.* (Translated by K. Wolf) New York: Glencoe-Free Press, 1950.

SIMONS, H.W. Requirements, problems, and strategies: A theory of persuasion for social movements. *Quarterly Journal of Speech.* 1970, 56:1-11.

SIMONS, H.W. Ethical problems of the Batesonian interventionists. Unpublished paper. 1977.

SIMONS, H.W. In praise of muddleheaded anecdotalism. *Western Journal of Speech Communication.* 1978, 42:21-28.

SKINNER, B.F. *Verbal behavior.* New York: Appleton-Century-Crofts, 1957.

SLUZKI, C. & BEAVIN, J. Simetria y complementaridad: Una definicion operacional y una tipologia de parejas. *Acta Psiquiatrica y Psicologica de America Latina.* 1965, 11:321-330.

SLUZKI, C. & RANSOM, D.C. (Eds.), *Double bind: The foundation of the communicational approach to the family.* New York: Grune & Stratton, 1976.

SMALL, A. *General sociology.* Chicago: University of Chicago Press, 1905.

STEINBERG, S. *Time Magazine.* April 17, 1978:92.

SUNDELL, W. The operation of confirming and disconfirming verbal behavior in selected teacher-student interactions. Doctoral dissertation, University of Denver, 1972.

SUTHERLAND, J.W. *A general systems philosophy for the social and behavioral sciences.* New York: Braziller, 1973.

SUTTON, M.K. Agreement, disclosure, gender, and perceived confirmation. Unpublished research, University of Denver, 1976.

SZASZ, T.S. *Ideology and insanity: Essays on the psychiatric dehuman-*

ization of man. Garden City, N.Y.: Doubleday, 1970.

TEDESCHI, J.T., SCHLENKER, B.R. & BONOMA, T.V. *Conflict, power and games.* Chicago: Aldine, 1973.

THAYER, L. *Communication and communication systems.* Homewood, Ill.: Irwin, 1968.

THONSSEN, L. & BAIRD, A.C. *Speech criticism.* New York: Ronald Press, 1948. (Second Edition with W.W. Braden, 1970.)

TOMPKINS, P.K. The rhetoric of non-oratorical forms. *Quarterly Journal of Speech.* 1969.

TOULMIN, S.E. Rules and their relevance for understanding human behavior. In T. Mischel (Ed.), *Understanding other people.* Oxford: Blackwell, 1974:185-215.

TOULMIN, S.E. *The uses of argument.* Cambridge: Cambridge University Press, 1958.

TURBAYNE, C.M. *The myth of metaphor.* New Haven: Yale University Press, 1962.

VARELA, F.J. A calculus for self reference. *International Journal of General Systems.* 1975, 2:5-24.

VON FOERSTER, H. An epistemology for living things. Urbana: Biological Computer Laboratory, University of Illinois, Report No. 93, 1972.

VON FOERSTER, H. Personal communication, 1979.

VON WRIGHT, G.H. Deontic logic. *Mind.* 1951, 60:1-15.

VON WRIGHT, G.H. *Explanations and understanding.* Ithaca: Cornell University Press, 1971.

WALTON, R.E. *Interpersonal peacemaking: Confrontations and third-party consultation.* Reading, Mass.: Addison-Wesley, 1969.

WATZLAWICK, P. A review of the double bind theory. *Family Process.* 1963, 2:132-153.

WATZLAWICK, P. *An anthology of human communication.* Palo Alto: Science and Behavior Books, 1964.

WATZLAWICK, P. A fragment from Patterns of psychotic communication (1969). In C.E. Sluzki & D.C. Ransom (Eds.), *Double bind: The foundation of the communicational approach to the family.* New York: Grune & Stratton, 1976a.

WATZLAWICK, P. *How real is real? Confusion, disinformation, commun-*

ication. *An anecdotal introduction to communications theory.* New York: Vintage Books, 1976b.

WATZLAWICK, P. Introduction. In P. Watzlawick & J.H. Weakland (Eds.), *The interactional view.* New York: Norton, 1977:xi-xv.

WATZLAWICK, P. *The language of change.* New York: Basic Books, 1978.

WATZLAWICK, P. & BEAVIN, J. Some formal aspects of communication. *The American Behavioral Scientist.* 1967, *10*:4-8.

WATZLAWICK, P. & WEAKLAND, J.H. (Eds.), *The interactional view: Studies at the Mental Research Institute, Palo Alto, 1965-1974.* New York: Norton, 1977.

WATZLAWICK, P., BEAVIN, J. & JACKSON, D.D. *Pragmatics of human communication: A study of interactional patterns, pathologies, and paradoxes.* New York: Norton, 1967.

WATZLAWICK, P., WEAKLAND, J.H. & FISCH, R. *Change: Principles of problem formation and problem resolution.* New York: Norton, 1974.

WAXWOOD, V.A. Intercultural and intracultural communication: A study of relationship cues in an interpersonal setting. Doctoral dissertation, University of Washington, 1976.

WEAKLAND, J.H. Communication and behavior: An introduction. *American Behavioral Scientist.* 1967, *10*:1-4.

WEAKLAND, J.H. The double bind theory by-self-reflexive hindsight. *Family Process.* 1974, *13*:269-277.

WEAKLAND, J.H. A comment by John H. Weakland. In C.E.Sluzki and D.C. Ransom (Eds.), *Double bind.* New York: Grune & Stratton, 1976a:106-108.

WEAKLAND, J.H. Communication theory and clinical change. In P.J. Guerin, Jr., (Ed.), *Family therapy: Theory and practice.* New York: Gardner Press, 1976c:111-128.

WEAKLAND, J.H. Pursuing the evident into schizophrenia and beyond. In M.M. Berger (Ed.), *Beyond the double bind.* New York: Brunner/Mazel, 1978:83-99.

WEAKLAND, J.H. Tribute to Gregory Bateson. Delivered to the ICA/SCA/SFSU conference on Human Communication from the Interactional View, Asilomar, February 1979.

WEAKLAND, J.H. Personal communication. 1980.

WEAKLAND, J.H., FISCH, R., WATZLAWICK, P. & BODIN, A. Brief therapy: Focused problem resolution. *Family Process.* 1974, *13*:141-168.

WEINSTEIN, E.A. The development of interpersonal competence. In D.A. Goslin (Ed.), *Handbook of socialization theory and research.* Chicago: Rand McNally, 1969:753-775.

WHEELWRIGHT, P. *Metaphor and reality.* Bloomington: Indiana University Press, 1962.

WHITE, R.W. Motivation reconsidered: The concept of competence. *Psychological Review.* 1959, 66:297-333.

WHITEHEAD, A.N. *Science and the modern world.* New York: Macmillan, 1925.

WHYTE, L. *Accent on Form.* New York: Harper, 1946.

WIEMANN, J.M. Explication and test of a model of communicative competence. *Human Communication Research.* 1977a, 3:196-213.

WIEMANN, J.M. A description of competent and incompetent communication behavior. Paper presented at the annual conference of the Speech Communication Association, Washington D.C., December 1977b.

WILDER, C. The Palo Alto group: Difficulties and directions of the interactional view for human communication research. *Human Communication Research.* 1979, 5:171-186.

WINSTON, A. Understanding and treating schizophrenics: A review of some contributions of communication and family systems theories. In M. Berger (Ed.), *Beyond the double bind.* New York: Brunner/Mazel, 1978.

WITTGENSTEIN, L. *Philosophical investigations.* New York: Macmillan, 1953.

WOLFF, W. *The expression of personality.* New York: Harper, 1943.

YALOM, I. *The theory and practice of group psychotherapy.* New York: Basic Books, 1970.

ABOUT THE AUTHORS

DEAN C. BARNLUND is Professor of Communication Studies at San Francisco State University. He has written books on interpersonal, group, and intercultural communication, the most recent being *The Public and Private Self in Japan and the U.S.* His theoretical and research papers have appeared in journals of psychology, anthropology, medicine, sociology, psychiatry, and communication. He is currently working on a study of communicative styles across cultures.

GREGORY BATESON was a natural scientist, anthropologist, cybernetician, and philosopher. His books include *Naven, Communication: The Social Matrix of Psychiatry,* (with Jurgen Ruesch), *Steps to an Ecology of Mind,* and *Mind and Nature: A Necessary Unity.* A book he wrote on art is being edited by Mary Catherine Bateson. At the time of his death in 1980, he was a member of the Board of Regents of the University of California and Resident Scholar at Esalen Institute.

ARTHUR P. BOCHNER is Associate Professor of Speech at Temple University. He has contributed more than 20 articles to national and international journals and is the author of several monographs and book chapters on interpersonal communication. He is interested in the nature of contradiction and paradox in human communication and is completing a book on *Relational Communication* for Addison-Wesley.

KENNETH BURKE, recipient of the 1981 National Medal for Literature, is a philosopher, rhetorical theorist, and literary critic. Best known of his 15 books are *A Grammar of Motives, A Rhetoric of Motives,* and *The Philosophy of Literary Form.* His books *Permanence and Change* and *Attitudes Toward History* will soon be reissued by University of California Press. He writes poetry and music at his farm in rural New Jersey.

KENNETH N. LEONE CISSNA is Assistant Professor of Communication at the University of South Florida. He has published in *Communication Education* and *Western Journal of Speech Communication,* and is co-editor of the *Journal of Applied Communication Research.* He is currently working on the role of confirmation and disconfirmation in group development and on strategies for interviewing.

VERNON E. CRONEN is Associate Professor of Communication Studies at the University of Massachusetts. His publications have appeared in *Communication Monographs, Human Communication Research, Communication Education, Journal of Social Psychology,* and elsewhere. He is currently working on the description of interactional logics.

DONALD G. ELLIS is Assistant Professor of Communication at Michigan State University. He has published in *Human Communication Research, Communication Monographs, Small Group Behavior,* and elsewhere. He is currently working in the area of relational communication.

B. AUBREY FISHER is Professor of Communication at the University of Utah. He is the author of *Small Group Decision Making* and *Perspectives on Human Communication* and is the editor of the *Western Journal of Speech Communication.* He is currently interested in communication as the process of negotiating relationships.

LINDA M. HARRIS is Assistant Professor of Human Development and Family Relations at the University of Connecticut. She has published in *Family Process* and has presented numerous conference papers. She is currently conducting research on paradoxical communication and family violence.

CLIFFORD KELLY   is Associate Professor of Communication at the University of the Pacific. He has published in *Human Communication Research, Communication Education,* and *Communication.* His research interests are in the assessment of interpersonal competence and in small group communication.

ROBERT NORTON is Associate Professor of Communication at Purdue University. He has published in *Human Communication Research, Communication Monographs, Journal of Personality and Social Psychology, Journal of Counseling Psycvhology, Communication Research, Small Group Behavior, Games and Simulation,* and elsewhere. He is currently working to establish a theory of communicator style.

W. BARNETT PEARCE is Professor of Communication Studies at the University of Massachusetts and president of the Eastern Communication Association. He is the author of *An Overview of Communication and Interpersonal Relations* and *Communication, Action, and Meaning: The Creation of Social Realities,* and co-author of *Communicating Personally.* He is currently working on an aesthetic and ethic of communication and on the analysis of communication strategies of those who have claimed ineffable experience.

L. EDNA ROGERS is Associate Professor of Communication and Director of Graduate Studies at Cleveland State University. She has published in *Communication Monographs, Human Communication Research,* and *Family Process,* and for five consecutive years authored or co-authored an ICA top-three ranked paper. She is currently working on the development of interactional methodologies and the dynamics of family systems.

EVELYN SIEBURG is a communication consultant in the San Diego area. She teaches communication and psychology courses for Chapman College and

Pepperdine University and is associated with the Family and Personal Relations Center of Pacific Beach and with Harris International, a La Jolla consulting firm.

HERBERT W. SIMONS is Professor of Speech at Temple University. He is the author of *Persuasion: Understanding, Practice and Analysis*, co-editor with Gerald Miller of *Perspectives on Communication in Social Conflicts*, and has contributed numerous articles on persuasion, conflict, and social change. His current interest remains in the area of persuasion.

STEPHEN TOULMIN is Professor of Social Thought and Philosophy at the University of Chicago. He is the author of numerous books on philosophy and the history of thought, from *Reason in Ethics* (1949) up to *Knowing and Acting* (1976). He is currently completing a large project on epistemological aspects of 20th century historical and scientific ideas, of which the first part was published in *Human Understanding* (1972), and he hopes, when this is completed, to return to philosophical ethics with a comparative study of "case reasoning" in morality and law.

HEINZ VON FOERSTER is Professor Emeritus of Biophysics, Physiology, and Electrical Engineering from the University of Illinois. He is the author of more than 100 scientific papers and editor of the Macy Conference proceedings on *Cybernetics: Circular Causal and Feedback Mechanisms in Biological and Social Systems (1949-1954)*. He established the University of Illinois Biological Computer Laboratory with Ross Ashby, Gotthard Gunther, Lars Lofgren, Humberto Maturana, Gordon Pask, Francisco Varela, and others. He now lives on the coast of Northern California.

PAUL WATZLAWICK is a Research Associate at the Mental Research Institute and Clinical Associate Professor of Psychiatry at Stanford University. He is sole or principal author of *Pragmatics of Human Communication, Change: Principles of Problem Formation and Problem Resolution, How Real is Real?*, and *The Language of Change*. He is currently working on a book about constructivist epistemology to be published in German.

JOHN H. WEAKLAND is a Research Associate at the Mental Research Institute and Clinical Assistant Professor of Psychiatry at Stanford University. He has authored or co-authored numerous articles, including "Toward a Theory of Schizophrenia" (with Bateson, Jackson, and Haley), is the co-author of *Change* (with Watzlawick and Fisch) and *Counseling Elders and Their Families* (with Herr), and co-editor of *The Interactional View* (with Watzlawick). He is currently Associate Director of MRI's Brief Therapy Center.

JOHN M. WIEMANN is Assistant Professor of Communication Studies at the University of California at Santa Barbara. He has published in *Human Communication Research, Journal of Communication, Communication Quarterly, Western Journal of Speech Communication, Communication Education*, and *Review of Educational Research*, and has contributed several book chapters. He is currently Kellogg National Fellow working on developing communication strategies for those who work with the disabled.

CAROL WILDER-MOTT is Assistant Professor of Communication Studies at San Francisco State University, Research Associate at the Mental Research Institute, and member-at-large of the Board of Directors of the International Communication Association. She has published both general and scholarly articles, the latter of which have appeared in *Journal of Communication, Human Communication Research, Communication Education,* and elsewhere. She is writing a book on social process.